THE CYBER PREDATORS

Ever wondered who lurks in the shadows of the Internet's vast landscape, balancing opportunity and risk? *The Cyber Predators* takes you on a revealing journey into the enigmatic world of Dark Triad/Tetrad personalities: psychopaths, Machiavellians, narcissists, and sadists, tackling the urgent issue of online crime as a global crisis. Drawing from cutting-edge research, this book synthesizes knowledge, exploring the motives and tactics that distinguish Dark Triad/Tetrad individuals. Offering unique expertise, it serves as an essential reference for scholars, practitioners, and the public, distinguishing itself with its consolidated and up-to-date approach. Navigating through diverse digital realms – from social media addiction to cyberbullying, hacking, and workplace deviance – this book unravels the complex interplay between Dark Triad/Tetrad personalities and cyber misconduct. Ideal for postgraduate students, it provides interdisciplinary insight, drawing from various scientific fields, making it a valuable resource for understanding cybercrime and its perpetrators.

AARON COHEN is Professor of Management at the University of Haifa. He has published about 100 papers in peer-reviewed journals. Noteworthy among his works are *Multiple Commitments in the Workplace: An Integrative Approach* (Taylor & Francis, 2003) and *Counterproductive Work Behaviors: Understanding the Dark Side of Personalities in Organizational Life* (Routledge, 2018).

THE CYBER PREDATORS

Dark Personality and Online Misconduct and Crime

AARON COHEN

University of Haifa

Shaftesbury Road, Cambridge CB2 8EA, United Kingdom

One Liberty Plaza, 20th Floor, New York, NY 10006, USA

477 Williamstown Road, Port Melbourne, VIC 3207, Australia

314–321, 3rd Floor, Plot 3, Splendor Forum, Jasola District Centre, New Delhi – 110025, India

103 Penang Road, #05–06/07, Visioncrest Commercial, Singapore 238467

Cambridge University Press is part of Cambridge University Press & Assessment,
a department of the University of Cambridge.

We share the University's mission to contribute to society through the pursuit of
education, learning and research at the highest international levels of excellence.

www.cambridge.org
Information on this title: www.cambridge.org/9781009416863

DOI: 10.1017/9781009416849

First published 2024

A catalogue record for this publication is available from the British Library

A Cataloging-in-Publication data record for this book is available from the Library of Congress

ISBN 978-1-009-41686-3 Hardback
ISBN 978-1-009-41685-6 Paperback

To Ruti Zohar for her endless support and encouragement and to Vana (and Mesi for a short time) for just being there for me.

Contents

List of Tables   *page* viii
Preface   ix

1   Dark Personalities and Cyber Misconduct: The New Territory   1

2   The Dark Triad/Tetrad and Social Networking Addiction   27

3   Dark Triad/Tetrad on Facebook and Other Social Networks   81

4   Dark Triad/Tetrad and Hate Behaviors: Cyber Aggression
    and Cyberbullying   110

5   Dark Triad/Tetrad and Hate Behaviors: Cyberstalking
    and Trolling   154

6   The Dark Triad/Tetrad Is above the Law: Cybercrime   198

7   The Dark Triad/Tetrad and Romantic Relationships in
    Cyberspace   231

8   The Dark Triad/Tetrad and Workplace Cyber Deviance   302

9   Conceptual and Practical Implications   320

References   332
Index   376

Tables

2.1 Summary of research findings on the relationship between
the Dark Tetrad/Triad and social network addiction   *page* 69
4.1 Summary of research findings on the relationship
between the Dark Tetrad/Triad and cyber aggression
and cyberloafing   148
5.1 Summary of research findings of the relationship between
the Dark Tetrad/Triad and cyberstalking and trolling   188
6.1 Summary of research findings of the relationship between
the Dark Tetrad/Triad and cybercrime   223
7.1 Summary of research findings of the relationship
between the Dark Tetrad/Triad and romantic relationships
in cyberspace   283
8.1 Summary of research findings of the relationship between
the Dark Tetrad/Triad workplace cyber deviance   318

Preface

Millions worldwide watched *The Tinder Swindler*, a British actual crime documentary film released on Netflix in February 2022. The film presents a true Israeli man, born Shimon Hayut, who traveled around Europe, presenting himself as the son of Russian-Israeli diamond tycoon Lev Leviev, alias the Diamond King. He used Tinder's dating application to contact women, presenting himself as Simon Leviev and tricking them into lending him the money he would never repay (Zhou, 2023). The frauds he was behind, allegedly, were very similar. He would charm women with generous gifts and take them to dinners on private jets using money he borrowed from other women he had previously conned. He would later pretend he was being targeted by his "enemies," often sending the same messages and images to each woman, indicating that he had just been attacked with a knife but that his bodyguard had saved him and was hurt. He then asked his victims to help him financially due to the breach of "security," supposedly hindering his use of his credit cards and bank accounts; the women often took out bank loans and new credit cards to help. He would then use the money gained through the deception to lure new victims while essentially operating a Ponzi scheme. Later, he would pretend to repay his victims by sending forged documents showing fake bank transfers and then breaking off contact with the victims. Sometimes, he would even go as far as to threaten them and use manipulation to get more money from his victims. It is estimated that he swindled $10 million from people across the globe (The Tinder Swindler, 2022; Osborne, 2022).

The Web has a crucial role in Shimon Hayut's cons. First, he used Tinder to introduce himself as Simon Leviev and to "hunt" his prey. Then, many parts of the "love bombing" stage occurred on Web applications. Then, after the "love bombing" stage, he used WhatsApp and other Web applications to show his victim a fake scene in which he or his bodyguard were in danger. Finally, the money he asked for was mostly transferred via the Internet.

Many who watched this film have shaken their head, wondering how women could be allegedly hoodwinked out of millions of dollars. To understand this, one must realize Shimon Hayut's personality and those of his victims. According to Campbell (2022), people with dark personality traits such as narcissism and psychopathy are likelier to perpetrate romance scams. These individuals lack empathy, lie for self-gain, and manipulate others. Narcissists are incredibly charming in the initial phases of a relationship, which hooks the target, but once the hook is in, control and exploitation ensue. According to Johnston (2022) and Christensen (2022), Hayut behaved like a psychopath. His pattern of deceit, manipulativeness, apparent indifference to the consequences of his actions, superficial charm, lack of empathy, and lack of remorse are all behaviors that certainly head us in that direction. According to Hillier and Greig (2022), Hayut's personality is shaped by the darker side of personality traits, namely, the Dark Triad traits (narcissism, psychopathy, and Machiavellianism) or Dark Tetrad (with the addition of sadism).

As for the victims, Campbell (2022) explained that for various reasons, some people are not successful in relationships, which puts them at risk of being scammed. The history of difficulty may stem from childhood (e.g., bad parenting) or low-quality adult relationships, but either way, these individuals are vulnerable to victimization. When a "partner" requests favors or breaks promises, those with a negative relationship history are inclined to remain committed and indulge the swindler rather than breaking it off. A more general explanation was advanced by Bohns (2022), who contended that Hayut's manipulations relied on the nature of most people to trust others over distrusting them, believing them over doubting them and going along with someone's self-presentation rather than embarrassing them by calling them out. The tendency to trust, believe, and go along with other people's explanations of events may seem disadvantageous.

Furthermore, these inclinations can indeed expose people. Nevertheless, without trust, there is no cooperation; without assuming others are telling the truth, there is no communication; and without accepting people for what they present to the world, there is no foundation for building a relationship. In other words, the very features that look like glitches when exploited are the essence of what it means to be human (Bohns, 2022). The fundamental nature of most people to trust others is the core ammunition of dark personalities, specifically the Dark Tetrad.

The Dark Triad/Tetrad and Cyber Deviance

Shimon Hayut is only one example. Many, like him, males and females, perform many unethical, misconduct, and criminal activities across numerous aspects of life. Romance frauds are only one example of one aspect. This book is about them and their misconduct and criminal activities in social media networks, the most popular platforms our days. The Dark Tetrad traits present four related personalities but are also independent

Narcissism is described as someone needing admiration and who lacks empathy for others. Other aspects are feelings of grandiosity, self-centeredness, and a sense of entitlement, through which they take advantage of others (VandenBos, 2007, APA Psychology Dictionary). Psychopathic personalities had been a synonym for antisocial personality disorder [...] "the presence of a chronic and pervasive disposition to disregard and violate the rights of others. Manifestations include repeated violations of the law, exploitation of others, deceitfulness, impulsivity, aggressiveness, reckless disregard for the safety of self and others, and irresponsibility, accompanied by lack of guilt, remorse, and empathy" (VandenBos, 2007, APA Psychology Dictionary, p. 65). Machiavellianism is defined as a personality trait marked by a calculating attitude toward human relationships and a belief that ends justify means, however ruthless. Machiavellians view other people more or less as objects to be manipulated to pursue their goals, if necessary, through deliberate deception (VandenBos, 2007, APA Psychology Dictionary).

A sadistic personality disorder is characterized by cruelty, aggression, and demeaning behavior (Chabrol et al., 2009). Sadism was defined as "cognitions and behaviors associated with the derivation of pleasure from inflicting physical or emotional pain on another person" (Porter & Woodworth, 2006, p. 486). This diagnosis appeared in the Diagnostic and Statistical Manual (DSM)-III-R (American Psychiatric Association, 1987) but was removed and no longer appeared in the DSM (Smith, 2021). However, some scholars consider this removal a mistake (Millon, 2011). In recent years, the interest in sadism has grown mainly because researchers sought that sadism should be added to the Dark Triad traits as an additional personality disorder despite its removal from the DSM (Johnson, Plouffe & Saklofske, 2019). A difference should be made between sadism and everyday sadism (Greitemeyer, 2015). Sadism can be characterized as deriving pleasure from being responsible for others' experiences of pain (Olckers & Hattingh, 2022; Liu et al., 2023). Everyday sadism is a nonclinical form of sadism. Everyday sadism can be conceptualized as a nonclinical form of sadism, differing from clinical sadism in that the individual does not harm others out of the need for cruelty but rather for the pleasure derived from the act (Greitemeyer, 2015; Porter et al., 2014; Perez del Valle & Hand, 2022; Lauder & March, 2023). Recent research has confirmed that everyday sadists find more pleasure in harming other people than nonsadists (Greitemeyer, 2015; Nocera et al., 2022). While the book will use the term sadist in all the following chapters, it should be noted that it relates to everyday sadists.

Online communication has become essential in modern society (Nocera et al., 2022), with 9 in 10 United States adults using the Internet (Pew Research Center, 2019). Most of the world now depends on computers, the Internet, and cellular technology. Individuals now own laptops connected via Wi-Fi, smartphones, and one or more video game systems that may be networked. Cell phones have become a preferred method of communication for most people, especially text messages. In addition, people have multiple email accounts and social networking profiles on various platforms for personal and business use (Holt, Bossler & Seigfried-Spellar, 2022). Social networking sites are an essential part of individuals' lives. People use social networking sites to maintain relationships, create new connections, and engage with events, people, and organizations.

Online social networking has no generalized definition, but it is defined by Boyd and Ellison (2007) as a web service that allows an individual to do three things: (a) generate a public or semipublic profile in a specific system, (b) create a list of users to interact with and browse through the list of contacts, and (c) see what was done by others within the system. There are many benefits of using social networking sites. They (a) elevate the ease in which individuals may form and create online communities, (b) improve collaboration and sharing of information, (c) can lead to the creation of new job roles, (d) allow users to be constantly connected to friends, (e) allow for ease of communication, information transfer, and (f) help break down social boundaries (Hussain, Wegmann & Griffiths, 2021). People are fond of online social networking for entertainment, social contacts, fun, fame, advertisement, and business. However, some people use social networking sites for evil purposes.

Over the past 20 years, digital communication has become increasingly important in the workplace and in individuals' lives. Social media has become popular with younger people as more diverse platforms have become available (Holt et al., 2022; Hand & Scott, 2022). In this era of technology, the popularity of online social networks is increasing among technologically strong and nontechnical people. The availability of the Internet is one of the primary reasons behind the high utilization of online social networking (Boyd & Ellison, 2007). Social networking sites, in particular, provide users with unique platforms to share their information through personalized web pages and interact with others using the Internet. These characteristics enable many people to use social networking sites to satisfy their self-expression needs. On the one hand, "weak tie" network platforms, that is, less reciprocal platforms that lack close emotional support, such as Twitter, satisfy the need of people to get the attention of many users while averting direct communication. On the other hand, the asynchrony of the Internet allows individuals to elaborate their information (Kong et al., 2021).

Compared to the past, making use of cyberspace and communication has increased. It has been expanded in the last decade due to the increasing growth of virtual social networks and free membership, as well as the facilitation of intelligent communication devices such as the increased number of advanced mobile phones leading to a gradual surge in the number of their users. The statistical information regarding this phenomenon is astonishing. Research suggests that 24% of teenagers use social networking sites constantly, and 71% use more than one social networking site. Recent statistics indicate that one-third of the individuals in the world and two-thirds of all Internet users are active social media users (Nikbin, Taghizadeh & Rahman, 2022). As of early 2017, about 2.8 billion people were members of at least one of these virtual social networks, while in 2010, only 0.97 billion of the world's population were members of one of these networks. It is also estimated that by 2020, the number of users of these social networks will increase to 2.95 billion (Soleimani Rad & Abolghasemi, 2021).

In current society, the Internet plays a fundamental role in interpersonal relationships. The Internet became a social environment that could boost positive self-views and had the exceptional ability to integrate into people's lives. There are now 4.57 billion Internet users worldwide, comprising 58.7% of the world's population (Holt et al., 2022). The Internet has changed human connection in profound ways, facilitating a range of diverse and new social relationships and interactions. (Hand & Scott, 2022). Many people around the world utilize social media as a means to connect and engage with others in different ways. For instance, 65% of American adults use Facebook, though there has been a substantial increase in the use of Instagram and LinkedIn to communicate. By contrast, WhatsApp is much more prevalent globally and is the number one messaging application across much of South America, Western Europe, Africa, and some parts of Asia (Holt et al., 2022).

Facebook is the largest social media site, with 2.85 billion active monthly users, while Twitter is also popular, with 340 million users. On Twitter, users can broadcast "tweets" of up to 280 characters, and other users can like, comment on, or "retweet" (share) them. Two ways in which Twitter differs from some other popular social media sites are the extent to which it is utilized heavily by celebrities as well as lay users and the fact that Twitter users who communicate do *not* know each other offline, in contrast to the majority of Facebook users/"friends" (Hand & Scott, 2022). The invention of the Internet and the advancement of its technologies have changed the world and human communication in profound ways.

Today, various online services and ever-evolving social networking sites are ubiquitous in the Western world and keep gaining popularity worldwide in most European countries. North America's Internet penetration is as high as 90% of the population (Bogolyubova et al., 2018). Over a billion people access social networking services daily to broadcast their personal lives, socialize with fellow users, or procrastinate. The heightened importance of social networking sites for social and political discourse has motivated users to join public discussions by expressing their viewpoints on different issues. The above-mentioned information emphasizes the massive use of social networking sites around the globe. While these instances can be seen as advantages, some experiences can make using mobile phones and the Internet more devastating than enjoying their spontaneity (Grigg, 2010). Unfortunately, this development has paved the way for new forms of virtual abuse, often leading to severe real-life consequences for their victims (Koban et al., 2018).

In addition to the stimulating advantages and benefits of social networking sites, there is a negative side to these profound developments. Information systems have "flattened" the world and facilitated communication and trade in ways that would have been impossible without them (Harrison et al., 2018); however, maladaptive innovations using new technologies have followed on the heels of legitimate transactions. The evolution of human behavior due to technological innovations has created unparalleled opportunities for crime and misuse. Over the last three decades, there has been a substantive increase in the use of technology by street criminals and novel applications to create new forms of crime that did not exist. The World Wide Web and the Internet also provide a venue for individuals who engage in crime and deviance to communicate and share information, which is impossible in the real world. As a result, we must begin to understand how and why these changes are occurring (Holt et al., 2022). What makes this new revolution of technology so appealing to misbehavior and crime?

Papapicco and Quatera (2019) provide a compelling logic to the previous question. Following the great Digital Revolution, the "fluid" woman/man changes the perception of what s/he lives and the essence of the experience, which is the "Who is," hence her/his identity: a re-written identity using the computer. Redefining your identity in a digital context is, in many ways, beneficial because it allows you to take time to rethink and choose descriptions, photos, or videos best suited to the desire to be constantly visible. In particular, the strong wave of social networks has initially differentiated the virtual and digital identity constructs. Virtual identity is the set of potentials, expectations, and imaginations that have not yet materialized online.

On the contrary, digital identity results from "rethinking in an online context." Subsequently, the distinction mentioned earlier was canceled with the predominance of the digital identity over the virtual one. It is multiple digital identities because it can be confirmed or disconfirmed, real but also fake, where the subjects can choose different ways to express themselves and interact with other subjects. Indeed, it is above all thanks to the endless possibilities of freedom offered by the Net and to this constant man–machine relationship, which gives rise to a new fragmented "Who," incapable also of distinguishing reality from virtuality, driven by the uncontrollable fantasy of being able to become another from themselves (Papapicco & Quatera, 2019).

Undoubtedly, if, on the one hand, the Net multiplies the possibilities of creating digital identities, on the other, lacking distinctive indices to depict, such as the tone of the voice or particular facial expressions, traits, that is, that belongs only to the person as dematerialized (a physical Chi), virtual spaces provide more freedom to avoid being identified. On the one hand, digital identity is in extreme need of anonymity because it allows open discussion of very intimate topics in relative security; on the other hand, however, the mere omission of the name could give rise to hostile behavior; it can be to encourage aggression because it makes the behavior more uninhibited, less conditioned by conventions and social norms. Anonymity is characterized by the desire not only to authenticate but also to act in an invisible and sometimes provocative manner: This is one of the darkest sides of the Web (Papapicco & Quatera, 2019).

The spread of the Internet has fundamentally changed the forms of interaction that people enter with each other and has created new opportunities for building their identity and self-esteem. On the one hand, by hiding their physical appearance, people can express themselves more freely and openly. By contrast, on the other, they can hide or fabricate their data, such as gender, education level, financial situation, and many others. This way, Internet users can express their "other self," often fundamentally different from the one that dominates in real life. This also applies to pathological personality traits that can be projected into cyberspace and treated as a specific social environment. Its structural and functional properties favor this, such as anonymity, the lack of nonverbal interaction indicators, asynchrony of interaction, and the lack of clearly defined standards. Unfortunately, these properties are also used to commit punishable offenses (Kong et al., 2021).

Another reason that makes cybercrime so attractive is the ubiquity of this technology that makes it easy for individuals to gain access to the tools necessary to offend with relative ease. The prices of computers have dropped substantially over the last decade, making it very easy to acquire such equipment. In addition, smaller portable computers, such as the iPad and smartphones, which can connect to the Internet through cellular technology, have also become common. As a result, offenders can readily acquire and access information from anywhere through these resources. If people cannot afford to buy these devices independently, they can always use computers in Internet cafes and public libraries for free or at a small cost. Thus, there are minimal barriers to computer technology globally. Also, technology acts as a force multiplier in that computer and computer-mediated technology allow a single person to engage in crimes that otherwise would involve multiple people and complex schemes to target such a significant number of victims. In online environments, offenders can target thousands of victims at a time worldwide within seconds (Holt et al., 2022).

Although these online connections are associated with positive social benefits, enabling quick and easy social interaction, the Internet also promotes a sense of anonymity and decreased accountability, self-awareness, and inhibition, which can encourage deindividuation. Online deindividuation may foster the manifestation of negative, online antisocial behavior, including cyberbullying, trolling, cyberstalking, and online aggression, collectively called cyber abuse (March et al., 2022). Further, some online antisocial behaviors may be illegal, criminal activity, such as cyber fraud and child pornography use, and thus approximate the definition of cybercrime. The online antisocial behaviors that characterize cyber abuse and cybercrime are not specific to a single culture and are considered a global issue (March, 2022). Online social networking has also become a significant platform for cybercriminals to perform several types of crimes. A considerable amount of data on social media is being utilized for several criminal purposes. The attacks' rate, types, and complexity are increasing drastically due to such big platforms where people are available relentlessly (Boyd & Ellison, 2007). Some harmful acts identified within these communication media are bullying, harassment, assault, abuse, and stalking. In the United Kingdom, for instance, cyberbullying has been used as a common phrase for most of these subsets of aggressive acts (Grigg, 2010).

Computers and computer networks (i.e., an interconnected collection of autonomous computers that allow an easy exchange of information between users) have become an integral part of American industry, business, and government. Consequently, their efficient operation is increasingly critical to the survival of the United States and its organizations. Unfortunately, however, next to supporting legitimate business activities and facilitating opportunities to interact with employees, clients, and vendors, the heavy reliance of large organizations on computers and computer networks increases their vulnerability to a wide range of cyber-dependent crimes (i.e., all these crimes that emerge as a direct result of computer technology and the Internet and that could not exist without it). Indeed, numerous reports suggest that large corporations and governmental agencies experience a wide range of computer-focused crimes, including system-trespassing (or hacking), website defacement, Distributed Denial of Service attacks, and malicious software infections, with an estimated $400 billion annual cost to the global economy from these crimes (Maimon et al., 2017).

Cybercrime is now a growing threat because, as aforementioned, the number of people using the Internet is increasing worldwide, and digital technology tools do not require specialist knowledge. Cybercrimes are committed not only by individuals but also by organized criminal groups. Particular attention should be paid to individuals exhibiting psychopathic personality traits, which pose an exceptionally high threat to Internet users. This risk is greater if the group of axial symptoms of psychopathy is accompanied by high intelligence. That is why Internet users who meet these criteria more often commit various cybercrimes, and their offenses are more harmful to victims. It should be remembered that victims of antisocial behavior online experience at least similar effects, both material and mental, as victims of criminals operating in real life. Some authors even claim that cybercrime leads to more severe and longer-lasting consequences, especially for the mental health of victims, for example, depression, chronic anxiety, and low self-esteem (Nicol, 2012; Jung et al., 2014). This group of people, also known as the Dark Triad traits, has the high potential to use the Web primarily for malevolence. Their behavior on social networking sites will be the focus of this book.

Research has focused on predictors of this behavior to understand how to respond to and manage online antisocial behavior. The Dark Tetrad has emerged as a subclinical trait strongly related to cyber abuse and cybercrime. A systematic review synthesizing the research on the Dark Tetrad personality traits (i.e., Machiavellianism, psychopathy, narcissism, and sadism) concluded that all the traits are with a range of antisocial online behavior (March, 2022; Olckers & Hattingh, 2022). There is a reason why Dark Tetrad personalities are attracted to social networking sites. Cyberspace creates conditions for creating a specific social environment in which the lack of face-to-face contact favors the appearance of the "disinhibition effect," as mentioned earlier. In such conditions, personality traits responsible for antisocial behavior can be enhanced in diversity and frequency. In addition, the basic features of cyberspace can have the effect of "psychological distancing" in some people, the essence of which is to perceive other Internet users as unreal, abstract beings (Perenc, 2022).

"The environment of computers, the Cloud, and the Internet make cyber fraudsters even more elusive than before. This behavior differs from what investigators are used to, and it is something they will have to adapt their methods to. Nevertheless, even cyber-crimes are still likely to be driven by the same psychological profiles found previously; only the behavior may have changed" (the Survey of Corporate responsibility reporting 2013, p. 17, as mentioned in Harrison, Summers & Mennecke, 2018). Of recent interest for social and personality psychologists and law enforcement defenses is the relationship between the Dark Tetrad and subversive behaviors that occur online via social networking sites, their applications, and related websites (Moor & Anderson, 2019).

Perence (2022) elaborates on why psychopaths favor cyberspace and its potential use for purposes that do not follow applicable legal order. These features are also relevant to narcissists as well as Machiavellians and sadists.

1. The anonymity of cyberspace. Psychopath uses this trait to hide or change their identity to avoid responsibility for their actions. In this context, while feeling "invisible" in cyberspace, s/he is convinced of the low probability of being caught and exposed to criminal sanctions. Although some psychopaths may realize that online

activity leaves some traces that may identify them, they think that the amount of these traces is small enough to give them anonymity and a sense of impunity.

2. The lack of nonverbal indicators of interaction between communicating people, such as physical appearance, eye contact, facial expressions, mime, and manner of expression. In such circumstances, interacting partners only need to rely on written words, which can often lead to misunderstandings and conflicts. For example, the mere lack of eye contact in interactions in cyberspace makes it difficult to identify a person committing a particular offense.

3. Asynchrony of interactions. This refers to a certain delay in communication in some online environments that use permanent messages, photo albums, and information that does not require their recipients to react in real time. Asynchrony makes cyberspace users less sensitive to current social norms because there are currently no "guards" who can stop someone's inappropriate behavior online. In addition, the absence of an Internet audience that could monitor the course of interaction means that users do not feel pressured to force them to comply with commonly accepted standards.

4. The lack of clearly defined norms. This promotes the occurrence of reprehensible behavior. Although some social networking sites require compliance with specific laws and policies, most users treat cyberspace as an open area for everyone that can be "conquered" without looking at legal regulations and social norms. Difficulties with implementing universally applicable social norms in cyberspace mean that, at present, one cannot speak of universal Internet culture. One consequence of this is the existence of social networking sites that allow anonymous users to publish all kinds of offensive content, such as calls for the persecution of specific groups of people, the promotion of racist theories, or the unlawful sharing of personal data (Perenc, 2022).

Those mentioned four basic features of cyberspace in practice work in a complementary manner, which promotes the expression of psychopathic features possessed by specific Internet users. In some people, the structural elements of cyberspace may also be conducive to adverse changes in the moral sphere, facilitating their involvement in socially unacceptable behavior. In this respect, they resemble the Dark Tetrads. It primarily relates to the role played by psychological distancing, which limits the influence of moral principles observed daily in direct contact between people. The lack of clearly defined social norms, typical of online contacts, is also essential, contributing to disregarding the potential consequences of offenses committed in cyberspace. This leads to the conclusion that in the case of many people, there is a violation of moral norms in relationships with others in cyberspace, even though these people generally follow these norms in genuine relationships (Perenc, 2022).

However, the intensity of violations in cyberspace is much more vigorous among Dark Tetrad personalities. The above-mentioned features of cyberspace seem to suit them perfectly. They feel highly comfortable performing cyber misbehavior and cybercrime, giving them a tool with a lower likelihood of being exposed and perhaps being accountable and punished. Therefore, the interest in the role of personality traits in determining offenses and deviant behavior in cyberspace has increased in recent years. According to Perenc (2022), there is a clear qualitative difference in personality profiles between cyber deviants and people in the general population who often use digital technology. People classified as cyber deviants generally have higher features, such as a tendency to manipulate and exploit others and no moral inhibitions. Many studies indicate the presence of a solid connection between the Dark Tetrad and cyber harassment, which means that the features of Dark Tetrad personalities occupy a central place in the personality profile of individuals making such offenses (Perenc, 2022).

The media reports increasingly on a variety of crimes performed using cyber. This issue has become a severe problem for society across the globe. Constraining from cyber abuse and crime becomes a vital need in a modern community. To succeed in this mission, there is also a need to understand it better and the personalities behind it, many of them dark personalities. This book responds to this challenge. The goal of this book will be to expose and explore the role of Dark Tetrad personalities in performing cyber misbehavior and crime. The chapters of the book will attempt to cover the issue thoroughly.

Chapter 1, the introduction, will present, define, and explain the two main concepts of the book. Then, it will elaborate on the main characteristics of each Dark Tetrad. Later, it will present the main forms of cyber misbehavior and cybercrime and their adverse outcomes. In its last comments, the chapter will present some main theories explaining why Dark Tetrad personalities are attracted to social media networks as a tool for perming their evil behaviors. Chapter 2 will focus on social media addiction. The chapter will argue that while a certain amount of extra time spent on social media networks can occur for many individuals, an addiction above normal behavior can characterize Dark Tetrad personalities. Finally, the chapter will cover issues of levels of addiction of Dark Tetrad to social network media, theories that explain the causes, and the adverse outcomes of being addicted to social media networking.

Chapter 3 will focus on the potential role of Dark Tetrad personalities on Facebook and other social media platforms. The first section will describe the importance and usage of Facebook in modern life. Then, the chapter will portray the benefits and potential damages included in Facebook. Next, it will present theories explaining Dark Tetrad personalities' attraction to Facebook. The chapter will review the relationship to Facebook for each Dark Tetrad personality. The assumption is that each of the three personalities has its own view and approach regarding the usage of Facebook. The chapter will also cover an important issue discussed in the literature: predicting Dark Tetrad personalities based on Facebook profiles and activities. Chapters 4 and 5 will concentrate on hate behaviors. Chapter 4 will focus on cyberbullying and aggression of Dark Tetrad personalities on social networking sites. Bullying and aggression are severe societal problems, and cyberbullying is no different. Cyberbullying can be viewed as rude/discourteous behaviors through Information and Communication Technologies. The chapter will review the different approaches and definitions of cyberbullying. It will later review the devastating outcomes of cyberbullying. The main parts of the chapter will be to discuss the role and the reasons for Dark Tetrad personalities to be involved in cyberbullying. This will be reviewed separately for each of the dark personalities. The chapter will end with a review of the latest research findings on the relationship between Dark Tetrad personalities and cyberbullying.

Chapter 5 will review Dark Tetrad personalities' involvement in cyber stalking, surveillance, and trolling. Cyberstalking is the stalking of others through electronic access and communication methods, such as using hidden webcams, global positioning system devices, and SpyWare to monitor the victim's behavior and pursuit and contact under anonymity through fake online profiles. First, the chapter discusses the differences between stalking and cyberstalking. The following section will review conceptual explanations for the involvement of Dark Tetrad personalities in cyber stalking and surveillance. The final section will present studies on the relationship between the Dark Tetrad personalities and cyber stalking and cyber surveillance. Cyber trolling and their relationship to Dark Tetrad personalities will be reviewed in the second section of Chapter 6. Trolling is an interpersonal antisocial behavior prominent within Internet culture across the world. Trolling behavior includes starting aggressive arguments and posting inflammatory, malicious messages in online comment sections to provoke, disrupt, and upset others deliberately. First, the chapter will review definitions and descriptions of cyber trolling. Then, theories about the reasons behind each Dark Tetrad trait's motives for using trolling behavior will follow. The chapter will later present research findings on the relationship between each of the four dark personalities and trolling.

Chapter 6 will cover one of the most important and devastating issues in cyber misbehavior, namely cybercrime. The chapter will start by describing the different forms of cybercrime, such as hacking, cyberattacks, phishing, insurance fraud, online consumer fraud, and more. The following section will present theories regarding the reasons behind each Dark Tetrad motive to perform cybercrimes. The final section of the chapter will present findings about the relationship between each Dark Tetrad trait and the different forms of cybercrime.

Chapter 7 will present another vital aspect regarding Dark Tetrad involvement in cyberspace: Dark Tetrad and intimate cyber relationships. First, the chapter will review the different forms of cyber abuse in romantic relationships, such as cyber dating, revenge pornography, and ghosting. Next, the chapter will review the specific role of each Dark Tetrad personality in cyber relationship abuse and the motives behind their behavior in this setting. Finally, the chapter will present research findings on this relationship.

Chapter 8 will focus on the work setting. The importance of understanding cyber misbehavior in the workplace and the devastating outcomes of cyber misbehavior will be presented first. After that, a description of the different ways of cyber misconduct in the work setting will be reviewed, such as cyberloafing, cyber aggression, and cyberbullying. Next, theories about Dark Tetrad personalities' motives for workplace cyber misconduct will follow. Finally, the chapter will end with presenting research findings about the relationship between the four dark personalities and cyber misbehavior in the workplace.

The book will end with Chapter 9, presenting the previous chapters' conclusions. The chapter will start with briefly reviewing the main findings presented in the earlier chapters. The conceptual contribution of the book will be explained later. The next section of the chapter will discuss the practical implications of understanding the impacts of Dark Tetrad cyber misbehaviors in the different settings presented in the book. Suggestions for better coping with Dark Tetrad cyber misconduct will follow this. The final section of the chapter will suggest future research agendas on this vital issue.

An important note is that both terms, Dark Triad and Dark Tetrad, will be used throughout the book. This is unavoidable. While the emphasis will be using the term Dark Tetrad most of the time, in empirical studies that examined the Dark Triad, this will be the term that will be used. The term Dark Tetrad cannot be used when an empirical study only examined the three Dark Triad traits: narcissism, Machiavellianism, and psychopathy. This rationale will guide the usage of the terms throughout the entire book.

This book provides a valuable perspective on one of the most important issues in modern society: cyberspace, cyber misbehavior, and cybercrime. Delving into these issues has become more vital now that rapid technological changes in cyberspace have had substantial effects on the current society around the world. In this new world of cyberspace, cybercrime and misbehavior have emerged as fundamental phenomena around the globe. Therefore, it is no surprise that this book relies on conceptual and empirical studies performed in recent years. A better understanding of this stunnable and worrying phenomenon can provide essential guides and tools to cope with the enormous potential damages of cybercrime and misbehavior.

CHAPTER I

Dark Personalities and Cyber Misconduct
The New Territory

1.1 The Dark Triad/Tetrad

At first, a more elaborated description of Dark Tetrad personalities is in place. The book is about their behavior, and to better understand their role in performing cyber deviance and cybercrimes, there is a need to know their characteristics. Therefore, a thorough description of their primary qualities will be presented here. Some of this description is based on the one advanced by Cohen (2016, 2018).

The Dark Tetrad is a constellation of four theoretically separable, albeit conceptually and empirically overlapping, personality constructs that are typically construed as interpersonally maladaptive: psychopathy, narcissism, Machiavellianism (Smith & Lilienfeld, 2013), and sadism. A narcissistic personality is marked by grandiosity, entitlement, and lack of empathy (Smith & Lilienfeld, 2013). Extreme self-aggrandizement is the hallmark of narcissism, which includes an inflated view of self, fantasies of control, success, and admiration, and a desire to have this self-love reinforced by others (O'Boyle et al., 2012). Machiavellianism, another constituent of the Dark Tetrad, is associated with disregarding the importance of morality and using craft and dishonesty to pursue and maintain power (Smith & Lilienfeld, 2013). Three interrelated beliefs define the Machiavellian personality: an avowed conviction in the effectiveness of manipulative tactics in dealing with other people, a cynical view of human nature, and a moral outlook that puts expediency above principle (O'Boyle et al., 2012). Psychopathy, the third element, has been described as impulsivity and thrill-seeking combined with low empathy and anxiety (Spain et al., 2014). Psychopathy is marked by the person's lack of concern for others, social regulatory mechanisms, impulsivity, and guilt or remorse when their actions harm others (O'Boyle et al., 2012).

In recent years, scholars suggested that the Dark Triad should be expanded to the Dark Tetrad with the addition of sadism, especially when investigating deviant online behaviors because sadism has predicted additional variance in these behaviors (Kircaburun, Jonason, & Griffiths, 2018a, 2018b; Kircaburun & Griffiths, 2018; Alavi et al., 2022; Gajda et al., 2022; Liu et al., 2023). The addition of subclinical sadism (dubbed "everyday sadism") to the triad has been proposed, as it explains antisocial behavior independently of that accounted for by the triad. Everyday sadism is an individual differences factor that captures the predatory motivation to cause harm or distress to innocent others and taking pleasure in doing so – which conceptually differs from those high in trait psychopathy to whom this harm is purely instrumental (Moor & Anderson, 2019; Perez del Valle & Hand, 2022).

The frequently used approach, which is applied here, is to conceptualize the Dark Tetrad as being multidimensional, that is, comprised of multiple traits (Wu & Lebreton, 2011; Olckers & Hattingh, 2022). Indeed, most research on the Dark Tetrad personality in the workplace was based on the multidimensional model (Schyns, 2015; Furtner, Maran, & Rauthmann, 2017). The characteristics common to the four Dark Tetrad constructs are highly salient: They all include the tendency to deceive, manipulate, and exploit others for selfish gains. However, as mentioned earlier, these four constructs have unique characteristics (Wu & Lebreton, 2011; Lee et al., 2013). The somewhat modest correlations among measures of the Dark Tetrad (e.g., ranging from 0.25 to 0.50) suggest that each contains a substantial amount of specific variance (Paulhus & Williams, 2002; Lee et al., 2013). This does not mean there is still a debate on treating the Dark Tetrad traits as unidimensional versus multidimensional. Some of this debate will be presented in the following section. This book will continue with the approach that each dimension should be treated separately despite their similarities. For this purpose, the following sections review in depth the main characteristics of each of the constituents of the Dark Tetrad.

1.1.1 Narcissism

The term narcissism, originally developed by Freud (1914/1991), was derived from the story of Narcissus, who, according to mythology, fell in love with his image in a reflecting pool. So moved was Narcissus by his reflection that he did not eat, drink, or sleep, resulting in his demise. Freud incorporated this term into his psychoanalytic theory to identify individuals who exhibit excessive self-admiration because of an unhealthy relationship between their ego and libido (Freud, 1914/1991). Since Freud coined the term, narcissists have been regarded as people who love themselves too much for their own good (Boddy, 2011). Today, narcissism often refers to a psychological personality disorder in the Diagnostic and Statistical Manual (DSM-IV) or a subclinical version of the trait, often studied by personality and social psychologists (Jonason et al., 2012).

Narcissism is a personality characteristic that describes individuals ranging from those who can function normally in society to those who are clinically impaired by their grandiose perception of themselves and their willingness to exploit others (Wu & Lebreton, 2011). Central to the clinical description of pathological narcissism is a core dysfunction related to managing intense needs for validation and admiration. When individuals fail or struggle to effectively manage these needs because of extreme or rigid behavior or impaired regulatory capacities, the frequent result is several negative psychological consequences that may be characteristically grandiose or vulnerable (Wright et al., 2013).

The psychoanalytic tradition regards narcissism as a defense against feelings of insecurity, inadequacy, or other psychic wounds. While Hogan and Fico (2011) found this view excessively speculative, they contended that the dark side tendencies originate in childhood. They framed the origins of these tendencies in terms of something resembling attachment theory. Hogan and Fico (2011) cited Millon and Grossman (2004), who noted that the narcissistic personality reflects the attainment of a self-image of superior worth, learned mainly in response to admiring and devoted parents. Destructive narcissism is a reaction to prolonged abuse and trauma in early childhood or adolescence. Narcissism is a defense mechanism that deflects hurt and trauma from the victim's "true self" into a "false self" that is omnipotent, invulnerable, and omniscient. This "false self" concept refers to individuals who present a self-concept that is not who they are but rather a facade of who they feel society thinks they should be. The false self is used to obtain any form of positive or negative attention to satisfy the narcissist's labile sense of self-worth. The false self is a "fabricated personality" that serves as a defense mechanism to avoid conflict or rejection (Herbst, 2014).

Thus, narcissists possess feelings of dominance, entitlement, and exploitation and display exhibitionism. As such, narcissism has been associated with self-enhancement, which involves convincing oneself and others that one is worthwhile, attractive, competent, and lovable (Wu & Lebreton, 2011). Schyns (2015) cited Babiak and Hare (2006), who put it clearly: "Narcissists think that everything that happens around them, in fact, everything that others say and do, is or should be about them (p. 40)." Narcissism is not necessarily pathological but has an independent developmental sequence that stretches from infancy to adulthood. In its healthy form, mature narcissism produces behaviors such as humor and creativity. However, pathological narcissism occurs when one cannot integrate the idealized beliefs one has about oneself with the realities of one's inadequacies. Pathological narcissists seek recognition from idealized parental substitutes as an emotional salve for their shortcomings (Rosenthal & Pittinsky, 2006).

It is useful to think of narcissism as having three components: the self, interpersonal relationships, and self-regulatory strategies (Brunell et al., 2008). As for the self, the narcissist self is characterized by positive "specialness," and uniqueness, vanity, a sense of entitlement, and a desire for power and esteem. Regarding personal relationships, narcissistic relationships contain low empathy and emotional intimacy. In their place, many shallow relationships range from exciting and engaging to manipulative and exploitative. Narcissists have several additional interpersonal strategies for maintaining self-esteem beyond simply controlling others or taking credit from them. For example, narcissists seek the admiration of others. They also strive to associate with high-status individuals from whom they can gain status by association. They will brag, show off, and otherwise draw attention to themselves or act colorfully to gain notoriety (Aplin-Houtz et al., 2023). Narcissists will shine when there is an opportunity for glory, but they will underperform when recognition is unavailable. As for self-regulatory strategies, these are strategies for maintaining inflated self-views. For example, narcissists seek out opportunities for attention and admiration, brag, steal credit from others, and play games in relationships. When narcissists are good at this, they feel good; they report high self-esteem and positive life satisfaction. However, when unsuccessful, they evidence aggression and sometimes anxiety and depression (Brunell et al., 2008; Campbell et al., 2011).

As a construct, narcissism appears widely in social personality, clinical psychology, and psychiatric literature. The social-personality literature conceptualizes narcissism as a normally distributed trait in the population, for which there is no qualitative cutoff (taxon) for elevated narcissism. Grijalva and Harms (2014) mention that the *Diagnostic and Statistical Manual of Mental Disorders* describes narcissism as a grandiose preoccupation with self-importance, the belief that one is unique and more important than others. Additional diagnostic criteria for a narcissistic personality disorder (NPD) include "fantasies of unlimited success," "hypersensitivity to criticism," "entitlement," "exploitativeness," and "a lack of empathy." Like other personality traits, narcissism exists from high to low levels

(Grijalva & Harms, 2014). In addition, narcissism relates to other "normal" variables, such as Machiavellianism and psychopathy.

According to Campbell et al. (2011), the clinical and psychiatric literature conceptualizes narcissism as an NPD, a continuing and flexible character structure associated with grandiosity, lack of empathy, and a desire for admiration. According to the "Diagnostic and Statistical Manual of Mental Disorders" (DSM) advanced by the American Psychiatric Association and the DSM-IV version of it, there are nine specific symptoms of narcissism (e.g., "Shows arrogant, haughty behaviors or attitudes"; "Believes that he or she is 'special' and unique and can only be understood by, or should associate with, other special or high-status people [or institutions])" (American Psychiatric Association, 2000). To be diagnosed as having an NPD, an individual must have five of the nine traits. Moreover, narcissism must also cause distress or damage. For example, if an individual feels good about themself, has good relationships, and performs at work reasonably well, they would not be considered to have an NPD. These criteria result in a relatively low prevalence point for NPD. By contrast, the prevalence of those with narcissistic symptoms (but without causing sufficient distress to cross the line into the clinical disorder) is much larger. This pattern of characteristics is sometimes known as subclinical narcissism (Campbell et al., 2011; Dow, 2023).

The trait narcissism's core aspects are similar to pathological narcissism: egotism, low concern for others, and dominant, aggressive, or manipulative behavior. However, trait narcissism is characterized by fewer neurotic and great self-enhancing tendencies than pathological narcissism (Treadway et al., 2017). Derived from an overidealized and grandiose self-concept, narcissists experience high yet unstable self-esteem, which drives their self-enhancing and narcissistic tendencies; however, these tendencies may be maladaptive in the long term. While high self-esteem is often theorized and measured as stable, narcissism is a variant of unstable self-esteem, the general category of which is believed to explain many of the maladaptive reactions exhibited by individuals with high self-esteem (Treadway et al., 2017).

Barry and Kauten (2014) found in a sample of at-risk adolescents that pathological narcissism was associated with reactive and proactive aggression, low self-esteem, anxiety, depression, social stress, and high contingent self-worth, even when controlling for nonpathological narcissism and exploitativeness. Pathological narcissism was also associated with negative perceptions regarding the quality of one's interpersonal relationships. Their findings showed that pathological and nonpathological factors were associated in opposite directions with self-esteem, anxiety, social stress, and the perceived quality of interpersonal relationships. Nonpathological narcissism was also associated with perceived positive relationships, self-reliance, and low social pressure. They concluded that neither of the two forms of narcissism stood out as clearly adaptive or advantageous, although nonpathological narcissism suggested fewer emotional difficulties. Barry and Kauten (2014) suggested that perhaps the two forms capture different underlying characteristics that influence a more personally insecure form of narcissism versus a more outwardly boastful and exploitative form of narcissism, which would be consistent with emerging research on adults.

1.1.2   Psychopathy

In common usage, a psychopath is a person with a personality disorder characterized by extreme callousness, liable to behave antisocially or violently to get their own way (Davidson et al., 1994). Psychologists define psychopathy as a particular constellation of antisocial behaviors and emotions, including shallow affect, low remorse, low fear, low empathy, egocentrism, exploitativeness, manipulativeness, impulsivity, aggression, and criminality (Wu & Lebreton, 2011; Jonason et al., 2012; Lee et al., 2013; Aplin-Houtz et al., 2023). Board and Fritzon (2005) contended that psychopathy, initially described by Cleckley (1941/1988), is a form of personality disorder. With a three-to-one ratio of men to women, psychopathy impacts 1–4% of the population, about 25% of the incarcerated population, and about 30% of domestic abusers (Dow, 2023).

Many researchers believe psychopathy includes two factors (Dow, 2023). The first is called primary or instrumental psychopathy (Lykken, 1995). This factor contains facets of psychopathy, such as shallow affect, low empathy, and interpersonal coldness. Individuals with profound levels of these traits are sometimes called "emotionally stable" psychopaths. Broadly corresponding to primary psychopathy are interpersonal and affective domains. Interpersonally, individuals are superficial, grandiose, and deceitful. Affectively, they lack remorse or empathy and do not accept responsibility. Lifestyle and antisocial domains equate with secondary psychopathy. In the first, individuals are impulsive and lack goals; in the other, they exhibit poor self-control and antisocial behavior. Babiak and Hare (2006) call attention to a predatory stare and empty eyes in the psychopath that can unsettle observers, indicative of a primitive, autonomic, and scary response to a predator (Hanson & Baker, 2017).

The second factor is secondary or hostile/reactive psychopathy. It comprises the socially manipulative and deviant facets of psychopathy and has been variously referred to as aggressive, impulsive, and neurotic psychopathy (Lykken, 1995; Jonason et al., 2012; Blickle & Schütte, 2017). Individuals with high levels of this factor tend to "act impulsively, 'without thinking', without giving themselves time to assess the situation, to appreciate the dangers, to foresee the consequences, or even to anticipate how they will feel about their actions when they have time to consider it" (Lykken, 1995). This self-centered impulsivity factor indicates that such individuals seek thrills, lack diligence, and are unconcerned with deadlines or responsibilities. Others have applied a four-factor model of psychopathy, consisting of interpersonal, affective, lifestyle, and antisocial factors (Williams, Paulhus, & Hare, 2007).

Researchers argue that the construct of the psychopathic personality should not be contaminated with the factors of criminality and socially deviant behavior because these elements are correlates of psychopathy rather than its core characteristics (Boddy, 2011). This fits with the view of psychopathy held by leading researchers in the field, such as Hare (1999), who have stressed that there are psychopaths who do not engage in criminal behavior and can function well in society. Other researchers distinguish between unsuccessful psychopaths, those who have criminal convictions, and successful psychopaths, those who have no criminal convictions or engage in no illegal, antisocial behavior. There is some empirical support for this viewpoint, especially from recent investigations of the concept of "successful" psychopaths (Board & Fritzon, 2005). "Successful" or "Corporate" psychopaths are said to be people with psychopathic personality disorder patterns but without the characteristic history of arrest and incarceration. Corporate psychopaths are thus opportunistic corporate careerists who lack any concern for the consequences of their actions and are ruthless in pursuing their aims and ambition (Board & Fritzon, 2005; Boddy, 2011; Fennimore & Sementelli, 2016; Cleckley, 1941/1988).

Wu and Lebreton (2011) cited Cooke and Michie (2001), who presented a three-factor model conceptualizing the multidimensionality of psychopathy. The latter authors argued that psychopathy is comprised of (1) an arrogant and deceitful interpersonal style, (2) a deficient affective experience, and (3) an impulsive and irresponsible behavioral style. In accordance with the first factor, highly psychopathic individuals believe they are superior to others and constantly engage in self-promoting behaviors. In addition, they are egocentric and put their interests before those of others. Such people believe that rules do not apply to them and that they deserve special treatment and are often critical of those they think pose a potential threat to them. The second characteristic is the psychopath's unique experience of affect. According to Wu and Lebreton (2011), researchers have suggested that a lack of guilt and conscience are the telltale signs of a psychopath. In addition, psychopaths do not experience anxiety or fear to the same extent as others, tend to be malicious toward others, are unlikely to experience embarrassment, and reside at the end of the dishonesty and manipulativeness spectrum. The final factor highlights that psychopaths are impulsive and irresponsible. As such, they are described as thrill seekers who often struggle to maintain long-term romantic, platonic, and work-related relationships. In particular, these individuals are ego-driven and seek immediate gratification for their needs.

1.1.3   Machiavellianism

The third component of the Dark Triad is Machiavellianism. Although somewhat related to narcissism and psychopathy, Machiavellianism is a trait in its own right (Jonason et al., 2012). Its name was inspired by the writings of Niccolo Machiavelli, a sixteenth-century Italian political theorist who outlined the strategies a new prince could use to establish and maintain political power (Lee et al., 2013). Jones and Paulhus (2009, 2014) drew attention to a neglected predecessor, the first-century military strategist Sun Tzu. Sun Tzu added planning, coalition formation, and reputation building to themes that resemble Machiavelli's. The strategies, highly pragmatic and devoid of traditional social virtues, eventually became associated with an opportunistic and deceptive "Machiavellian" personality (Jonason et al., 2012). Wu and Lebreton (2011) cited in their review Wilson, Near, and Miller's (1996) definition of Machiavellianism: "A strategy of social conduct that involves manipulating others for personal gain, often against others' self-interest (p. 285)."

Machiavellianism describes a personality construct characterized by a cynical view of human nature and a deceitful and calculated interpersonal style (Christie & Geis, 1970). A person not concerned with conventional morality has no interpersonal affect and gross psychopathology, has a low ideological commitment, and is willing and able to manipulate others by any means, including deceit, is called Machiavellian. Machiavellianism has also been described as socially manipulating others for personal gain (Boddy, 2011; Aplin-Houtz et al., 2023). The main characteristics of the Machiavellian personality are also demonstrated in the Mach-IV scale, developed by Christie and Geis (1970), which has been widely used to assess this construct. The MACH–IV scale is comprised of 20 items that are phrased as recommendations, quasi-facts, or statements (e.g., "Anyone who completely trusts anyone is asking for trouble"). People who endorse such items have been found to (a) think in a cold, strategic, and pragmatic way, (b) have cynical, misanthropic, and negativistic views, (c) be emotionally detached and callous, (d) be agentically (e.g., for money, power, status) rather than communally (e.g., for love, family, harmony) motivated, and (e) use duplicity, exploitation, and manipulation tactics to push through their self-beneficial goals (Rauthmann, 2013).

Machiavellians were characterized as people who, in general, negatively perceive others as weak and untrustworthy. At the same time, their pragmatic morality enables them to follow the rule that "the end justifies the means." The dominant symptom is coldness, implying emotional detachment, lack of empathy, and disregard for the needs and aims of a partner. Research showed that Machiavellians not only have a common perception system but also eagerly try to manipulate their partners and use lies, deception, and cheating in situations where it is profitable for them to do so and when it increases the chances of reaching their goals. It could be said that the Machiavellian can act unethically whenever it pays off (Bańka & Orłowski, 2012; Dow, 2023).

Wu and Lebreton cited Christie and Geis (1970), who argued that individuals high in Machiavellianism could be identified using four key characteristics. First, these individuals lack empathy for others and are instead suspicious of them. This tendency toward suspiciousness may make these individuals less likely to be swayed by social influence, as they anticipate exploitation and selfishness during interpersonal interactions. Furthermore, high Machiavellians perceive others as less cooperative and generous than those low in Machiavellianism. Second, high Machiavellians have lower levels of affect when interacting with others. They not only experience difficulties in identifying their own emotions but also lack basic interpersonal skills. High Machiavellians approach others with a sense of detachment and lack of emotional involvement. Thus, these individuals can approach problems logically without interfering with affective states. Because they are prone to emotional detachment, it has been suggested that high Machiavellians are less cooperative and compliant than low Machiavellians. Third, high Machiavellians possess an aberrant view of morality and are willing to engage in immoral and unethical acts that go against convention, including manipulating, deceiving, and exploiting others.

Research has suggested that high Machiavellians are less likely to help others in emergencies. Fourth, high Machiavellians focus on their agendas with no regard for others. Machiavellians are willing to do whatever is necessary to achieve their own goals and are goal- rather than people-oriented. These individuals are not motivated by concern for others but by their purposes; as such, they are willing to manipulate others for personal gain. High Machiavellians are also more ambitious, adept at lying, seek to dominate others, and are more likely to assume control over situations than low Machiavellians (Wu & Lebreton, 2011; Dow, 2023).

1.1.4 Sadism

In their review of the literature on psychopathy and aggression, Porter and Woodworth (2006) have proposed an affective motive that may mediate the relationship between psychopathy and unprovoked aggression. According to them, sadism may explain acts of unprovoked aggression and violence. O'Meara, Davies, and Hammond (2011), after an extensive review of the literature, developed the following definition for sadistic personality: The term sadistic personality describes a person who humiliates others, shows a longstanding pattern of cruel or demeaning behavior to others or intentionally inflicts physical, sexual, or psychological pain or suffering on others to assert power and dominance or for pleasure and enjoyment.

The sadistic personality is unique among the Dark Tetrad, involving an appetite for cruelty instead of callous indifference. Only sadistic individuals are willing to pay the price (perform a tedious task) for the opportunity to harm others (Paulhus, Curtis, & Jones, 2018; Nocera et al., 2022; Liu et al., 2023). Therefore, the expanded model of the dark traits with sadism will deepen our understanding of amoral and antisocial personality dispositions, which could result in practical implementations (Međedović & Petrović, 2015). Conceptually, sadism is associated with deriving enjoyment from hurting others and seeking opportunities to do so (Lauder & March, 2023; Liu et al., 2023). Although psychopathy is also associated with hurting others, aggressive behavior may result from boredom or occur for instrumental gain, as opposed to the enjoyment of cruelty. Individuals high in psychopathy will only hurt others when it is easy and convenient, consistent with the tendency of high-psychopathy individuals to be impulsive and seek out short-term thrills despite long-term consequences (Buckels, Jones, & Paulhus, 2013).

Smith (2021) mentioned that criteria for the condition were listed in the DSM 3-R as a pervasive pattern of at least four of the following, which had emerged by adolescence:

Use of physical cruelty or violence in relationships to establish
  dominance (not simply for secondary gain, like robbery).
Humiliates/demeans people in the presence of others.
Unusually harsh treatment/discipline towards someone under their
  control.
Amusement from witnessing the psychological/physical pain of others,
  including animals.
Has lied to harm/inflict pain on others.
Operates through intimidation or terror to get others to comply.
Restricts the autonomy of people they are close to (i.e., the spouse
  must always be accompanied, and children are not allowed out of
  the home).
Fascination with violence, weapons, and torture/injury.

Characterized by cruel, aggressive, manipulative, and demeaning behavior directed toward others, sadistic individuals tend to display recurrent aggressive and evil behavior, as abusiveness and violence are common in the sadist's social relationships. Higher scores in everyday sadism are associated with verbally, physically, and/or psychologically injuring others, inspired by a hedonic value of being cruel (Buckels et al., 2013). There are several subtypes of sadism, including sexual sadists (Perez del Valle & Hand, 2022), criminal sadists (Owen, Noble, & Speed, 2017), political sadists (Blain, 2022), and everyday sadists (Greitemeyer, 2015) who enjoy witnessing others being injured or humiliated. Everyday sadism can be further delineated into dynamic behavior targeted at a victim (e.g., Internet bullies or playing first-person murder video games) or passive behavior (e.g., watching cage/bullfighting, enjoying stunt prank shows, or watching violent movies) (Dow, 2023).

Reidy, Zeichner, and Seibert (2011) examined 137 men who viewed photographs depicting violent imagery, completed a lexical decision task to assess state affect, and competed in a laboratory-based aggression paradigm. Their findings showed that sadism (i.e., faster reaction times to happiness words following violent imagery) was associated with a higher risk for unprovoked aggression. Also, psychopathy was not associated with sadism, and psychopathy and sadism independently predicted unprovoked aggression. Johnson et al. (2019), in a sample of 615 undergraduate students, found that construct validity for subclinical sadism was supported through negative correlations with agreeableness, honesty–humility, emotionality, and conscientiousness. Finally, Hughes and Samuels (2021) concluded that despite such overlaps with psychopathy, everyday sadism had received sufficient support from researchers, arguing that sadism is also a unique construct that should be included in the modified tetrad of dark personality traits.

1.1.5   Similarities and Differences among the Dark Tetrads

One of the issues that evoked researchers' interest is the similarities and differences between the three traits. This issue has given rise to many debates about whether the four traits should be treated as multidimensional because of their differences or merged into one construct because of their similarity. According to the general approach, the Dark Triad consists of three overlapping but distinct personality variables: narcissism, Machiavellianism, and psychopathy (Boddy, 2011; Furtner et al., 2017). Psychopaths differ from people classified as having a narcissist personality in that narcissists have emotions, feelings, and thus a conscience and are troubled by their behavior. Psychopaths, on the other hand, with their lack of emotions or conscience, are not. Machiavellianism, similar to corporate psychopathy, has no regard for moral standards and promotes the idea that the end justifies the means. It also advocates a cynical, political approach to management, including using a fraudulent persona when necessary and using force, if necessary, to achieve desired ends. Corporate psychopaths have the ruthlessness, charm, and cunning to get to the top of any organization. Therefore, it is the corporate psychopaths who may be the successful ones in the organizational setting (Boddy, 2011).

Machiavellians may also achieve success, but they may not quite make it because they lack the natural cruelty of the corporate psychopath. A Machiavellian personality does not imply that the individual lacks the conscience displayed by psychopaths, but it has broad similarities to many definitions of a psychopathic personality (Boddy, 2011). While narcissism involves excessive self-aggrandizement and psychopathy involves an antisocial nature lacking in empathic concern, Machiavellianism is characterized by a manipulative, self-serving social strategy comprised of three main components: cynicism, manipulation, and the view that the ends justify the means (Jonason et al., 2012). Robertson et al. (2016) also discussed the similarities and differences between the three traits. According to them, all three Dark Triad traits share a lack of honesty and humility (e.g., sincerity and fairness), but each trait adds additional components. Machiavellian individuals are adept at skillful manipulation and are cynical about other people. The narcissism component of the Dark Triad emerged from the clinical research studies of individuals who lack empathy and display inflated self-worth and need for admiration. Individuals with high levels of psychopathy exhibit high impulsivity and low anxiety about the consequences of their behavior.

According to Jones and Paulhus (2014), whereas psychopaths act impulsively, abandon friends and family, and pay little attention to their reputation, Machiavellians plan, build alliances, and do their best to maintain a positive reputation. The element of impulsivity is crucial in distinguishing psychopathy from Machiavellianism. When overlap was controlled in research studies, these assertions were supported: Machiavellians are strategic rather than impulsive, and they avoid manipulating family members (Barber, 1998) and any other behavioral tactics that might harm their reputation, such as feigning weakness. The critical elements of Machiavellianism appear to be (a) manipulation, (b) callous affect, and (c) a strategic-calculating orientation. Narcissists may always be too obviously egotistical in their efforts to get promoted unopposed. Narcissistic behavior is marked by manipulation and callousness, such as Machiavellianism and psychopathy (Jones & Paulhus, 2014).

Research discussing and examining whether the three traits should be treated as unidimensional or multidimensional is not entirely conclusive. This should be considered by scholars who study the Dark Triad. Jones and Figueredo (2013) concluded from their two studies that manipulation and callousness are necessary and sufficient components of an evil personality. This assertion is supported by the fact that it was found that the latter two traits (i.e., the traits called the "dark core") accounted for all the non-within-scale interrelationships in the Dark Triad. This malevolent core seems to be a common element in all antagonistic variables. Jones and Figueredo contended that while all malicious traits have a dark core of covariance, their behavioral, attitudinal, and belief-related components make them unique. For example, Machiavellians have a dark personality with a cold, calculating, long-term, and strategic style. Psychopathy is a dark personality with an impulsive and antisocial style, while narcissism is a dark personality with an egotistical style.

Rauthmann and Kolar (2012) examined the perceived "darkness" of the Dark Triad traits narcissism, Machiavellianism, and psychopathy. Their findings showed that narcissism was perceived more favorably than Machiavellianism and psychopathy. Their explanation to the result was that some narcissistic attributes might alter people's perceptions, such as narcissists' (a) charmingness, (b) physical attractiveness, and (c) relatively higher conscientiousness and achievement motivation. This could help explain narcissism's perceived desirability. Moreover, themes such as seeking attention, admiration, and status (covered in the Dirty Dozen scale) may be inherently more desirable than Machiavellian and psychopathic themes of exploitation and callousness. Their findings also showed that people's judgments of others versus themselves differed. While all three traits were less desirable for the self than for others, this was interestingly reversed for consequences for others: People tended to judge the consequences of their behavior as less detrimental to others than when others, in general, enacted the same behavior.

McHoskey, Worzel, and Szyarto (1998) found that Machiavellianism is associated with psychopathy in general and specifically with both primary and secondary psychopathy. They concluded that Machiavellianism is a global measure of psychopathy that assesses but confounds both the unique and common sources of variance associated with primary and secondary psychopathy. According to them, this finding provides a framework for understanding seemingly inconsistent results in the literature on Machiavellianism that has precluded its integration with psychopathy. For example, the consistent positive association between Machiavellianism and anxiety has prevented its smooth integration with psychopathy because anxiety is an antithetical characteristic of psychopathy. However, recognizing the implications of the distinction between primary and secondary psychopathy with anxiety and the nature of Machiavellianism relative to the difference between primary and secondary psychopathy erodes the mystery surrounding this association (McHoskey et al., 1998).

Wisse, Barelds, and Rietzschel (2015) found, based on data collected from 306 pairs of Dutch employees and their direct supervisors (most worked in commercially oriented (service) organizations (e.g., shops, financial institutions, health-care organizations, etc.), a positive relationship between employee narcissism and supervisor ratings of (all subscales of) innovative employee behavior. They also found that employee Machiavellianism was negatively related, and employee psychopathy was unrelated to supervisor ratings of creative employee behavior. They contended that this testifies to the importance of differentiating between the Dark Triad personality traits. One factor that may explain these differential findings is that Machiavellians and psychopaths, more strongly than narcissists, lack communal tendencies and interpersonal orientations and generate more negative perceptions in others. An interesting study conducted by Jonason (2014) on a sample of American employees found that narcissism and psychopathy were linked to political conservatism. On the other hand, Machiavellianism was associated with low rates of political liberalism, not political conservatism. Jonason concluded that political conservatism is informed by traits such as the Dark Triad, predisposing individuals to desire social dominance.

While the previously discussed findings support some discriminant validity among the three traits, it should be noted that there is evidence to suggest otherwise. In their study, Bertl et al. (2017) assessed the factorial structure of the Dark Triad in a large community-based sample (N = 2463). Structural equation modeling indicated that a better fit for a single latent dark core is obtained than when assuming that the Dark Triad traits are independent constructs. The researchers concluded that the assumption that the three traits represent conceptually distinct but overlapping constructs is questionable. If these traits could be best characterized as distinct yet overlapping, then modeling the Dark Triad as a three-trait hierarchical factor structure should show the best fit. However, their results indicate that this is not the case.

In addition, meta-analysis findings (Muris et al., 2017) did not yield a compelling reason to include all three traits when studying their role in transgressive human behavior. The findings of Muris et al. showed that correlations among the Dark Triad constituents were quite substantial, suggesting conceptual redundancy. Therefore, while the dominant approach is to treat the Dark Triad as multidimensional, there is evidence that in some cases and samples, one dimension represents the concept better than three. This means that, before researchers analyze their data, they would be best advised to examine the dimensionality of the concept in their specific data to decide whether they should treat the concept as multi- or unidimensional.

Later studies have focused on how sadism can be incorporated into the Dark Triad traits as an independent facet. Chabrol et al. (2009) found that psychopathic, narcissistic, and Machiavellian traits were correlated moderately with sadistic traits. They suggest that all four of these constructs are overlapping but distinct and propose calling the association of psychopathic, narcissistic, Machiavellian, and sadistic traits the "Dark Tetrad" of personality traits. Some people's interpersonal style seems entirely constructed around sadistic behavior (Smith, 2021).

Johnson et al. (2019) found that the Dark Triad traits were positively correlated with subclinical sadism, suggesting that sadism, Machiavellianism, psychopathy, and narcissism share common elements. Interestingly, each sadism subscale correlated most strongly with psychopathy, but these correlations were not high enough to suggest that psychopathy and sadism can be reduced to the same factor. In other words, the facets of sadism still carry sufficient unique variance. They concluded that their results distinguished vicarious, physical, and verbal sadism from psychopathy, narcissism, and Machiavellianism and also replicated past relationships between subclinical sadism and relevant personality traits. At the factor level, subclinical sadism can be distinguished from psychopathy by its facets, loaded separately from psychopathy. Therefore, according to them, their study's findings support the position of subclinical sadism as an additional and unique in a revised Dark Tetrad of personality (Alavi et al., 2022; Gajda et al., 2022).

Buckels et al. (2013) found that sadists, psychopaths, narcissists, and those low in empathy and perspective took aggressed against an innocent person when aggression was easy. Of those with dark personalities, however, only sadists increased the intensity of their attack once they realized that the innocent person would not fight back. Sadists were the only dark personalities willing to work (i.e., expend time and energy) to hurt an innocent person. They concluded that together, these results suggest that sadists possess an intrinsic appetitive motivation to inflict suffering on innocent others – a motivation that is absent in other dark personalities. Inflicting suffering on the weak is so rewarding for sadists that they will aggress even at a personal cost.

Plouffe, Smith, and Saklofske (2019) examined the Sadistic Personality scale in 638 Canadian undergraduate students. Their results support the scale's psychometric qualities and the position of sadism within the Dark Tetrad. It should be noted that the sadism scale had the highest correlation with psychopathy compared to narcissism and Machiavellianism. This conclusion was supported by a cross-national study in Russia, Greece, Serbia, and the United Kingdom (Plouffe et al., 2023). Liu et al. (2023) developed and validated the Chinese form of the short Dark Tetrad scale across four studies in a large sample (total N = 3,181). The findings showed that the four subscales are correlated but also distinct regarding factor structure and criterion correlations. This finding supports incorporating sadism into the Dark Triad traits as an independent facet. The findings of Liu et al. (2023) also demonstrate that the Dark Tetrad concept applies to other cultures, such as the Chinese culture, and not only to Western cultures. Similar findings and conclusions were found in a sample of 429 participants from Portugal (Pechorro et al., 2023).

While some researchers use sadism as part of the Dark Tetrad (Hughes & Samuels, 2021; Pechorro et al., 2023), others still rely on the Dark Triad traits (Leite, Cardoso, & Monteiro, 2023). Scholars should always consider the high correlation between sadism and psychopathy scale, including subclinical sadism, to form a "Dark Tetrad" personality (Kowalski et al., 2021;

Blötner & Beisemann, 2022). Therefore, one should not overlook the conceptual implications of the findings that of the Dark Triad traits, subclinical sadism is closely related to psychopathy (Johnson et al., 2019). Bonfá-Araujo et al. (2022) concluded, based on a meta-analysis review, that the sadism dimension likely yields incremental validity to the previous Dark Triad proposal, although the discriminant validity of sadism relative to the remaining Dark Tetrad factors still deserves a closer investigation.

1.1.6 Cyber Misconduct and Crime and Its Consequences

1.1.6.1 Cyber Misconduct and Crime

Harmful online behavior can take a variety of forms. One of the principal terms used here, cyber misconduct, is not the only one for this behavior. Many include antisocial online behaviors (Moor & Anderson, 2019). Cyber aggression is the most general term given to describe socially undesirable online behaviors in the existing research literature; cyberbullying is usually used to describe bullying behaviors in cyberspace; and other terms such as online harassment and trolling have been used to describe malicious behaviors conducted with modern technologies (Bogolyubova et al., 2018). Cyber abuse and cybercrime are rightfully global issues, as both are associated with significant negative impacts. As Harrison et al. (2018) mentioned, online consumer fraud was reported to cost individuals almost $1 billion annually (IC3, 2015). Online interactions facilitate online consumer fraud through various communication media. Common online consumer fraud practices include misrepresenting assets during the sale and nondelivery of goods or services.

Moor and Anderson (2019) mentioned seven popular mobile phone applications (Facebook, Instagram, Pinterest, Snapchat, LinkedIn, Twitter, and WhatsApp) that provide immediate and readily available social connectivity and can result in variations to negative online behaviors such as trolling and harassment, and the sending of nonconsensual redistribution of explicit images. It also should be noted that there is some overlap among the different cyber misconducts discussed here. Sometimes, it is not easy to differentiate between them. However, each cyber misbehavior mentioned here has unique characteristics regarding its usage and features. These variations affect how Dark Tetrad uses them for performing cyber misconduct as each kind of cyber application led to unique features in how Dark Tetrad utilizes it for abuse.

Experiencing online antisocial behaviors has similar psychopathological outcomes as experiencing traditional harassment, including depression, anxiety, and low self-esteem. Unlike more traditional, face-to-face anti-social behaviors, victims of online antisocial behavior are often targeted in the perceived safety of their home, aggravating the victim's perceived vulnerability and well-being. Online antisocial behaviors are considered to be more pervasive than traditional antisocial behaviors and have a longer-lasting impact on the victim (March, 2022). There is no doubt that many of the individuals who use social media sites for malicious purposes have dark personalities. As mentioned earlier, this book focuses on four personalities known as the Dark Tetrad traits: psychopaths, narcissists, sadists and Machiavellians and their relationship to cyber misbehavior and cybercrime.

1.1.6.2   Consequences of Cyber Deviance and Cybercrime

Antisocial online behaviors are any deviant behavior (or the purposeful absence of any expected behavior) that is perpetrated online that has negative online or offline consequences for the target (including self-directed behaviors) (Moor & Anderson, 2019). The spread of digital communications, especially the Internet, has created new opportunities for psychopaths to engage in criminal activity, which may vary in the frequency and extent of damage it can cause to its victims. The most serious are disseminating computer viruses, cyberbullying, and impersonating another person or institution for phishing. However, offenses using the Internet and mobile telephony (cyber offenses) are also committed by people belonging to the general population (Perenc, 2022).

According to Jabłońska and Zajdel (2020), "Problematic Internet use" refers to a condition where people's difficulty controlling their Internet use negatively influences their social life, relationships, and mental health. According to them, risk factors related to problematic Internet use remain unclear, but psychological traits are seen as potential vulnerability factors for this phenomenon. Research with adolescents supports an association between excessive Internet use for social connection, accompanied by feeling unable to control Internet usage as "Internet attachment," and finds it leads to greater loneliness and irritability when offline and greater cyber victimization. In addition, greater media use at night is associated with disturbed sleep and depression and anxiety symptoms in adolescents (Hayes et al., 2020).

One of the main negative consequences of cyber misconduct is the damages it costs to the victims. The negative consequences for the victims of cyberbullying mirror those of traditional bullying, increasing rates of depression, anxiety, and alcohol dependence (Moor & Anderson, 2019). Hayes et al. (2020) informed based on their study that in terms of psychopathology symptoms, cyber aggressors/victims reported higher levels of emotion dysregulation, depression, and anxiety. Slonje and Smith (2008) found that picture/video clip bullying had a high impact. This kind of cyberbullying is the most obviously public and can show the victim in embarrassing or hurtful situations. This is because of the large audience size (if the picture/clip was on the Internet) and the concreteness effect, that is, actually seeing the picture/clip. The fear of not knowing who had seen the picture/clip is also a reason for some participants (Slonje & Smith, 2008). Email and text messages seem to be less harmful than traditional bullying. This is because email bullying is not as personal since the victims often did not know who the bully was and thought the email could have been meant for anyone and not specifically for them. In addition, emails are possibly less used and less salient for this adolescent age group than text messaging and mobile phone calls (Slonje & Smith, 2008).

Revenge porn proclivity, as well as the nonconsensual dissemination of "sexts" are behaviors that are contingent on a nonconsenting dissemination of confidential, sensitive material, and the perpetrators of such behaviors can cause severe and damaging consequences to their victims (who are most commonly women). Moreover, this behavior captures the unempathetic callousness exercised by the trait psychopathy in their affinity for short-term action for instant gratification and cruel relationship abandonment (Moor & Anderson, 2019).

A growing body of research demonstrates that exposure to cyberbullying in children and adolescents is associated with emotional distress, adverse changes in body image, depression, substance use, and suicidal behaviors. In adults, there are indications that victims of such behaviors are more likely to experience psychological distress, develop symptoms of depression, and exhibit problematic alcohol use. Moreover, it has been demonstrated that victimization and engagement in harmful online behaviors, such as cyberbullying, may be associated with maladjustment (Bogolyubova et al., 2018).

Cyber misconduct has severe damages when performed in the workplace. Charlier et al. (2017) mentioned Randazzo and colleagues (2004), who report that cyber misconduct in work organizations is most often associated with a financial loss for the organization, a result of either direct theft or cost incurred in repairing the damage done to online systems as a result of this misconduct. Other reported harm to organizations included damages to business operations and organizations' reputations. Charlier et al. (2017) contended that these cases are drawn from examples where individuals were caught and subsequently charged with a crime. There are undoubtedly many more instances of cyber misconduct in the workplace where perpetrators have not been caught or have not been formally charged with a crime. It is also possible that many employees who are caught engaging in cyber misconduct experience a variety of organizational sanctions, including warnings, probation, or termination, rather than facing criminal charges.

Another aspect of cyber misconduct in the workplace is the damage it causes to employees. Cyber misconduct in the workplace could be categorized as involving communication (such as communicating mistreatment in the form of bullying, incivility, aggression, or sexual harassment) or the acquisition of information or objects (such as identity theft or fraud). Such cyber misconduct that takes place using information and communication technologies, such as email, text messaging, or other computer technologies, violates workplace norms and threatens to harm or results in harm to individual employees (Charlier et al., 2017).

1.1.7 Dark Triad/Tetrad and the Inclination to Perform Cyber Misconduct

The rising popularity of social networking sites raises the question of whether and how personality differences are manifested in them. As demonstrated in this book, personality differences play an essential role in social networking sites' motivations and how users create and maintain their identity on them (Kapidzic, 2013). Harmful online behavior is a multifaceted problem and can be approached differently. One of the most notable psychological approaches to this problem is assessing dark personalities (Bogolyubova et al., 2018). The domain of dark personality traits is an area of investigation relating to interpersonal online misconduct due to strong links between these traits and socially destructive and malevolent behavior (Craker & March, 2016; Olckers & Hattingh, 2022).

The online environment includes various social networks, such as Facebook, Twitter, Instagram, LinkedIn, WhatsApp, and Messenger. By nature, dark personalities are more motivated to perform misconducts and criminal activities. However, to perform illegal and/or unethical behaviors, one has to be capable of deceiving the other party. Consequently, in our case, individuals with Dark Tetrad personalities must believe they can successfully deceive victims into committing misconducts. The effects of the capabilities of a perpetrator are rooted in how they increase various forms of power and influence exchanges. Thus, technical capabilities may aid in some types of misconducts, whereas interpersonal communication skills may be helpful in other contexts. To perform cyber misconducts and crime, Dark Tetrads should have the capabilities to be able to use the Internet in a way that will foster in their victims a false sense of trust so that they may gain some advantage and influence over their victims (Harrison et al., 2018).

Even when an individual possesses the skills necessary to commit fraud, that person must recognize that some exploitable opportunity exists. As predators, Dark Tetrad personalities always ensure that the environment provides the best conditions to attack (Cohen, 2016, 2018). In the case of cyber deviance, the individual should be able to identify specific applications and channels that will provide an excellent opportunity to exploit the trust of another for gain intentionally, and the likelihood of being caught or punished seems remote. The predators should also be able to recognize naivety, gullibility, or a lack of cleverness in potential victims that they may exploit (Harrison et al., 2018). This might be easier for Dark Tetrad in direct interpersonal, face-to-face interaction, but it requires different capabilities when identifying the potential victims' weaknesses on the Internet. Finally, the Internet provides predators attractive opportunities for misconducts, often resulting from weak controls and procedures that may mask the perpetrator's misconducts and crimes. For example, the anonymity of individuals engaged in multiple online transactions can increase the opportunity for fraud by reducing the likelihood that the perpetrator can be subsequently identified and held accountable (Harrison et al., 2018).

The following section will present the unique characteristics of each dark personality in performing cyber deviance and crime.

1.1.7.1 Narcissists

Social media is an environment where people with narcissistic traits can meet their psychological needs, such as the need to be admired and receive constant positive feedback on their physical appearance. Narcissism refers to a grandiose sense of self-importance, superiority, and entitlement, which may direct individuals to problematic social media use via preoccupation with self-promotion in social media via selfies and other tools. Concerning cyber aggression, narcissists are expected to function well in online environments because of the shallowness of online relations and the controllability of online self-presentation. Narcissism is also associated with more intense use of social networking sites and more extensive online networks (Pabian, De Backer, & Vandebosch, 2015).

The personality trait of narcissism, which involves a grandiose but unstable view of one's abilities, uniqueness, and social attraction, contributes to exhibitionistic and self-centered thoughts and actions in social media in different ways. The Dynamic Self-Regulatory Processing Model explains how narcissists pursue and maintain their inflated self-concept by gaining attention and admiration from others on social networking sites. Narcissistic social media users benefit from the large audience provided by social networking platforms, seeking positive feedback to recover from perceived social rejection. As a result, online social behavior, such as frequently posting photographs, status updates, and self-promotional and sexually provocative content, increases due to operant conditioning. Thus, the number of likes has become the secondary reinforcement for experiencing a positive emotional affect (Hernández et al., 2021).

Vaknin (2008) argued that to the narcissist, the Internet is an alluring and irresistible combination of playground and hunting grounds, the gathering place of numerous potential sources of narcissistic supply, a world where false identities are the norm and mind games the bon ton. Furthermore, it is beyond the reach of the law, the pale of social norms, and the strictures of civilized conduct. The Internet is an extension of the real-life Narcissistic Pathological Space but without its risks, injuries, and disappointments. In the virtual universe of the Web, the narcissist vanishes and reappears with ease, often adopting myriad aliases and nicknames. S/he can thus fend off criticism, abuse, disagreement, and disapproval effectively and in real time – and preserve the precarious balance of his infantile personality. Narcissists are, therefore, prone to Internet addiction (Vaknin, 2008).

1.1.7.2 Machiavellians

Individuals scoring high in Machiavellianism tend to be assimilative and self-oriented, generally showing little concern for others and may, therefore, not be interested in serving as role models. Machiavellians showed greater concern for themselves (self-oriented secondary goals) than for the interaction, likely due to their self-oriented and manipulative streak. Machiavellians are characterized by manipulating and exploiting others, which involves obtaining much information about potential victims. Since Facebook users often publish intimate personal data on their sites, individuals with high Machiavellianism are eager to collect this information for malicious purposes at the appropriate time. This also applies to rumors often disseminated in cyberspace (Rosenberg & Egbert, 2011; Lai et al., 2023).

Machiavellian adults employ manipulation tactics, such as making others feel ashamed, embarrassed, or guilty to navigate their offline social world. Protective self-monitoring may facilitate this manipulation and allow the Machiavellian man or woman to avoid detection and associated consequences such as loss of reputation or retaliation. Both men and women with high levels of Machiavellianism also employ self-monitoring online. The use of impression management strategies on Facebook by Machiavellian men and women may reflect a conscious effort to avoid being perceived as manipulative or exploitative. The dual nature of these friendships may increase the importance of online self-monitoring as offline friends may detect dishonest or misleading information (Rosen et al., 2013; Abell & Brewer, 2014). Besides their deceptive, manipulative, and exploitative nature, Machiavellians fear social rejection, which may cause them to prefer online communication, where they can manipulate others more easily. Machiavellians can feel more comfortable conducting activities on the Internet rather than communicating with others face to face (Ibrahim, 2010; Perenc, 2022).

1.1.7.3 Psychopaths

Psychopaths have less compassion toward others, lie more, enjoy lying, and take more risks. In an online context, it has been found that individuals high in psychopathy tend to make unpleasant and aggressive comments to others. Psychopathy has a significant relationship with online gaming motives. Additionally, individuals with high psychopathy use social media to engage in cybersex to fulfill their extra stimulation and sensation needs. Thus, it can be said that individuals high in psychopathy desire pleasure and enjoyment by using social networking sites such as Instagram.

Moreover, psychopaths do not like uncertain feelings and are thus motivated to reduce such feelings. Individuals with high intensity of this trait badly bear the feeling of uncertainty, so they are strongly motivated to remove or reduce it. Increased uncertainty makes the person uncomfortable and motivates him/her to act to reduce it. One way to achieve this is to collect as much information about the surrounding environment as possible, which gives them control over it. Therefore, they engage in surveillance on social networking sites to reduce such feelings of uncertainty. People with high-intensity psychopathic traits will often surveil and supervise others on Facebook, with a sense of uncertainty as an intermediary variable (Ibrahim, 2010; Perenc, 2022).

Psychopaths are motivated to use social networking sites such as Instagram for social motives (achieve social benefits), coping motives (a desire to escape from pressure or discomfort from uncertainty), and enhancement motives (seek pleasure and enjoyment) (Nikbin et al., 2022).

Psychopathy has been positively correlated with many deviant behaviors on social networks, such as creating conflicts, provoking discussions that offer erroneous information to create chaos, and violating rules or regulations. Psychopaths may engage in cybersex using social media to fulfill their need for sensation and extra stimulation (Perenc, 2022). Another intriguing effect of research on the discussed issues was the discovery of the relationship between the features of psychopathy and narcissism and sending autographs to cyberspace, the so-called "selfie." Moreover, it turned out that people promoting themselves on the web (e.g., on Facebook) show a greater than average intensity of narcissism, which also belongs to the psychopathic personality traits (Ibrahim, 2010; Bilal, Nadeem, & Saleem, 2022; Perenc, 2022).

1.1.7.4 Sadism

Any psychological mechanism that inhibits empathy would help release the sadistic impulses of those rewarded by cruelty. The anonymity of the Internet minimizes a powerful deterrent, that is, social repercussions. Hence, it is the ideal venue to unleash latent malevolence (Buckels et al., 2019). Sadists obtain pleasure from cruel behaviors, and they are even willing to work for the opportunity to hurt an innocent victim. Everyday sadists, more than others, seek opportunities to indulge their appetites for cruelty (Greitemeyer, 2015; Nocera et al., 2022), and social networking provides them with many such opportunities. Because sadists derive enjoyment and pleasure from inflicting physical or emotional pain and humiliation on others (Chung et al., 2019; March & Steele, 2020), they tend to perform cyberbullying and cyber trolling behaviors as they bring personal enjoyment and pleasure from attacking others and seeing them suffer (Alavi et al., 2022; Gajda et al., 2022; Liu et al., 2023). With the number of users on social media, it is easy for everyday sadists to indulge their need for cruelty as they have a large variety of victims to choose from (Olckers & Hattingh, 2022). Online antisocial behavior then seems more driven by sadistic pleasure than by callousness, strategic considerations, or a threatened ego (van Geel et al., 2017; Nocera et al., 2022).

Sadistic individuals might be stimulated by hurting others and seeing the victims suffer as they find it gratifying, which becomes more effortless and anonymous in cyberspace (Brown et al., 2019). Environmental and situational factors may influence sadistic behaviors. Underlying sadistic interests and tendencies can be increased, especially among those with higher baseline levels (Themelidis & Davies, 2021). A sadistic personality promotes reward-motivated (appetitive-controlled) cyber aggression

(Gajda et al., 2022). Not only do individuals with high trait sadism enjoy harming others, but they are willing to endure personal strain and sacrifice just for the opportunity to do so (March & Steele, 2020). Sadism has a residual predictor role in problematic antisocial online behaviors when included in the model with the Dark Triad traits, which may indicate that, despite its overlap with other traits, sadism should be added to the Dark Triad to form the Dark Tetrad (Kircaburun & Griffiths, 2018; Kircaburun et al., 2018a; Liu et al., 2023). Therefore, theoretically, researchers should find Dark Tetrad a more valuable and complete model of personality traits as the role of sadism may prove integral as an explanatory mechanism for antisocial behaviors in cyberspace (Alavi et al., 2022; Liu et al., 2023). It should be noted that relative to the Dark Triad, sadism has a relatively small research base from which to conclude (Reidy et al., 2011).

Kircaburun et al. (2018b) explained the relationship between sadism and online gaming in that most of the gamers in the study were playing violent games (role-playing games and first-person shooter games). According to them, sadism is associated with the amount of violent video game play when other personality traits are controlled for. Sadists enjoy humiliating others, cruelty, and deviant behaviors. Arguably, it would be expected that those with sadistic tendencies might play video games to escape into a world where they can hurt others and exercise their fantasies of hurting and killing, which they may find challenging to do without severe consequences in the real world. They may become dependent on gaming because of their need to have what they perceive as pleasant feelings. Such gamers would also want to compete and beat others to humiliate them to make themselves feel superior.

1.1.8 Research Evidence

Strong evidence exists for the relationship between dark personalities and cyber misconduct (Olckers & Hattingh, 2022). Moor and Anderson (2019) performed a systematic literature review of the evidence for these relationships and found 26 studies that reveal these traits are related to many forms of cyber misconduct. Based on a thorough literature review of empirical studies, they concluded that psychopathy and sadism are the strongest correlates of online behaviors that are (a) the most interpersonally belligerent and (b) the easiest for the perpetrator to remain anonymous. For example, the online behaviors of trolling, cyber aggression, cyberbullying, and technology facilitating sexual violence are all uniquely predicted by psychopathy or both psychopathy and sadism. However, these traits do not drive behaviors that are not as interpersonally antagonistic (or at least not as consistently or to the same degree). For example, problematic social media usage is more strongly related to narcissism than other traits, and sending unsolicited explicit images is more strongly related to Machiavellianism. Moor and Anderson (2019) concluded that all four traits could uniquely predict antisocial behavior despite commonly covarying with their fellow triad.

There is also empirical evidence for the relationship between the Dark Tetrad and cyber misconduct. For example, Hayes et al. (2020) found that students who reported engagement in cyber aggression showed higher levels of maladaptive personality traits and psychopathology symptoms compared to students who did not report aggression. They concluded that dark traits consistently predict aggressive behavior in frequency and severity. Furthermore, these traits are associated with impulsiveness, frustration intolerance, and lack of empathy, factors that place individuals at risk for harming others and thus could explain opportunistic cyber aggression.

Jabłońska and Zajdel (2020) found in a sample of 384 online users from Poland that higher Dark Triad traits are associated with higher problematic Internet use. All the Dark Triad's components were associated linearly with problematic Internet use: Their highest levels were displayed by respondents with high problematic Internet use. Lopes and Yu (2017) argued that the Dark Triad personalities have different motivations and beliefs that may impact the behavior they display. According to them, narcissists are more frequent users of Facebook. Psychopaths and Machiavellians tend to display antisocial behavior, including trolling and acting against the law.

Kircaburun et al. (2018b) found in a sample of 421 gamers that different personality traits and online gaming motives were associated with different levels of problematic online game use. Narcissism was indirectly associated with problematic online gaming via the escape motive among role-playing gamers and the total sample. Sadism was directly associated with problematic online gaming among first-person shooter gamers and indirectly with problematic online gaming via escape, competition, and fantasy motives among the total sample. Psychopathy and Machiavellianism had no direct relationship with problematic online gaming. Kircaburun et al. (2018b) concluded that Dark Tetrad should also be considered when considering theoretical models involving problematic gaming use, online gaming motives, and preference for different games.

CHAPTER 2

The Dark Triad/Tetrad and Social Networking Addiction

2.1 Social Network Addiction: Definition and Conceptualization

With the increasing Internet usage, social networks have become a modern phenomenon. Recent statistics show that active digital users were 4.66 billion on the Internet, 4.32 billion on mobile Internet, and 4.2 billion on social media by January 2021 (Statista, 2021). People use social networks for various purposes, such as playing games, socializing, spending time with each other, and communicating. In addition, the social network provides them with opportunities for self-disclosure, self-presentation, and impression management. However, social network use, regarded as a popular leisure activity worldwide, also risks becoming problematic given the results of models that explain the excessive and compulsive use of social networks, as well as its similarities to behavioral and chemical addictions, problematic social network use, and addictive use of social networks is represented in the literature as a specific form of Internet addiction (Kircaburun, Demetrovics, & Tosuntaş, 2019).

The online environment includes various social networks, such as Facebook, Twitter, Instagram, LinkedIn, WhatsApp, Messenger, and more (Necula, 2020). Excessive Internet use can lead to Internet addiction, which includes a heterogeneous spectrum of Internet-related activities that can potentially cause problems – such as gaming, shopping, gambling, or social networking – for the individual. Since the mid-1990s, Internet addiction has been recognized as a new type of addiction and a mental health problem showing signs and symptoms like other established addictions (Hussain & Pontes, 2018, 2019). Social networking site addiction can also be perceived as manifesting in excessive involvement in social networking sites, being driven by a solid motivation to log on to or use social networking sites, and dedicating a significant amount of time and effort to social networking sites. Such activities negatively affect other social activities, studies/jobs, interpersonal relationships, and/or psychological health and well-being (Andreassen & Pallesen, 2014).

Cheng and Li (2014) examined the prevalence of Internet addiction. Their dataset included 164 prevalence figures from 80 reports, including 89,281 participants from 31 nations across seven regions. A random-effects meta-analysis showed a global prevalence estimate of 6.0%. In addition, they found that the prevalence rate of Internet addiction varies across world regions. In detail, the highest prevalence rate of 10.9% was found in the samples from the Middle East. Furthermore, prevalence rates of 8.0% in North America, 7.1% in Asia, 6.1% in South-East Europe, 4.3% in Oceania, and 2.6% in North-West Europe were reported. Prevalence rates in Germany are estimated to be around 1–2% of the general population. Moreover, Internet addiction prevalence was higher for nations with greater traffic time consumption, pollution, and dissatisfaction with life in general. The researchers also found that Internet addiction prevalence is inversely associated with quality of life, as reflected by subjective (life satisfaction) and objective (quality of environmental conditions) indicators.

From a formal medical perspective, Internet addiction has not yet been introduced in the Diagnostic and Statistical Manual of Mental Disorders as a Psychiatric Disorder (American Psychiatric Association, 2013). However, according to the American Psychological Association (APA) (2013), the clinical diagnosis of Internet Gaming Disorder comprises a behavioral pattern encompassing persistent and recurrent use of the Internet to engage in online games, leading to significant impairment or distress over a period of 12 months as specified by the endorsement of at least five out of the following nine criteria: (i) preoccupation with Internet games; (ii) withdrawal symptoms when Internet gaming is taken away; (iii) tolerance, resulting in the need to spend increasing amounts of time engaged in Internet games; (iv) unsuccessful attempts to control participation in Internet games; (v) loss of interest in previous hobbies and entertainment as a result of, and with the exception of, Internet games; (vi) continued excessive use of Internet games despite knowledge of psychosocial problems; (vii) deceiving family members, therapists, or others regarding the amount of Internet gaming; (viii) use of Internet games to escape or relieve negative moods; and (ix) jeopardizing or losing a significant relationship, job, or education or career opportunity because of participation in Internet games (APA, 2013). These symptoms can be generalized to Internet addiction in general.

An interesting typology was advanced by Jin, Wang, and Ji (2019), who differentiate between negative Internet adaptation and positive Internet adaptation. Negative Internet adaptation is manifested in Internet Interpersonal

Orientation (e.g., ignoring genuine interpersonal relationships and being addicted to social networking), Academic Escape (e.g., surfing the Internet to escape from schoolwork), and Internet problem behaviors (e.g., cyberbullying and browsing pornographic and violent websites). On the other hand, positive Internet adaptation is manifested in relational Internet use, which includes complying with network norms, engaging in the rational expression on the Internet, and rejecting negative Internet information.

From a scientific and practical point of view, several definitions and approaches seek to capture the notion of addiction to the social network. For example, Kircaburun and Griffiths (2018a) used the term "problematic Internet use" to describe a range of similar and overlapping online addictive, compulsive, and excessive behaviors. They mentioned that several terms had been widely used to describe complex Internet engagement, including "Internet addiction," "Internet-use disorder," "excessive Internet use," "Internet dependency," and "compulsive Internet use." However, these terms describing problematic online use often employ similar diagnostic criteria. According to them, problematic Internet use (i.e., social networks, online gaming, online gambling, online shopping, and online sex) has been referred to as the preoccupation with and loss of control over Internet use that leads to impairments in one's social, personal, and professional life as well as psychological health and well-being (e.g., occupation and education), and sleep and eating patterns (Andreassen, 2015; Kircaburun & Griffiths, 2018; Kircaburun et al., 2018a).

Social network addiction is considered a behavioral addiction. Some might argue that "social networking site addiction" represents an unnecessary pathologizing of a normal behavior extreme (Andreassen, 2015). However, behavioral addictions can be like substance addictions in many ways, including natural history, phenomenology, tolerance, comorbidity, overlapping genetic contributions, neurobiological mechanisms, and response to treatment. In fact, in recent years, many studies have shown that social network addiction has standard features of both behavioral addictions (such as gambling and sex addiction) and chemical addictions (such as alcohol and substance addiction) (Andreassen, 2015; Savci, 2019). According to Tahoon (2020), social network addiction is the inability to control the use of social networks. Social network addiction, also called social network disorder (Tang, Reer, & Quandt, 2022), is a behavioral problem that causes a constant urge to communicate with other people on the social network even though there is no immediate necessity for such interaction. Consistent evidence shows that people who spend more time on social network platforms, specifically Facebook, report higher addictive tendencies (Chung et al., 2019). As a result, the use of social networks becomes uncontrolled and compulsive among addicted individuals (Kircaburun et al., 2019).

Such excessive use has been explained using general addiction models (Chung et al., 2019). In this context, problematic social network use is defined by Andreassen and Pallesen (2014) as being overly concerned about the social network, being driven by an uncontrollable motivation to log on to or use the social network, and devoting so much time and effort to the social network that it impairs other important life areas. Facebook has created a wave of communication addiction. It has become a platform for social communication, fostering relationships, and a source of unbound entertainment. People update their statuses on their Facebook pages; even minute details of day-to-day life are sometimes updated. Some people habitually upload their self-taken pictures to get noticed by their peers. Sharing personal moments is very much in vogue. Friends on social networking sites are seldom friends in real life. Large numbers of friends and followers on social networking sites are regarded as indices of a high social quotient. This has led to "virtual world addiction." This addiction is limited to interactive visual media, for example, social media such as Facebook. Nevertheless, scientists predict the future of virtual reality to be a computer-stimulated pseudo-environment with extreme potential for addiction (Bhattacharyya, 2015).

2.2   Specific Forms of Social Network Addiction

Social network addiction can take several forms. One of the most common is problematic smartphone use (Pearson & Hussain, 2015; Servidio, Griffiths, & Demetrovics, 2021) or, to use a more specific term, phubbing. This term was created due to the intensive usage of smartphones. Phubbing – a portmanteau of the words "phone" and "snubbing" – refers to the group of behaviors that occur when an individual focuses on their mobile phone at the expense of interacting with the people they are face-to-face with at the time (Garrido et al., 2021). A human being needs to communicate in life. Humans must share information or express feelings and thoughts that help them establish relationships with others. Communication is vital in life and the workplace, where people spend most of their time. Nowadays, it has become more complex than ever due to the increase in the technology-driven life of people. The different tools that advanced technology brings us, especially our smartphones, enable us to live at the touch of a button, creating ease of use for everything. We can see people looking at their phones everywhere, and smartphones have become integral to us. The communication process has its share of this. In today's digital society, new communication problems that disrupt the interpersonal linkages of face-to-face interaction are being created because of mobile tools. The previously mentioned phubbing is another issue that has been added to these communication problems in recent years (Kanbur & Kanbur, 2021).

Phubbing is marked by excessive and increasingly uncontrolled use of smartphones that cause daily-life disturbance (Balta et al., 2019). It is the compulsive usage of a device that is constantly at hand and is hard to resist, even when the device is banned, for example, while driving (Pearson & Hussain, 2015). It can be thought of as a modern social phenomenon that people commonly experience. The term explains the behavior of people looking at their phones instead of engaging in social interaction. Phubbing regularly occurs in social interactions, with sample phubbing behaviors including reading/sending text messages and checking social networks instead of interacting with physically present companions. Moreover, phubbing tends to be hypocritical, with phubbers reporting feeling annoyed and ignored when somebody else phubs them. Significantly, phubbing threatens fundamental human social needs, leading to deflated affect or negative emotional experiences (Kanbur & Kanbur, 2021).

Social network craving has also become an often-researched topic in the literature in recent years. As mentioned by Savci (2019), social network craving is defined as "a strong desire/urge" to use a social network or as "a strong desire or sense of compulsion" to use the social network. Social network craving is essential to social network addiction (Savci & Griffiths, 2019). Another disturbing form of addiction is gambling. Over the past decade, gaming disorder has garnered media and scientific attention, revealing its harmful consequences, such as lower academic performance, sleep problems, depression, mood problems, increased anxiety, and fatigue. Considering these findings, the World Health Organization (WHO, 2018) officially included gaming disorder as a diagnosable disease in the 11th edition of the International Classification of Diseases. Thus, there is a need to examine further the causes of gaming disorder, especially concerning motivation and personality traits (Tang, Reer, & Quandt, 2020).

Kircaburun et al. (2022) pointed to a new type of online activity, another kind of addiction, namely Addictive Mukbang Watching. Mukbang videos typically include a solo eater, known as the broadcast jockey (BJ), who consumes a large quantity of food during the broadcast while communicating with the watching viewers. This communication can be interactive and real time or via more linear channels such as YouTube. The high correlations between all Dark Triad traits and Mukbang Watching (Kircaburun et al., 2022) suggest that Dark Tetrads are attracted to extreme behaviors that provide them the thrill they seek.

2.3   Outcomes of Social Network Addiction

Internet addiction is a disorder that carries a risk of social problems and is seen in the early ages of young people. It accompanies other psychiatric disorders and sometimes leads to new ones. Furthermore, researchers have confirmed that Internet addiction can be seen together with attention-deficit/hyperactivity disorder, social phobia, and depression; a tendency toward addiction in the family increases the risk of Internet addiction. In addition, chatting in chat rooms, sharing experiences via messages, and the time adolescents spend together are increasing daily. As a result, some adolescents show symptoms of Internet addiction or pathological/unhealthy Internet use. Thus, their daily lives are negatively affected (Eksi, 2012). Internet addiction has a prevalence rate of 6% across 31 nations from seven world regions and is associated with significantly aversive individuals (March, 2022).

Social network addiction can devastate the individuals involved and their surroundings. Research has revealed the detrimental effects of social networking site addiction on several functioning domains, including well-being, interpersonal relationships, self-esteem, and life satisfaction (Lee, 2019). Social network addiction might reduce interest in social activities, studies, employment, interpersonal relationships, and psychological well-being (Tahoon, 2020). Andreassen, Pallesen, and Griffiths (2017) have proposed that social network addiction among individuals is also seen because of the individuals' desire to reduce negative emotional stress and forget personal problems. Individuals who suffer from such issues spend time on social networks. This behavior gradually leads to a situation in which the amount of time the individual spends on getting the desired satisfaction on the social network is excessive. Next, they become anxious, irritable, and bored when they cannot use social networks. Such individuals have great difficulty controlling, stopping, or reducing the use of social networks. They usually ignore their hobbies, partners, family members, and relationships. Therefore, social network addiction is considered an unfavorable consequence, with a loss of ability to control it (Andreassen, 2015).

Andreassen and Pallesen (2014) argue that addicts typically spend significant time thinking about social networking sites and how they can free up more time for online social networking (salience). Often, they spend much more time on the social network than they initially intended, as they must spend increasingly more time on the network to attain the same level of pleasure (tolerance). They use social networking sites to reduce their guilt, anxiety, restlessness, helplessness, and depression and to forget about personal problems (mood modification). If prohibited from visiting social networking sites, addicts typically become stressed, restless, troubled, or irritable (withdrawal). They do not heed the advice of others to reduce the time they spend on social networking. When they try to cut down on social networking, they are typically unsuccessful (relapse). Social networking site addicts assign lower priority to hobbies, studies/jobs, leisure activities, and exercise, and they ignore their partners, family members, or friends because of social networking sites (conflict). Social networking site addicts often use social networking sites so much that it negatively influences their health, sleep quality, relationships, and well-being (Andreassen & Pallesen, 2014; Andreassen, 2015; Chung et al., 2019; Tang et al., 2022).

Another adverse outcome of social network addiction is technostress. The term technostress was coined by Brod (1984). It is widely understood as the "inability to adapt or cope with new computer technologies in a healthy manner (Brod, 1984, p. 16)." There exists a range of symptoms that people experience from technostress. These are headaches, mental exhaustion, panic, helplessness, insomnia, loss of temper, irritability, anger, and frustration. Hours in front of the computer can lead to physical symptoms such as backache, neck and shoulder stiffness, and reduced job satisfaction and productivity. Jobs that have an increased likelihood of developing technostress should employ adequate preventive measures like periodic assessments to check the effects of technostress on the physical and emotional aspects of the employee. There should be workshops organized for employees not only to impart knowledge and enhance their technical skills but also to make them aware of the deleterious effects of technostress. Information technology troubleshooters should help maximize the system's accessibility and strive to make the employees more comfortable with the system (Bhattacharyya, 2015; Rohwer et al., 2022).

When phubbing occurs, smartphones add the interaction between two sides as a third person. It might be hurtful for a person to be phubbed, affecting social interaction and becoming the reason for adverse psychological outcomes. Phubbing can be seen as threatening to relationships. It is also possible for a person to be either phubbed (victim of phubbing) or phubber (perpetrator of phubbing). This behavior can be seen everywhere with the growing number of phubbees and phubbers daily (Kanbur & Kanbur, 2021). Phubbing creates various negative results, such as lower conversation intimacy and depression. It can be considered a particular type of ostracism or social exclusion that threatens the fundamental needs of belongingness, self-esteem, meaningful existence, and control. Phubbing harms people's feelings, causes lower moods, creates a negative emotional experience, and negatively affects communication quality and relationship satisfaction. Additionally, partner phubbing endangers relationship satisfaction, impairs life satisfaction, and increases signs of depression. Earlier research on phubbing has emphasized that phubbing predicts social disconnectedness (Kanbur & Kanbur, 2021).

According to Balta et al. (2019), empirical research has shown that problematic smartphone use can lead to severe psychological and physical impairments among individuals, including elevated depression, anxiety, and stress, lower sleep quality, and decreased physical activity. Balta et al. contended that personality traits and adult attachment are among the core psychological elements that can help explain individuals' problematic and addictive use of mobile phones (see also Pearson & Hussain, 2015). Pearson and Hussain (2015) argued that evidence suggests that overdependence on smartphones can lead to destructive public health inferences. Smartphones provide us with unparalleled connectedness, but the psychological cost is unknown. The depth of such relationships might not be equal to real-life communications, and they might be engaged to raise self-esteem by feeling popular – an indicator of narcissism (Pearson & Hussain, 2015).

2.4 The Dark Triad/Tetrad and Social Network Addiction

2.4.1 Reasons for Dark Triad/Tetrads' Attraction to Social Media Networking

Cheng and Li (2014) advanced two overarching explanations for the prevalence of Internet addiction – accessibility and quality of (real) life. The accessibility hypothesis suggests that greater Internet availability might foster a greater engagement in online activities, increasing susceptibility to Internet addiction (Naidu et al., 2023). Providing a distinct perspective, the quality of (real) life hypothesis predicts that Internet addiction prevalence is related to poor quality of real life. In the present cyber age, people might immerse themselves into the virtual world of the Internet to escape the stress they experience in the real world. As the virtual and real worlds become blurred, individuals encountering more frequent real-life problems are more motivated to use the Internet as a coping mechanism. It is thus reasonable to infer an inverse link between Internet addiction and the quality of (real) life (Cheng & Li, 2014).

However, in recent years, the association between personality characteristics and social network addiction has become one of the most investigated topics in the literature (Kumpasoğlu et al., 2021). According to Curtis and Jones (2020), narcissism, Machiavellianism, and psychopathy comprise the Dark Triad, characterized by antisocial behaviors, callousness, and egocentrism. Therefore, examining the relationship between these personality traits with undesirable tendencies and social network disorder is reasonable. Many studies with people showing elevated levels of Dark Triad personality traits have shown that a predisposition to the Dark Triad was related to addictive behavior. For instance, the relation between the problems of individuals with narcissistic personality characteristics in self-regulation strategies, the compulsive use of smartphones, especially alcohol and substance use, and social network addiction has often been emphasized. Similarly, Machiavellianism was associated with substance addiction (e.g., cocaine) and Internet addiction. It has been reported that individuals with psychopathy personality traits are prone to substance, gambling, Internet, and social network addictions (Kumpasoğlu et al., 2021).

Indeed, the problematic use of social networks is associated with antisocial traits, with the discovery that there is a direct relation between the features of the Dark Triad and social network addiction (Kircaburun et al., 2018a). These traits are associated with reward and sensation-seeking, which may be satisfied through the use of social media platforms, allowing individuals to showcase their achievements and ambitions to a broader audience (Turan et al., 2023). A social network is an environment where people with narcissistic traits can meet their psychological needs, such as being admired and receiving constant positive feedback on their physical appearance (Lopes & Yu, 2017). Machiavellians can feel more comfortable conducting Internet activities rather than communicating face-to-face with other people (Kircaburun & Griffiths, 2018). Psychopathy has been positively correlated with many deviant behaviors on social networks such as creating conflict, provoking discussions that offer erroneous information to create chaos, and violating rules or regulations (Lopes & Yu, 2017). For narcissists, addiction stems from the desire to regulate emotions and stabilize self-esteem. Psychopaths resort to addictive behaviors due to disinhibition, which favors the use of substances concerning psychopathy (Jauk &

Dieterich, 2019). Narcissists with mental disorders, such as depression or anxiety, lose self-confidence and cannot present themselves favorably to others (Brailovskaia, Margraf, & Köllner, 2019). Therefore, these people tend to take refuge online, increasing the risk of becoming dependent on social networks (Campbell et al., 2004).

The following will provide more specific reasons for each of the dark personalities. According to Nikbin et al. (2022), narcissists believe they are special, unique, and superior and behave in an attention-seeking and exhibitionistic way to maintain their self-esteem and gain attention. Tendencies toward excessive self-promotion, entitlement, and grandiosity characterize narcissism (Curtis & Jones, 2020). Narcissistic individuals feel the need to receive approval and admiration frequently. This need is easily met on social networks. Therefore, narcissistic individuals are a risk group for social network addiction. Machiavellianism is characterized by tendencies toward manipulation, deceit, and exploitation for personal gain, while psychopathy is characterized by impulsivity, thrill-seeking, and lack of empathy. Reflecting dark tendencies in social networks, Machiavellianism is associated with the frequency of dishonest self-promotion, self-monitoring, and psychopathy, surveilling others on social networks. In addition, Machiavellians tend to engage in strategic planning in social interactions. These individuals use more self-presentation tactics on social networks. Such behaviors lead to problematic social network use (Nikbin et al., 2022; Savci, 2019).

Psychopathy is associated with the frequency of posting selfies and trolling online. Hence, individuals with high dark personality traits use social networks to express their dark tendencies. Furthermore, the reinforcing gratification cycle from social networks might lead to social network disorder (Tang et al., 2022). Personality traits such as psychopathy, narcissism, and Machiavellianism have unique characteristics that can lead to pathological Internet use. Individuals with a high tendency to psychopathy are often impulsive and careless. Therefore, these individuals are more vulnerable to problematic Internet pornography. Finally, individuals with a high tendency toward (Savci, 2019).

2.4.2   Theories for the Linkage between Dark Triad/ Tetrad Personalities and Social Network Addiction

Hussain et al. (2021) and Tang et al. (2022) advanced the interaction of the Person-Affect-Cognition-Execution model (I-PACE) developed by Brand et al. (2019) to explain the emergence and maintenance of addictive behaviors. According to the Person-Affect-Cognition-Execution model, the development of disordered forms of Internet use (such as social network disorder) results from the interplay of a person's characteristics, motivations, situation, cognitive and affective components, and gratifications. Therefore, examining how specific personality traits and associated use motives are related to social network disorder might help to find at-risk groups and prevent the development of addictive use forms. Furthermore, the use of the Person-Affect-Cognition-Execution model should contribute to the development of a deeper understanding of the factors underlying social network disorder by examining the interplay between dark personality traits, social network use motives, and social network disorder (Hussain et al., 2021; Naidu et al., 2023).

According to the I-PACE model, general predisposing factors (e.g., personality traits) are related to behavior-specific predisposing variables, such as particular needs and motivations. People's network use is goal-directed, intended to gratify specific needs expressed as motives. Compared to offline gratifications, the ease of obtaining gratifications from social networks reinforces some individuals' tendency to rely increasingly on social networks for their needs, leading to addictive use. Such motivations as entertainment, communication, relationship maintenance, and self-expression are examined (Tang et al., 2022). Given that individuals high in dark personality traits were associated with specific social network behaviors (e.g., self-promotion, selfies) that expressed their tendencies, it is reasonable to assume that their behaviors are similarly motivated. Dark personality traits' relationship to social network disorder is mediated via motivations for escapism, fantasy, competition, and skill development. Therefore, it can be expected that the social network mediates the associations between the individual dark personality traits and motivations of entertainment, communication, and self-expression, except for relationship maintenance (Tang et al., 2022; Naidu et al., 2023).

Tahoon (2020) contended that dark personalities are related to reward-seeking in a certain sense. The social network provides such individuals with the ability to reveal their desires and achievements to a vast number of individuals. Social network use might positively increase dark personality traits by providing online relationships that compensate for the lack of real-life social relationships. Similarly, narcissistic individuals use social networks to improve their self-promotion. In comparison, psychopathic individuals find a suitable place in social networks to show their negative attitudes without anxiety about suffering a penalty. In addition, using social networks among Machiavellians provides an outlet for self-promotion and self-monitoring.

Narcissism is relevant to social network addiction because social networks can help narcissists conceal their illicit side by choosing what they want to share to boost their ego. Machiavellianism is relevant to social network addiction because the social network provides an opportunity for Machiavellian individuals to cheat or trick people online easily, given that the standard of morality is subjective. Psychopathy is also relevant to social network addiction. The social network is a widely preferred platform for psychopaths to displace their impulsive yet reckless attitudes in a venue where disciplinary actions are less likely to be taken than in real life (Siah et al., 2021).

According to Balta et al. (2019), individuals with dark traits have standard and unique features that might result in problematic smartphone use. For instance, narcissists might be more prone to problematic smartphone use, given their desire for approval and admiration, manifesting in biased online self-presentation. Machiavellianism is associated with interpersonal manipulation and deceptive self-promotion, which can lead to cyberbullying, cyber trolling, and cyberstalking (which can make individuals susceptible to smartphone preoccupation). Psychopathy is associated with impulsivity, recklessness, and emotion dysregulation, causing psychopaths to struggle to control their urges to spend long hours on their smartphones for pleasure and sensation-seeking purposes. Dark Triads have unique features that might lead to pathological online use (Chung et al., 2019). Individuals high in psychopathy are often impulsive and reckless and are more willing to engage in unsolicited Internet pornography. Narcissistic people constantly need approval and admiration, placing them more at risk of developing social network addiction. Highly Machiavellian people tend to show strategic planning in their social interactions and have been shown to employ more self-presentation tactics on Facebook (Chung et al., 2019).

Tang et al. (2022) asserted that social network uses the motivations of entertainment, communication, self-expression, and relationship maintenance, which, to a certain extent, are tendencies of dark personality traits. For example, narcissistic tendencies toward grandiosity lead to seeking attention and praise, which is tapped by communication motivation, and self-promotion tendencies are tapped by self-expression motivation. Machiavellianism's positive relationship to self-expression motivation is belied by the Machiavellian tendencies of manipulation, deceit, and exploitation, as they instead present false information about themselves. Psychopathic thrill-seeking tendencies might be tapped by the entertainment motivation of occupying their time. Psychopaths might entertain themselves by engaging in antisocial behaviors such as trolling.

According to Tang et al. (2020), given the affordances of online games, individuals with elevated levels of dark personality traits might indulge in seeking to achieve online fame and wealth, manipulating others to serve them, engaging in reckless behaviors with few physical consequences, and obtaining rewards more efficiently than is possible in offline contexts. More specifically, narcissists play due to the motivation for escapism through their need for admiration. It is easier to self-promote in a gaming world through displays of virtual wealth and abilities for other players to admire. Online gaming provides an escapist avenue from offline contexts as there are few consequences for socially aversive behaviors, making it attractive to individuals with dark personality traits. Personal gain is a Machiavellian characteristic. Those with this characteristic are motivated to gain higher gaming abilities; for narcissists, recognizing their skills is appealing, while psychopaths find it appealing to fight against opponents more skilled than they are. Narcissists are motivated to play with friends to seek admiration and praise. Machiavellians are motivated to have friends to manipulate and exploit, while psychopaths' impulsivity and thrill-seeking motivate them to seek similar others in gaming (Tang et al., 2020). While regarding psychopaths, research has not shown the utility of psychopathy to predict problematic (i.e., addictive) online gaming behavior, there is evidence that psychopathy is related to other problematic behavior when gaming, such as disruption and aggression. The utility of psychopathy in predicting disruptive online gaming can be attributed to the critical psychopathy characteristics of aggression and self-centeredness (March, 2022).

Menzel, Meier, and Maier (2023) relate the Dark Triad traits to the intention to cheat on gaming. They contended that gamers with high Machiavellianism tend to be manipulative. They intend to manipulate online games to gain unfair advantages. Similarly, gamers with high narcissism try to dominate others, which aligns with their cheating to surpass other gamers. Finally, gamers with a high level of psychopathy are characterized by thrill-seeking. They cheat because they enjoy showing divergent behavior without being caught by other gamers and game publishers.

According to Hussain et al. (2021), individuals with maladaptive personality traits appear at higher risk of developing addictive behavior, especially when they have impairments in regulating emotions. Moreover, the maladaptive personality traits differ in their effect on developing and maintaining problematic social networking use. According to Hussain et al., narcissism could be identified as a direct risk factor. Individuals who desire admiration and self-enhancement, such as narcissists and those who show reduced empathy for achieving individual goals, have more significant difficulties controlling their social networking site use (Kristinsdottir et al., 2021). This could be because most social networking sites allow users to present an ideal self and explicitly control their impression management. It might be assumed that this control and the desire for ideal self-presentation could become obsessive, resulting in the urge to obtain positive feedback for the user's profile or new status updates.

More interestingly, Hussain et al. (2021) suggested that the mechanisms for individuals with psychopathic and Machiavellian tendencies appear different. According to them, individuals who are impulsive, nonempathetic, selfish, manipulative, and ruthless (see psychopathic and Machiavellian) seem to have difficulties regulating their emotions, which could make them more vulnerable to developing problematic social networking use. A dysfunctional coping style could be described as a reinforcement mechanism that enhances the risk of problematic Internet use when specific personality traits are investigated. The disability of handling emotions might be associated with a dysfunctional coping style. It could show a more fear-driven approach. Individuals with maladaptive personality traits try to compensate for this dysfunctional emotion regulation strategy by using social networks, resulting in repeated behavior and problematic use.

Internet addiction disorder can also be described as unmanageable Internet use and changeable behavioral design when restrained. It can be explained as an inclination toward obsessive Internet use that disturbs the individual's normal functioning. The maladaptive internet-using behavioral pattern, hereafter termed Internet addiction disorder, is described as the inability to control one's use of the Internet, which contributes to mental, community, or occupational problems (Iftikhar & Tariq, 2014). According to Chung et al. (2019), there is also evidence that the Dark Triad traits are related to other addictive behaviors. For instance, cocaine-addicted individuals have reported significantly higher Machiavellianism scores than stimulant-naïve controls. Greitemeyer and Sagioglou (2017) and Gonzalez and Greitemeyer (2018) found that all Dark Tetrad, particularly sadism, is related to the amount of time spent on violent video games. Psychopathy, narcissism, Machiavellianism, and sadism are associated with increased substance use and the risk of problematic gambling behavior. However, everyday sadism shares a common core with the Dark Triad but is conceptually distinct in that everyday sadists enjoy harming others (Gonzalez & Greitemeyer, 2018; Olckers & Hattingh, 2022).

The following sections will present specific theories for each dark personality trait.

2.4.2.1 *Narcissism and Addictive Online Behavior*

Three general classes of theoretical models predict elevated social network use on the part of narcissistic individuals: self-enhancement, fit, and trait models (McCain & Campbell, 2018; Monacis et al., 2020; Kristinsdottir, Gylfason, & Sigurvinsdottir, 2021). According to the self-enhancement model, the social network represents favorite environments for gaining admiration, fulfilling self-enhancement needs, and reinforcing the narcissistic self-image. The social network can be a valuable platform for promoting and enhancing the self, so narcissistic individuals will be drawn to social networks to fulfill self-enhancement needs (Kristinsdottir, Gylfason, & Sigurvinsdottir, 2021).

According to Savci et al. (2021), social network use might provide individuals with unlimited and selected social connections that ease narcissistic personality beliefs and strengthen individuals' narcissistic tendencies. Consequently, social network use might unconsciously feed individuals' narcissistic tendencies. Individuals with narcissistic personality beliefs might have a permanent need for social approval and a desire to be liked. Therefore, they might be more at risk of developing social network addiction. The narcissistic behavior patterns seen on social networks come about because of favorable conditions that trigger and are conducive to narcissism. The social network will be "sticky" for narcissistic individuals because once involved, the narcissistic individual will find a favorable environment for gaining admiration and esteem, reinforcing the narcissistic self (McCain & Campbell, 2018).

A second model is the fit model, which considers social network use to encourage wide but shallow social networks as a good fit for narcissistic skills and abilities. Individuals with grandiose narcissism prefer emotionally shallow social relationships and associate themselves with high-status others (Kristinsdottir et al., 2021). For example, individuals high in grandiose narcissism prefer emotionally shallow social relationships and publicly associate with high-status others. As a result, they make good first impressions and are often seen as more attractive. Likewise, because narcissists enjoy having social influence, they tend to occupy more central positions in their social networks. Given this, it is reasonable that grandiose narcissism is consistently associated with having more friends on social networking sites (McCain & Campbell, 2018).

Finally, the essential personality traits associated with narcissism suggest a trait model of narcissism. This model posits that individuals characterized by the grandiose quality of narcissism, including high extraversion, openness, and low agreeableness, tend to have more friends and generate more content on social networks (Kristinsdottir et al., 2021). Nikbin et al. (2022) contended that narcissistic individuals maintain extreme self-centeredness, arrogance, egoism, a lack of emotions, and a desire to show an unreal image. People with characteristics of narcissism usually love themselves more than any other things. Narcissists spend significant time on social networks, where they have more "friends" and portray themselves. Addiction to Instagram results in broader and higher approval and admiration from others. Narcissism was also indirectly associated with Instagram addiction via conformity, enhancement, and coping motives. Users with high narcissistic traits use Instagram to enhance their psychological states, avoid disapproval from others, and avoid negative feelings. Individuals with high narcissism scores are less agreeable and constantly require ego reinforcement and admiration. Thus, it can be said that they have problematic social relationships in their offline lives, in which they cannot get the admiration they wish, feel that they are left out and not liked by others, and do not have enjoyable feelings. Thus, they try to find alternatives for satisfying their unmet needs offline. For narcissists, Instagram provides an opportunity to gain admiration and success (Nikbin et al., 2022; Rajesh & Rangaiah, 2022).

For narcissists, addiction stems from the desire to regulate emotions and stabilize self-esteem. Narcissists who have a mental disorder, such as depression or anxiety, lose self-confidence and become unable to present themselves favorably to others. Thus, these people tend to take refuge in the online environment, which increases their risk of becoming dependent on social networks. Narcissism is positively correlated with dependence on social networks because networks such as Facebook, Instagram, and Snapchat offer people with narcissistic traits a space to feed their egos. They use these social networks to receive constant feedback, especially positive feedback, from others (Necula, 2020; Rajesh & Rangaiah, 2022).

According to Nikbin et al. (2022), individuals high in narcissism engage in deceptive self-promoting behaviors such as selfie-editing and selecting photographs that are flattering for purposes such as attention-seeking, admiration, and escaping boredom. Narcissists engage in such behaviors to receive comments on their photos, which can function as a form of reinforcement in terms of group cohesiveness. Using a platform such as Instagram might help narcissists experience heightened belongingness and admiration, be perceived positively, and appear "cool." In addition, narcissists use interpersonal relationships to confirm their positive illusions of physical desirability. Narcissism is linked positively to liking and commenting on friends' photos to gain popularity with those friends. Therefore, it can be said that a platform such as Instagram enables individuals to gain attention and admiration, escape boredom, experience higher belongingness, appear relaxed, maintain self-esteem, and increase their sense of self-importance, all of which are highly attractive to narcissists.

Finally, the Internet is one of the best spreaders of the narcissism epidemic. Narcissists are fond of the Internet because it allows them to present themselves as they wish via social networking sites. Additionally, it is said that these social networking sites reinforce narcissism and the superficial sentimental relationships that narcissists need (Eksi, 2012). Narcissism was associated with using social networks rather than playing games on the Internet because, on social platforms, individuals can present themselves favorably to receive admiration from other users (Casale & Fioravanti, 2018). Narcissism is positively correlated with dependence on social networks because networks such as Facebook, Instagram, and Snapchat offer people with narcissistic traits a space to feed their egos. Such people use these social networks to receive constant feedback from others, especially positive feedback (Andreassen et al., 2017; Rajesh & Rangaiah, 2022).

According to Hussain and Pontes (2018, 2019), the relationship between narcissism and Facebook activity might be related to the fact that narcissists have an imbalanced sense of self, fluctuating between grandiosity concerning explicit agency and low self-esteem concerning implicit communion and vulnerability. Based on a literature review, they contended that the current findings suggest that high-frequency technology use and technology addiction are linked to increased levels of narcissism. However, this finding is not straightforward, as recent studies have failed to replicate it in the context of generalized Internet addiction. This suggests that the interplay between narcissism and technological addiction is complex and might be mediated by more variables.

Based on a systematic literature review, Casale and Banchi (2020) suggested that narcissism might not have consistent effects across social media platforms, and some key differences between the platforms might exist. In other words, different social networking sites differ in how they facilitate narcissistic needs satisfaction, which, in turn, is associated with problematic use. Casale and Banchi (2020) concluded, based on their review, that Facebook might be particularly appealing to both grandiose and vulnerable narcissists because it is an ideal tool for self-promotion as users can frequently post status updates, comments, or photos of themselves and reasonably expect timely and frequent positive feedback. Therefore, narcissists are more likely to be at risk for problematic Facebook use than at risk for a more general difficulty in regulating one's own use of online social media.

2.4.2.2   *Grandiose in Comparison to Vulnerable/Covert Narcissist*

Studies investigating the association between narcissism and social networking sites have focused on the grandiose form and neglected the vulnerable form (Casale & Fioravanti, 2018). However, the online–offline nexus is a potentially fruitful but fraught place for the vulnerable narcissist. The ubiquity of social networks represents both an opportunity and a risk as individual struggles to integrate and synthesize their feelings of inadequacy with their need for admiration. Specifically, the relationships between narcissism and associated online outcomes are conditional based on narcissistic subtypes. Thus, it is suggested that the potentially different impact of grandiose and vulnerable manifestations of narcissism should be considered when hypotheses are generated regarding the role of narcissism in online contexts (Grieve & March, 2021).

Vulnerable narcissism, or "covert" and "hypersensitive" narcissism, is characterized by a defensive and insecure sense of grandiosity associated with low self-esteem, shame-proneness, shyness, and hypersensitivity to the evaluation of others. Vulnerable narcissists are more interested in setting up and controlling their privacy than grandiose narcissists, even though both narcissists are more interested in using online social platforms for self-presentation purposes than non-narcissists (Casale & Fioravanti, 2018). Vulnerable narcissism might contribute more to the problematic use of social networking sites than grandiose narcissism. People who are highly vulnerable narcissistic feel anxious in face-to-face interactions and more comfortable online, which might lead to problematic social network use (Fegan & Bland, 2021).

In Big Five terms, grandiose narcissism is composed of high extraversion and openness and low agreeableness; extroverts have been shown to have more extensive social networks and spend more time and generate more content on social networking sites. Thus, narcissists' tendency to have more friends and generate more content on social networks might, in part, be linked to their extraversion. By contrast, vulnerable narcissism is associated with low agreeableness and neuroticism, suggesting more anxiety or discomfort associated with social network use. Grandiose narcissists are much more sensitive to and motivated by potential reward than potential punishment. This creates a tendency toward approach-oriented social behavior, which might explain why those high in grandiose narcissism generate more content, especially self-promoting content, with little concern for privacy on social networking sites. By contrast, vulnerable narcissists, high in both approach and avoidance motivation, are more cautious about obtaining praise, showing more concern for privacy, and putting more effort into impression management (i.e., taking multiple selfies before picking one, cropping and editing pictures) than grandiose narcissists. The earlier discussion suggests that traits associated with grandiose narcissism are better for the social network than those associated with vulnerable narcissism (McCain & Campbell, 2018; Fegan & Bland, 2021).

Grieve and March (2021) explained that individuals high in vulnerable narcissism should be invested in the face-to-face interaction that they are having, wanting to ensure that they appear to be good conversational partners with fascinating and witty insights. However, while this might be the case, the power of the social network might reinforce the highly contingent feelings of superiority and fragile self-esteem associated with vulnerable narcissism. Such individuals will be more likely to prioritize engagement with their smartphones, perceiving that the social network is ubiquitous and has greater scope to influence a broader social sphere. Related to the larger social networking sphere, grandiose narcissists should care little for the content others are posting and can access via the phone. This is because their grandiosity and ego are such that they assume others are less interesting than they are. Their belief in social dominance means they have nothing to fear regarding what others might post (given that others are likely to admire them). However, because total trait narcissism is associated with self-centered thoughts and behaviors, and phubbing has been conceptualized as a selfish behavior in which an individual favors their online self over social interaction with others, it is possible that while grandiose narcissism might have some effect, the potential role of grandiose narcissism concerning phubbing is unclear (Grieve & March, 2021).

Grandiose narcissists might use online interactions to compensate for a lack of sociability and social networking. However, this attempt to obtain social benefits via the Internet puts them at risk of problematic Internet use (Casale & Fioravanti, 2018). Problematic use of social networking sites might be driven by unmet needs in face-to-face interactions, thus supporting theoretical models that argue that those who try to obtain social benefits via the Internet are more likely to experience adverse outcomes associated with their Internet use. Casale and Fioravanti (2018) concluded that grandiose and vulnerable narcissists might prefer online social inter-actions because social network applications represent an ideal setting for satisfying narcissistic needs. Users can manipulate information by choos-ing what to disclose and what to hide. In addition, social networking sites might allow narcissists to manage their self-presentation efforts better, thus increasing their chances of receiving admiration that they cannot achieve in face-to-face exchanges.

In line with Kong et al. (2021), social networking sites can be dichot-omized into active and passive. Social networking sites provide oppor-tunities for vulnerable narcissistic individuals to promote themselves. Vulnerable narcissists fear their relationships with others because they seek to protect themselves from shame and potential negative evaluations dur-ing their search for admiration. Conversely, they are more likely to prefer online social interactions using platforms with less reciprocation. These behaviors displayed by vulnerable narcissists might be passively perceived by others, with these passive behaviors in social networks being called pas-sive social networking sites (Garcia et al., 2023).

Grieve and March (2021) explained that vulnerable narcissism is based on contingent ideas of superiority and stems from fragile self-esteem. By contrast, grandiose narcissism is conceptualized as inflated ideas of self-importance and grandiosity. Vulnerable narcissism is also associated with separation insecurity and anxiousness. The researchers argued that individ-uals high in vulnerable narcissism would have a more heightened sensi-tivity to – and more significant investment in – new information about themselves that might be on their smartphones, as the social network is widespread. Finally, they contended that the fundamental characteristics of narcissistic vulnerability (such as looking for approval, seeking valida-tion, and being sensitive to interpersonal rejection) function as drivers of problematic phone use in the form of (antisocial) phubbing behaviors.

Brailovskaia et al. (2023) explained that individuals with high levels of vulnerable narcissism often lack the social competence to achieve their interaction partners' attention and admiration in face-to-face contact, which is of great importance for their narcissistic core. Negative emotions often accompany this failure (Garcia et al., 2023). Vulnerable narcissists tend to employ dysfunctional coping strategies to reduce the negative state. Social media likely provides them with a less harmful alternative to escape the negative emotions of failure. Moreover, by the positive feed-back of other users, vulnerable narcissists could compensate for the lack of offline attention and admiration. This compensation could foster their positive emotions. However, intensive social media use serves only as a functional coping strategy in the short term.

Grieve, Lang, and March (2021) advanced an alternative explanation for the relationship between narcissistic vulnerability and phubbing. According to this explanation, it might simply be that vulnerable narcissists prefer to interact online rather than face-to-face. Unlike offline social interaction, online social interaction is asynchronous and controllable, and social networks allow users to curate the images they present carefully. Thus, for those high in vulnerable narcissism, online social interactions afford effective self-presentation to maximize the presentation of positive self-aspects while hiding self-aspects associated with their shame and self-doubt (Grieve & March, 2021). If so, vulnerable narcissists might engage in phubbing not only because the phone allows them to meet contingent self-esteem needs via a potentially influential and readily accessible audience but also because they prefer interacting in the online environment where they more easily manufacture their desired self-presentation. Grieve et al. (2021) argued that their explanation is consistent with the Uses and Gratifications Theory. This theory posits that network users are actively motivated to have their individual needs gratified through network engagement.

Moving even further, Balcerowska and Sawicki (2022) emphasized the heterogeneous nature of narcissism. In a three-sample study in Poland (N = 1,659; one student's sample and two general samples), they focused on four aspects of narcissism (i.e., admirative narcissism, communal narcissism, rivalrous narcissism, and vulnerable narcissism), arguing that there might be different underlying narcissistic motives in terms of the relationship to social networking site addiction. Their results showed that all four aspects of narcissism were positively related to social networking site addiction. However, only rivalrous, communal, and vulnerable narcissism aspects were independent predictors of social networking site addiction. The findings discussed earlier emphasize the importance of a multidimensional perspective when analyzing the relationship between narcissism and social network addiction.

2.4.2.3 Psychopathy and Addictive Online Behavior

Psychopathy is a personality disorder characterized by a lack of remorse, a lack of morality in one's actions, insensitivity, and heartlessness. Psychopaths engage in problematic online behavior due to their maladaptive coping strategies and desire to obtain higher sensations. Therefore, engaging with Instagram might help them cope with feelings of deficiency or negative emotions. It is expected that those with psychopathic tendencies and greater feelings of uncertainty tend to engage in Instagram surveillance in a maladaptive way to gather information about their surrounding environment and to enhance their feelings of control, which might drive their addiction to Instagram. In addition, excessive use of Instagram allows them to escape reality and forget about their problems (Nikbin et al., 2022).

Psychopaths might become so attentive to and interested in the deviant behaviors mentioned earlier that they become dependent on social networks, as they provide a favorable environment for these activities. Psychopaths tend to have absolute power and control in any situation, so they are eager to follow and investigate the problems of others or what other people post on their profiles to satisfy this desire to maintain power. Social networks, such as Facebook, Instagram, and Snapchat, are platforms that ease deviant behaviors (Necula, 2020). Psychopaths resort to addictive behaviors due to disinhibition, which favors the use of substances concerning psychopathy (Necula, 2020). Psychopaths are often impulsive, reckless, and more willing to engage in antisocial online behaviors. They use social network platforms to express their hostile and aversive attitudes without fear of punishment (Monacis et al., 2020).

Compared to people with low levels of psychopathy, those with higher levels spend more time online and on social networks. Because dysfunctional impulsivity is a characteristic of trait psychopathy, addiction is strongly associated with impulsivity. This can be attributed to characteristics of social networks that are attractive to individuals with high psychopathy. Specifically, the social network might be an attractive platform to these individuals, as they can use it to (anonymously) express their hostile and aversive attitudes without fear of punishment (Necula, 2020).

2.4.2.4 *Machiavellians and Addictive Online Behavior*
Machiavellians are characterized as exploitative, calculating persons with strategic orientation and manipulative skills. They enjoy trolling others, influencing and praising others for getting their things done, and using people for their ends. These characteristics might lead to the addictive and problematic use of Instagram for enjoyment and self-promotion. Fear of social rejection results in attempts to avoid disapproval from others. Individuals with such characteristics neutralize social rejection by adding more friends to their network to increase their acceptance. Machiavellianism is an important trait that can lead to higher moral

disengagement – another essential predictor of antisocial online behaviors. In addition to sadistic and psychopathic motivations (e.g., harming others, seeing them suffer), Machiavellian predispositions such as giving up moral values easily and lacking remorse can be unique predictors of antisocial online behaviors, especially among men (Nikbin et al., 2022; Kircaburun et al., 2018a).

As Machiavellianism predicts self-oriented goals in social networks, such people engage excessively and deceptively with Instagram to gain more friends and achieve their goals. Machiavellianism is also linked to self-monitoring and self-promotion on social networking sites such as Facebook. Such individuals engage in self-promotion on social networking sites such as Facebook for egoistic and self-serving motives. Machiavellians use several tactics to self-present themselves profitably. Furthermore, Machiavellians are more prone to surveillance on Facebook, as they want to enhance their "advantageous" information. They also enjoy gossiping and discussing absent third parties. Machiavellians might engage in activities that enhance their need for attention and admiration. Also, Machiavellians use social networks for deceptive self-promotion, partly to avoid social rejection. Thus, those high in Machiavellianism are expected to use social networking sites such as Instagram to seek pleasure, obtain social acceptance, and avoid social rejection and negative feelings (Nikbin et al., 2022).

Machiavellians and psychopaths follow or investigate others on social networks, especially Facebook, and are prone to manifesting antisocial behaviors online, such as behaviors that lead to conflict and actions against the law. Machiavellianism has led to intense follow-up by other users, especially gossip approval. However, for people with psychopathic traits, Facebook investigation has been linked to intolerance of uncertainty (Necula, 2020). Machiavellians tend to show strategic planning in social interactions, employing more self-presentation tactics on social network platforms (Monacis et al., 2020). People with high Machiavellianism are manipulative, ambitious, and exploitative. The Internet can be a new medium where people can easily present their attitudes (Błachnio et al., 2023).

It should be noted that some scholars pointed to a moderate relationship between Machiavellianism and social network addiction (Demircioğlu & Göncü Köse, 2021). One explanation for the possibility of a nonsignificant relationship between Machiavellianism and social network addiction is that individuals high in Machiavellianism might more often use communication channels other than social media to manipulate others and engage in impression management. Therefore, they might find direct communication channels more efficient than online channels. Moreover, direct communication channels such as face-to-face interaction might provide immediate rewards for such individuals. Therefore, there is a need for studies that will compare the frequency of using direct communication channels with the frequency of using social networks among individuals who score high on Machiavellianism and those who score low on Machiavellianism (Demircioğlu & Göncü Köse, 2021).

2.4.2.5   Sadism and Addictive Online Behavior

Sadistic individuals enjoy humiliating others, cruelty, and malevolent behaviors (Balta et al., 2019). This may lead to addictive online behavior because the more time they spend on social networks, the more opportunities they have to find a victim on the net. Most explanations of the relationship between sadism and addictive online behavior are based on gaming addiction. First, violent games can provide virtual satisfaction for individuals motivated by cruelty needs. In these scenarios, sadistic individuals might find ways to express and strengthen their sadistic needs, causing virtual harm to others and being aggressive. Sadistic individuals are drawn to violence more than nonviolent or neutral games and more aggressive/offensive type-hero in-game, being more fascinated with weapons than others. Lastly, playing such games can be a way in which sadists improve their mood, as they might encounter, in virtual environments, gratification for fantasies that would be punishable in the real world (Bonfá-Araujo et al., 2022).

Behavioral research suggests that everyday sadists actively seek opportunities to indulge their appetite for cruelty, so it appears a plausible explanation that particularly everyday sadists are attracted to violent video games, possibly due to the opportunity to cause virtual injury and death. This reasoning aligns with the selection hypothesis proposing that highly aggressive individuals are more likely to seek out violent media content than less aggressive individuals. On the other hand, the socialization hypothesis proposes that exposure to violent content causes the user to become more aggressive over time. Therefore, the positive association between everyday sadism and the amount of violent video game play could also be due to violent video game exposure increasing the player's sadistic tendencies (Greitemeyer & Sagioglou, 2017; Gonzalez & Greitemeyer, 2018).

It should be noted that research on sadism and addictive online behavior is in its early stages. The reason is that sadism has been included as an addition to the Dark Triad traits only in recent years and not by all scholars in the field.

2.5 Research Findings

Po, Sher, and Liu (2023) conducted a bibliometric analysis of 396 articles published from 2011 to 2021. Through a cluster analysis of keywords, they found that the influence of negative and dark personality traits remains prevalent in social media addiction research. Furthermore, these articles are the most numerous and most recent in terms of average publication year, supporting the psychology-driven nature of this field, especially from the perspective of personality psychology. This section will focus on the empirical findings of studies that have examined the relationship between Dark Tetrad traits and different dimensions of social network addiction. First, studies that have examined the relationship between all four Dark Tetrad traits and different forms of social network addiction will be reviewed. After that, studies examining the relationship between one dark personality trait (or two traits) and social network addiction will be presented. In addition, the empirical studies will be categorized into Western versus non-Western cultures. The categorization across cultures is based on the contention that dark traits might be less expressed in collectivistic cultures characterized by strong social control (Aluja et al., 2022). Dark Triad characteristics such as manipulativeness, self-importance, and lack of empathy are incompatible with the characteristics of social harmony in collectivistic cultures (El Keshky et al., 2022). Therefore, a stronger relationship between the Dark Tetrad and cyber deviance and crime, including social network addiction, is expected in Western societies.

After Section 2.5.6, a table summarizing the empirical studies' main findings will be presented and briefly analyzed.

2.5.1 The Dark Triad/Tetrad and Social Network Addiction

2.5.1.1 Western Cultures

Sindermann et al. (2018) performed two studies in Germany to understand the relationship between the Dark Triad of personality and internet-use disorder (IUD). The first sample included 468 participants, and the second included 472 participants. The findings showed that Machiavellianism and psychopathy were positively linked to tendencies toward unspecified IUD in both samples and males and females. No significant associations were found in males regarding the relationships between tendencies toward specific IUDs and the Dark Triad. In females, the trait of Machiavellianism/ psychopathy and tendencies toward internet-shopping disorder, the trait of psychopathy and tendencies toward internet-pornography-use disorder, and the trait of Machiavellianism and tendencies toward internet-communication disorder were significantly positively correlated. No robust pattern of associations between narcissism and unspecified/specific forms of IUD was found across (sub)samples. However, their findings show positive associations between the traits of Machiavellianism and psychopathy (on a subclinical level) with tendencies toward IUD, especially unspecified. The authors concluded that the relationships with tendencies toward specific forms of IUD seem more complex, with differential personality correlates for each specific IUD.

Hussain et al. (2021), in a sample of 555 participants from the United Kingdom, found that Machiavellianism, psychopathy, and narcissism explained 33.5% of the variance in problematic social networking use. Hussain et al. (2021) also found that male users scored higher in all Dark Triad traits. Tang et al. (2022), based on a nationally representative sample of 1,865 German Internet users, found that each dark personality trait had positive direct and indirect associations with social network disorder via entertainment, communication, and self-expression motivations. Unexpectedly, relationship maintenance had different indirect effects for each dark personality trait. A negative indirect effect was found for narcissism, a positive indirect effect for psychopathy, and a nonsignificant indirect effect for Machiavellianism.

Monacis et al. (2020) found that a sample of Italian students partially supported the positive narcissism and psychopathy-social network addiction associations. As for Machiavellianism, no significant relationship was found. Indeed, because Machiavellians show an ego drive (i.e., the tendency to derive satisfaction from successful persuasive attempts and a tendency toward independence), they were not likely to employ selfitis activities as tactics and strategies on the social network, given their strong sense of independence. Consequently, the lack of codependence (the combination of both dependence/addiction) was empirically supported among all three groups. The hypothesized mediating role of selfitis behavior in the relationships between narcissism and social network addiction and between psychopathy and social network addiction was confirmed.

In their study among a sample of German adults, Tang et al. (2020) found that psychopathy and Machiavellianism were directly associated with higher gaming disorder scores. However, narcissism was not. Furthermore, the indirect effects on gaming disorder scores via escapism were found for all dark personality traits; social motivation mediated for psychopathy and Machiavellianism, but achievement was not a significant mediator. Thus, the relationship between narcissism and gaming disorder is fully mediated via escapism, while psychopathy and Machiavellianism are partially mediated.

Servidio et al. (2021) examined 457 Italian smartphone users recruited online through a snowball sampling. They found a direct and significant association between narcissism and problematic smartphone use. According to them, individuals with narcissistic traits might use smartphones for self-promotion and self-presentation on social networking sites (such as Facebook and Instagram), given their disposition to these behaviors; positive mood modification, achieved by satisfying the desired gratification, might develop into problematic smartphone use. Their findings also showed that psychopathy and Machiavellianism were not associated with problematic smartphone use. According to Servidio et al. (2021), this result contradicts other reported significant associations.

Freyth, Batinic, and Jonason (2023) examined 243 German speaking who used Instagram and/or Facebook. They correlated behavioral data of the two most prominent social networks – Instagram and Facebook – with the Dark Tetrad facets. In general, the Dark Tetrad facets were associated with Instagram use. By contrast, the Dark Tetrad facets were almost entirely uncorrelated with Facebook use. They explained that this finding supports the difference between Instagram, a highly visual social media application, and Facebook, which developed into a general platform with different and more text-based interactions. Indicating the link between Instagram use and the Dark Tetrad facets supports the assumption of using mating tactics on visual social media such as Instagram but not on Facebook. Furthermore, relationships between personality and social media usage intensity were probably almost completely limited to the Dark Tetrad facets. High-scoring individuals seek mating purposes online and prefer the environment because of possible success (i.e., better fitness pay-offs and niche specialization).

Barberis et al. (2023) found in a sample of 788 Italians that the Dark Triad was positively correlated with problematic use of social media and social media engagement, both directly and mediated, via fear of missing out. Individuals who have a propensity to exploit others and a tendency to seek admiration may tend to overuse social media due to intense concerns about missing out on potentially rewarding social experiences that would bolster their maladaptive personalities. They concluded that individuals who have a propensity to exploit others and a tendency to seek admiration may tend to overuse social media due to intense concerns about missing out on potentially rewarding social experiences that would bolster their maladaptive personalities.

2.5.1.2   Non-Western Cultures

Siah et al. (2021) found, in a sample of 219 Malaysian undergraduate students recruited from a university, that not all Dark Triad personality types were associated with social network addiction. Only a significant positive association was found between narcissism and social network addiction. Furthermore, they found no significant association between psychopathy traits and social network addiction and between Machiavellianism and social network addiction.

In an English survey among 315 Omani Instagram users in different regions across Oman, Nikbin et al. (2022) found that narcissism, Machiavellianism, and psychopathy were linked positively and significantly to Instagram addiction. Their findings imply that individuals with high narcissism, Machiavellianism, and psychopathy extensively involve themselves in others' statuses or photo/video uploads or try to compensate for their superiority, ambition, and recklessness by building relationships on Instagram. In addition, they use Instagram excessively to view others' profiles or hobby profile uploads, such as technology, sports, cars, celebrities, or any other topic that draws their interest (Nikbin et al., 2022). Nikbin's findings showed that narcissism has the highest effect on Instagram addiction among the three Dark Triad traits. Nikbin et al. (2022) also found that Machiavellianism is directly associated with Instagram addiction and mediates the conformity motive. Finally, Nikbin found that psychopathy has a direct association with Instagram addiction via the role of the coping motive.

Tahoon's (2020) findings in a sample of Egyptian students showed that narcissism did not affect social network addiction. However, the results also showed that psychopathy indirectly influenced social network addiction by mediating social interaction. Nevertheless, the Machiavellian personality indirectly and negatively affected social network addiction. Among 204 Malaysian undergraduate students, Lee (2019) found that secondary psychopathy was linked to risky decision-making, poor inhibition, and high impulsivity, which will induce excessive use of social networking sites or addiction. Therefore, the findings suggested that a high degree of secondary psychopathy elevates the risk of addiction to social networking sites. Their findings showed that the traits of narcissism and Machiavellianism were not significant predictors of social networking site addiction. According to Lee (2019), individuals with high Machiavellianism traits might prefer other social networking or interaction forms to achieve their goals. Moreover, individuals with salient features of Machiavellianism engage in greater self-monitoring to disguise their manipulative tendencies. In this light, these individuals are less likely to be impulsive. With the absence of poor self-control central to the development of social networking site addiction, the trait of Machiavellianism did not correlate significantly with social networking site addiction.

Lee and Lim (2020) examined Internet addiction among 166 undergraduate students from Malaysia. Their findings showed that psychopathy was the weakest predictor of Internet addiction. The strongest predictor was narcissism, which also intensified the risk of technology addiction. They contended that Machiavellianism might have weakened the strength of psychopathy as a predictor of Internet addiction, as both are theoretically overlapping. Their findings also showed that the entry of the five-factor model traits further weakened the strength of Machiavellianism and psychopathy as predictors of Internet addiction. They concluded that these results suggest that the five personality traits are redundant in the presence of the three dark traits (Lee & Lim, 2020).

Chung et al. (2019) examined a Malaysian sample. First, Android 5.0+ smartphone users were asked to install the Social Tracker mobile application developed by PopCornBox Games to obtain participants' actual time spent on social network applications. iPhone users retrieved this information using the built-in Battery Usage feature. Next, a Social Network Usage form was developed to record the application's on-screen duration for the past two to seven days (the available data varied depending on whether the smartphone had been powered down and restarted before retrieval, causing the settings to be reset). Finally, the average screen time per day, in minutes, was calculated. Chung et al. (2019) found that psychopathy was the only Dark Triad trait positively associated with the addictive use of social networks. According to Chung et al. (2019), one interpretation of the positive psychopathy–addiction association is that social networking sites might provide a venue for aggressive online behaviors in which people high in psychopathy are prone to engage. In other words, psychopathic individuals might be motivated to use social networks to express their dark traits extensively.

Jin et al. (2019) examined 1,927 middle school students from four middle schools in Beijing and Kunming. They examined the relationship between the Dark Triad and positive and negative Internet adaptation. Jin et al.'s (2019) findings showed that, in general, the Dark Triad negatively predicted positive Internet adaptation and positively predicted negative Internet adaptation. The three Dark Triad dimensions had more predictive power for negative than positive Internet adaptation. The close correlation between the Dark Triad and negative Internet adaptation showed that adolescents who scored higher in the Dark Triad were more likely to develop negative adaptation behaviors, such as escaping from school using the Internet, avoiding relationships, and engaging in Internet problem behaviors. Jin et al. (2019) also found that psychopathy was a stronger predictor of Internet adaptation than Machiavellianism or narcissism. They advanced a possible reason for this finding, claiming that individuals with high psychopathy are impulsive, lack empathy and responsibility, and have negative social adaptation characteristics. Because Internet adaptation is a unique social adaptation, it should be highly correlated with psychopathy (Jin et al., 2019).

Kircaburun et al. (2019) found among 761 participants from Turkey that problematic social network use was positively associated with Machiavellianism and narcissism but not psychopathy. Demircioğlu and Göncü Köse (2021) found that psychopathy was directly and positively associated with social network addiction. Expected positive paths from the two other Dark Triad personality traits, namely, Machiavellianism and narcissism, to SMA were insignificant. Savci (2019) found, among 296 students from Turkey, that social network craving significantly and positively predicted narcissism, Machiavellianism, and psychopathy.

In a sample of 251 men and 295 women who completed an online survey promoted in Yaşar University's distance learning center in Turkey, Balta et al. (2019) found that narcissism and psychopathy were related to problematic smartphone use. No significant direct relationship was found between Machiavellianism and problematic smartphone use. According to Balta et al. (2019), the direct relationship between narcissism and problematic smartphone use is consistent with the existing literature, which found that narcissistic individuals had higher problematic smartphone use. Individuals with narcissistic traits might use smartphones for self-promotion and self-presentation on virtual platforms (such as social networking). Given their proneness to these behaviors, positive mood modification by obtaining desired gratifications might develop into problematic use.

In a sample of 547 high school students in Turkey, Demircioğlu and Köse (2022) found that psychopathy fully mediated the relationship between attachment avoidance and social media addiction. They explained that psychopathic tendencies triggered by high attachment avoidance are likely to lead individuals to engage in impulsive acts and uncontrolled behaviors such as social media addiction. Contrary to their expectations, the associations of Machiavellianism and narcissism with social media addiction and cyberbullying were insignificant. They explained that in contrast to individuals who score high on psychopathy, Machiavellians' level of social media usage may depend on the context. Individuals with high scores on Machiavellianism may use or avoid social media depending on perceived benefits, contacted individuals, or the context.

A possible explanation for the insignificant relationship between narcissism and social media addiction found in their study may be that the narcissism scale used measured the general (unidimensional) narcissism rather than vulnerable and grandiose narcissism as separate dimensions of the construct. It is highly likely that individuals who score high on grandiose narcissism excessively use social media for self-promotion and activities that aim to boost their self-esteem further (e.g., taking filtered selfies). Therefore, each "like" would please them and reinforce their use of social media, contributing to social media addiction. On the other hand, social media may not be advantageous for individuals who score high on vulnerable narcissism since even minor negative feedback would damage their fragile self-esteem.

Necula (2020) found a positive correlation between narcissism and social network addiction in a sample of adults from Romania. A weak correlation was found between Machiavellianism and social network addiction. Finally, a weak correlation between psychopathy and social network addiction was also found. However, it was greater than the earlier two. Kumpasoğlu et al. (2021) found in a sample of 364 participants from Turkey a significant relationship between psychopathy and Machiavellianism personality traits and social network addiction and a lack of a significant relationship between narcissism and the social network. They explained that features of different social network platforms could change the type of usage for narcissistic personalities. For instance, Facebook could be more suitable for narcissistic people to present themselves and satisfy their narcissistic needs than Twitter. Therefore, in their study, the lack of a significant relationship between narcissism and social networks could result from assessing social network use without differentiating between platforms.

Xu et al. (2022) examined in a sample of 740 Chinese undergraduate students the psychological mechanisms underlying the link between the Dark Triad and Internet gaming disorder, taking into account psychological needs and negative coping styles with stress and other problems. Their findings showed that Machiavellianism and psychopathy could predict Internet gaming disorder through sequential mediation of basic psychological needs satisfaction and negative coping styles, and narcissism could predict Internet gaming disorder only via the negative coping styles. Machiavellianism and psychopathy showed a much stronger relationship with Internet gaming disorder than narcissism.

Salimi et al. (2023) found a direct relationship between a composite scale of the Dark Triad and social media addiction among 370 high school students in Iran. The specific correlations between each of the dark traits and social media addiction were relatively high. Kiziloglu et al. (2021) found relatively modest but significant correlations among 514 Turkish private-sector employees between Machiavellianism, narcissism, and social media addiction. There was no significant relationship between psychopathy, sadism, and social media addiction. Hussain et al. (2023) found in a sample of 400 university students from Pakistan weak correlations between Machiavellianism and narcissism and social media addiction. No significant relationship was found between psychopathy and social media addiction. Turan et al. (2023) found, in a sample of 497 Turkish adolescents, that the Dark Triad mediates the relationship between ostracism and social media addiction. The study findings suggest that the Dark Triad may serve as an underlying mechanism that explains the relationship between ostracism and social media addiction.

Nwufo, Nnadozi, and Beluonwu (2023) examined Internet addiction among 300 high school students in Nigeria. Their findings showed that Machiavellianism and psychopathy were significantly related to Internet addiction, while narcissism was not. A similar finding was found by Shrivastava (2023) among 94 participants from India. In a sample of 591 Hispanic college students, Garcia et al. found that narcissism and psychopathy were positively and significantly related to phubbing. They explained that based on the politeness theory, individuals with low empathy usually have limited politeness for others, thus disregarding conflict and other people.

One immediate impression from the studies mentioned earlier is that there are fewer studies on this issue in Western than non-Western cultures. Based on the existing studies, there is evidence that the relationship between dark personalities and social network addiction is slightly stronger in Western cultures. More research on Western cultures is needed.

2.5.2   Narcissism and Social Network Addiction

Gnambs and Appel (2018) performed a meta-analysis review based on 289 effect sizes from 57 studies (total $N = 25,631$) on the association between trait narcissism and social networking. Their meta-analysis involved data from 16 countries on 4 different continents. Their findings showed an overall relationship between social networking site behaviors and grandiose narcissism of average $r = 0.17$ that replicated across a variety of conditions: Narcissism was equally predictive of activities on Facebook, Twitter, or other social networking sites; the relationship did not vary with the gender composition or the age of the participants. According to general interpretation guidelines, this relationship is small to moderate. However, its size is similar to the effect sizes found in many of the studies in Table 2.1. The findings also showed that the relationship was stronger for grandiose narcissism than for vulnerable narcissism (the latter association was nonsignificant). Their data further indicate that narcissists have a larger circle of contacts on social networking sites, are particularly inclined to upload photos, and tend to feel strongly connected to Facebook. Thus, although narcissists spend more time on social networking sites, they display specific usage patterns.

Their findings showed that the size of the social networking sites behavior–grandiose narcissism link varies with the cultural background. Whereas the relationship was comparable in individualistic and collectivistic countries, the social networking sites' behavior–narcissism link was particularly strong in societies in which social stratification is considered to be fixed and where citizens' place in society appears to be a given country with considerable power distance. In these countries, social networking sites provide rare opportunities to express self-entitlement and uniqueness and are, therefore, relatively more attractive for grandiose narcissists. Gnambs and Appel (2018) concluded that contradictory results in previous studies could partly be explained by variations in the respondents' cultural backgrounds.

In another meta-analysis based on 21 studies that dealt with Facebook addiction and narcissism, Rajesh and Rangaiah (2022) showed an average positive correlation (0.228) between narcissism and Facebook addiction. According to them, the various features of Facebook allow narcissistic individuals to promote their grandiosity, which satisfies their need for admiration. Individuals high in narcissism tend to engage in ego-enhancing activities through Facebook, such as displaying their ambitions and endorsing their successes. These kinds of activities are met with rewards in the form of likes and comments. These activities might gratify narcissistic individuals, as they repeat this action and get addicted to it.

In a cross-national study that examined three clusters of personality characteristics, including narcissism (the only Dark Triad trait examined in the study), in 14 countries, Kalaitzaki et al. (2022) found that narcissism was a significant correlate of problematic mobile phone use in five countries (Brazil, Columbia, UAE, Finland, and Romania). No significant relationship was found in the other countries (Italy, Ecuador, France, Peru, Chile, Turkey, Greece, Iran, and Pakistan). The relationship between narcissism and problematic mobile phone use in the entire sample ($N = 7,531$) was significant (0.086; $P < 0.001$).

2.5.2.1 Western Cultures

Bergman et al. (2011) contended that the rise in levels of narcissism among Millennials, together with the increased usage of social networking sites, raises the question of whether a connection exists between the two. Their study of 374 undergraduate students in the United States examined the link between narcissism and social networking site activities and motivation for social networking site activities. Their results showed that narcissism did not relate to the amount of time spent on social networking sites, frequency of status updates, posting a picture of others, or checking up on social networking sites with friends. However, narcissism predicted the reasons why Millennials use social networking sites, such as having as many social networking site friends as possible, wanting their social networking site friends to know what they are doing, believing that their social networking site friends are interested in what they are doing, and having their social networking site profiles project a positive image. Bergman et al. (2011) concluded that Millennials' general usage of social networking sites is a sign of the times. While narcissists in the Millennial generation do not appear to use social networking sites more often than non-narcissists, their reasons for doing so are different.

In a large Norwegian sample, Andreassen et al. (2017) found that narcissism was positively related to the addictive use of social networks and appeared to have a small-to-medium-sized effect after basic sociodemographics were controlled, therefore being meaningfully related to the construct. Facebook, Instagram, Snapchat, and other social network applications might serve as ideal social arenas for individuals who appreciate and are attracted to ego-enhancing activities, as they enable individuals to bolster their egos based on instant feedback from potentially large numbers of other individuals. It could be speculated that individuals with elevated narcissistic traits use social networks excessively because these online platforms fulfill a need for affiliation and confirm the sense of an idealized self.

Pearson and Hussain (2015) performed a study of 256 participants (71% females) recruited via opportunity sampling from a United Kingdom university and the Internet via social networking sites and smartphone forums. The findings showed a significant positive relationship between narcissism levels and smartphone addiction. This suggests that the more narcissistic a person is, the more likely they are to be addicted to their smartphone. According to Pearson and Hussain (2015), the qualitative results supported the idea that smartphones create narcissistic traits in people who otherwise do not show high levels of narcissism, as most of those showing self-serving personalities did not have a narcissistic personality disorder. This contention supports the theory that advanced technologies such as smartphones influence the narcissism epidemic. Furthermore, the results showed that young males were most likely to have a narcissistic personality disorder.

Hussain, Griffiths, and Sheffield (2017) used an online survey to examine 640 United Kingdom smartphone users. Their findings showed that problematic smartphone use (as discussed earlier) and time spent using smartphones were positively related to narcissism, suggesting that increased smartphone use can lead to narcissistic traits. However, no association was found between narcissism and problematic smartphone use, a scale based on the nine criteria that define Internet Gaming Disorder according to the fifth edition of the Diagnostic and Statistical Manual of Mental Disorders (DSM-5). They explained that this unexpected finding arose because the study sample had very few narcissistic individuals or was not motivated to use smartphones for narcissistic purposes. Calvert et al. (2021), in a sample of 185 American individuals recruited voluntarily through online platforms such as social networks and college class forums, found no significant relationship between more narcissism and increased gaming use.

2.5.2.2 Non-Western Cultures

Iftikhar and Tariq (2014) examined 100 participants from different educational institutes in Pakistan. The results revealed a positive relationship between narcissistic tendencies and Internet addiction among adolescents. Savci et al. (2021) examined 305 high school students in Turkey. They found that social network addiction increases narcissistic personality beliefs. In a sample of 596 participants from Turkey, Savacı, Bayraktar, and Özen (2021) did not find a significant relationship between narcissism and social network addiction.

Using a longitudinal design, Hou et al. (2023) surveyed 1,196 Chinese students. Their findings showed that narcissism at time 1 was related to more problematic social networking sites use at time 3. According to Hou et al., this finding was in line with previous studies reporting that individuals who score highly on narcissism are more likely to engage in various problematic social networking sites use. Hou et al. (2023) explained that people with higher narcissism tend to be more egocentric, with a strong desire for admiration and attention. To this end, they need a larger audience.

2.5.3   The Dimensionality of Narcissism and Social Network Addiction

McCain and Campbell (2018) collected data from 62 samples of published and unpublished research (N = 13,430). They performed a meta-analysis concerning the relationships between grandiose and vulnerable narcissism and (a) time spent on social media, (b) frequency of status updates/tweets on social media, (c) number of friends/followers on social media, and (d) frequency of posting pictures of oneself or selfies on social media. The findings suggested that grandiose narcissism was positively related to all four indices (range of average correlations of the four forms of media use, r = 0.11–0.20). Vulnerable narcissism was not significantly related to social media use (range of average correlations of the four forms of media use, r = 0.05–0.42). However, smaller samples made these effects less confident. According to McCain and Campbell (2018), individuals with grandiose narcissism appear to have more friends, post more frequent status updates, and post more pictures of themselves on social networks than non-narcissists.

However, two of these relationships – narcissism and the number of friends and frequency of status updates – appear to be moderated by culture in that they are significantly higher in Russian samples. Asian samples did not differ significantly from United States or European samples, which is inconsistent with past research showing that Asian countries, which tend to have collectivistic cultures and interdependent self-construal, have different relationships between narcissism and social network use. However, Russia is considered to have an attenuated collectivistic culture with both individualistic and collectivistic elements, which might have a unique effect on the relationship between narcissism and social network use.

The finding that individuals high in grandiose narcissism more often update their statuses also appears to be moderated by sample type. Specifically, the relationship was most robust for Internet samples, which were not specific to any particular age group or location and were nonsignificant for adolescent samples. It might be that individuals who have a stronger relationship between narcissism and status updates were more likely to sign up for these studies (McCain & Campbell, 2018). The finding that individuals high in grandiose narcissism post pictures of themselves more often on a social network also appears to be moderated by the platform. This finding was nonsignificant for Instagram-only studies but was more robust in studies that did not specify a platform (McCain & Campbell, 2018).

2.5.3.1 Western Cultures

Fegan and Bland (2021) examined 115 participants from the United Kingdom. Their findings showed that levels of vulnerable narcissism were related to time spent on social networks and frequency of posting to the social network. However, this was related more to oversensitivity than to the egocentricity part of vulnerable narcissism. Their results showed that oversensitivity to judgment and preoccupation with what others think drives a greater frequency of social network usage than the more egocentric self-absorption and self-centeredness trait of vulnerable narcissism. Indeed, vulnerable narcissists often experience high levels of anxiety in social interactions. Therefore, they avoid social contacts offline in favor of social networking sites, where they can carefully plan and control self-presentation. However, this might contribute to further excessive immersion into the online world and the development of problematic social network use that can negatively affect well-being.

Fegan and Bland (2021) also observed that people who scored higher in oversensitivity were more likely to use social networks as soon as they woke up, when they went to bed, and when they were in the bathroom. On the other hand, egocentricity was linked to checking one's phone during mealtimes. Both factors of vulnerable narcissism were linked to checking social networks in social situations, that is, when in the physical company of other people. Spending more time on the social network, especially during social situations, further reduces real-world connections and friendships opportunities. In addition, oversensitivity but not egocentricity is significantly associated with concerns about likes and comments on social networks. Furthermore, they observed that people who use social networking sites to post images, videos, and updates on their lives had higher oversensitivity scores but not higher egocentricity scores. The earlier discussion suggests that vulnerable narcissism is related to caring about likes and comments and is driven explicitly by oversensitivity to feedback from others (Fegan & Bland, 2021).

Grieve and March (2021) examined 250 Australian adults. They found that phubbing behaviors were predicted by vulnerable narcissism. However, their data revealed no predictive effect of grandiose narcissism on phubbing behaviors. Grieve et al. (2021) examined 402 smartphone users, also from Australia. Their findings showed that narcissistic vulnerability predicted a preference for online social interaction, which predicted phubbing. The mediation effect suggested that those with vulnerable narcissism might engage in phubbing because they prefer interacting with people online compared to those with whom they are face-to-face. According to Grieve et al. (2021), the online environment eases control over self-presentation. They contended that their results show that a preference for online inter-actions – a product of low social self-efficacy and higher social anxiety – in those with narcissistic vulnerability might result in unregulated, inappropriate phone-checking behavior.

However, Grieve et al. (2021) noted that while the vulnerable narcissist might prefer online social interactions, increasing phubbing, the characteristics associated with vulnerable narcissism (i.e., contingent self-esteem) still directly predict phubbing behavior. Grieve et al. (2021) concluded that phubbing allows those high in narcissistic vulnerability to meet contingent self-esteem needs through access to a potentially broad online audience and that those individuals prefer interacting with others in the online environment because it allows them to curate their self-presentation more carefully. They also argued that this interpretation of their findings is consistent with the Uses and Gratifications Theory.

In a convenience sample of 550 undergraduate students from Italy, Casale and Fioravanti (2018) found that grandiose narcissism traits were more strictly related to Facebook addiction than vulnerable narcissism traits. Their findings supported the idea that the need for admiration mediated the relationship between grandiose narcissism and Facebook addiction levels. They also found that the need to belong has a mediating role in the association between Facebook addiction levels and grandiose narcissism, often linked to problematic face-to-face interactions and relationship dissatisfaction. Fegan and Bland (2021) examined 115 participants in the United Kingdom and found a significant relationship between vulnerable narcissism and social network use, particularly concerning oversensitivity.

Balcerowska et al. (2023) examined the relationship between four dimensions of narcissism (admirative, communal, rivalrous, and vulnerable narcissism) and social networking site addiction in Germany ($N = 781$) and Poland ($N = 1,165$). They also examined whether positive reinforcement expectancies could mainly explain the relationship between self-enhancement–based aspects of narcissism and social networking site addiction. By contrast, negative reinforcement expectancies could mainly explain the relationship between self-protection–based aspects of narcissism and social networking site addiction.

Their findings showed that all dimensions of narcissism were positively associated with social networking site addiction, except communal narcissism in Poland. Balcerowska et al. (2023) concluded that given that the explanations linking narcissism to social networking site use were primarily based on the assumption that social networking sites are convenient platforms for ego-boosting activities, their research puts the addiction perspective into emphasis, showing that narcissistic ego protection might be as crucial as ego boosting in social networking sites addiction research. Furthermore, regarding narcissism as a personality risk factor, social networking site addiction might be viewed not only as a result of a maladaptive gratification-seeking process but also as a compensatory strategy to cope with psychosocial stressors.

Brailovskaia et al. (2023) examined the relationship between vulnerable narcissism and addictive social media use among a sample of males ($N = 365$) and females ($N = 380$) in Germany. The relationship was significant in both samples but more robust for males. However, they found only minor effects of the gender differences. Therefore, these differences should not be overemphasized, and the question of gender-specific differences in addictive social media use remains to be checked. However, they found higher values of vulnerable narcissism and addictive social media use in men than in women, allowing some preliminary assumptions on the higher levels of addictive tendencies in their male participants.

2.5.3.2 Non-Western Culture

Choi et al. (2011) examined 56 participants from South Korea. Male middle school students with Internet addiction tendencies (addiction tendency group, $N = 27$) and regular students (control group, $N = 29$) were recruited. They compared covert narcissistic propensity in adolescents with Internet addiction tendencies to normal adolescents. Further, they investigated the correlation between such propensities and anonymity in cyberspace, presence feeling and interactivity in Internet gaming, and achievement motivation in adolescents with Internet addiction tendencies. Choi et al. (2011) found that compared to the control group, the addiction tendency group showed significantly higher scores on all subscales of the covert narcissism scale and the scale of presence feeling and interactivity in

Internet games. They also found that in the addiction tendency group, the scores on several subscales of the covert narcissism scale were significantly positively correlated with the scale of presence feeling in Internet games, anonymity in cyberspace, and interactivity in Internet games. However, in the control group, the scores of several subscales on the covert narcissism scale were significantly negatively correlated with the score on the achievement motivation scale. They were significantly positively correlated with the score on the interactivity scale in Internet games. There were no other significant correlations between the scores on the subscales of the covert narcissism scale and the scores of either presence feeling in Internet games or anonymity in cyberspace. Choi et al. (2011) concluded that adolescents with a tendency toward addiction to the Internet showed higher covert narcissistic propensities than normal adolescents and that the covert narcissistic tendencies were related to presence feeling in cyber games as well as anonymity in cyberspace.

Eksi (2012) examined 508 vocational high school students in Istanbul (male = 331). According to the results of the research, the trait of a narcissistic personality, "entitlement" significantly predicts "deprivation" in Internet addiction and "controlling difficulty." Moreover, the trait of narcissistic "superiority" significantly predicts "social isolation" in Internet addiction.

2.5.4   *Machiavellianism and Social Network Addiction*

Błachnio et al. (2023) found among 748 participants from Poland a direct and significant relationship between Machiavellianism and Facebook intrusion only for females in their structural equation modeling analysis. Kircaburun et al. (2018a) found a direct association between Machiavellianism and social network addiction among a sample of undergraduate students in Turkey. They also reported that Machiavellianism was indirectly associated with social network addiction via cyberbullying and cyberstalking. However, this association was significant only in the total sample and among men.

2.5.5   *Psychopathy and Social Network Addiction*

de Jesus Costa, Simoes, and Relva (2023) examined the associations between psychopathic traits and Internet addiction. They tested the mediating effect of Internet addiction between psychopathic traits (e.g., interpersonal manipulation, callous affect, and erratic lifestyle). Their sample constituted 249 students from Portuguese universities. The results revealed that 73.5% of the participants presented a mild and moderate addiction rate. According to them, university students use the Internet continuously and become addicted to it. Furthermore, an erratic lifestyle was positively associated with Internet addiction.

Regarding the degree of addiction, in the interpersonal manipulation dimension, individuals with a moderate degree of addiction presented a higher average than regular users. According to de Jesus Costa et al. (2023), it is possible to conject that these individuals have a greater opportunity to perform their devious behaviors online since the existence of punishment may be more limited in these contexts. In conclusion, de Jesus Costa et al. (2023) contended that the results of their study showed that psychopathic traits correlate and positively predict Internet addiction and cyber dating abuse. They also argued that psychopathic traits are related to the development of Internet addiction, which, in turn, can be related to the development of cyber abuse.

Bilal et al. (2022) found in a sample of 160 undergraduate students from Pakistan a strong relationship between cyberpsychopaths and cybersex addiction. They concluded that the impulsive nature of psychopaths, their emotional mood dysregulation, and their lack of empathy toward others are the traits that make them fit to develop cybersex addiction.

2.5.6 Sadism and Social Network Addiction

Greitemeyer and Sagioglou (2017) examined the relationship between sadism, Dark Triad, and exposure to violent video games among 743 participants in the United States. Their longitudinal study addressed the interplay between everyday sadism and exposure to violent video games over time. Their findings showed that the relationship between everyday sadism and violent video game play is bidirectional. On the one hand, everyday sadists are more attracted to violent video games than others. However, on the other hand, violent video game play increases the player's sadistic tendencies. Overall, it appears that a downward spiral is at work in that everyday sadists prefer to play violent video games in the first place, and their desire to cause harm is then further strengthened by previous violent video game play. Taken together, of the Dark Tetrad and trait aggression, everyday sadism had the most robust association with the amount of violent video game play, suggesting that the observation that avid players of violent video games score higher than others on everyday sadism is not a byproduct of them having other forms of socially aversive personalities

Instead, causing virtual harm during video game play appears particularly attractive to individuals with urges for cruelty above the population average (i.e., everyday sadists) (Greitemeyer & Sagioglou, 2017).

Gonzalez and Greitemeyer (2018) performed a similar study to that of Greitemeyer and Sagioglou, albeit cross-sectional, among 613 Austrian, German, and US-American students and community members. They found, similarly to Greitemeyer and Sagioglou (2017), that everyday sadism is a strong predictor of the amount of violent video game play. Importantly, this relationship held when controlling for the impact of other facets of the dark side of human personality, including the Dark Triad trait. They concluded that causing virtual harm while playing violent video games is particularly attractive to individuals who enjoy harming others (i.e., everyday sadists).

Balta et al. (2019), in a sample of 251 men and 295 in Turkey, found that sadism accounted for an additional 3% of problematic smartphone use. Also, sadism was positively related to fearful attachment, and in turn, a fearful attachment was positively associated with problematic smartphone use. Sadism was directly associated with problematic smartphone use among women. Balta et al. explained that women with more sadistic impulses might become problematic smartphone users in attempts to stalk others in online contexts, which has been associated with problematic social media use. Sadistic individuals engage in cyberbullying and cyberstalking. These obsessive behaviors may promote preoccupation and fear of missing out, leading to excessive engagement and problematic smartphone use.

****

Table 2.1 summarizes the findings regarding Dark Triad traits and social network addiction forms. The table focuses on the correlations between the two. However, in some cases where correlations were not reported, the table presents the relationship between the two based on the statistical analysis presented in the relevant study. The findings revealed that the relationship between Dark Triad personalities and forms of social site addiction is modest. This suggests that the relationship between dark personalities and social network addiction is moderated and mediated by variables representing situational constraints. Also, there is a need for more research on this relationship in Western cultures. Future research should continue the search for essential moderators and mediators that intervene in the relationship between dark personality traits and social network addiction.

Table 2.1 *Summary of research findings on the relationship between the Dark Tetrad/Triad and social network addiction*

Study	Sample size	Type of social network addiction	Gender	Age (mean)	MTurk or similar	Country	Occupation	Education	Narcissists	Psychopathy	Machiavellianism	Sadism
Hussain et al. (2021)	555	Social media addiction	55% male	33.32	Yes	United Kingdom	70% employed	NR	0.294***	0.347****	0.343***	NE
Ifrikhar & Tariq (2014)	100	Internet Addiction Test	50% female	18	No	Pakistan	Students	50% B.A. and above	0.09	NE	NE	NE
Tang et al. (2022)	1,865	Social media disorder	48.5% male	27.65	No	Germany	NR	NR	0.32***	0.47***	0.47***	NE
Nikbin et al. (2022)	315	Instagram addiction	80% female	71.7% age 18–25	No	Oman	NR	80% B.A. and above	Highest effect	Significant effect	Significant effect	NE
Casale & Fioravanti (2018)	535	Facebook addiction	50.08% female	22.7	No	Italy	Students	Undergraduate students	GN = 0.013*** VN = 0.025***	NE	NE	NE
Sindermann et al. (2018)	468	Internet-use disorder	28% male	29.6	No	Germany	Students and university staff	Students	0.03 (partial Spearman corrected for age)	0.32*** (Partial Spearman corrected for age)	0.24*** (Partial Spearman corrected for age)	NE
Sindermann et al. (2018)	472	Internet-use disorder	30.3% male	23.2	No	Germany	Mostly students	Students	0.00 (partial Spearman corrected for age)	0.29*** (Partial Spearman corrected for age)	0.30*** (Partial Spearman corrected for age)	NE
Lee et al. (2021)	230	Social networking addiction	42.5% male	21.46	No	Malaysia	Undergraduate students	Students	Significant relationship (Structural model)	No significant relationship (Structural model)	No significant relationship (Structural model)	NE
Tahoon (2020)	247	Social media addiction	64.37% female	19.98	No	Egypt	Undergraduate students	Students	0.00	0.43*	0.44*	NE

Table 2.1 (*cont.*)

Study	Sample size	Type of social network addiction	Gender	Age (mean)	MTurk or similar	Country	Occupation	Education	Correlations			
						Sample characteristics			Narcissists	Psychopathy	Machiavellianism	Sadism
Necula (2020)	290	Social media addiction	78.6% female	22.5	No	Romania	NR	65.2% high school; 32.4% above high school	0.08*	0.18**	0.14*	NE
Kumpasoğlu et al. (2021)	364	Social media addiction	60.2% female	24.02	No	Turkey	Students	7.7% high school; 92.3% B.A. and higher	-0.01	0.26***	0.13*	NE
Monacis et al. (2020)	490	Social media addiction	53.1% female	21.23	No	Italy	Students	Students from secondary schools and university	0.146**	0.179***	0.151**	NE
Savci et al. (2021)	305	Social media disorder	52.4% female	Between 14 and 18 years old	No	Turkey	High school students	High school students	0.39**	NE	NE	NE
Choi et al. (2011)	56	Internet addiction	100% male	About 13.7 years old	No	Korea	Middle school students	Middle school students	Higher VN relates to higher addiction	NE	NE	NE
Andreassen et al. (2017)	23,532	Social media addiction	65% female	35.8	No	Norway	Variety	47.8% B.A. and above	0.06**	NE	NE	NE
Bergman et al. (2011)	361	Frequency of engagement in SNS activities	53.6% male	20.77	No	USA	Undergraduate students	Undergraduate students	-0.04	NE	NE	NE
Lee (2019)	204	SNS addiction	60% female	22.94	No	Malaysia	Undergraduate students	Undergraduate students	0.07	0.25***	0.11	NE
Lee & Lim (2020)	166	Internet addiction	50% female	20.28	No	Malaysia	Undergraduate students	Undergraduate students	0.21**	0.34**	0.36**	NE
Chung et al. (2019)	128	Social media addiction	52.3% female	19.73	No	Malaysia	University students	University students	0.21*	0.03	-0.01	0.08

Study	N	Construct	% female	Mean age	Online platform	Country	Sample 1	Sample 2				
Chung et al. (2019)	128	Social media usage	52.3% female	19.73	No	Malaysia	University students	University students	0.05	0.03	−0.06	0.14
Kircaburun et al. (2019)	761	Social media addiction	64% female	20.70	No	Turkey	Undergraduate students	Undergraduate students	0.22***	0.15***	0.23***	NE
Jin et al. (2019)	1,927	Negative Internet adaptation	59% male	15.07	No	China	Middle school students	Middle school students	0.24***	0.41***	0.38***	NE
Demircioğlu & Göncü Köse (2021)	229	Social media addiction	67.9% female	21.51	No	Turkey	University students	University students	0.04	0.25**	0.24**	NE
Savci (2019)	296	Social media craving	60% female	22.17	No	Turkey	University students	University students	0.45***	0.31***	0.32***	NE
Calvert et al. (2021)	185	Gaming use	60% female	23.51	No	USA	Students and a variety of employees	74.60% at least some college education	No significant relationship.	NE	NE	NE
Calvert et al. (2021)	185	Pornography use	60% female	23.51	No	USA	Students and a variety of employees	74.60% at least some college education	0.28***	NE	NE	NE
Tang et al. (2020)	1,502	Disordered use of digital games	53.6% male	27.62 (range: 14–39)	No	Germany	Students, employees, and retirees	24% university degree	0.24***	0.36***	0.37***	NE
Li et al. (2022)	322	"Phubbing"	56.2% female	25.6 (range: 18–53)	Online survey platform	China	NR	NR	VN = 0.44*** GN = 0.06	NE	NE	NE
Pearson & Hussain (2015)	256	Smartphone addiction	71% female	29.2	No	United Kingdom	35% students; others with a variety of occupations	35% students	0.13*	NE	NE	NE
Hussain et al. (2017)	640	Problematic smartphone use	65.6% female	24.89 (range: 13–69)	No	United Kingdom 86% United States 3.3% Canada 0.5%	68.6% of students; 23.6% employed	68.6% students	0.01	NE	NE	NE
Hussain et al. (2017)	640	Time spent on smartphone	65.6% female	24.89 (range: 13–69)	No	United Kingdom 86% United States 3.3% Canada 0.5%	68.6% of students; 23.6% employed	68.6% students	0.10*	NE	NE	NE
Balta et al. (2019)	546	Smartphone addiction	54% female	NR	No	Turkey	University students	University students	0.25***	0.10*	0.21***	0.26***

Table 2.1 (cont.)

Study	Sample size	Type of social network addiction	Gender	Age (mean)	MTurk or similar	Country	Occupation	Education	Narcissists	Psychopathy	Machiavellianism	Sadism
						Sample characteristics			Correlations			
Savacı et al. (2021)	506	Social media addiction	70.6% female	29.1% (18–24); 29.1% (25–29); 30.2% (30–49); 15.6% (above 50)	No	Turkey	22.3% of students; others – a variety of occupations	63.4% B.A. and above	No significant correlation	NE	NE	NE
Ekşi (2012)	508	Internet addiction	66.2% male	30.9% 1 (5 and under); 53.5% (16–17); 15.6% (18 and plus)	No	Turkey	Vocational high school students	Vocational high school students	Significant paths between dimensions of narcissism and dimensions of Internet addiction	NE	NE	NE
Servidio et al. (2021)	457	Problematic smartphone use	73.3% female	23–49	No	Italy	NR	NR	0.31***	0.06	0.17***	NE
Servidio et al. (2021)	457	Daily social media use (hours)	73.3% female	23–49	No	Italy	NR	NR	0.11*	−0.02	−0.01	NE
Fegan & Bland (2021)	115	Social media use	77% female	23–17	No	United Kingdom	Students & citizens	Students & citizens	VN is positively related to Social Media Use	NE	NE	NE
Grieve & March (2021)	250	"Phubbing"	80.8% female	23–21	No	Australia	NR	NR	VN = 0.26***; GN = 0.02	0.06	0.07	NE
Grieve et al. (2021)	402	"Phubbing"	75% female	23–49	No	Australia	NR	NR	VN = 0.26***; GN = 0.03	0.10*	0.14**	NE
Lee et al. (2022)	169	SNS addiction	53% male	15–40	No	Malaysia	High school students	High school students	Dark Triad composite = 0.19**			NE
Akat et al. (2022)	506	"Phubbing"	70.7% female	22–41	No	Turkey	Undergraduate students	Undergraduate students	0.35***	0.21***	0.35***	NE

Study	N	Type	Gender	Age	Online panel	Country	Sample 1	Sample 2	Narcissism	Psychopathy	Machiavellianism	Sadism
Balcerowska & Sawicki (2022)	456	SNS addiction	70.3% female	21.37	No	Poland	Undergraduate students	Undergraduate students	Leadership = 0.06 Grandiose = 0.13** Entitlement = 0.13** Communal = 0.07	NE	NE	NE
Balcerowska & Sawicki (2022)	402	SNS addiction	69.4% female	39.40	Ariadna online survey	Poland	NR	NR	Admiration = 0.09 Rivalry = 15** Communal = 16**	NE	NE	NE
Balcerowska & Sawicki (2022)	608	SNS addiction	57.1% female	43.90	Ariadna online survey	Poland	NR	NR	Admiration = 23** Rivalry = 0.22** Communal = 0.32** Vulnerable = 0.24**	NE	NE	NE
Kircaburun et al. (2022)	222	Addictive mukbang watching	69% female	21.68	No	Turkey	University students	University students	0.37***	0.60***	0.45***	0.63***
Wang et al. (2022a)	4,172	SNS addiction	48% female	16.41	No	China	High school students	High school students	0.200***	NE	NE	NE
Musetti et al. (2022)	344	Cognitive preoccupation	76.5% female	23.80	No	Italy	NR	NR	VN = 0.27**	NE	NE	NE
Musetti et al. (2022)	344	Compulsive use	76.5% female	23.80	No	Italy	NR	NR	VN = 0.26**	NE	NE	NE
Freyth et al. (2023)	243	Instagram time	43.21 female	42.81	No	German speaking	NR	NR	Agentic extraversion = 0.13 Self-centered antagonism = 0.27** Neurotic narcissism = 0.01	Meanness = 0.11 Boldness = 0.12 Disinhibition = 0.03	Machiavellian views = -0.03 Machiavellian tactics = 0.04	Verbal sadism = -0.06 Physical sadism = -0.05 Indirect sadism = 0.03
Freyth et al. (2023)	243	Instagram sessions	43.21 female	42.81	No	German speaking	NR	NR	Agentic extraversion = 0.06 Self-centered antagonism = 0.32** Neurotic narcissism = 0.07	Meanness = -0.05 Boldness = 0.11 Disinhibition = 0.07	Machiavellian views = 0.04 Machiavellian tactics = 0.15	Verbal sadism = 0.05 Physical sadism = 0.01 Indirect sadism = 0.06

Table 2.1 (cont.)

Study	Sample size	Type of social network addiction	Sample characteristics						Correlations			
			Gender	Age (mean)	MTurk or similar	Country	Occupation	Education	Narcissists	Psychopathy	Machiavellianism	Sadism
Freyth et al. (2023)	243	Facebook time	43:21 female	42.81	No	German speaking	NR	NR	Agentic extraversion = −0.09 Self-centered antagonism = −0.010 Neurotic narcissism = 0.04	Meanness = 0.14 Boldness = 0.01 Disinhibition = 0.01	Machiavellian views = 0.12 Machiavellian tactics = 0.01	Verbal sadism = 0.05 Physical sadism = −0.05 Indirect sadism = −0.04
Freyth et al. (2023)	243	Facebook sessions	43:21 female	42.81	No	German speaking	NR	NR	Agentic extraversion = 0.03 Self-centered antagonism = −0.04 Neurotic narcissism = −0.05	Meanness = 0.09 Boldness = 0.09 Disinhibition = 0.02	Machiavellian views = 0.15* Machiavellian tactics = 0.04	Verbal sadism = 0.06 Physical sadism = −0.04 Indirect sadism = −0.04
Kircaburun et al. (2018a)	761	Social media addiction	64% female	20.70	No	Turkey	Undergraduate students	Undergraduate students	0.22***	0.15***	0.23***	0.22***
Kircaburun et al. (2018a)	761	Daily social media use	64% female	20.70	No	Turkey	Undergraduate students	Undergraduate students	0.07	0.03	0.06	0.11*
Kircaburun et al. (2018b)	421	Problematic online gaming	100% male	20.82	No	Turkey	NR	NR	0.21**	0.05	0.07	0.15**
Kircaburun et al. (2018b)	421	Amount of gaming	100% male	20.82	No	Turkey	NR	NR	−0.03	0.08	−0.06	0.02
Kircaburun & Griffiths (2018)	772	Internet addiction	64% female	20.72 (18–28)	No	Turkey	University students	University students	0.20***	0.15***	0.24***	0.20***

Study	N	Measure	Gender	Age (range)		Country	Sample	Sample				
Greitemeyer (2015)	225	Violent video game exposure	72% female	25.1	No	Austria	Students/employees of an Austrian university	Students/employees of an Austrian university	NE	NE	NE	Physical sadism = 0.25*** Verbal sadism = 0.25***
Greitemeyer (2015)	340	Violent video game exposure	69% female	24.2	No	Austria	Participants of an Austrian university	Participants of an Austrian university	0.03	0.13*	0.12*	Physical sadism = 0.21*** Verbal sadism = 0.10
Greitemeyer & Sagioglou (2017)	743	Violent video game exposure (time 1)	55.2% female	35.7 (18–79)	Yes	United States	Amazon Mechanical Turk	Amazon Mechanical Turk	0.09* (Time 1)	0.18*** (Time 1)	0.15*** (Time 1)	0.35** (Time 1)
Greitemeyer & Sagioglou (2017)	743	Violent video game exposure (time 2)	55.2% female	35.7 (18–79)	Yes	United States	Amazon Mechanical Turk	Amazon Mechanical Turk	0.08* (Time 1)	0.22*** (Time 2)	0.19*** (Time 2)	0.40*** (Time 2)
Greitemeyer & Sagioglou (2017)	743	Violent video game exposure (time 2)	55.2% female	35.7 (18–79)	Yes	United States	Amazon Mechanical Turk	Amazon Mechanical Turk	0.07 (Time 1)	0.20*** (Time 1)	0.18*** (Time 1)	0.38*** (Time 1)
Gonzalez & Greitemeyer (2018)	613	Violent video gameplay	68.8% female	26.7 (16–81)	No	Austrian, German, and US-American	477 Students 136 community members	477 Students 136 community members	0.18***	0.38***	0.21***	0.36***
Fox & Rooney (2015)	800	Time on SNSs	100% male	29.29 (18–40)	No	United States	NR	NR	0.19***	0.09**	0.13***	NE
Freyth & Batinic (2021)	555	Average daily use time on smartphone	41.8% female	43.09	No	Germany	NR	NR	0.24*	0.04	0.33***	NE
de Jesus Costa et al. (2023)	249	Internet addiction	82.7% female	21.38 (17–49)	No	Portugal	Universities students	Universities students	NE	Interpersonal manipulation = 0.107 Callous affect = 0.066 Erratic lifestyle = 0.211* Criminal tendencies = 0.078	NE	NE

Table 2.1 (cont.)

Study	Sample size	Type of social network addiction	Gender	Age (mean)	MTurk or similar	Country	Occupation	Education	Narcissists	Psychopathy	Machiavellianism	Sadism
						Sample characteristics			Correlations			
Perez del Valle & Hand (2022)	672	Problematic pornography use	22.3% female	26.14 (18–72)	No	Native English and native Spanish speakers	NR	NR	0.014	0.180**	0.197**	Physical sad = 0.144** Verbal sad = 0.199** Vicarious sad = 0.210**
Lyons et al. (2019)	225	Facebook use	72.9% female	22.18 (17–40)	No	United Kingdom	NR	NR	0.12	0.07	0.36**	
Gylfason et al. (2021)	139	Facebook use (h/day)	85.6% female	25.2% (under 25) 51.8% (25–34) 22.9% (above 34)	No	Iceland	NR	NR	0.135	0.076	0.146	0.146
Brubaker et al. (2021)	438	Hours per day on Reddit	44.6% female	NR	No	USA	NR	27.2% have some college education; 37.3% 4-year college degree; 20.9% have an advanced degree.		Composite scale 0.041		NE
Ferenczi et al. (2017)	573	Time on Facebook	59% female	30.79	90% A.T.	USA	65% employed full or part-time	20% full or part-time student	Male = 0.14* Female = −0.01	NE	NE	NE

Author	N	Behavior	Gender	Age		Country						
Menzel et al. (2023)	192	Cheating intention in gaming	33.33% female	44.79% (20–29) 19.79% (30–39) 26.04% (above 40)	No	Germany	NR	NR	0.43***	0.68***	0.70***	NE
Blachnio et al. (2023)	748	Facebook intrusion	56% female	22.05	No	Poland	Undergraduate students and their Facebook friends	Undergraduate students and their Facebook friends	NE	NE	0.16** For females N = 420	NE
Blachnio et al. (2023)	748	Facebook intrusion	56% female	22.05	No	Poland	Undergraduate students and their Facebook friends	Undergraduate students and their Facebook friends	NE	NE	0.13* For males N = 328	NE
Petit & Carcioppolo (2020)	147	Compulsive Internet behavior	80% female	NR	No	USA	Undergraduate students	Undergraduate students	0.004	0.19*	0.24**	NE
Jin et al. (2022)	1,921	Online deviant behavior	40.45% female	15.03 (11–18)	No	China	Middle and high school students	Middle and high school students	0.29***	0.36***	0.32***	NE
Balcerowska et al. (2023)	781	Social networking site addiction	77% female	25.71 (18–86)	No	Germany	NR	NR	Communal = 0.15** Admirative = 0.27** Rivalrous = 0.41** Vulnerable = 0.39**	NE	NE	NE
Balcerowska et al. (2023)	1,165	Social networking site addiction	76% female	24.79 (18–59)	No	Poland	NR	NR	Communal = 0.03 Admirative = 0.20** Rivalrous = 0.32** Vulnerable = 0.34**	NE	NE	NE
Brailovskaia et al. (2023)	365	Addictive social media use	100% male	28.78 (18–73)	No	Germany	60.5% students, 37.8% employees	60.5% students, 37.8% employees	Vulnerable = 0.514***	NE	NE	NE
Brailovskaia et al. (2023)	380	Addictive social media use	100% female	29.71 (18–65)	No	Germany	61.8% students, 37.4% employees	61.8% students, 37.4% employees	Vulnerable = 0.391***	NE	NE	NE

Table 2.1 (cont.)

			Sample characteristics							Correlations			
Study	Sample size	Type of social network addiction	Gender	Age (mean)	MTurk or similar	Country	Occupation	Education	Narcissists	Psychopathy	Machiavellianism	Sadism
Demircioglu & Köse (2022)	547	Social media addiction	49.9% female	15.8	No	Turkey	High school students	High school students	0.12**	0.32**	16**	NE
Paul (2009)	377	Time spent online	53.11% female	20	No	USA	University Students	University students	NE	Impulsive thrill-seeking = -0.07 (for female) Antisocial behavior = 0.03 (for female) Interpersonal manipulation = 0.08 (for female) Cold affect = 0.06 (for female)	NE	NE
Paul (2009)	377	Time spent online	53.11% female	20	No	USA	University Students	University students	NE	Impulsive thrill-seeking = 0.10 (for male) Antisocial behavior = -0.03 (for male) Interpersonal manipulation = 0.16* (for male) Cold affect = 0.03 (for male)	NE	NE
Salimi et al. (2023)	370	Social media addiction	NR	15.05 (14–18)	No	Iran	High school students	High school students	0.41**	0.46**	0.44**	NE
Barberis et al. (2023)	788	Social media engagement	75% female	24.22 (18–35)	No	Italy	72% – students; 16% – employee; 5% – freelance	56% – high school diploma; 38% – university degree		Composite scale 0.18**		NE

Study	N	Variable	Gender	Age		Country	Sample (occupation)	Sample (education)		Composite		NE
Barberis et al. (2023)	788	Problematic use of social media	75% female	24.22 (18–35)	No	Italy	72% – students; 16%– employee; 5% – freelance	56% – high school diploma; 38% – university degree		Composite scale 0.32**		NE
Barberis et al. (2023)	788	Fear of missing out	75% female	24.22 (18–35)	No	Italy	72% – students; 16%– employee; 5% – freelance	56% – high school diploma; 38% – university degree		Composite scale 0.32**		NE
Leite et al. (2023)	773	Internet addiction	60.4% female	27.39 (19–78)	No	Portugal	NR	Mean years of educative = 13.06	0.254***	0.168***	0.336***	NE
Sparavec et al. (2022)	239	Prosocial motives to use social media	54.8% female	31.11 (18–85)	No	Australia	NR	NR	0.20*	0.19*	0.13	NE
Sparavec et al. (2022)	239	Antisocial motives to use social media	54.8% female	31.11 (18–85)	No	Australia	NR	NR	0.35***	0.48***	0.37***	NE
Kiziloglu et al. (2021)	514	Social media addiction	41% female	All above 21 years	No	Turkey	Private-sector employees	NR	0.17***	−0.06	0.17***	0.03
Xu et al. (2022)	740	Internet gaming disorder	36.4% female	18–25	No	China	Undergraduate gamers	Undergraduate gamers	0.15***	0.40***	0.43***	NE
Hussain et al. (2023)	400	Social media addiction	52.8% female	24.83 (17–41)	No	Pakistan	University students	University students	0.171**	0.097	0.114*	NE
Hou et al. (2023)	1,196	Problematic social media use Time 1	70.2% female	19.59	No	China	University students	University students	Time 1 = 0.19***; Time 2 = 0.18***; Time 3 = 0.12***	NE	NE	NE
Hou et al. (2023)	1,196	Problematic social media use Time 2	70.2% female	19.59	No	China	University students	University students	Time 1 = 0.13***; Time 2 = 0.33***; Time 3 = 0.24***	NE	NE	NE
Hou et al. (2023)	1,196	Problematic social media use Time 3	70.2% female	19.59	No	China	University students	University students	Time 1 = 0.10**; Time 2 = 0.25***; Time 3 = 0.32***	NE	NE	NE
Turan et al. (2023)	497	Social media addiction	60.2% female	14.98 (13–1?)	No	Turkey	High school students	High school students	0.30**	0.40**	0.35**	NE

Table 2.1 (cont.)

Study	Sample size	Type of social network addiction	Gender	Age (mean)	MTurk or similar	Country	Occupation	Education	Correlations			
									Narcissists	Psychopathy	Machiavellianism	Sadism
Nwufo et al. (2023)	300	Internet addiction	54.3% female	16.68	No	Nigeria	High school students	High school students	β = −0.11	β = 0.15*	β = 0.23**	NE
Shrivastava (2023)	94	Social media addiction	50% female	18–26	No	India	NR	NR	0.010	0.344**	0.342**	NE
Garcia et al. (2023)	452	Phubbing: nomophobia	77.2% female	19.97	No	United States/Mexico	College students (border-region university)	College students (border-region university)	0.013	0.195*	0.191*	NE
Garcia et al. (2023)	452	Phubbing: interpersonal conflict	77.2% female	19.97	No	United States/Mexico	College students (border-region university)	College students (border-region university)	0.056	0.282*	0.144*	NE
Garcia et al. (2023)	452	Phubbing: self-isolation	77.2% female	19.97	No	United States/Mexico	College students (border-region university)	College students (border-region university)	−0.047	0.294*	0.163*	NE
Garcia et al. (2023)	452	Phubbing: problem acknowledgment	77.2% female	19.97	No	United States/Mexico	College students (border-region university)	College students (border-region university)	0.027	0.128*	0.113*	NE
Bilal et al. (2022)	160	Cybersex addiction	50% female	21.27	No	Pakistan	Undergraduate students	Undergraduate students	NE	Cyber-psychopathy = 0.71**	NE	NE

Note: AT = Amazon Turk; NR = not reported; NE = not examined; GN = grandiose narcissism; VN = vulnerable narcissism; SNS = social network sites.
$p < 0.05$; ** $p < 0.01$; *** $p < 0.001$.

CHAPTER 3

Dark Triad/Tetrad on Facebook and Other Social Networks

3.1 The Prevalence of Facebook

Facebook is among the most popular social networks. In 2021, over 4.26 billion people were using social media worldwide, which is projected to increase to almost six billion in 2027 (Statista, 2023c). During the fourth quarter of 2022, 3.74 billion people used at least one of the company's core products (Facebook, WhatsApp, Instagram, or Messenger) monthly (Akhter et al., 2022; Statista, 2023c). Facebook is a platform that enables users to share information, form new relationships, and maintain their existing relationships. Because of these functions, Facebook can considerably affect people's social lives and has caught the attention of researchers worldwide. However, Facebook is not about just signing in. Facebook allows its users to perform a variety of functions. For example, they can passively view content, such as others' photos, videos, posts, or statuses, or create their content and directly interact with others by posting photos, videos, and opinions, sending messages, chatting, and commenting on the posts of others (Akhter et al., 2022).

Facebook has been the dominant social media for years, and most studies on social networking sites have focused on Facebook. Nevertheless, the trend is changing, which can especially be seen among teenagers. As a social networking platform, Instagram is becoming more popular among Millennials and Generation Z. Instagram will reach 1.22 billion monthly active users by 2023 (Djuraskovic, 2023). Despite the increasing popularity of Instagram, most previous studies have focused on addiction to other social networking sites, that is, Facebook. In fact, despite findings that Instagram can result in problematic use or addiction, only a few studies have explored the impact that Instagram, as a social networking platform, has on its users. While there are similarities between social networking sites, each has unique features with different motives for use and sources of gratification for users. Instagram's features allow users to edit and upload photos and videos, receive likes and comments, follow other profiles, and be followed by others. Recently, Instagram added a new feature enabling users to broadcast live streams. In addition, restriction on photo downloads is another triggering factor for using Instagram. All such features drive Instagram users to spend excessive time on the platform (Nikbin et al., 2022).

Facebook, Instagram, and other platforms have become part of life for many individuals across the globe. However, there are potential draws to Facebook and Instagram that attract the attention of malevolent personalities. Facebook allows its users to create their profiles, upload their photos and videos, and send messages (both private and public). It has a broad reach, as comments or posts can reach thousands of people, primarily through the "liking" and "sharing" mechanisms. These mechanisms allow cyberbullies to efficiently distribute offensive or unwanted information about their victims. Instagram, such as Facebook, also makes it easy to set up new, anonymous profiles for cyberbullying purposes. The speed and size of the distribution mechanism allow hostile comments or humiliating images to go viral within hours (Kircaburun et al., 2019). This chapter focuses mainly on Facebook, the platform that has received the most scholarly attention, but will also review Dark Triad behavior on other social networking sites, including Instagram.

3.2   Theories for the Use of Facebook and Other Platforms

The motives for using Facebook are rooted in two social needs: the need for belonging and the need for self-presentation. The need to belong denotes the intrinsic drive to associate with others and gain social acceptance, while the need for self-presentation refers to the constant process of impression management (Nadkarni & Hofmann, 2012). The motives for using Instagram are self-expression and social interaction, making it easier for individuals to present their ideal selves. Snapchat is used to communicate with the immediate environment (Kircaburun et al., 2019). The rapid evolution of social media networks such as Facebook, Twitter, and YouTube has allowed users to communicate information by interacting with the community. However, there is a dark aspect to these social networks, as there is always a possibility that users might misuse the power that mechanisms such as status updates, images, text, and public profiles afford them (Asghar et al., 2021).

Geary, March, and Grieve (2021) advanced the Uses and Gratifications Theory as a conceptual framework for explaining Dark Triad activity on

Facebook and other social networking sites. This theory posits that individuals actively choose and use traditional media and that this choice is based on how media gratifies their needs. Uses and Gratifications Theory has also been applied to social media, where users actively consume and create content to gratify their needs. Various gratifications are obtained from the use of social media. For example, Facebook users may gratify self-worth and integrity, information-seeking, and friendship and connection needs. Using Pinterest as a primarily visual medium may gratify entertainment and virtual exploration needs, and using YouTube may gratify needs for entertainment, interaction, information seeking, and escape. The use of social media may even generate new needs, such as promoting the need to stay constantly connected (e.g., the fear of missing out). Compared to Facebook, Twitter, Snapchat, YouTube, Google+, and WhatsApp, users of Instagram are more likely to use the platform to create and present themselves as more prevalent than in reality. Instagram seems strongly related to motives likely to underpin inauthenticity in self-presentation. The uses and gratifications framework would suggest that the features of Instagram allow these self-presentation needs to be met.

Individual differences play a crucial role in the Uses and Gratifications Theory because gratifications sought will vary depending on an individual's personality. In line with this, there is evidence that gratifications around self-presentation on Facebook arise from individual differences in grandiose and vulnerable narcissism. Grandiose narcissism is characterized by overconfidence and exhibitionism. It is posited to be driven by self-enhancement strategies, where one may employ extreme displays of charisma, boldness, and extroversion to fulfill one's needs for attention and admiration from others. Vulnerable narcissism is described as a more subordinate and defensive form of narcissism, where grandiosity is motivated by feelings of inadequacy, negative affect, and incompetence. Authentic self-presentation on Facebook is associated with higher levels of grandiose narcissism. Individuals high in vulnerable narcissism (combined with low self-esteem) are less likely to present themselves authentically online, too (Geary et al., 2021).

As vulnerable narcissism is more associated with stress related to fear of social rejection than grandiose narcissism, individuals high in vulnerable narcissism may guard their social media privacy by employing inauthentic self-presentation as a protective strategy. Further, individuals high in grandiose narcissism may engage in authentic self-presentation online as they believe their true self is to be admired. Further, given the associations between trait Machiavellianism and strategic online self-presentation, it is reasonable to expect trait Machiavellianism will be associated with more inauthenticity on Instagram. Finally, based on the characteristics of psychopathy, there is reason to expect primary psychopathy (i.e., calculation and deceit) and secondary psychopathy (i.e., impulsivity) to predict inauthentic and authentic self-presentation on Instagram, respectively (Geary et al., 2021).

3.3   Dark Triad/Tetrad on Facebook

Garcia and Sikström (2014) focused on Facebook updates. They contended that the Dark Triad traits might be expressed in status updates because people are usually internally motivated to use Facebook to increase social capital (i.e., benefits from interaction with others) and fulfill social-grooming needs, such as gossip and monitoring social group members. Garcia and Sikström (2014) suggested that when people interact with others on Facebook using status updates, they may use language related to malevolent traits in the Dark Triad and neurotic behavior. The statuses of individuals scoring high in these traits seem "odd" and "negative." In these cases, people reading status updates might experience the adverse effects of social networking.

Nikbin et al. (2022) focused on Instagram. They argued that individuals high in narcissism might be prone to excessive use of social media due to high engagement with activities such as selfie-editing and deceptive self-promotion behaviors. Machiavellianism has also been linked to addiction to social media. Because of their fear of social rejection, individuals high in Machiavellianism heavily use social media networking in problematic ways for deceptive self-promotion and interpersonal manipulation. Individuals high in psychopathy engage in problematic online behaviors as a maladaptive coping strategy and for sensation seeking. Thus, individuals high in the Dark Triad traits of narcissism, Machiavellianism, and psychopathy are more vulnerable to problematic Instagram use.

Withers et al. (2017) explained the relationship between the Dark Triad and the level of acceptance of violations of moral behavior as outlined in the Facebook Community Standards. First, they analyzed the levels at which users accepted Facebook Community Standards violations as a predictor of subjects' liability to engage in such behaviors. This is because subjects are likely reluctant to disclose their violations. Next, they focused on three deviant activities: nudity, hate speech, and graphic and violent content. According to Withers et al. (2017), individuals exhibiting high narcissism find nudity acceptable on social networking sites because it allows them to express their self-love and receive admiration while also being a channel for them to be critical of and devalue others. In addition, this need to devalue others may extend beyond nudity, and they may contribute to social networking sites through verbal comments and postings.

Withers et al. (2017) further contended that Machiavellians had been shown to use aggressive interactions to dominate and exploit other users. They argued that hate speech and propaganda are also used for domination and oppression. Psychopathic behavior is manipulative, sensation-seeking, and lacks empathy and remorse. Using hate speech and posting highly violent or graphic images or graphic descriptions of violent events causes viewers aversion, disgust, and other unpleasant reactions. In theory, those who post these images or engage in hate speech do so to manipulate others or because they take sadistic pleasure in these acts.

3.3.1 Research Findings

The following studies were all performed in Western cultures.

Withers et al. (2017) examined 145 American social networking site users from diverse backgrounds and ages. Their findings contradicted the expectation that narcissism was negatively correlated to nudity, hate speech, and violent graphic content. As expected, Machiavellianism was positively correlated to all three deviant behaviors. Also, in support of the expectation, psychopathy was positively correlated with nudity and hate speech behaviors. However, quite interestingly, psychopathy and violent graphic content had a negative correlation and contradicted the expectation (Withers et al., 2017).

Geary et al. (2021) examined how grandiose narcissism, vulnerable narcissism, primary psychopathy, secondary psychopathy, and Machiavellianism predict authentic self-presentation on Instagram. They surveyed 542 Australian Instagram users. Their findings showed that higher levels of vulnerable narcissism and Machiavellianism predicted lesser degrees of congruence between the true self and the projected self on Instagram (i.e., inauthenticity). However, grandiose narcissism, primary psychopathy, and secondary psychopathy were not significant predictors of authentic self-presentation on Instagram. Instead, they concluded that inauthentic self-presentation on Instagram might be best attributed to fragile ego and low self-worth (i.e., vulnerable narcissism) and strategic, tactical, and measured manipulation (i.e., Machiavellianism).

Nitschinsk, Tobin, and Vanman (2022) examined 322 participants in the United States, Canada, United Kingdom, and Australia for Dark

Triad traits and online self-presentation styles and beliefs. They found that both Machiavellianism and psychopathy were associated with adaptability (the extent to which someone is versatile in their self-presentation online) and inauthentic self-presentation. Machiavellianism was additionally associated with beliefs that online environments allow for freedom in self-presentation (the extent to which someone believes online environments make it easier to express oneself). Finally, those high in narcissism presented an authentic self online and believed that online environments are not beneficial to self-presentation. They concluded that those with dark dispositional tendencies use – or do not – the affordances of online environments for self-presentation, depending on their goals.

Garcia and Sikström's (2014) examined 304 participants in the United States. Their study showed that the semantic content of Facebook updates predicted psychopathy and narcissism. People with high levels of these traits had more negatively valued words in their updates and more "odd" semantic representations than those with low levels. Their findings also showed that narcissism was also related to the number of Facebook friends, while Machiavellianism was negatively correlated with the time spent on Facebook.

The previous arguments and findings show that the relationship between the Dark Triad and Facebook and/or Instagram activities is quite complex. More research is needed before we can make any solid conclusions. Another important observation is that trait sadism is hardly examined in the context of Facebook or Instagram. Also, most of the studies are based on samples from Western cultures. Section 3.4 presents the relationship between narcissism, including dimensions of narcissism and Facebook use (or other social media sites), and the specific relationship between Machiavellianism, Psychopathy, and Facebook use.

3.4   Narcissism and Facebook

Unsurprisingly, considerable media attention has been paid to narcissism and social networking. For several reasons, online communities have been indicated as a fertile ground for narcissists to self-regulate. First, this online setting allows users to establish and maintain hundreds of superficial relationships (i.e., virtual friends) and emotionally detached communication (i.e., wall posts and comments). While these sites can serve a communicative purpose among friends, colleagues, and family, other registered users can initiate requests to be friends, meaning an individual's social network can snowball rapidly beyond a user's immediate work and life contexts. Second, social networking sites are highly controlled environments that allow owners absolute power over self-presentation. Users can carefully curate the image they present using text-based features such as "About Me," "Notes," and "Status Updates" and can select attractive self-promoting photographs. This virtual arena allows narcissists to pursue an infinite number of trivial "friendships" and affords them endless opportunities for self-promotion (Mehdizadeh, 2010).

Users typically select a profile picture on Facebook to display on their profile page. Below the profile picture, the "View Photos" link indicates the number of photos in which the user has been "tagged" (identified) by themselves or others identified by oneself or others. The "Friends" box displays the user's total number of "friends" added on Facebook. There is also a "wall" on the profile page where friends can post short messages. Users can also post messages or "status updates" on their walls as frequently as they like. Among the various features, the profile picture has been posited as the essential means for self-presentation because it represents the individual on the online platform and appears in search results alongside every online interaction, such as wall posts. Moreover, photos can be constructed and refined to conceal flaws. As is to be expected, college and adolescent social networking site users were found to choose profile pictures they perceive to appear more physically attractive (Ong et al., 2011; Kim & Kim, 2019).

Such activities regarding positive self-presentation are more evident on sites such as Facebook, where users can make public "identity statements" that they may not normally do offline. These statements can take explicit (i.e., autobiographic descriptions) and implicit (i.e., photos) forms, enabling people to publicly display their hoped-for possible selves. Narcissism, especially, is linked to prominent aspects of self-presentation, such as the frequency of status updates or the amount of self-promoting content displayed. Social networking sites provide narcissists with both an audience and a stage for highly controlled self-presentation (Mehdizadeh, 2010; Kapidzic, 2013).

Because of the abovementioned features of social networking sites, they are favorable for manifesting narcissistic behavior. This is because they offer individuals an environment to present a curated construct of themselves to an audience (Kapidzic, 2013). Research indicates that individuals with high narcissism have a highly inflated, positive self-concept and are concerned with their physical appearance. The abovementioned contention is reflected in the online profiles of narcissists. Research on the relationship between narcissism and social networking sites indicates a significant link between higher levels of narcissism and more attractive appearance in profile pictures, higher ratings of the profile owner's attractiveness, and content that persuades the viewer of the account holder's positive traits (Kapidzic, 2013).

Marshall, Lefringhausen, and Ferenczi (2015) contended that narcissistic individuals tend to be self-aggrandizing, vain, and exhibitionistic. They seek attention and admiration by boasting about their accomplishments and taking particular care of their physical appearance. This suggests that their status updates will more frequently reference their achievements and diet and exercise routine. Moreover, the choice of these topics may be motivated by using status updates to gain validation for inflated self-views. This is consistent with the positive association of narcissism with frequent status updates, posting more self-promoting content, and seeking to attract admiring friends to one's Facebook profile.

3.4.1   Research Findings

Indeed, the abovementioned contentions regarding narcissists on Facebook received support from several empirical studies. As in Chapter 2, the studies will be categorized into those performed in Western cultures versus those performed in non-Western cultures.

3.4.1.1   Western Cultures

Buffardi and Campbell (2008) analyzed the Facebook profiles and personality traits of 129 undergraduate students in an American university. They found that narcissism is measurable in the number of friends and wall posts posted between friends. However, narcissism was unrelated to the length of an individual's self-description on the site. As for written content, narcissism is positively (but only marginally) related to self-promoting information about the self and negatively related to entertaining quotes. Similarly, regarding image content, narcissism is positively associated with main photograph attractiveness, self-promotion, and sexual provocativeness. Regarding the overall impression of the social networking site, strangers rated narcissistic individuals as more agentic (but not more communal) and more narcissistic.

Furthermore, the strangers' impressions of narcissism and agency uniquely predicted site owners' narcissism. Narcissistic impressions related to the Facebook page content features associated not only with narcissistic personality scores but also to three additional features: the quantity of information listed about the self, self-promoting pictures, and provocative pictures. Finally, the study revealed that the impression of narcissism is based primarily on the number of social interactions and the extent to which the Website owner is self-promoting and attractive in their main photo.

Buffardi and Campbell (2008) concluded that narcissism on social networking sites is very similar to its expression in other social domains. Narcissism is related to more social relationships, self-promoting presentation, and the perception of having many agentic characteristics. Only two differences between narcissism in the "real world" and online communities were found. The narcissists' quotes were judged to be less entertaining than those of non-narcissists. In addition, the narcissists were judged to be more attractive based on their photos than the non-narcissists.

In a sample of 294 American undergraduate college students, Carpenter (2012) examined two socially disruptive narcissism elements that would predict a particular pattern of Facebook behaviors. Grandiose exhibitionism was related to Facebook behaviors that afforded extensive self-presentation to as large an audience as possible via status updates, photos, and attaining large numbers of friends. Entitlement/exhibitionism was related to antisocial behaviors such as retaliating against negative comments about oneself, reading others' status updates to see if they are talking about oneself, and seeking more social support than one provides. In some cases, self-esteem was negatively related to these narcissistic Facebook behaviors. Carpenter's findings also revealed that these individuals are more likely to accept friend requests from strangers, tag themselves more often, update their newsfeeds more frequently, respond more aggressively to derogatory comments about them, and change their profile pictures more often.

Marshall et al. (2015) examined 555 Facebook users residing in the United States. Their findings showed that narcissism was positively associated with posting updates about achievements and with using Facebook for validation. Moreover, using Facebook for validation and communication predicted the frequency of updates about achievements over and above the control variables and traits. The association of narcissism with posting updates about achievements was significantly mediated by using Facebook for validation, as is consistent with narcissists' tendency to boast of gaining attention. They also found that narcissism was positively associated with posting about diet/exercise. However, using Facebook for self-expression rather than validation was positively associated with posting updates about diet/exercise over and above the control variables and traits. Self-expression mediated the association of narcissism with updating about diet/exercise, suggesting that narcissists may broadcast their diet and exercise routine to express the personal importance they place on physical appearance (Marshall et al., 2015). In addition, they found that narcissism rather than self-esteem was associated with receiving more likes and comments to one's updates. They revealed that more frequent updates about their achievements mediated the tendency for narcissists to report receiving more likes and comments. Thus, narcissists' publicizing of their achievements was positively reinforced by the attention and validation they crave.

Rosen et al. (2013) found, in a sample of 1,143 adult students from the Southern California area, that increased use of Facebook for impression management and more Facebook friends predicted more signs of narcissism. According to Rosen et al. (2013), this corroborates the many studies showing how social media provides a platform for narcissists. In addition, narcissism predicts using Facebook to occupy time, pursue leisure interests, and interact with romantic interests, over and above extroversion, suggesting that narcissists enjoy the exhibitionistic nature of social networking sites (Ong et al., 2011).

In a sample of 100 Facebook users randomly recruited at York University (Canada), Mehdizadeh (2010) found a significant relationship between individuals who scored higher on narcissism, the number of times Facebook was checked daily, and the time spent on Facebook per session. The findings also showed significant positive relationships between narcissism and self-promotion in profile pictures, photos, status updates, and the "Notes" section. However, the "About Me" section found no relationship between narcissism and self-promotion.

The findings showed some interesting gender differences. For example, males displayed more self-promotional information in the "About Me" and "Notes" sections than women. Conversely, women displayed more self-promotional profile pictures. Although no research has examined gender differences in types of self-promotional domains, particularly in online settings, this premise supports simple socialization processes. Specifically, gender roles influenced narcissistic females' tendency to include revealing, flashy, and adorned photos of their physical appearance and trends in narcissistic males to highlight descriptive self-promotion reflecting intelligence or wit in the "About Me" section (Mehdizadeh, 2010).

Ryan and Xenos (2011) found in a sample of 1,324 self-selected Australian Internet users that Facebook users are more likely to be extroverted and narcissistic. However, they also have stronger feelings of family loneliness. They concluded that their findings validate previous research and substantiate that Facebook particularly appeals to narcissistic and exhibitionistic people. Facebook specifically gratifies the narcissistic individual's need to engage in self-promoting and superficial behavior.

Smith, Mendez, and White (2014) developed and examined a model to explain the relationships between narcissism, concerns over privacy, vigilance, and exposure to risk on Facebook. They surveyed a sample of 236 adult users in the United States. They found that increased narcissism was associated with increased risk exposure and lower vigilance on Facebook despite greater concern for privacy and security. They concluded that not posting is inconsistent with narcissistic personalities, and narcissists will be more active on Facebook than less narcissistic users.

Aspects that attracted the attention of several researchers are the way narcissists present their profiles and profile photos. Kapidzic (2013) focused on what motivations guide narcissistic individuals in selecting a prominent feature of an online profile, the profile picture. They examined 288 students from communications courses at a large Midwestern university. Kapidzic's (2013) findings showed that Facebook users with higher levels of narcissism have different motivations than those with low levels of narcissism when selecting profile pictures on Facebook. Narcissistic individuals not only have a highly positive concept of themselves but also need constant external affirmation. Kapidzic's (2013) findings imply that narcissistic individuals are highly motivated to display their positive traits on social networking sites. The results also suggest that narcissistic individuals strive more than others to present their online audience with the best possible image of themselves. The findings showed that narcissists select images that emphasize the attractiveness and personality of the user. The motivation to emphasize looks and personality in profile pictures might be connected to the striving for positive feedback through admiring comments and "likes." Narcissistic individuals consider themselves highly attractive and might consider displaying their looks an easy way to gain admiration. Furthermore, they consider themselves special and unique and seem motivated to post pictures portraying their personality, lifestyle, and activities.

Kapidzic (2013) also focused on selecting pictures for self-presentation. Narcissists' main characteristics are low intimacy striving, viewing oneself as superior, and overestimation of own attractiveness. According to Kapidzic (2013), narcissists continually engage in a dynamic construction of self internally and through interpersonal interactions. It follows that narcissistic individuals are more concerned with the impressions they make and might be more highly motivated than others to garner positive feedback from their environment. Online interactions, especially on social networking sites, are favorable for impression management, as they can present a selective version of the self to one's network (Ong et al., 2011). When choosing profile pictures, narcissistic individuals may, thus, be motivated to emphasize features that will result in positive feedback and admiration (Kapidzic, 2013; Ong et al., 2011).

Ozimek et al. (2018) examined four samples; most participants were German students. The only requirement for participation in their studies was using a Facebook account. In all four studies, they used the same design and the same measures. Following the Social Online-Self-Regulation Theory, they assumed that vulnerable narcissism should positively correlate with Facebook use after statistically controlling for grandiose narcissism. Most of the evidence was in favor of the theoretical perspective. Their findings showed that the overall index of Facebook activity was consistently related to vulnerable narcissism. However, they also found that grandiose narcissism did not predict Facebook activity after controlling for vulnerable narcissism.

Ozimek et al. (2018) concluded that grandiose and vulnerable narcissists have similar goals, that is, gaining admiration. Nevertheless, they differ in their means of attaining the primary goal of narcissistic interest. Vulnerable narcissists use Facebook to attain self-regulatory goals (e.g., increasing their self-esteem, fostering positive self-presentation, and gaining the admiration of others). By contrast, grandiose narcissists (who are, in general, more socially integrated than vulnerable narcissists) do not depend heavily on social networking sites to attain their self-regulatory goals. In conclusion, Ozimek et al.'s study contributed to the working out of a theoretical framework in which vulnerable narcissism is the main predictor of the amount of Facebook activity mediated by social comparison orientation.

3.4.1.2 Non-Western Cultures

Ong et al. (2011) examined four Facebook profile features – profile picture, status updates, social network size, and photo count – of which the former two features present self-generated content while the latter two present system-generated content. Their sample was 275 adolescents from two government secondary schools in Singapore. The findings showed that even after accounting for extroversion, more narcissistic adolescents rated their Facebook profile pictures as more physically attractive, fashionable, glamorous, and "fabulous" than their less narcissistic peers. This suggests that more narcissistic adolescents select physically appealing profile photos to self-present on Facebook. This finding supports the current understanding that more narcissistic individuals are more acutely concerned about their physical appearance than less narcissistic individuals are.

Furthermore, selecting self-perceived profile photos as more physically appealing is consistent with other self-regulatory strategies that more narcissistic individuals adopt to affirm the positive illusions of their physical appearances, as described in previous research. For example, narcissists have more Facebook friends, wall posts, and profile pictures rated by others as more physically attractive and self-promoting than the profile pictures of non-narcissists. In this regard, narcissists may have selected more attractive photos of themselves to affirm their inflated beliefs.

Kim and Kim (2019) examined 179 university students in South Korea. Their Instagram photos were analyzed regarding colorfulness, color diversity, and color harmony. A total of 25,394 photos were analyzed. Their findings showed that narcissism was not related to the color features of their photos, such as color matching or variation. They explained that this finding might be due to the difference between Facebook and Instagram. Facebook is mainly aimed at building and maintaining social relationships. In contrast, on Instagram, users post about what they want to post, and it is not assumed that uploaders are closely related to their followers. Therefore, it is possible that trait, such as narcissism, is manifested differently in different platforms.

Several preliminary conclusions result from the studies reviewed earlier. First, the relationship between narcissism and Facebook use attracts much attention among scholars. The findings show that narcissists find Facebook or Instagram important platforms that supply their ego and self-esteem needs. At the same token, the question that remains open is the lack of attention on trait sadism and Facebook use. Another observation is that most of the studies were performed in Western cultures.

3.5 Machiavellians, Psychopathy, and Facebook

There are few studies on the nature of Machiavellian activities on Facebook (Abell & Brewer, 2014). In addition, few studies have focused solely on psychopathic individuals and their behavior on Facebook. Furthermore, as mentioned earlier, there are hardly any studies on sadism and Facebook use. However, initial findings are consistent with the notion that Machiavellianism influences online behavior and that motivations for Facebook activity are self-centered rather than cooperative. Machiavellian Facebook users are more concerned with themselves than the "friends" they are interacting with on Facebook. Aggressive interactions allow Machiavellian men and women to dominate and exploit other users (Abell & Brewer, 2014).

In a sample of British university employees, Abell and Brewer (2014) found that Machiavellianism (cynicism, emotional detachment, and a willingness to manipulate others) influences online behavior. Machiavellian adults use manipulation tactics, such as making others feel ashamed, embarrassed, or guilty to navigate their offline social worlds. Protective self-monitoring may facilitate this manipulation and allow the Machiavellian individual to avoid detection and associated consequences such as loss of reputation or retaliation. The abovementioned findings demonstrate that people with high Machiavellianism also employ online self-monitoring. Machiavellians' use of impression management strategies on Facebook may reflect a conscious effort to avoid being perceived as manipulative or exploitative. The dual nature of these friendships may increase the importance of online self-monitoring, as offline friends may detect dishonest or misleading information.

The abovementioned study also found differences between men and women. Specifically, their study shows that Machiavellian women were more dishonest in their self-promotion and were more relationally aggressive toward Facebook friends. In addition, findings indicate that Machiavellian men engaged in more self-promotion online. Finally, Machiavellians of both sexes engaged in higher levels of self-monitoring on Facebook than those with low levels of Machiavellianism.

In a study of 477 American Facebook users, Rosenberg and Egbert (2011) found that individuals who are manipulative and tend to exploit situations and people for their benefit, also known as high Machiavellians, do not show concern for secondary interaction goals and therefore are not likely to employ role-modeling tactics on Facebook. A possible explanation for this finding is that individuals scoring high in Machiavellianism tend to be assimilative and self-oriented, generally showing little concern for others and may not be interested in serving as role models. Machiavellians showed greater concern for themselves (self-oriented secondary goals when interacting with others). This is likely due to their self-oriented and manipulative streak. As for psychopaths, the little we know from the research is that individuals with a higher level of psychopathy may use Facebook to increase their social status and monitor and manipulate social groups. Further, the Facebook statuses of these individuals appeared to lack appropriate social and verbal filters (March, 2022).

3.6   Detecting Dark Personalities Based on Facebook

Two specific issues concerning Facebook and the Dark Triad have received particular attention. The first is the behavior of dark personalities regarding selfies. More specifically, dark personalities behave differently when taking and sharing selfies. These behaviors can assist in detecting them. The second concerns whether and how dark personalities can be identified based on the content of their posts. The assumption is that posts by individuals with Dark Triad traits differ from Facebook users in the norm. This distinction can provide another tool for detecting them.

3.6.1 selfitis

Recent research has documented the popularity of "selfies," as pictures taken of oneself and shared on social media (March, 2022). Technological advances, including the rise of virtual social networks, the facilitation of virtual communication devices, easy Internet access, free membership on networks, and the increase in smartphone use, have facilitated the phenomenon of user selfies posted online. For example, Google reports that its Android devices take 93 million selfies per day, and in one poll, 18-to-24-year-olds reported that every third photo they take is a selfie (Broz, 2023). This increase in selfies and postings on virtual social networks led to the introduction of selfies in the Oxford Dictionary as the International Word of the Year in 2013. According to the definition, a selfie is a photo that a person usually takes with a smartphone or webcam and shares through virtual social networks (Oxford Dictionaries, 2013).

Monacis et al. (2020) explained that "selfitis" represents an obsessive-compulsive desire to take photos and share them via social media to compensate for the lack of self-esteem and fill an intimacy gap. Balakrishnan and Griffiths (2018) empirically showed the existence of "selfitis" as a potential behavior to add to technologically related mental health disorders. They developed a psychometric scale, the Selfitis Behavior Scale (SBS), which classified individuals into one of three categories: borderline, acute, and chronic. Balakrishnan and Griffiths' starting point was that even though posting selfies allows individuals to express their self-oriented actions and establish their individuality and self-importance, other psycho-social-environmental factors might generate different selfie behaviors. The SBS comprises six subcomponents:

Environmental enhancement (i.e., to feel good and show off to others in specific locations);
social competition (i.e., to get more "likes" on social media);
attention seeking (i.e., to gain attention from others);
mood modification (i.e., to feel better);

self-confidence (i.e., to feel more positive about oneself); and subjective conformity (i.e., to fit in with a social group and peers) (Balakrishnan & Griffiths, 2018).

However, some people seem more inclined than others to take selfies and share them on social networks. Some psychological and personality factors of individuals may affect this phenomenon; also, taking selfies has a psychological effect on individuals (Soleimani Rad & Abolghasemi, 2021). Based on their review, Vander Molen et al. (2018) concluded that the self-promoting and duplicitous behaviors of individuals higher on the Dark Triad traits (particularly for narcissists and psychopaths) are manifested in their Facebook content. As mentioned by Vander Molen et al. (2018), based on previous research, those higher in the Dark Triad traits are frequent Facebook users and use Facebook in ways consistent with the nature of the traits. For example, narcissists tend to have many Facebook "friends," have more Facebook-based social interactions, post "selfies," and post a large amount of information about themselves. Machiavellians engage in self-promoting behaviors (e.g., tagging themselves in photos) on Facebook. Psychopaths tend to post selfies and photographs of socially inappropriate and risky behaviors. All the abovementioned suggests that Dark Triad personalities invest in their selfie posts more than people who do not have these personality disorders.

Unsurprisingly, researchers have examined the relationship between Dark Triad traits and their unique behavior in posting selfies. Monacis et al. (2020) examined 490 Italian participants and found positive narcissism-selfitis and psychopathy-selfitis behavior associations in a sample of Italian students. The finding of a direct relationship in the total sample and a partial relationship for males and females confirmed these relationships. In this study, no significant relationship was found for Machiavellians. Monacis et al. (2020) explained that narcissists and psychopaths are ego-driven. However, unlike Machiavellians, they are self-vs-others-oriented since they tend to satisfy their self-reinforcement by emotionally dealing with others and, therefore, depend on others.

Similarly, the primary dependence is further strengthened by selfitis activity, which not only represents an apparent gratifying means of being connected with others by posting selfies on social media but may also promote the addictive use of social media. According to Monacis et al., Machiavellians show an ego drive (i.e., the tendency to derive satisfaction from successful attempts at persuasion and an independence tendency). So, for Machiavellians, Monacis et al. (2020) argue that selfies are not likely to be employed as a tactic and strategy on social media, given their strong sense of independence.

In a sample of 202 undergraduate students selected by cluster sampling from the faculties of an Iranian university, Soleimani Rad and Abolghasemi (2021) found that selfie-taking individuals have higher scores on narcissism and Machiavellianism than non–selfie-takers. These differences indicated that selfie-takers have more narcissistic and Machiavellian traits than non–selfie-takers. However, no significant difference was observed in the psychopathy trait. Therefore, it can be said that taking selfies and sharing them is closely related to narcissism and is a way to attract the attention and admiration of others, which in part satisfies the narcissistic needs of individuals as well. People who consider themselves attractive and better than others take headshots and share them on virtual social networks to show others their attractiveness and beauty, resulting from this narcissistic image.

Machiavellianism believes that the ends justify the means and that speaking should be based on the person's will. Therefore, taking selfies and sharing them in different situations is a way to show off what they want to project and attract other people's attention. Thus, projecting an ideal self can explain why taking and sharing selfies relates to Machiavellianism, as demonstrated in Soleimani Rad and Abolghasemi's (2021) study. In the case of psychopaths, others' feedback is not essential and does not gratify them. Therefore, since the feedback of others on virtual social networks is a factor in taking and sharing selfies, psychopathic people tend to be indifferent to selfies. However, conversely, due to their characteristic drives to humiliate and ridicule others on virtual social networks, psychopaths may tend to write negative comments about the selfies of others (Soleimani Rad & Abolghasemi, 2021).

Stuart and Kurek (2019) investigated the mediating effects of selfies and those taken to appear physically attractive (i.e., sexualized selfies) on the relationship between narcissism and cyber behaviors. They examined 262 young women from New Zealand who reported taking selfies. Their findings showed that selfie behavior mediated the effects of narcissism on cyber behaviors. Narcissism was measured using a multidimensional approach: Four maladaptive sub-factors of the Pathological Narcissism Inventory were used to assess elements of a narcissistic personality. These four factors comprised two elements of grandiose narcissism, exploitativeness, and grandiose fantasy, and two of vulnerable narcissism: entitlement rage and contingent self-esteem.

The authors mentioned that exploitativeness was associated with taking more selfies and self-sexualizing selfies. In turn, exploitativeness was also indirectly (via selfies) and directly associated with increased negative cyber behaviors. According to Stuart and Kurek (2019), one of the reasons for these associations may be that individuals high in exploitativeness tend to manipulate situations to profit in some way. For the young women higher in exploitativeness in their study, taking selfies may be a goal-driven activity utilized to exploit the conditions of the digital environment, garnering attention as their desired outcome.

However, because they relied on the evaluations of others, individuals with higher levels of grandiose narcissism may be at risk of both acting out and experiencing diminishing self-worth when they do not receive the approval or attention from others they desire. Therefore, while young women high on exploitativeness may be self-sexualizing to elicit a response from their networks to increase feelings of empowerment and self-worth, they may inadvertently put themselves at greater risk of peer rejection and social isolation. In addition, because young women who post provocative images are subject to a double standard, where the broader peer groups often disparage overt sexualization, these young women may become the target of online aggression (Stuart & Kurek, 2019).

Alongside the results supporting the relationship between grandiose narcissism and selfie behavior, they also found a positive association between contingent self-esteem (a component of vulnerable narcissism) and sexualized selfies. The authors contended that, compared to those high in grandiose narcissism, individuals high in vulnerable narcissism often rely on covert forms of self-enhancement to mitigate feelings of inadequacy and inferiority. The study found that contingent self-esteem was not significantly associated with taking selfies, but it was associated with taking sexualized selfies. These results suggest that young women who believe their self-worth is conditional on the approval of others may be more likely to engage in self-sexualization and, in turn, be more likely to be victimized. This potentially indicates that young women who base their self-worth on the opinions of others believe portrayals of desirability are a means of achieving such approval. However, they may fail to assess the risks of this behavior (Stuart & Kurek, 2019).

Fox and Rooney (2015) found in a sample of 800 men from the United States that narcissism is associated with posting selfies and editing photos self-shared on social networking sites, both of which may qualify as the type of self-promotional social networking site behaviors that are more common in narcissists and as cheating strategies. Because narcissists value their physical appearance and male narcissists overestimate their attractiveness, they may be compelled to share more pictures of themselves on social networking sites and edit their photos to maximize attractiveness. Those high on Dark Triad traits are willing to engage in several manipulative tactics to secure short-term sexual partners, and manipulating one's appearance on social media might be one of them. Further, because narcissists are prone to social comparison, narcissists may present these edited and optimized images in the social context of social networking sites as a strategy to convey their perceived superiority to others. The fact that narcissists engage in more photo-editing behavior also corresponds to the underlying insecurity associated with narcissism.

Fox and Rooney (2015) also found that psychopathy predicted posting selfies, although it did not predict editing them. Psychopathy is characterized by impulsivity and a lack of self-control, which may explain why psychopaths do not edit photos of themselves despite posting more selfies. They also lack appropriate filters for their Facebook content, as a recent content analysis of textual Facebook posts revealed. However, this lack of filtering and impulsivity in social networking site posting may benefit some psychopathic men. According to Fox and Rooney (2015), psychopathic men appearing reckless or impulsive on SNSs may help attract mates.

Fox and Rooney (2015) did not identify any relationships between Machiavellianism and social networking use, posting selfies, or editing photographs of the self. According to them, one possibility is that Machiavellians may recognize that social networking site–based communication is not universally effective for achieving their goals, given that much social networking site activity is visible to the network (if not the public in general). Thus, Machiavellians may not rely disproportionately on social networking sites and instead use various channels (such as texting or face-to-face communication) strategically depending on their goals. It should be noted that Fox and Rooney's (2015) data were collected only from men.

Scott et al. (2018) found in a sample of 264 participants, most of them from the United Kingdom and Europe, that narcissism positively predicted the frequency of posting a range of self-promoting photos but negatively predicted the likelihood of posting family and significant other, demonstrating that narcissists post more of self-promoting photos, but are more likely to neglect other categories altogether.

A different view regarding psychopathy was advanced by March (2022) based on previous studies on this relationship. According to March, people with higher levels of psychopathy posted many selfies daily. They were less likely to experience negative emotions during the selfie process (i.e., posting a selfie and gaining likes and comments on a selfie). Specifically, the higher an individual's level of psychopathy, the less likely they are to experience negative emotions in reaction to likes, comments, etc. This lack of negative affect experienced from selfie feedback is due to the callous, unemotional nature of trait psychopathy. Also, individuals with high psychopathy seek excitement combined with characteristic impulsivity and may post selfies to create excitement when bored (March, 2022).

The findings discussed earlier support the expected strong relationships between taking and posting selfies and narcissism. While studies support the relationship between psychopathy and posting selfies, the relationship is more complex for Machiavellians. It seems that Machiavellians are more cautious in posting selfies and perhaps do not need the self-esteem provided by selfies as narcissists do.

3.6.2   Content

One of the exciting aspects of Facebook, Instagram, Twitter, and other social media is that their content enables the detection of dark personalities. The idea that one can gain insight into an individual's psychological characteristics and function by studying how this person uses language has been around for some time (Bogolyubova et al., 2018; Marengo & Settanni, 2023). According to this idea, there should be a relationship between linguistic expressions and dark personality traits. More specifically, the content on such networks can be acquired and analyzed to identify individuals with Dark Triad traits. To exemplify this contention, according to Bogolyubova et al. (2018), narcissistic individuals who use language on social networking sites have unique features that can be attributed only to them. More specifically, narcissism is associated with a propensity for I-talk (frequent use of personal pronouns). In addition, individuals scoring high on psychopathy and Machiavellianism used more swear words, more verbal makers of anger, and fewer first-person plurals and positive emotion words (Sumner et al., 2012).

It should be noted that many of the studies reviewed ahead used an automated approach to studying language, starting from the assumption that linguistic content and style differ between individuals. Measurements are based on word count. These studies attempt to detect dark personalities using their pattern of activities by applying computational models for Dark Triad personalities, covering machine learning and deep learning-based techniques. The aim is to develop an automated method to filter Dark Triad personalities from non–Dark Triad personalities using textual content on social media sites. Many researchers adopting this approach have used Linguistic Analysis and Word Count (LIWC-22), which reports the number (proportion) of words in a document related to each category.

This program calculates the percentage of words in each text that fall into one or more of over 80 linguistic, psychological, and topical categories, indicating various social, cognitive, and affective processes (Ahmad et al., 2020; Asghar et al., 2021; van der Vegt, Kleinberg & Gill, 2022).

Bogolyubova et al. (2018) analyzed 1972 Russian Facebook users' language to identify instances of dark personality traits employed in their online communication. The most notable observation from their data was that Machiavellianism is associated with posting fewer and shorter posts. In addition, there were no positive correlations between this dark trait with morphological, lexical, and semantic features. One interpretation is that the Machiavellian propensity for manipulating others and controlling one's public image leads social networking site users with this trait to disclose less about themselves and maintain a careful façade in online communication. Highly narcissistic individuals were likelier to write longer posts and employ longer sentences than Machiavellian subjects. This is consistent with theoretical models of narcissism that highlight tendencies to exhibit oneself and attract attention. Highly narcissistic individuals were characterized by employing semantic clusters revolving around social interaction, self-image, status, and reflections on one's mental processes. The results of their study do not support the existence of a relationship between first-person singular pronoun use and narcissism.

Finally, for individuals scoring high in psychopathy, two semantic features primarily characterized their language use. First, their posts often referred to basic needs and satisfaction or politics and authority-related issues. Focus on political terms was also evident at the level of lexemes used by these study participants (Bogolyubova et al., 2018). Some of the findings of this study are specific to Russian culture, and there is a need to replicate them in other countries and cultures.

Osterholz, Mosel, and Egloff (2023) examined personality expression, impression formation, and the consensus and accuracy of zero-acquaintance personality judgments that were based on people's Instagram accounts. Self- and informant reports of the Big Five personality traits, self-esteem, and narcissism were collected from 102 Instagram users. Screenshots of Instagram users' profiles were taken, including up to the 102 latest available Instagram posts. Several Instagram cues were objectively retrieved, counted, and rated by independent trained cue coders from the screenshots. One hundred unacquainted observers then judged the Big Five traits, self-esteem, and narcissism based on Instagram screenshots only. They found that narcissism was positively correlated with Instagram activity, which was linked to observers' narcissism judgments. They also found that self-esteem and narcissism judgments based on Instagram accounts converged significantly with Instagram users' personality self-reports, informant ratings, and self-informant composite scores of these traits.

Vander Molen et al. (2018) investigated the extent to which active Facebook users could make accurate judgments about Dark Triad traits in the posts of other users. They tested whether unacquainted observers can accurately interpret these dark expressions from the content of dark individuals' Facebook profiles. In their experiment design, 145 American undergraduate students in 34 groups provided Dark Triad self-ratings and rated their group members on these traits based on Facebook profiles. Their results revealed that observer accuracy is low to moderate for narcissism but nonexistent for psychopathy and Machiavellianism.

Hancock, Woodworth, and Boochever (2018) examined 110 undergraduate students at a large United States research university. Their study focused on detecting psychopaths based on the content of their posts across three types of online communication (email, Facebook, and social networking sites text messaging). Their findings showed that in online communication, participants higher in psychopathy referred less often to their conversation partner, used more psychological distancing, produced less comprehensible text, and used more interpersonally hostile language, such as anger and swear words. However, participants higher in psychopathy did not focus more on basic needs or less on higher-level needs in online communication. By contrast, a positive relationship between basic needs and psychopathy scores was observed in the elicited narratives, one of the few instances where associations emerged in the narratives but not online communication. For instance, narratives are more likely to explain why a person acted (e.g., "At the birthday party, I just wanted to eat the cake because I was starving"). Finally, psychopathy scores were not correlated with conjunctions, suggesting that participants higher in psychopathy did not use more cause-and-effect statements.

According to Hancock et al. (2018), speech difficulties, such as lack of cohesion or increased speech disfluencies, are also apparent in text-based online communication contexts with reduced readability. Evidence of increased anger and swearing in online communication is consistent with psychopaths' proclivity for interpersonal manipulation and the poor behavioral controls associated with callous affect, specifically for anger. For example, one participant wrote in an email: "I do not wish to talk to you anymore about anything ever again. I am glad that this is over because talking to you is like sticking a spoon in my ass." The same participant had the following Facebook status updates: "Dead," "Bored," "Tired,"

"Fighting with her again," and "Hate everyone." According to Hancock et al. (2018), psychopaths are known for their impulsivity. Their increased usage of swear words and anger words could indicate their reduced ability to control the type of language they produce (e.g., adverse) in natural discourse.

Hancock et al. (2018) concluded that discourse patterns of participants higher in psychopathy showed evidence of narcissism and psychological distancing, produced less comprehensible text, and used more words indicative of an interpersonally hostile style, including more anger and swear words. There may be features unique to online communication that afford a better opportunity to spot these linguistic traces of psychopathy or online interactions that are more likely to trigger or prompt these differences. Regardless, according to Hancock et al. (2018), their results reinforce the theory that individual personality characteristics, such as psychopathic tendencies, can be reflected in discourse patterns found in online communication.

Yuan, Hong, and Wu (2020b) examined how the language features linked to power on Facebook can predict whether a user belongs to a Dark Triad personality. In their study, participants were asked to allow the researchers to access their Facebook, particularly their Facebook posts. Then, the LIWC-22 was used to analyze the content of the posts and compare it to the participants' self-reported personality variables, attitudes, or demographic information.

They examined 879 Chinese junior high school students and analyzed 2,497 posts, which consisted of a total of 10,364 words. Their findings concluded that language features on Facebook reflecting an individual's need for power are predictive of Dark Triad traits. Specifically, language features such as I-words, negative emotion, and clout are positively related to Machiavellianism. Those who use the first-person pronoun to express themselves online tend to have high Machiavellianism. Language features such as analytic, I-words, and social words were indirectly associated with the need for power via narcissism. They found that psychopathy was positively related to authenticity. In addition, analytic language was negatively related to psychopathy. Their findings showed that individuals with high psychopathy tend to use less formal or logical language and focus on their here-and-now and personal experiences.

Van der Vegt et al. (2022) recruited 800 participants through Prolific Academic's online crowdsourcing platform. Only adult United Kingdom citizens with English as their first language were eligible. The participants produced a unique dataset of 789 abusive messages directed at politicians. Their study examines statistical relationships between the demographics of text authors and (abusive) language, then uses a machine learning approach to predict personality, age, and gender, based on language in the texts. Results showed that personality traits, including the Dark Triad, could be determined within 10% of their actual value. The authors concluded that even though they found statistically significant relationships between language use and demographics, prediction performance was poor compared to previous author profiling research. Therefore, they suggest that further research is needed before author profiling systems can be of significant value within the context of abusive language and threat assessment.

Hassanein et al. (2021) propose a prediction method for the Dark Triad traits by analyzing personality characteristics identified as personal values and needs that can be extracted from users' text on social media. More specifically, personal values were based on the personality characteristics inference like the "Big Five," and the value features are based on Schwartz's personal values theory. The proposed features are employed singly and combined with machine learning techniques for predicting the triad classes. A labeled dataset from Twitter for 863 users from Egypt was used. The experimental study indicated that the proposed personality characteristics of values and needs features could classify the Dark Triad traits with an accuracy of up to 70%, surpassing existing related work that employs traditional textual features. Furthermore, their findings showed that personal values have the highest accuracy for the Dark Triad prediction, with an average accuracy of 67.3%. Furthermore, the features were the best predictors of Machiavellianism and Narcissism traits.

Asghar et al. (2021) used a deep neural network model called Bi-LSTM. First, they acquired the required dataset from social media sites such as Facebook and Twitter. For example, they used the hashtag "#psychopath" to crawl the tweets they needed using a Python-based library, namely, Tweepy. Then, to annotate each review text/tweet in the acquired dataset into a psychopath and non-psychopath class, they performed manual annotation by assigning the task to three human annotators (psychiatrists), each of them assigned a class label: "psychopath" or "non-psychopath." In this way, they received three votes for each tweet. The class label is selected based on the majority voting scheme, that is, a tweet having two votes for "psychopath" and one for "non-psychopath" is tagged as "psychopath." The required dataset contains 601 user-input text samples from Pakistan. The proposed Bi-LSTM model, when applied to the labeled dataset, yielded the best performance results in terms of precision (85%), recall (85%), score (86%), and accuracy (85%) (Asghar et al., 2021).

Ahmad et al. (2020) also applied a deep neural network, Bi-LSTM, for Dark Triad prediction. The dataset was collected from social media sites such as Twitter and Facebook. The Tweepy library, based on Python (Rivera, 2021), extracted the relevant tweets using the hashtag "#dark-triad (psychopath)." They found that the proposed method produced improved results (AUC = 0.82) concerning the benchmark work. However, Ahmad et al. (2020) concluded that the study had certain drawbacks, including limited dataset size, using only one dataset, and using a single deep neural network model.

Similarly, Alotaibi, Asghar, and Ahmad (2021) tried detecting psychopathic classes from Twitter users with a hybrid deep learning model. Their study aimed to build an automated method to classify the available textual content on social networking sites into psychopaths and non-psychopaths. Their study applied a deep learning model called CNN-LSTM to classify input text into a psychopath or non-psychopath categories. The proposed system performed the following tasks: (i) dataset collection, (ii) data processing, (iii) formation of the feature vector, (iv) feature extraction with CNN, (v) preservation of sequential information with LSTM, and (vi) prediction.

The required data were collected from social media sites using the hashtag psychopath (#psychopath) using a Python-based library, namely, Tweepy. The collected dataset was transformed into an Excel file. Psychiatrists were asked to manually label the dataset by assigning a class label, that is, "psychopath" or "non-psychopath," to each tweet. As a result, three votes were obtained for each tweet. Using the majority voting scheme, a tweet with the maximum number of votes was assigned a particular label. For example, a tweet having two votes for "psychopath" and one vote for "non-psychopath" was tagged under the "psychopath" class.

In the proposed CNN-LSTM model, a CNN was combined with LSTM neural network since, in recent years, both models have shown great success and are considered integral components of deep learning models. Meanwhile, the LSTM was utilized to handle the issue of limited contextual information by learning the contextual information to detect psychopathic behavior from online texts. The performance of the proposed model was evaluated with state-of-the-art methods, and the experimental results showed that the proposed model outperformed the other methods in terms of its accuracy (91.67%), precision (0.93), recall (0.92), and F-measure (0.91).

Sumner et al. (2012) examined the extent to which it is possible to determine antisocial personality traits based on Twitter use. This was performed by comparing the Dark Triad personality traits of 2,927 Twitter users from 89 countries with their profile attributes and use of language. In addition, each participant's historic Twitter post content was analyzed using the standard categories provided in the Linguistic Inquiry and Word Count (LIWC) 2007 software. Their analysis showed that in terms of linguistic analysis, people higher in scores of psychopathy and Machiavellianism tend to use more swear words and more words associated with anger. In addition, both traits were significantly negatively correlated with first-person plurals and words associated with positive emotion. The major differences between psychopathy and Machiavellianism are the frequency of words associated with sex, relativity, motion, and time.

Narcissism displayed far less overlap with psychopathy and Machiavellianism, most notably in the significant negative correlations between narcissism and common verbs. They also found relationships between language and psychopathy, specifically in relation to swearing, anger, and negative emotions. A statistical analysis of Twitter profile attributes, such as the number of friends and followers, showed the most statistically significant relationships related to narcissism. People with higher scores in narcissism tended to have more followers and friends and a more significant number of followers per friend. Narcissism was also positively correlated with influencing other users through online behavior. Sumner et al. (2012) concluded that while the Dark Triad constructs are related, they are not equivalent. Also, they concluded that their predictive models, which used crowd-sourced machine learning algorithms, provide advantageous prediction rates but are imperfect in predicting an individual's Dark Triad traits from Twitter activity.

Preotiuc-Pietro et al. (2016) studied how the Dark Triad traits are related to observable Twitter behavior, such as platform usage, posted text, and profile image choice. They collected all public posts of Twitter users up to the most recent 3,200 posts in their history using the Twitter Search API, which resulted in a final dataset of 491 users who produced a total of 536,579 tweets, which they tokenized with a Twitter-specific tokenizer. Their analysis showed that narcissism is associated with an expression that is both positive ("favorite," "beautiful") and somewhat banal ("breakfast," "place"). In addition, the topics positively associated with narcissism also display facile, sanguine language: discussions of reality TV competitions, weekend plans, and cheerfulness. Together, these patterns suggest a surface-level pleasantness characterized by narcissistic personalities and a possible chronic assumption that others are interested in their mundane activities and interests.

Users high in narcissism have profile images that are less likely to be grayscale and more likely to feature a single face instead of multiple ones and include smiling. Again, these behaviors characterize a desire to present oneself positively and be at the center of attention. For profile features, narcissism was positively associated with geo-enabled tweets – suggesting Twitter use from mobile – and negatively associated with duplicated posts, @-mentions, and hashtags. The lack of duplicated posts hints at carefully curating the Twitter timeline. Hashtags and @-mentions are ways of inviting others to participate in Twitter interactions. The negative relationship implies that narcissists prefer to control their social media spaces more tightly, perhaps because of a fear of external criticism. Importantly, they also have a higher proportion of tweets that are favored at least once, consistent with narcissists' preference for regular, positive feedback.

As for psychopathy, the content of posts associated with users high in psychopathy is coarse, angry, and violent ("killed," "injuries," "furious") and characterized by negative emotionality. The correlated LIWC features carry a high level of negativity and morbidity; they are also not driven by the same words in each category, implying that psychopathy is not simply associated with a specific kind of negativity but rather a wide range. However, although psychopathy was significantly associated with negative emotions, many were driven by the same words, for example, "lost" or "bad." Certain topics suggest an interest in violent events such as wars or criminal acts. Noteworthy is that one of the topics associated with psychopathy describes a more "positive" form of aggression ("courageous," "freedom"). These topics are a good reflection of the sensation-seeking and impulsivity displayed by people high in psychopathy. Psychopaths' profile pictures are only associated with less saturation, which may suggest less planning or conscientiousness in taking or choosing a photo. In profile features, psychopathy was negatively associated with posting URLs and explicitly asking for followers. This latter finding may indicate a lower level of concern with social approval.

The findings specific to narcissism and psychopathy explain the seemingly paradoxical nature of the Dark Triad results. Narcissists talk about prosaic events with a veneer of positivity, while psychopaths angrily talk about violence and death. Although these two traits are positively correlated, they reveal distinct types of behavior. Machiavellianism shows the fewest relationships out of the three traits. The distinctive words associated with Machiavellianism feature more spam advertisement posts, suggested by words such as "affordable," "bingo," "application," and "entering." Being high in Machiavellianism may be associated with fewer scruples about allowing advertisements to be part of their communications. The topics associated with Machiavellianism include those associated with the general Dark

Triad focused on cars and driving, which has no theoretical association with Machiavellianism.

More notable is a topic focused on expressing gratitude, which could be considered a form of gaining social capital. No LIWC categories and emotions correlated with Machiavellianism above-and-beyond age, gender, psychopathy, and narcissism. There are also no relationships between profile pictures and profile features. Users high in Machiavellianism post fewer URLs and fewer retweets, showing that these users post advertisements and more personal messages such as thank-yous. In conclusion, Machiavellianism contains surface-level charm and social orientation in common with narcissism, while it also has cynicism and lack of concern for ethics in common with psychopathy. It may simply be that few behaviors distinguish Machiavellianism above and beyond its more extreme counterparts within the Dark Triad.

Preotiuc-Pietro et al. (2016) used all the previously derived features to create a predictive model of the three Dark Triad traits and a composite score. They found that, except for psychopathy, the textual topic features obtained the best prediction results. In the case of psychopathy, the LIWC textual categories obtain a better performance. They explained that this is probably due to the more syntactical usage patterns by uses high in psychopathy, which are captured through some LIWC categories. In rest, the predominantly semantic information performed best. Other consistently good predictive features are the shallow textual features and the emotions, albeit these do not offer significant performance when predicting Machiavellianism. Image features perform poorly over the three traits but provide significant accuracy for predicting the combined score. Profile features also perform poorly in all traits except narcissism.

Finally, Azzahra and Sihwi (2022) used the Support Vector Machine method to predict Dark Triad personality tendencies through Twitter analysis. Support Vector Machine is an algorithm generally used to classify text using the term index weight as a feature. From the results of this study, based on analyzing 75 active accounts, the classification with the highest accuracy is 73.3%.

The current status of studies using computational models for predicting Dark Triad personalities is well summarized by Gunasekara and Senaratne (2019). They contended that considering the related work, most of the research on predicting psychopaths using text on social media performed well in general clustering. However, the researchers had poor accuracy when classifying individuals (Marengo & Settanni, 2023). According to them, studies have proven the importance of the factor structure of the psychopath checklist. Furthermore, they concluded that factorial classification in psychopaths makes it possible to subcategorize identified psychopaths into other groups. This allows us to identify what kind of psychopaths we deal with and study them from a clear perspective. Therefore, developing an accurate model for classifying individuals as psychopaths and dividing psychopaths into clusters according to factor structure will help address this gap in the research by identifying psychopaths and factorial classification using social media. Gunasekara and Senaratne's (2019) argument might also be relevant to the three other dark personalities: Machiavellians, Psychopaths, and Sadists.

CHAPTER 4

Dark Triad/Tetrad and Hate Behaviors
Cyber Aggression and Cyberbullying

4.1 Terminology and Review of the Concepts

4.1.1 Cyber Aggression as the Higher-Level Construct

Cyber aggression is defined as "intentional harm delivered by the use of electronic means to a person or a group of people, irrespective of their age, who perceive(s) such acts as offensive, derogatory, harmful or unwanted" (Grigg, 2010, p. 152). Online aggression among adolescents is believed to result from biological, cognitive, emotional, and social transitions. However, it has become clear that adults of all ages, meaning early (19–29), middle (30–64), and late (65+) adults, are involved in online aggression (Pabian & Vandebosch, 2023). Grigg proposes that behaviors using mobile phones or the Internet to conduct bullying, harassment, stalking, abuse, assault, or hostility, as well as violent behaviors such as "happy slapping," "outing," and "flaming," be classified under the term "cyber aggression." According to this definition, it is also possible to include bystander roles in a cyber-aggressive environment (e.g., in cases of "happy slapping") as part of the construct of cyber aggression.

Cyber aggression is an umbrella term given to socially undesirable online behaviors encompassing cyber harassment, cyberbullying, and other forms of online aggression (Brown, Hazraty, & Palasinski, 2019; Grigg, 2010; Pyzalski, 2012). Cyber aggression is a broader construct than cyberbullying in that cyberbullying involves repetitive behavior and a power differential, whereas these criteria do not define cyber aggression. Thus, cyberbullying studies are relevant to cyber aggression but may need to assess the full scope of the broader cyber aggression construct (Nocera et al., 2022). Cyber aggression is a derivative form of traditional aggression. Cyber aggressive behavior is a new form of aggressive behavior resulting from the development of the Internet, which involves intentionally using the Internet and mobile phones to harm others (Zhang & Zhao, 2020).

Throughout this book, the overarching term cyber aggression will refer to any act of violence that falls under this general definition. According to Grigg (2010), it is acknowledged that the field of cyberbullying is new. Therefore, research in this area should consider a broader perspective that embraces any negative behaviors of Internet and mobile phone users and not be limited to current definitions of cyberbullying. "Cyber aggression" describes broad negative behaviors that may occur when people use the Internet. This term includes repeated and unrepeated acts that are likely to cause harm to the intended recipient(s) of the message(s). However, because many studies refer to cyberbullying rather than cyber aggression, this book will address the concept of cyberbullying in a specific section. It should be noted, however, that there may be some overlap between the concepts of cyberbullying and cyber aggression.

Before focusing on cyber aggression and its dimensions as the primary constructs discussed in this chapter, some characteristics of aggressive behavior must be described. Björkqvist, Lagerspetz, and Kaukiainen's (1992) theory posits that aggressive behavior does not decrease over time; individuals engage in different types of aggressive behavior dependent upon their behavior abilities. This theory was refined to suggest that individuals engage in a risk/benefit analysis, such that they engage in aggressive behaviors that provide a high level of benefits (e.g., distress of a target) at relatively low risk (e.g., social exclusion or physical harm). For individuals who can accurately read social situations, this means a movement toward more covert/indirect (e.g., manipulating an individual to "explode," causing them to lose face in front of their peers) or relational (e.g., spreading gossip or otherwise attacking another's social relationships) forms of aggression. The age of an individual, their gender, their experience with specific types of aggressive behavior, and their personality traits (e.g., the Dark Tetrad, described later) may play essential roles in determining that individual's abilities and, thus, the type of aggressive behavior in which they engage.

Several features of cyber aggression distinguish it from overt and relational forms of aggression implemented without electronic assistance. First, one of the essential aspects is the lack of nonverbal cues in online communication. This has been the focus of the cues-filtered-out theories that generally regard communication via computers as less "rich" as it does not allow for all contextual information (i.e., nonverbal cues) to be transmitted similarly to face-to-face interactions. Consequently, perpetrators of bullying could be less aware of the effect of their behavior on their victim when bullying online instead of offline, which might further reinforce cyberbullying behavior (Vranjes et al., 2017).

Second, whereas the perpetrator is usually known for traditional aggression, online communication offers many opportunities for the perpetrator to stay anonymous. This is problematic because it hinders the victims of negative behavior from acting against their abusers. It also limits the victim's control over the situation, making this bullying uniquely harmful. These indications may include the nature of the harmful acts (e.g., making someone's work impossible), the context of the acts (e.g., via the workplace intranet), or the information disclosed (e.g., the perpetrator refers to work-related issues). Technology allows some aggressors to remain anonymous, facilitating aggression by reducing accountability. However, aggressors who do not conceal their identities may still benefit from a degree of "invisibility" that comes with indirect forms of aggression, primarily when delivered via online platforms (i.e., the perpetrator not being personally known to the victim, deletion of aggressive comments) (Vranjes et al., 2017; Nocera et al., 2022).

Another important aspect of online communication is its intrusive nature. Victims of traditional aggression can usually escape bullying from colleagues, supervisors, subordinates, or others related to the work context (e.g., clients) while at home. However, online communication allows the transgression of the private/public boundary: Individuals can communicate everywhere (i.e., at home and work) and at any time (i.e., during and after work hours). Because of this, it may be much harder for the victims of cyberbullying to escape this behavior. Furthermore, the online environment allows violators to access private information previously unattainable in face-to-face interaction. The aspects of pervasiveness and boundarylessness, which relate to behaviors invading someone's personal life and making individuals feel pursued, are reoccurring themes in people's experience of cyberbullying (Vranjes et al., 2017).

Also, a power imbalance (social, psychological, or physical) between the target and the perpetrator is a defining characteristic of aggression. However, the aspect of power imbalance changes meaning online. "Power" in the online context can be argued to stem from technological opportunities (i.e., availability of online content or characteristics of computer-mediated communication such as anonymity), allowing individuals low in power in a physical context to be still perpetrators of cyberbullying in the online environment (Vranjes et al., 2017).

In addition, aggression and cyber aggression can be aimed directly (e.g., insults) and indirectly (e.g., gossiping) at the victim. However, compared to traditional aggression, indirect cyber aggression behavior has the potential to reach a much larger audience. This relates to the viral reach of a negative cyber act: the volume of online or offline message viewing, sharing, and forwarding by Internet users. Other vital features of cyber aggression involve the increased accessibility of the victim to the perpetrator and the potential for a larger audience than is typical in traditional bullying. In addition, victims of cyber aggression may never feel safe from perpetrators who can aggress at any time from any location and publicize their attacks (Vranjes et al., 2017; Nocera et al., 2022).

Finally, private information that was never meant for the public eye can be exposed to and consulted by a broad online audience. This invasion, together with the constant threat of public exposure or its actualization, makes this kind of activity incredibly distressing, even after a single occurrence. Furthermore, if made public, the negative behavior, which was only committed once from the perpetrator's perspective, can be repeated by others who can frequently access, view, share, and repost this information (Vranjes et al., 2017).

4.1.2 *Cyberbullying and Cyber Harassment*

As argued in Section 4.1.1, cyberbullying and cyber harassment are subdimensions of cyber aggression. Bullying is a form of abuse based on an imbalance of power. It can be defined as an aggressive, intentional act or behavior conducted by a group or an individual repeatedly and over time against a victim who cannot easily defend herself/himself. Researchers distinguish several main types of bullying (Slonje & Smith, 2008). The most common categories are physical, verbal, indirect, and relational. Physical aggression includes hitting, kicking, punching, and taking or damaging belongings; attacks on the property might be considered separately. Verbal aggression includes teasing, taunting, and threatening. Both these are usually direct and face-to-face types of aggression. During the 1990s, the scope of aggression broadened to include indirect aggression (carried out via a third party), relational aggression (aimed at damaging someone's peer relationships), or similar social aggression (done to damage self-esteem and/or social status). Most researchers now consider indirect aggression, such as spreading nasty stories, and relational/social aggression or social exclusion, such as telling others not to play with someone, as forms of bullying (Slonje & Smith, 2008). It may take various forms, including cyber, which occurs in cyberspace.

However, a new form of bullying has emerged, labeled "cyberbullying," in which aggression occurs through modern technological devices, specifically mobile phones or the Internet (Wang, Nansel, & Iannotti, 2011). Cyberbullying is commonly defined as the repeated use of technology to harass and cause distress to others (March, 2022). The explanation of cyberbullying is derived from the term bullying by adding "electronic forms of conduct" to its definition. Though some researchers argue whether cyberbullying is the "same wine" in an old bottle, studies have shown that bullying and cyberbullying differ. The main differences between the two types of bullying are anonymity, publicity, the connection between bully and victim, and the time and space limits. Since publicity and anonymity worsen the effect of bullying, cyberbullying can be considered a more severe form of bullying (Ildirim, 2021). In addition, cyberbullying may include flaming (a brief online fight using profanities and hostile languages), harassing (repeatedly sending offensive messages to someone), slandering (spreading malicious rumors) (Lai et al., 2023), masquerading (pretending to be someone else), and exclusion (intentionally excluding a person from an online group) (Balakrishnan et al., 2019; March, 2022).

Research on this topic is still early; cyberbullying only appeared in recent years, as the use of electronic devices such as computers and mobile phones has increased (Slonje & Smith, 2008). There is a range of reasons why someone might perpetrate cyberbullying behaviors, including revenge, jealousy, boredom, and seeking approval. Due to the highly detrimental psychological, physical, and emotional consequences, much research has explored its predictors to manage and prevent cyberbullying (March, 2022).

Online harassment is offensive behaviors conducted through electronic media to harm and embarrass another person intentionally. Online harassment behavior is seen as a form of verbal or sexual aggression. In addition, victims also experience cyberstalking, receiving inappropriate and/or pornographic messages, as well as threatening messages. Online harassment differs from cyberbullying in that most harassment incidents are not repetitive; they only happen once.

Researchers have found that many youths are victims of traditional bullying and cyberbullying. There is growing literature on the causes and effects of cyberbullying. Personality is among the factors related to cyberbullying and online harassment (Ildirim, 2021). This will be elaborated on in later sections. Section 4.2 will focus on cyberbullying because this specific behavioral construct generally attracts the most attention, particularly concerning its relationship to dark personality traits.

4.2 Cyberbullying

Social media bullying has been defined as any bullying that occurs over digital devices, including cell phones, computers, and tablets. These instances of bullying can occur through SMS, text, social media platforms, and other forums. Social media bullies often send posts or share harmful content about another individual. The shared information is often personal and private, meant to cause embarrassment or humiliation to the target. Social media bullying includes repeated threats and attacks toward a target intended to cause harm to the target, including physical or mental abuse. The United States Department of Health and Human Services (2018) concluded that, unlike traditional bullying, cyber and social media bullying usually comprises mental torture rather than physical threats. The fact that a perpetrator can constantly attack the target at any time makes the issue of cyber or social media bullying a severe issue. This form of bullying can have a lasting effect on the target. It may create a permanent, negative online record that may be accessible to and misunderstood by schools, employers, and colleagues. In addition, the target is often identified as a threat in a manner unique to the perpetrator's perception (Herron, 2021).

Cyberbullying is an intentional act to incur injury or damage over time by using computers, cell phones, and other electronic devices against others who cannot prevent or stop this behavior. In addition, the invisibility of the aggressor, the increased potential of the number of spectators, and the lack of "safe spaces" for the victim could be significant problems of cyberbullying. Thus, the perpetrator remains anonymous and unaccountable and could post messages to a large audience without socially visible consequences. Therefore, cyberbullying offers an ideal forum to harass others, taking advantage of the feeling of impunity (Sánchez-Medina, Galván-Sánchez, & Fernández-Monroy, 2020). The literature provides several more definitions of cyberbullying besides those mentioned previously. These definitions reflect the variety of perspectives on cyberbullying and can lead to a better understanding of this behavior. For example, Giumetti et al. (2012) defined cyberbullying as rude/discourteous behaviors occurring through information and communication technologies.

According to Vyawahare and Chatterjee (2020), cyberbullying can be of two types: direct and indirect cyberbullying. Direct cyberbullying involves only two people, the bully and the victim, whereas, in indirect cyberbullying, a group of people can get involved. An excellent example of indirect cyberbullying is a post on social media to make fun of someone, and many people comment on it and share it. As for direct cyberbullying, recent literature suggests focusing on the victim's and bully's perspectives (Alipan et al., 2015; Kallis & Meluch, 2021). According to this view, the bully uses information and communication technology to target one or more people directly or indirectly, whereby (1) the bully's goal is to harm the victim intentionally. Repetition can also help establish intentionality and cyberbullying, in which the bully continuously conducts a harmful behavior toward the same victim; (2) the behavior is perceived as intentional and harmful as defined by a victim. A one-off attack can also be considered cyberbullying as the negative impact on the victim may be just as severe as frequent attacks, and (3) a bystander observes that behavior has negatively affected another person or that such behavior would likely negatively affect the bystander if directed toward herself/himself. A bystander may also perceive the behavior as intentional and aggressive (Alipan et al., 2015, p. 12).

Indirect cyberbullying has a significant and more dangerous impact. More specifically, this form of cyberbullying often involves multiple parties, the most prominent being the bullies, victims, bully victims, and bystanders. Bullies perpetrate a bullying incident; victims are bullied, and bystanders witness a bullying/victimization incident online. Bullying victims results in a vicious cycle in which a victim turns into a bully and vice versa. There is a consensus across studies that cyberbullies have a profile of being aggressive, manipulative, and exploitative, whereas victims often have low self-esteem. In addition, some studies differentiate between bullies and aggressors, whereby the latter refers to someone who once engaged in an offensive behavior (Balakrishnan et al., 2019).

According to Scott et al. (2020), although much of this abuse can include private communication between the perpetrator(s) and victim, it also often manifests in the publicly visible online record (e.g., Facebook timeline or Twitter page). Of all the social media platforms, Facebook, Twitter, YouTube, ASKfm, and Instagram have been listed as the top five networks with the highest percentage of users reporting having experienced cyberbullying. According to the Warranting Theory (DeAndrea, 2014), these publicly visible abusive messages constitute behavioral residue and, as such, would carry weight in the impressions formed of targets and may contribute to a stereotyped impression based on their content.

This may be especially true for celebrity victims whom observers may think are disingenuous with their online communications to self-promote. Thus, they may deserve any abuse directed toward them (Vyawahare & Chatterjee, 2020).

An interesting form of cyberbullying is the diffusion of misleading information on social networks (Maftei, Holman, & Merlici, 2022). Fake news refers to misleading or false articles spread on social networks. The diffusion of misleading information, namely fake news, on social networks causes an impact on the civil life of people in terms of psychological, financial, and so on, making it difficult to lead their life in society (Srinivas, Das, & Pulabaigari, 2022). Srinivas et al. (2022) found using a large dataset of news articles that fake news spreaders who propagate gossip and political fake posts on social media are, in addition to other personality characteristics, narcissists and psychopaths.

Another form of cyberbullying was advanced by Ehman and Gross (2019), who contend that a specific name for the subset of sexually orientated cyberbullying behaviors currently does not exist. They defined sexual cyberbullying as "any sexually aggressive or coercive behavior facilitated through the use of electronic media (i.e., text messages, social networking sites, cell phone applications, etc.)" (Ehman & Gross, 2019, p. 80).

4.2.1   *The Effects of Cyberbullying on the Victims*

People of all age groups may suffer from the shameful act of cyberbullying. Cyberbullying can have very harmful effects on the psychological health of the victim and the bully. Cyberbullying is more harmful than traditional bullying because it can quickly turn into indirect cyberbullying, and victims cannot escape anywhere. Depression and isolation are major effects of cyberbullying. Many victims report emotional, concentration, and behavioral issues (Olckers & Hattingh, 2022). These victims will also likely report frequent headaches, recurrent stomach pain, and sleeping difficulties. An extreme result of cyberbullying can be a suicide attempt (Vyawahare & Chatterjee, 2020).

Vyawahare and Chatterjee (2020) also state that cyberbullying impacts male victims and perpetrators because they become more aggressive and get addicted to alcohol consumption or cigarette smoking. Female victimization results in internalizing behaviors, such as isolation, depression, or suicide attempts. Through social networks, many teenagers, as well as adults, are suffering from cyberbullying. Almost 50% of the youth in the United States have admitted to being bullied. Nevertheless, these victims usually hide their victimization for different reasons. Teenagers or adolescents fear that the device may be taken away from them. Adults are embarrassed to acknowledge that they are being bullied and fear being misunderstood by their peers or family members. Hence, identifying and reporting cyberbullying is vital for identifying victims and taking action to help them. It is also required to save society from the damage cyberbullying is causing (Vyawahare & Chatterjee, 2020).

Cyberbullying is particularly problematic because as schools, parents, and communities attempt to combat it, perpetrators find new and creative ways to victimize others through evolving technologies (e.g., new cell phone applications, social networking websites, and messaging programs). Cyberbullying is a prevalent problem affecting between 20% and 40% of youths, typically via mobile phones and the Internet. Students report varying motivations for cyberbullying, including revenge, jealousy, boredom, and seeking (Goodboy & Martin, 2015). Cyberbullying harms victims in many ways, including educational functioning and mental health. Regarding educational functioning, cyberbullying victims show increased school absences and decreased concentration, educational achievement, and performance. They also show higher levels of anxiety, increased symptoms of depression, suicide ideation, self-harm, and suicide attempts than their peers. The undesirable effects of cyberbullying are also evident in reactive aggression, instrumental aggression, depression, and somatic symptoms. Mental health problems, drug abuse, and low self-esteem have also been found in both victims and perpetrators of cyberbullying (Safaria et al., 2020).

The effects of broader cyber aggression are similar to those seen in victims of cyberbullying. The victims of cyber aggression may experience various negative emotions (e.g., anger, sad, depression, and fear), some psychiatric and psychosomatic problems (e.g., insomnia, headaches, substance abuse, and eating disorders), several social function disorders (e.g., high level of social anxiety, poor concentration, and losing interest in things), and suicidal ideation (Zhang & Zhao, 2020). Victims also reported receiving little or no support from friends or authorities. Although the population generally underestimates the severity of online abuse and its impact on victims, individuals differ in how abusive incidents are interpreted (Scott et al., 2020).

An interesting aspect of victimization is that those with dark personalities tend to perceive themselves as victims of cyberbullying. For example, Cheng and Lee (2022) contended, based on their findings, that individuals with high Machiavellianism and psychopathy are prone to being victims of cyberbullying. They tend to be victims of cyberbullying due to an innate need for social attention or social dominance. The inclination to release certain inappropriate information to assert social saliency in online settings may have induced victimization among those with salient Machiavellianism. Those with high psychopathy are also prone to cyber victimization. They do not discriminate against their online victims, and thus, individuals with a high level of psychopathy have the propensity to undermine individuals with high social status. In addition, these individuals are reckless in regulating the content that they share online (Amon et al., 2023). The significant relationship between this Dark Triad personality trait and cyber victimization may reflect the consequence of such a tendency. Individuals with high psychopathy also tend to indulge in controversial topics on social media that might invite aggression from others. When combined with the proclivity to challenge those with prominent social status, those with high psychopathic tendencies are vulnerable to cyberbullying.

Narcissism is not related to cyber victimization because individuals with high levels of narcissism do not perceive themselves as victims of cyberbullying. The inflated ego of these individuals may be protective against aversive online experiences. Cheng and Lee (2022) concluded that online vulnerability applies to some Dark Triad personality traits. It is possible that the observed vulnerability in online settings is not interpreted as a sign of weakness among those with high Machiavellianism and psychopathy. This implies that other factors underlie the perceived online vulnerability among those with salient Dark Triad personality traits.

4.3 The Dark Triad/Tetrad, Cyber Aggression, and Cyberbullying

Identifying the antecedents of cyberbullying perpetration is crucial to reducing cyberbullying and eliminating the detrimental consequences of cyberbullying victimization. Recently, cyberbullying studies have begun to explore the roles of user personalities in cyberbullying perpetration, with the majority focusing on Dark Triad/Tetrad models (Demircioğlu & Çıkan, 2021; Balakrishnan et al., 2019; Sánchez-Medina et al., 2020; Achuthan et al., 2022; Zhang et al., 2022). According to Antoniadou, Kokkinos, and Markos (2019), personal characteristics (e.g., personality traits) result from an interplay between biological and environmental factors. Therefore, their effect on an individual's behavior relates to the given situation or the individual's perception of it. In this sense, personal characteristics are dynamic since they can result in different behavior expressions.

Hence, it can be assumed that personality traits can predict cyberbullying behavior (Sánchez-Medina et al., 2020).

The abovementioned argument leads to the search for personality traits that are more predictive of performing cyberbullying. Antoniadou et al. (2019) contend that the characteristics of cyberspace might facilitate the expression of psychopathic traits and contribute to disinhibited online acts. Most cyberbullies spend a considerable amount of time online and engage in risky online behaviors, but there are essential individual/personality differences that predict bullying behavior beyond the characteristics of Internet use (Goodboy & Martin, 2015; Peterson & Densley, 2017). For instance, cyberbullies tend to lack self-control and sensitivity; they tend to be higher in psychoticism and verbal aggressiveness and lower in empathy. Low empathy is the most reported individual risk factor for cyberbullying. In addition, those high in the Dark Tetrad may be less likely to perceive abusive incidents from the victim's point of view and appreciate the potential impact such abuse might have on the recipient. Similarly, reduced empathic responsiveness and moral disengagement may increase potential cyberbullying behaviors (Goodboy & Martin, 2015; Zhang et al., 2022).

All the abovementioned characteristics point to the Dark Triad/Tetrad as the personality traits distinguishing cyberbullies from their peers. Specifically, individuals scoring high in the Dark Tetrad of personality traits – psychopathy, narcissism, Machiavellianism, and sadism – may likely underplay the severity of online abuse and attribute more blame to victims (Hand et al., 2021). In addition, the tetrad members tend to show that the four traits have different patterns of associations with aggression, whether self-reported, observer-reported, or behavioral. Many recent studies include three or four traits of dark personalities. This multivariate methodology helps control for the overlap among members, thereby avoiding possible misattribution of the effect of one tetrad member to another unmeasured member (Paulhus et al., 2018).

Much like traditional bullying enacted face to face, cyberbullying should be associated with the Dark Tetrad (Goodboy & Martin, 2015; Brown et al., 2019). Given the collective findings that suggest the Dark Triad traits predict traditional bullying and negative Internet behavior, these traits should also predict cyberbullying (Baughman et al., 2012; Goodboy & Martin, 2015; Brown et al., 2019; Leite et al., 2023). Studies exploring the relationship between cyberbullying and darker personalities have shown that cyberbullying behavior appears more often with these four traits. As for the specific relationship between each dark personality and cyberbullying, there are varied results (Wang et al., 2022b). The bulk of such research has involved the Dark Triad (all barring sadism), but work with the Dark Tetrad is growing (Paulhus et al., 2018).

Evidence shows that all four traits positively relate to bullying (Baughman et al., 2012; Goodboy & Martin, 2015; Brown et al., 2019). However, in recent years, sadism has also been incorporated into the Dark Triad to form the Dark Tetrad due to the similarities with the other three personality traits (Brown et al., 2019). The sadistic personality is unique among the Dark Tetrad, involving an appetite for cruelty instead of callous indifference. In addition, only sadistic individuals are willing to pay the price (e.g., perform a tedious task) for the opportunity to harm others (Paulhus et al., 2018). Sadism may uniquely predict antisocial behavior because over and above callousness toward the suffering of others (i.e., psychopathy), calculated aggression (i.e., Machiavellianism), or lashing out because of a threatened ego (i.e., narcissism), sadists enjoy the suffering of others (Van Geel et al., 2017). Brown et al.'s (2019) findings indicate that in an ethnically diverse sample, Machiavellianism and psychopathy are better predictors of cyberbullying than narcissism or sadism. However, sadism showed itself as a legitimate predictor of cyberbullying.

According to Lopes and Yu (2017), in contrast to psychopaths, narcissists display a self-serving schema of firm beliefs about their distorted sense of self-importance and grandiosity. Hence, their underlying motivation is not necessarily to cause harm to others but to socially compare themselves favorably to other perceived essential people. This can help them maintain their inflated views of themselves, thus protecting their self-esteem. Like narcissists, Machiavellians have also been characterized by self-interest, such that they will manipulate, deceive, and exploit others to achieve their goals. Previous literature shows positive intercorrelations between Machiavellianism and narcissism, and these two personalities are similar concerning manipulating and exploiting others to promote self-advancement and success. This suggests that narcissists and Machiavellians may be only motivated to bully when this leads to personal gain and self-advancement. By contrast, psychopaths seem to bully not only to self-advance but also simply because they derive pleasure or enjoyment from harming other people just for fun (Lopes & Yu, 2017).

All Dark Tetrad personality factors influence individuals' cognitions and perceptions of social situations. Individuals high in Dark Tetrad factors are higher in levels of Schadenfreude, lower in empathy, generally hold negative perceptions of others, and utilize fewer cues when making assessments of others' vulnerability. In addition, those high on psychopathy and Machiavellianism are more likely to perceive social situations as competitive and those high on narcissism perceive fewer social restrictions. This demonstrates fundamental differences in how individuals high in Dark Tetrad perceive others and social situations. It suggests they may interpret antisocial online behaviors in a way that could impact their perceptions of victims and the acts perpetrated against them (Scott et al., 2020).

According to Gibb and Devereux (2014), each trait may influence the perception of risk/benefit associated with engaging in aggressive behaviors. As for Machiavellianism, individuals high in this trait may engage in cyberbullying to solidify, maintain, or establish their place within their social network due to the relatively low risk associated with these behaviors and the potentially considerable influence on their social network. Individuals high in narcissism may engage in cyberbullying because they feel socially invulnerable (i.e., they believe that their social status is such that there is a low level of social risk associated with the behavior; Gibb & Devereux, 2014). Traits associated with subclinical psychopathy include high impulsivity and engagement in thrill-seeking behavior, low levels of empathy, and low social anxiety. These individuals' low levels of empathy have been linked to reactive and proactive aggression, which in turn have been linked to bullying behavior (see Azami & Taremian, 2021). The emergence of sadism as the primary predictor in the online context suggests that anonymity can unleash the darker side of human nature (Paulhus et al., 2018). Therefore, sadism should be included as another essential trait, even though its relationship with cyberbullying has been examined only recently.

Gammon et al. (2011) proposed that the Dark Triad traits are particularly relevant to cyber harassment. Narcissism is a stable trait characterized by statements of exaggerated self-worth, grandiosity, arrogance, and entitlement. To protect their fragile ego, narcissists make substantial efforts to augment their self-view through exaggerated accounts of dominance and continually seeking affirmation from others. These relationships with others protect the narcissist's fragile ego unless the exaggerated views of the narcissist are questioned, which often leads to aggressive or hostile responses from the narcissist. Rather than forming close personal relationships, narcissists are likely to form bonds that will preserve their façade of superiority and will attempt to maintain their exaggerated self-views at all costs, usually at the expense of others who must bear the burden of constant self-aggrandizing and hostile reactions to ego threat. People with subclinical psychopathy are impulsive, thrill-seeking, carefree, easily bored, and lacking empathy and remorse. In addition, the behavior of psychopaths tends to be excessively selfish and manipulative, and they demonstrate no compunction for hurting others while pursuing their agendas.

Machiavellianism is characterized by cold calculation, instrumentality, and the strategic manipulation of others to achieve desired goals. These goals are often tied to money or power rather than community building or interpersonal relationships. Rather than act reactively or impulsively, Machiavellians are noted for their cool detachment from conflict situations. Little research has tied Machiavellianism to overt acts of aggression. Research suggests that high Machiavellians are prone to betraying others, especially when they feel that no retribution is possible. However, the research suggests that Machiavellians are not prone to revenge motives because they view revenge as a maladaptive strategy (Gammon et al., 2011).

Following the earlier discussion, Gammon et al. (2011) propose that individuals high on narcissism and psychopathy are likely to engage in cyber harassment behavior after specific triggering events. By contrast, those high on Machiavellianism are not likely to engage in cyber harassment. Gammon et al. contend that the traits of narcissism and psychopathy contribute to aggression via ego threat and physical threat provocations, respectively. Given this, the triggering event for narcissists is likely to be interpreted as threatening to one's ego, such as a personal insult by a customer service representative. By contrast, the triggering event for psychopaths is a situation likely to be interpreted as a physical threat, such as being physically bullied. Given their high level of self-control, being slighted as a consumer may be less likely to be encoded as a provocation by those high in Machiavellianism. Thus, when Machiavellians view provocation as an opportunity for strategic gain, they may betray, aggress, or seek revenge. Extended to the cyber harassment domain, Machiavellians may only engage in the behavior if they view it as leading to economic goal attainment (Gammon et al., 2011).

Sadists may engage in cyberbullying simply because they are stimulated by hurting others and seeing the victims suffer as they find it gratifying, which becomes more accessible and anonymous in cyberspace (Kircaburun et al., 2018a, 2018b; Brown et al., 2019). Therefore, theoretically, researchers should find the Dark Tetrad to be a more valuable and complete model of personality traits than the Dark Triad, as the role of sadism may prove integral as an explanatory mechanism for antisocial behaviors in cyberspace (Alavi et al., 2022).

Sari and Adriani (2022) explained that narcissistic personalities tend to be more self-centered, consider themselves unique human beings, and like to be the center of attention. Hence, their energy is more focused on themselves than others. Individuals with narcissism tend to have higher cognitive empathy because they need more understanding to ensure others pay attention and make themselves the center of attention. The time they have is more used to make themselves the center of attention than cyberbullying. In comparison, a psychopath tends to lack empathy, remorse, selfishness, indifference, and impulsiveness. A psychopath tends to hurt and retaliate directly without hiding her/his identity from others. S/he does not care if his behavior will destroy her/his reputation. Meanwhile, individuals with Machiavellianism will make plans first before hurting others because they do not want their behavior to be known by others, so it will destroy the reputation they already have. Therefore, the Machiavellian personality will choose to do cyberbullying because apart from being able to realize their plans to hurt others, their reputation will remain safe and well maintained.

Some scholars focused only on specific dark personality traits and their relationship to cyber aggression and cyberbullying. Section 4.3.1 focuses on specific explanations of these personalities.

4.3.1   Psychopathy, Cyber Aggression, and Cyberbullying

The literature suggests that psychopathy predicts cyber aggression and abuse better than milder uncivil online behavior (March, 2022). Therefore, some researchers focus on this dark personality trait and its relationship to cyber aggression and cyberbullying. According to Lopes and Yu (2017), beliefs and associated cognitions are part of the self under a cognitive-behavioral framework. Other schemas act as lenses through which information is perceived and appraised. Thus, determining behavior, in turn, will help to maintain the beliefs. The inherent belief that characterizes psychopathy is that it is acceptable for others to be manipulated and hurt for the individual's benefit and by an underlying sadistic motivation to cause harm to others (both psychological and physical) that ultimately will give pleasure to the psychopath. This sadistic streak motivates psychopaths to bully and prey on people who catch their attention to use them for their benefit and self-advancement (e.g., bullying and blackmailing famous individuals for social connections and gains).

Therefore, bullying behavior will maintain the psychopaths' sadistic beliefs and motivation by providing them with feelings of pleasure derived from provoking harm to essential people, socially salient and attractive. Moreover, although psychopaths may be motivated to bully weak and vulnerable victims, they are also aware that they can obtain more from weaker and lower-status victims by showing false sympathy and modesty, thus gaining their trust. This is because vulnerable victims usually have lower self-esteem and self-confidence, are more gullible, and are more willing to trust (which makes them easier to manipulate) than mentally strong victims. Therefore, bullying vulnerable and less popular individuals does not give as much sadistic pleasure to psychopaths as bullying famous people does. This is simply because bullying vulnerable low-status individuals does not necessarily pose a challenge to psychopaths; it is too easy to do and does not necessarily bring any benefit or pleasure to psychopaths (Lopes & Yu, 2017; Peterson & Densley, 2017).

March (2022) also explained why psychopathy should predict cyberbullying behaviors. This trait is characterized by high impulsivity, thrill-seeking behavior, and low levels of empathy and has previously been associated with traditional bullying behavior. Unlike other dark personality traits, the predatory nature of psychopathy may motivate these individuals to seek online victims to bully in an attempt to inflict emotional and psychological harm. Further, individuals with higher levels of psychopathy feel little remorse, as they often disregard the distress they cause. According to Antoniadou et al. (2019), Internet users may exhibit online disinhibition, which refers to the tendency to feel less inhibition and concern for the consequences of one's actions in the online world. Overall, the user may not be aware of the consequences of online behavior in real life. They contend that psychopathy is necessary when studying online behavior because users with such traits exhibit tendencies for disinhibited behaviors that may be exacerbated online. Therefore, when studying the association of psychopathic traits with online disinhibition, a distinction should be made between primary and secondary psychopathy since they differ significantly in the individual's behavioral tendencies and empathic abilities.

4.3.2 Narcissism, Cyber Aggression, and Cyberbullying

Narcissists display higher activity levels on social media platforms and exhibit increased self-promoting and self-enhancing behaviors. Narcissists are also found to use social media networks for self-enhancement and to develop and exploit shallow and short-term online friendships to bolster their social status and self-esteem (Kurek, Jose, & Stuart, 2019). In the case of narcissism, there is a need to consider the dimensionality of this personality trait when dealing with cyber aggression and cyberbullying. According to Fan et al. (2019), narcissism's inflated and depleted aspects constitute two separate disorders of the self: the exhibitionistic and closet narcissistic disorders, based on the fusion of a grandiose self-representation with an omnipotent object representation. Specifically, the exhibitionistic narcissist has an inflated, grandiose self-perception maintained by receiving attention and admiration from others. By contrast, the closet narcissist has a deflated, inadequate self-perception derived from the dependency on and admiration of those idealized others. In this sense, the covert narcissist, unlike the overt narcissist, may have more maladaptive features, including a shy demeanor, hypersensitivity to criticism and failure, and a lack of self-confidence. Empirical evidence also supports the conceptual distinction between overt and covert narcissism (Brown et al., 2019; Fan et al., 2019).

Each type of narcissism predicts different types of aggression, the former being more active denigration of others and the latter being a form of apparent self-belittlement at the emotional cost of others. Cyberbullying and cyber aggression are believed to be defense mechanisms against low self-esteem (Brown et al., 2019). Fan et al. (2019) explained that according to the theory of threatened egotism, aggression is a means of defending a highly favorable self-view against someone who seeks to undermine or discredit that view. Hence, individuals with either overt or covert narcissism are more likely than others to act aggressively against people. These aggressive behaviors appear in different forms, including bullying others via electronic means. Given narcissists' frequent disrespect and disregard for others, their behaviors may engender negative behaviors from others. They are also more likely to retaliate against or exclude others in the cyber context due to their tendency to bully others. Similarly, victims may be attacked online by narcissistic cyberbullies, as those victims have learned the bullying behaviors and need to externalize the strain resulting from the experiences of victimization. In brief, overt and covert narcissism may be associated with cyberbullying perpetration and victimization (Fan et al., 2019).

Fan et al. (2019) argued that the hostile attribution bias framework also sheds light on possible connections between narcissism and aggression. A hostile attribution bias interprets others' intent as hostile when social cues fail to indicate a clear intent. Individuals with hostile attributions of intent tend to display more aggressive behaviors. Facial expressions and verbal and emotional cues are lacking in the cyber environment. This lack of information may be more challenging for covert narcissists, who are more sensitive about interpersonal relationships than overt narcissists. Covert narcissists may be more likely to perceive the information they receive as aggressive, and their antisocial behaviors are more likely to be motivated by this hostile attribution bias. In addition, due to the anonymity and elimination of physical strength in virtual space, covert narcissistic individuals can efficiently utilize different media online to retaliate against those who bully them.

However, covert narcissists are introverted, vulnerable, emotionally unstable, lack confidence, and have socially avoidant interpersonal styles. Hence, it might be difficult for them to succeed in interpersonal communication, and they may be more vulnerable to online bullying. From this perspective, we hypothesize that overt and covert narcissism positively correlates with cyberbullying perpetration and victimization. However, covert narcissism substantially affects cyberbullying more than overt narcissism (Fan et al., 2019).

According to Fan et al. (2019), individuals with high levels of covert narcissism are sensitive to others' evaluations and more likely to express indirect forms of aggression, such as anger and hostility. Without a physical presence, cyberbullying happens in chiefly covert and indirect ways (e.g., excluding someone in chat rooms), which may help to explain why covert narcissists are aggressive in the cyber environment. However, covertly narcissistic individuals may be easily bullied online due to personal characteristics, such as high neuroticism, lack of confidence, vulnerability, and socially avoidant interpersonal styles. In addition, covert narcissists might perceive themselves as victims of cyberbullying to soften the negative implications of poor performance in various domains of life (e.g., they might justify a poor academic performance by believing that they would have performed better if no one attacked them), to make their accomplishments seem more impressive (e.g., they could emerge victorious against all odds, although they were frequently bullied), or to justify treating people with similar disregard (e.g., they might justify bullying other people by attributing this behavior to others' bullying behavior toward them). Hence, they may become a relatively high-risk group in cyberspace, and efforts toward prevention or intervention should be targeted at this group (Fan et al., 2019).

As for overt narcissists, Fan et al. (2019) explained that their characteristics may make them likely to develop good interpersonal relationships both offline and online. Therefore, fewer interpersonal problems or conflicts experienced by overt narcissists might reduce the likelihood of involvement in cyberbullying, which is, by its very nature, a potential result of troubled relationships. So naturally, there is a need for more theory and empirical studies on this vital issue.

4.3.3   Machiavellianism, Cyber Aggression, and Cyberbullying

High Machiavellianism involves self-interest, deception, and seeing others as tools or mechanisms for pursuing and achieving goals. Engaging in manipulative behaviors coupled with the desire to promote self-interest and goals increases the risk of antisocial and aggressive behaviors, including cyberbullying involvement (Paulhus & Williams, 2002; Wright et al., 2022). In addition, they often have no reservations about using exploitative practices to achieve goals. These characteristics increase the likelihood of engaging in antisocial and aggressive behaviors. Cyberbullying might be a strategy that adolescents with high Machiavellianism characteristics use to promote their self-interest and goals. They might have few or zero qualms about engaging in such harmful behaviors as they might consider their peers a means to an end. Because of their aggressive behavioral strategies, they might also be at risk of being targeted by cyberbullying (Paulhus & Williams, 2002; Wright et al., 2022).

4.3.4   Sadism, Cyber Aggression, and Cyberbullying

Since most past conceptualizations of dark personalities did not include sadism, it is not well understood how sadism interacts with cyberbullying. Some studies found that when sadism is incorporated into the models, it becomes the strongest predictor of cyberbullying. Perpetrators of cyberbullying may enjoy seeing the victims in distress to gain pleasure (Kurek et al., 2019; Alavi et al., 2022). Sadistic individuals exhibit the highest levels of enjoyment of their own adversarial and provocative online behaviors. This observation suggests that these individuals do it for the "LULZ" (i.e., aggressive laughter derived from another person's distress or discomfort)(Kurek et al., 2019). Shahnawaz, Nasir, and Rehman (2020) contended that with increasing Internet usage, subclinical sadism is also on the rise leading to cyber aggression/cyberbullying/trolling. In light of such observations, sadism can be used to screen potential perpetrators in clinics or school settings. Alavi et al. (2022) further contend that if sadism as a trait is found to be significantly correlated with cyberbullying alongside the Dark Triad, future researchers should consider investigating online behaviors from the lens of the Dark Tetrad as a whole.

4.4 Research Findings

Many empirical studies have examined the relationship between Dark Triad personalities, cyber aggression, and cyberbullying. These studies' main findings and conclusions are reviewed in the following sections. A summary of the quantitative studies is presented in Table 4.1 and will be discussed later.

It is essential to start this review with a meta-analysis that provides a quantitative summary of the studies on this issue. Demircioğlu and Çıkan's (2021) meta-analysis aimed to investigate the effects of the Dark Triad personality traits on cyberbullying perpetration with the moderating role of participants' age group. Relevant databases were systematically reviewed. Only studies are written in Turkish and English, and studies that reported at least one Pearson correlation coefficient between study variables were included. In total, 22 study findings were integrated ($k = 22$, $N = 12,967$ for Machiavellianism – cyberbullying; $k = 24$, $N = 12,533$ for narcissism – cyberbullying; and $k = 18$, $N = 10,885$ for psychopathy – cyberbullying). Study samples were comprised of adolescents, university students, and adults. The findings revealed that the overall effect sizes of psychopathy, narcissism, and Machiavellianism on cyberbullying were significant ($r = 0.36$, $p \leq 0.001$; $r = 0.22$, $p \leq 0.001$; $r = 0.31$, $p \leq 0.001$, respectively). Furthermore, age was found to moderate the link between psychopathy and cyberbullying.

The following review of specific studies will categorize the empirical studies into Western versus Non-Western cultures. Such categorization will enable a comparative perspective on the relationship between Dark Triad traits, cyber aggression, and cyberbullying. As mentioned in Chapter 2, in collectivist cultures, more control mechanisms might discourage Dark Tetrad from cyber aggression and cyberbullying because of the high probability of exposure (Aluja et al., 2022; El Keshky et al., 2022). Shahnawaz et al. (2020) contended in this regard that Western research suggests that sadism may prove to be the best predictor of cyberbullying and cyber aggression. Examining this association outside of Western culture can strengthen its empirical basis.

4.4.1 Western Cultures

Giumetti, Kowalski, and Feinn (2022) examined 317 students from two United States universities who participated in both Times 1 and 2. Their findings showed that of the three Dark Triad traits, only Machiavellianism significantly predicted cyberbullying perpetration and victimization. According to them, from a theoretical standpoint, this finding supports the role of personality processes in predicting aggressive behavior. Because people who score high on Machiavellianism tend to be manipulative, low in empathy, and calculating, cyberbullying perpetration may be one of their outlets for interpersonal manipulation. Although the positive relationship between Machiavellianism and cyberbullying perpetration was not surprising, the nonsignificant relationships of psychopathy and narcissism with cyberbullying perpetration in the model are surprising. They explained these findings as a result of the differences in the gender composition of the sample and lower levels of narcissism in the current study compared to previous research.

In a sample of 297 undergraduate and graduate students from a Western university in the United States, Gibb and Devereux's (2014) results differ from those of Giumetti et al. (2022). Their study found that Machiavellianism and narcissism were nonsignificant predictors. However, individuals who scored high on a measure of subclinical psychopathy were more likely to report engaging in cyberbullying. They explained that this finding supports the idea that some behaviors might be retaliatory, as individuals high on psychopathy tend to be more impulsive and less empathetic than others. For these individuals, the instant gratification of knowing that they are potentially causing harm to another may drive their behavior and increase their propensity to engage in similar behaviors (Gibb & Devereux, 2014).

In a study of United States undergraduate students, Goodboy and Martin (2015) examined the relationships between the Dark Triad and cyberbullying behavior. Cyberbullying was defined in the survey as two-dimensional: visual-based cyberbullying and text-based cyberbullying. Their findings showed that Machiavellianism, psychopathy, and narcissism were positive correlates of both visual-based and text-based cyberbullying reports. However, these associations were small to moderate, suggesting that dark personalities play some role in cyberbullying tendencies. One of their more interesting findings was that psychopathy was revealed to be the unique predictor of the three traits, suggesting that this trait may be more problematic than the others. Goodboy and Martin (2015) explained this by relying on Jones and Paulhus (2010), who contended that individuals with Dark Triad traits are predisposed toward aggression but that psychopaths tend to be aggressive even when unprovoked.

Nocera and Dahlen (2017, 2020) examined the relationships between Dark Tetrad personality traits and cyber aggression in a college student sample (N = 297–317) in the United States. Their finding showed that all the dark personality traits were positively correlated with cyber aggression perpetration and victimization. When combining them into a predictive model and taking respondent gender into account, grandiose narcissism, psychopathy, and sadism predicted the perpetration of cyber aggression. They concluded that it would be premature to dismiss Machiavellianism and vulnerable narcissism as relevant to cyber aggression; however, their findings suggest that they may be less involved than the other traits. When focusing on the previously reviewed United States samples, it seems psychopathy is the strongest predictor of cyberbullying.

Van Geel et al. (2017) examined whether the Dark Tetrad predicts traditional bullying and cyberbullying. Their sample comprised 1,568 participants from 17 senior vocational high schools in the Netherlands. Concerning the Dark Tetrad and traditional bullying, they found that Machiavellianism, psychopathy, and sadism were predictors of traditional bullying, but narcissism was not. Concerning cyberbullying, sadism was a significant predictor, whereas narcissism and psychopathy were marginally significant, and Machiavellianism was insignificant. Van Geel et al. (2017) conclude that their study points to the possibility that sadism is more predictive of antisocial online behavior than Dark Triad traits; online antisocial behavior then seems more driven by sadistic pleasure than callousness, strategic considerations, or a threatened ego.

Interestingly, the relationship between the Dark Tetrad traits and cyberbullying was weaker than with bullying. Moreover, sadism was a unique predictor of traditional bullying when the Dark Triad and Big Five were controlled. Van Geel et al. (2017) attributed this to the possibility that beyond a strategic instrument to achieve dominance (Machiavellianism) and callousness toward victims and thrill-seeking (psychopathy), seeing victims suffer may be a fundamental reason behind traditional bullying behaviors.

Pabian et al. (2015) investigated the relationship between the Dark Triad and cyber aggression on Facebook among adolescents in Belgium. Their findings showed that only psychopathy, not Machiavellianism and narcissism, were related to cyber aggression on Facebook over 14–18 years old. Furthermore, no significant relation was found when controlling for a potential mediation effect of Facebook intensity between narcissism and cyber aggression. This finding is quite similar to the findings in the United States.

March and Marrington (2021) examined the relationship between the Dark Triad and antisocial and prosocial behaviors using a sample of 283

participants recruited via social media (e.g., Facebook, Reddit) advertisements. The participants were predominantly English speakers from
Australia (80.4%) and the United States. Their findings showed that
the Dark Triad traits significantly positively influenced antisocial online
behavior. According to them, using the Internet for antisocial purposes
(e.g., "being mean" and "showing off") may be attributed to the Dark
Triad's opportunistic, exploitative interpersonal styles. However, quite
interestingly, they found that narcissism was a significant, positive predictor of prosocial online behavior. They concluded that future research
could explore if prosocial online behavior is associated with more grandiose or vulnerable forms of narcissism.

Brown et al. (2019) also found that the Dark Triad predicts cyberbullying in a sample of 1,310 United Kingdom recruited through social media.
More specifically, Machiavellianism and psychopathy are better predictors
of cyberbullying than narcissism. A significant positive correlation between
psychopathy and the cyberbullying tendency was found in both genders,
which, according to them, is consistent with previous research. Their results
showed that Machiavellianism was a significant predictor for cyberbullying
for both genders, even though male participants often scored higher. The
findings generalize across white, Black, and Asian participations.

Kurek et al. (2019) examined the relationship between Dark Tetrad
and cyber aggression among 709 high school students in New Zealand.
Because Machiavellianism showed unacceptable reliability, it was omit-
ted from the data. The findings showed that only sadism was a significant
direct predictor of cyber aggression. Both narcissistic and psychopathic
tendencies indirectly predicted cyber aggression through the mediation of
both false self-perceptions and online disinhibition. Kureka et al. (2019)
concluded that of the dark personality traits, it is the sadistic youth who
engage in cyber aggression that may be more intrinsically motivated and
find particular pleasure or amusement in this behavior.

Leite et al. (2023) found in a sample of 773 Internet users from Portugal
a strong and positive relationship between the Dark Triad traits and online
harassment. Sánchez-Medina et al. (2020) found in a convenience sampling
of 374 higher education students from the Canary Islands (Spain) that two
dimensions of the Dark Triad (psychopathy and Machiavellianism) were
significantly related to sexual cyberbullying behaviors. However, their
study focuses on a form of cyberbullying that is not examined frequently,
and more studies are needed to validate the findings of this research.

The final study reviewed here examines second-world country. The
term "second world" has been used to cover countries more stable and

developed than the offensive term "third-world" countries but less stable and less developed than "first-world" countries (Chen, 2020).

In a sample of 251 participants from Poland recruited from social media advertisements, Gajda et al. (2022) found that sadism, Machiavellianism, and psychopathy were positively associated with cyberbullying and cyber victimization. These results indicate that cyberbullying perpetration may be associated not only with a callousness that characterizes Machiavellianism, psychopathy, and sadism, but also with the manipulativeness characteristic of Machiavellianism and psychopathy and the enjoyment of cruelty present in sadism. Furthermore, the finding from path analysis indicated that, when controlling for shared variance between Dark Tetrad traits, only sadism appeared to be significantly associated with cyberbullying. This may indicate that callousness and enjoyment of cruelty may fuel cyberbullying perpetration the most. Furthermore, they suggested that a sadistic personality promotes reward-motivated (appetitive-controlled) cyber aggression. Thus, from the Dark Tetrad perspective, cyberbullying appears to be related to enjoying cruelty, which is the essence of sadism.

Their findings also showed that narcissism was weakly correlated with cyberbullying and not significantly correlated with cyber victimization. They contend that narcissistic individuals could engage in cyberbullying only in a particular situation of ego threat aiming at face restoration. Thus, future studies should investigate the frequency of cyberbullying and its motivations to better describe the role of narcissism in cyber aggression (Gajda et al., 2022).

Pabian and Vandebosch (2023) examined 2,000 adults in the Netherlands. Their findings showed significant and, in some cases, high correlations between the Dark Tetrad and online aggression perpetration, online moral disengagement, and online aggression victimization. Their path model showed significant positive associations between all traits and online moral disengagement, except for narcissism. Pabian and Vandebosch concluded that adults who scored higher on Machiavellianism, psychopathy, and sadism agreed more strongly with beliefs that excuse their immoral or harmful behavior online, but this was not true for narcissists. Pabian and Vandebosch (2023) also examined the mediating role of online moral disengagement in the relationships between the Dark Tetrad and online aggression perpetration. Their findings showed a small significant indirect association for psychopathy and sadism but not for the two other traits. They concluded that online moral disengagement is a less important risk factor for online aggression than traditional moral disengagement.

A broader view of the findings from studies performed in Western culture emphasizes psychopathy and sadism as an essential determinants of cyber aggression and cyberbullying. At the same time, narcissism seems to have a weaker effect among the three dark personalities. A possible explanation for this finding is that narcissism typifies Western societies (Foster, Campbell, & Twenge, 2003), and its negative features are less dominant. Future studies should examine this possible explanation.

4.4.2   Non-Western Cultures

In a sample of 675 Chinese college students (296 men and 379 women), Zhang and Zhao (2020) found a positive association between dark personality traits and cyber aggression in adolescents. Based on their findings, they contend that psychopathy can significantly predict cyber aggression, which may be because psychopathic individuals tend to be less empathic, are more callous and are more likely to engage in aggression. Furthermore, in cyberspace, the anonymity of the Internet may promote the cyber-aggressive behaviors of Machiavellian individuals. Therefore, their study revealed that Machiavellianism positively correlates with adolescents' cyber aggression. In addition, they found a significantly positive correlation between narcissism and cyber aggression. Narcissistic individuals tend to be self-centered and exploitative; the Internet's anonymity could exacerbate their disregard for others and their belief that aggression is acceptable and justifiable (Zhang & Zhao, 2020).

Jin et al. (2022) found in a sample of 1,921 middle and high school students in China that adolescents who scored higher on the Dark Triad and lower on perceived parental monitoring and self-control were likelier to have online deviant behaviors. Psychopathy was more strongly associated with online deviant behavior than Machiavellianism and narcissism. They explained that individuals with high psychopathy are more likely to have different cognition from other people than individuals with high Machiavellianism or narcissism. They tend to regard some general interpersonal interaction as a provocation to themselves, thus showing strong aggression and being more likely to develop retaliatory online. Jin et al. also found that the Dark Triad partially mediated the relationship between perceived parental monitoring and online deviant behaviors.

In a sample of 501 high school students in China, Zhang et al. (2022) found a direct relationship between the Dark Triad and moral disengagement. They also found that moral disengagement mediated the connection between the three dark personalities and adolescents' cyber aggression. Adolescents high on Dark Triad personality traits are more prone to justifying immoral consequences, leading to a rise in cyberattacks. Zhang et al. (2022) conclude that their findings align with similar results in Western cultures. One of their interesting findings is that all subsets of Dark Triad personality traits are more strongly associated with cyber aggression for girls than boys.

Safaria et al. (2020), in a sample of 2,407 adolescents from 11 cities in Indonesia, found that all three Dark Triad traits have significant positive correlations with cyberbullying. Multiple regression analysis showed that Machiavellianism emerged as the strongest predictor of cyberbullying, followed closely by psychopathy and narcissism. Adolescents with a Dark Triad personality are likelier to bully others on social media. The Dark Triad personality plays a role in increasing cyberbullying conduct. They also contend that one factor that might have allowed Machiavellianism to develop into cyberbullying is the ability of the bully to hide their identity on the Internet, enabling them to deceive the victims.

In a sample of 425 Iranian high school students, Azami and Taremian (2021) found that the Dark Triad did not significantly increase or decrease the chances of cyberbullying, cyber victimization, or cyberbullying victimization as such. In another study, Afzal, Latif, and Siddique (2021) collected data from 200 adolescents in Pakistan. Correlational analysis revealed no significant relationship between a combined scale of the Dark Triad and cyberbullying.

Alavi et al. (2022) examined the relationship between the Dark Tetrad and antisocial cyber behaviors (i.e., cyberbullying and cyber trolling) in the Malaysian context using structured equation modeling (SEM). The findings among 323 young Malaysian adults revealed that Machiavellianism had no relationship with cyberbullying and cyber trolling, and narcissism had a positive relationship with cyberbullying. However, there is no relationship with cyber trolling, and psychopathy and sadism positively correlate with cyberbullying and cyber trolling. According to them, the main theoretical implication of their study is that it further supports the use of the Dark Tetrad in studies on personality and antisocial cyber behaviors over the Dark Triad. In line with past studies involving sadism as a variable. Their study found sadism to be an essential predictor of cyber-bullying and cyber trolling behaviors. Therefore, theoretically, researchers should find the Dark Tetrad to be a more valuable and complete model of personality traits as the role of sadism may prove integral as an explanatory mechanism for antisocial behaviors in cyberspace.

Shahnawaz et al. (2020) examined the relationship between sadism and cyber aggression among 207 adolescents aged 16–19 in India. They found a strong association between sadism and cyber aggression. They explained that the defining feature of sadism is hurting others, which is the prototypical aspect of the personality of such individuals made possible and easier in the cyberworld as the victim is not physically present. Moreover, the diffused nature of the identity of the perpetrators that aggravates such virtual aggression is also alarming. They further concluded that their findings established the construct validity of the sadism scale in the Indian culture and provided cross-cultural support to the emerging relationship between sadism and cyber aggression. Sari and Adriani (2022), in a sample of 943 high school students from Indonesia, found using path analysis that only Machiavellianism significantly affected cyberbullying positively, while narcissism and psychopaths did not influence cyberbullying.

In a sample of 547 high school students in Turkey, Demircioğlu and Köse (2022) found a strong effect of psychopathy on cyberbully-ing. They explained that impulsivity, avoiding others, lack of empathy, and negative affectivity are among the main characteristics of psychopa-thy. Therefore, psychopathic tendencies, partially shaped by attachment avoidance, are likely to lead individuals who score high on these tenden-cies to engage in cyberbullying since they are indifferent to the feelings of others and highly impulsive. However, contrary to their expectation, the associations of Machiavellianism and narcissism with cyberbullying were insignificant.

In short, findings from non-Westernized cultures are not consistent. Therefore, it is impossible at this stage to make any generalization based on the findings in these societies. There is a strong need for more studies to reach firmer conclusions.

4.4.3   Comparative Studies

Comparative studies offer great value for better understanding the relation-ship between the Dark Tetrad and cyber aggression. Unfortunately, not many such studies exist, but even the few that exist can contribute. The following study (Wright et al., 2020) was performed in three non-Western countries. The total sample was 1,631 adolescents from China (n = 683), India (n = 480), and Japan (n = 474). Wright et al. (2020) found evidence that the role of the Dark Triad of personality traits in cyberbullying perpetration is not universal and varies by country. Their findings showed that narcissism and callous and unemotional traits were positively associated with cyberbullying perpetration for Chinese and Indian adolescents but not for Japanese adolescents. In addition, the relationship between Machiavellianism traits and cyberbullying perpetration was found for Indian adolescents only. Considering these findings, the associations between the Dark Triad of personality traits and cyberbullying perpetration are inconsistent across different countries. Wright et al. (2020) explained that the caste-based system in India promotes attitudes conducive to bullying, and bullying typically occurs in social groups because of significant disparities in social status. Endorsing individualism, along with the caste-based system and disparities in social status in Indian culture, might increase Indian adolescents' cyberbullying perpetration, especially when they possess the characteristics associated with the Dark Triad of personality traits, including a lack of empathy and guilt, the promotion of self-interests and goals, and a lack of concern with the feelings of others.

According to Wright et al. (2020), the Chinese culture values relational hierarchy, which promotes obedience to social hierarchies and a desire to order relationships by status. The hierarchical nature of Chinese adolescents' relationships combined with characteristics of the Dark Triad of personality (e.g., having little empathy and guilt, being unconcerned with others' feelings) might increase their perpetration of cyberbullying. However, Wright et al. (2020) did not find that Machiavellianism and cyberbullying perpetration were linked among Chinese adolescents. This finding might reflect the collectivistic orientation of Chinese culture, which does not promote self-interest and goals. Like the Chinese or Japanese culture, collectivistic culture values a patient, gentle, and harmonious life and is less relationally hierarchical, with characteristics that do not promote aggressivity. Given these values, it might be less likely for Japanese adolescents to engage in cyberbullying perpetration and for the Dark Triad of personality traits to increase this propensity. Their findings support this proposal as these personality traits were not linked to cyberbullying perpetration among Japanese adolescents (Wright et al., 2020).

In a later study, Wright et al. (2022) performed a one-year longitudinal study to examine, among other goals, the relationships between Machiavellianism and cyberbullying perpetration among adolescents from China (N = 683), Cyprus (N = 480), India (N = 480), and the United States (N = 813) adolescents. The importance of this study results from the fact that it compares Western and non-Western cultures. Their findings revealed that Machiavellianism characteristics and popularity goals were positively associated with cyberbullying victimization and perpetration in all countries, suggesting that these risk factors have potentially universal effects on cyberbullying involvement. Their study applied the social-ecological perspective and proposed that differences would be found among adolescents in different countries; however, they found more similarities between the adolescents than differences.

In a sample of 743 individuals (44% from Austria, 52% from Germany, and 4% from other European countries), Schade, Voracek, and Tran (2021) found that Dark Triad traits are associated with more self-reported cyberbullying behavior. In addition, secondary psychopathy, but also primary psychopathy, was associated with more cyberbullying among both men and women. The associations with both primary and secondary psychopathy highlight that cyberbullying may either be an impulsive or a strategic form of aggression, depending on the perpetrator's profile. They also found an association between grandiose narcissism and cyberbullying and between vulnerable narcissism and cyberbullying behavior, particularly among men. Finally, they found that Machiavellianism was directly and indirectly associated with cyberbullying.

Hossain et al. (2022) posit that cyberbullying is a complex and multidimensional phenomenon that should be explained as a triadic configuration of the Big Five and Dark Tetrad with demographic attributes. Their 313 responses (158 from the United States and 155 from India) showed that to commit cyberbullying, a social media user must be a psychopath (necessary condition) with high Machiavellianism. High psychopathy and sadism are also sufficient to commit cyberbullying. Alternatively, cyberbullying is less likely for a social media user with low psychopathy and sadism, low narcissism and sadism, or low narcissism and psychopathy, even with high Machiavellianism. These five configurations within the Dark Tetrad sufficiently explain the high and low scores on their measure of cyberbullying.

Again, it is vital to compare the Dark Tetrad behavior across cultures. There is a need for many more studies like those reviewed earlier to get a firm conclusion about cross-cultural differences in Dark Tetrad cyber aggression and cyberbullying. Such an understanding can increase our ability to explain the roots of this behavior.

4.4.4 Cyberbullying of Celebrities

Celebrities are among the appealing populations to examine cyber aggression and cyberbullying. This specific issue has received growing attention among scholars. Shabahang et al. (2023) reported based on a sample of 1,175 Iranian Internet users, that celebrities were perceived as Machiavellian, narcissistic, and psychopathic simultaneously, but at different levels. Above all, celebrities were more perceived as narcissistic by the participants. They concluded that people attributing Dark Triad characteristics to celebrities tend to dislike celebrities more than others. According to Shabahang et al. (2023), characterizing celebrities as deceptive, selfish, and manipulative is unsurprising, as many are aware of celebrity scandals and misleading celebrity endorsements. Celebrities are often viewed as narcissistic and undeserving of their stature in society. The findings of Shabahang et al. (2023) explain why celebrities are an attractive target for cyberbullying.

In an interesting study, Scott et al. (2020) examined how different types of tweets by celebrities, as well as observers' Dark Triad personality scores, influence attributed victim blaming and perceived abuse severity. More specifically, they examined how the type of tweet written by celebrities (identity claims; negative, neutral, or positive) and the volume of abusive responses by followers (behavioral residue; low or high) affected participants' attribution of victim blaming to the celebrity and participants' perceptions of incident severity. More importantly, they examined whether participants' Dark Triad traits impacted their perceptions of victim-blaming and severity. In an experimental design of 184 United Kingdom university Twitter users, they presented to the participants celebrity tweets and later measured participants' Dark Triad personality traits. Their finding showed that Machiavellianism, narcissism, and psychopathy positively associated with victim blaming in the harmful tweet condition. Regarding abuse severity, narcissism and psychopathy were inversely associated with perceived severity in the harmful tweet condition.

Further, psychopathy was inversely related to perceived severity in the positive tweet condition. Those high in psychopathy perceived abusive tweets as less severe regardless of the original tweet's valence. By contrast, those high in narcissism only perceived less severity when the original tweet was negative. They further revealed that narcissism was a significant independent predictor of victim blaming in the negative tweet condition, but Machiavellianism and psychopathy were not. Narcissism was the only significant independent predictor of perceived severity in the negative tweet condition. This suggests that victim blaming following negative tweets increases as narcissism increases, while the perceived severity of abusive tweets decreases (Scott et al., 2020).

Scott et al. (2020) also found that psychopathy was a significant predictor of perceived severity in the positive tweet condition alone: Those high in psychopathy were likely to perceive abuse as less severe when the celebrity tweet was positive. As the tweets used in the positive tweet condition arguably reflected the celebrity's success and happiness, participants high in psychopathy may believe that celebrities deserved the resulting abuse. A key characteristic of psychopathy is a fundamental belief in superiority over others; those high in the trait often view interactions with others as competitive. According to Scott et al., when celebrity tweets were positive, those high in psychopathy may have viewed the abusive responses as justified to "bring the celebrity down." This is because psychopaths tend to experience envy or contempt for those they perceive to be in a more prosperous position than themselves.

Scott et al. (2020) found that Machiavellianism did not significantly predict victim blaming or perceived severity in either condition. Their explanation for this finding was that Machiavellianism is underpinned by attitudes and behaviors aimed at achieving success at all costs, with little consideration or concern for how one's behavior might impact others. The central interaction in the present study does not reflect an opportunity for a Machiavellian individual to prosper personally so that they may be indifferent to the incident. Therefore, while Machiavellianism may predict engagement in cyberbullying behavior, which could be used as an advancement tool, it does not appear to predict attitudes regarding cyber abuse committed by or expressed toward others.

A similar study examined 125 United Kingdom volunteers. One difference between this study and the previous one is the addition of sadism to the Dark Triad traits. Hand et al. (2021) found that psychopathy was a significant predictor of the perceived severity of abuse that followed positive tweets by the victim. The association between psychopathy and perceived severity was also found by Scott et al. (2020), whose results indicated that psychopathy was a significant predictor of perceived severity in the positive tweet condition. This suggests that positive initial tweets by celebrities and lay users reduce the perceived severity of abuse the victim receives in those high in this trait.

However, Hand et al. (2021) also found that psychopathy predicts perceived severity following negative tweets. They explained that it might be that those high in psychopathy view the abuse as less severe because the initial negative tweets insinuate that the individual can handle the abuse they receive. Again, due to their feelings of superiority, they may view a lay-user target as even more inferior than the celebrity targets used by Scott et al. (2020) and may be more likely to attribute a minimized impact on the victim. Hand et al. (2021) also found that Machiavellianism predicts the perceived severity of abuse following neutral victim tweets only. The fact that Machiavellianism was not predictive of victim blaming or perceived severity in the negative or positive tweet condition aligns with the findings of Scott et al. (2020). However, Hand et al.'s (2021) study indicates that Machiavellianism may be relevant when the victim's initial tweet is neutral in valence. Given the goal-oriented nature of Machiavellianism, it may be that these individuals view any neutral social media posts as futile and non–goal-directed. For this reason, they may demonstrate less sympathy for the impact of the abuse on the victim.

Interestingly, Hand et al. (2021) found that narcissism was not a significant predictor of victim blame or perceived severity of abuse. This is in contrast to the findings of Scott et al. (2020), who found narcissism was the sole predictor of victim blaming and perceived severity following negative tweets by celebrities. A fundamental aspect of narcissism is heightened ego-threat monitoring, which makes those high in this trait quick to respond negatively and aggressively to potential ego threats (real or imagined). The lay users portrayed in this experiment represented a lesser threat to those high in narcissism than the successful and wealthy celebrities portrayed in Scott et al.'s study. Those high in narcissism may find it harder to relate to the "everyday person" given their feelings of eminence and, therefore, may be somewhat disinterested and unresponsive to observed instances of abuse.

As for sadism, their findings indicated that sadism predicted victim blame in instances where the abuse bore no relation to the valence of the initial tweet. Hand et al. (2021) contended that while previous literature indicates that sadism is a significant predictor of engagement in cyberbullying and trolling behaviors, their study is the first to consider sadistic attitudes toward abuse perpetrated by others. As those high in this trait exude pleasure in witnessing the pain or distress of others, it is unsurprising that this trait also predicts higher attribution of blame to a victim of cyber abuse. According to Hand et al. (2021), their findings suggest that the pleasure sadists experience at others' misfortune comes not from the perpetration of the abuse itself but from its presumed negative effect on the unobserved reaction of the victim – the outcome of which remains the same regardless of the abuse perpetrator.

In sum, for observations of online abuse against lay users, psychopathy predicts perceived severity following positive or negative initial tweets, whereas Machiavellianism predicts perceived severity following neutral tweets (Hand et al., 2021). When observing abuse against celebrities, narcissism predicts both victim blaming and perceived severity following negative tweets, and psychopathy predicts perceived severity following positive tweets (Scott et al., 2020). Observer sadism scores predicted victim blame regardless of the valence of victims' initial tweets. Observers scoring high in the Dark Tetrad are less able to perceive online abuse from the victims' perspective or understand the negative impact that such actions may cause (Hand & Scott, 2022).

Hand and Scott (2022) examined 309 United Kingdom participants in another study that examined similar research questions. Their findings showed that participants who scored more highly in Dark Triad characteristics (Machiavellianism, narcissism, and psychopathy) were likelier to blame victims and perceive incidents as less severe. Psychopathy and Machiavellianism both negatively correlated to both victim blaming and perceived severity. Hand and Scott explained that all three Dark Triad traits are associated with low empathy levels, a reduced ability to take others' perspectives, and an inability to relate to the viewpoint of victims and understand the negative impact of abuse. Individuals in psychopathy think of themselves as superior to others and highly competitive. Such individuals may view abuse as bringing others down and increasing their position by comparison. For celebrities, who may be considered to occupy an elevated position, this could be viewed as "taking them down."

By contrast, lay victims may be viewed as inferior, so their abuse impact will likely be minimized. Individuals high in Machiavellianism are focused on achieving success without concern for how their actions might impact others. For this reason, they might be less sympathetic to any victim of abuse and not be as sensitive to the severity of abusive incidents (Hand & Scott, 2022).

Finally, Hand et al. (2022), in an experiment with 197 United Kingdom participants, found that user-generated content (i.e., Initial Tweet Valence) was the largest contributor in explaining attributed victim blame variability; however, Machiavellianism was found to contribute to the model as observers' Machiavellianism increased, as did their likelihood of attributing victim blame. This is in line with the findings of Hand and Scott (2022). However, unlike previous research investigating perceptions of male victims, there was no attributed victim blame for narcissism (as per Scott et al., 2020) or psychopathy (as per Hand & Scott, 2022), or sadism. These contrasting model structures suggest a different interplay between victim-generated content and observer Dark Triad characteristics when victims are female celebrities as opposed to male celebrities and/or male laypersons.

The findings also showed no evidence of a linear relationship between observer narcissism nor sadism and perceived incident severity, regardless of Initial Tweet Valence. There was mixed evidence for a relationship between observer Machiavellianism and psychopathy on perceived incident severity, which seemed to depend on victim-generated content (i.e., Initial Tweet Valence). The findings also showed that the Volume of Abuse received and Initial Tweet Valence explained more variability than observer characteristics; however, observer Machiavellianism contributed significantly to this model. However, there was no place in the regression model of perceived incident severity for narcissism or psychopathy (as per Hand & Scott, 2022; Hand et al., 2021; Scott et al., 2020) or sadism. This may suggest that those high in Machiavellianism find it particularly difficult to grasp the risk that online abuse may pose to a female victim. As with victim blame data, this suggests a different interplay between victim-generated and abusive content received.

4.5 Detecting Cyberbullies Based on Their Personality

Another important research trend is the detection of cyberbullies or cyber aggressors' dark personalities based on the content of their posts. Balakrishnan, Khan, and Arabnia (2020) and Balakrishnan et al. (2019) developed a cyberbullying detection model based on user personality. They contend that studies still need to incorporate users' personalities in automatically detecting cyberbullying. Most studies revealed the empirical findings from survey-based studies, attempting to examine relationships between personality traits and cyberbullying perpetration. Balakrishnan et al. (2019) contend that their study differs because they aimed to investigate whether users' personalities can be used collectively and individually to automatically detect cyberbullying based on their textual communication, using a technique from artificial intelligence (i.e., Random Forest). They used Twitter as the social media platform of choice for their study.

Their model aims to recognize bullying patterns among Twitter communities based on relationships between personality traits and cyberbullying. Random Forest, a well-known machine-learning algorithm, was used for cyberbullying classification (i.e., aggressor, spammer, bully, and normal), applied in conjunction with a baseline algorithm encompassing seven Twitter features (i.e., number of mentions, number of followers, and following, popularity, favorite count, status count, and number of hashtags). Their findings based on 9,484 tweets in the first study and 5,453 tweets in the second indicate that factoring in a user's personality greatly improves cyberbullying detection mechanisms. More specifically, their findings showed that psychopathy impacted cyberbullying more than narcissism and Machiavellianism, significantly improving online bullying detection.

Balakrishnan et al. (2019, 2020) conclude that their findings demonstrate the emergence of psychopathy as a significant predictor for cyberbullying, compared to Machiavellianism and narcissism. Unlike Machiavellians, who are more likely to harm others if the perceived benefits are high and the personal risk is low, and narcissists, who tend to harm others when their sense of self feels threatened, psychopaths are predatory, callous, and fearless. The predatory nature of psychopaths, for example, may drive these individuals to seek potential victims to inflict emotional and psychological harm, as they also wholly disregard the distress they cause others. This probably explains why the trait has been consistently found to predict antisocial behaviors, including cyberbullying (Balakrishnan et al., 2019, 2020). Balakrishnan et al. (2019, 2020) concluded that knowledge of each user's traits could help distinguish between individuals with tendencies to engage in cyberbullying and those who do not and that this will enable a more effective detection mechanism as opposed to identifying them solely based on the use of abusive words, or platform features.

The following section will present empirical studies concentrating on each of the Dark Tetrad personalities.

4.6 Psychopathy and Cyberbullying and Cyber Aggression

Charalampous et al. (2021) examined 407 high school students randomly selected from six schools in urban and rural areas in Nicosia, Cyprus. The results indicated that the interrelationships among psychopathic traits, moral disengagement, school climate, and cyberbullying and cyber victimization were differentiated based on the level of participants' self-reported psychopathy and their gender. Based on the findings, it seems that cyberbullying directly relates to psychopathic traits for boys, only for students with high psychopathy. Moral disengagement does not relate to cyberbullying for this group, even though both psychopathic traits and perceived aggressive attitudes significantly affect moral disengagement. Therefore, for boys reporting high psychopathic levels, psychopathy is the key variable affecting cyberbullying levels. Moral disengagement is a side effect of high psychopathy without relation to cyberbullying perpetration.

By contrast, for boys reporting low psychopathy levels, moral disengagement has a robust significant relationship with cyberbullying, and psychopathic traits do not affect cyberbullying or moral disengagement. Therefore, negative psychopathy does not affect cyberbullying perpetration, nor does moral disengagement. However, in this case, moral disengagement is the key variable influencing cyberbullying, with school climate also playing a significant role as a determinant of moral disengagement. Lastly, for boys with moderate levels of psychopathy, cyberbullying is not significantly predicted by any of the variables in the hypothesized models.

Charalampous et al. (2021) reported that, for girls, the results differed significantly. The psychopathy trait was a significant predictor for cyberbullying regardless of the levels of self-reported psychopathy. Nevertheless, the coefficient of this effect was considerably higher for girls high in self-reported psychopathy levels than those with moderate or low such levels. By contrast, moral disengagement and perceived aggressive attitudes significantly affected cyberbullying for girls high in self-reported psychopathic levels. However, this was not true for girls in the low and moderate psychopathy groups. Thus, for girls' psychopathy is an essential determinant of cyberbullying perpetration for all levels of self-reported psychopathy, with this effect being more substantial for high-psychopathy girls. Moral disengagement seems to affect cyberbullying only for high-psychopathy girls and is related indirectly to psychopathy through the latter's effect on perceived aggressive attitudes.

Charalampous et al. (2021) argued that one explanation for this finding might be traced to gender socialization differences that lead to different reactions to ethical dilemmas by men and women. Societal norms expect women to be communal and expressive, whereas men are expected to be agentic and instrumental. Thus, moral disengagement affects cyberbullying for girls only for the high and moderate psychopathy group since girls seem to apply moral justifications for their actions much more when socioemotional dysfunction – associated with psychopathic traits – is present.

As for cyber victimization, the findings of Charalampous et al. (2021) showed that only psychopathy was a significant predictor of cyber victimization, and this effect was in place only for high-psychopathy boys. However, in that instance, the magnitude of the predictor exceeds the magnitude of psychopathy on cyberbullying. Thus, boys reporting high psychopathy seem likelier to be cyber victims than bullies. Nevertheless, the partition of the participants into different subgroups based on gender and self-reported levels of psychopathy in their study further revealed significant differences in how psychopathy relates to cyber victimization for individuals reporting different levels of psychopathy. Finally, moral disengagement was predictive of higher involvement in cyberbullying in low-psychopathy boys and high-psychopathy girls, supporting the idea that cognitive distortion facilitates bullying as it limits the possibilities that the person will take responsibility for his/her actions, will sympathize with the victim and will try to take the agency to do something about bullying incidents.

Antoniadou et al. (2019) examined the relationship between psychopathic traits and online disinhibition in 1,097 Greek junior high school students. A correlation analysis showed that psychopathic traits and social anxiety were positively related to online disinhibition, thus indicating that they may be context-dependent and differently manifested online.

4.7   Narcissism, Cyberbullying, and Cyber Aggression

Fan et al. (2019) examined 814 students recruited from two schools in central China (53.3% male). Participants were in the 7th, 8th, 10th, and 11th grades. Their findings showed that covert narcissism positively predicts cyberbullying perpetration and victimization, whereas overt narcissism predicts neither perpetration nor victimization.

4.8   Machiavellianism and Cyberbullying and Cyber Aggression

In a sample of 879 adolescents from four junior high schools in East China, Yuan, Liu, and An (2020a) found a strong direct relationship between Machiavellianism and cyberbullying. However, their findings also showed that Chinese adolescents with high levels of mindfulness and low levels of Machiavellianism engage in less cyberbullying through the development of empathy.

4.9　Sadism, Cyberbullying, and Cyber Aggression

In a sample of 404 emerging adult volunteers recruited from Amazon's Mechanical Turk website and currently living within the United States, Nocera et al. (2022) found that sadism and psychopathy predicted cyber aggression perpetration. According to them, the dimensions of psychopathy and sadism coincide with some motives for cyber aggression perpetration among emerging adults (e.g., disinhibition relating to negative affect as a motive, boldness relating to thrill-seeking behaviors such as deprecating humor, and meanness relating to retaliation motives). In addition, they found that moral disengagement partially mediated these relationships, suggesting that it may be one mechanism through which dark personality traits are connected to cyber aggression.

Their findings also showed that examining psychopathic and sadistic traits in the same model demonstrated that both predict cyber aggression perpetration even when considered together. According to this study, this finding supports the contention that these dark personality traits are overlapping but distinct and suggests that both are likely to clarify why some emerging adults perpetrate cyber aggression (Nocera et al., 2022).

******

Table 4.1 shows a summary of the findings presented in this chapter. A review of the table shows a moderate relationship between dark personalities and cyber aggression and bullying. First, it should be noted that there is an underrepresentation of studies that examined the Dark Tetrad. Most of the studies in the table focused on the Dark Triad. There is a need for more research that includes sadism within the framework of dark personalities. Viewing the relatively small size of the correlations presented in the table, an immediate conclusion is that the relationship between dark personalities and cyber aggression and bullying is not direct. There are possibly moderators and mediators that affect the magnitude of this relationship. The table also reveals that most of the samples used in these studies consist of adolescents. There is little representation of adult and working individuals' samples. This fact means it is quite difficult to generalize from the results presented here to the general population. There is a growing need to examine older populations and working individuals and not rely too much on findings based on samples from elementary, high school students, and university students.

Table 4.1 *Summary of research findings on the relationship between the Dark Tetrad/Triad and cyber aggression and cyberloafing*

Study	Sample size	Type of behavior	Gender	Age (mean)	MTurk or similar	Country	Occupation	Education	Correlations			
									Narcissists	Psychopathy	Machiavellianism	Sadism
Van Geel et al. (2017)	1,568	Cyberbullying	61.9% female	17,58 (16–21)	No	Netherlands	Senior vocational high schools	Senior vocational high schools	0.177***	0.278***	0.172***	0.313***
Van Geel et al. (2017)	1,568	Traditional Bullying	61.9% female	17,58 (16–21)	No	Netherlands	Senior vocational high schools	Senior vocational high schools	0.234***	0.410***	0.268***	0.363***
Wright et al. (2020)	683	Face-to-face bullying perpetration	52% male	11–14	No	China	Two middle schools	Two middle schools	0.18***	0.22***	0.33***	NE
Wright et al. (2020)	480	Face-to-face bullying perpetration	52% boys	11–15	No	India	Six middle schools	Six middle schools	0.08*	0.24***	0.15**	NE
Wright et al. (2020)	474	Face-to-face bullying perpetration	39% boys	11–14	No	Japan	Two middle schools	Two middle schools	0.07	0.12***	0.24***	NE
Wright et al. (2020)	683	Cyberbullying perpetration	52% boys	11–14	No	China	Two middle schools	Two middle schools	0.24***	0.34***	0.33***	NE
Wright et al. (2020)	480	Cyberbullying perpetration	52% boys	11–15	No	India	Six middle schools	Six middle schools	0.33***	0.37***	0.36***	NE
Wright et al. (2020)	474	Cyberbullying perpetration	39% boys	11–14	No	Japan	Two middle schools	Two middle schools	0.12**	0.08*	0.21***	NE
Fan et al. (2019)	814	Cyberbullying perpetration	53.3% male	14.67 (11–18)	No	China	Middle and high school students	Middle and high school students	Overt = 0.26***; Covert = 0.35***	NE	NE	NE
Fan et al. (2019)	814	Cyberbullying victimization	53.3% male	14.67 (11–18)	No	China	Middle and high school students	Middle and high school students	Overt = 0.27***; Covert = 0.38***	NE	NE	NE

Study	N	Measure	Gender	Age		Country	Sample	Sample				
Charalampous et al. (2021)	407	Cyberbullying	55.3% female	16.01 (15–18)	No	Nicosia, Cyprus	High school students	High school students	NE	Direct relationship for girls. Direct relationship for boys with high psychopathy	NE	NE
Brown et al. (2019)	2,100	Cyberbullying perpetration scale	62.4% female	22.48	No	United Kingdom	NR	NR	Significant positive relationship	Significant positive relationship	Significant positive relationship	Significant positive relationship
Gibb & Devereux (2014)	297	Cyberbullying	61% female	22.70	No	USA	Undergraduate and graduate students	Undergraduate and graduate students	No significant relationship	Positive significant relationship	No significant relationship	NE
Zhang & Zhao (2020)	675	Cyber aggression	56.1% female	19.64 (17–22)	No	China	College students	College students	0.11**	0.37***	0.32***	NE
Schade et al. (2021)	743	Internet trolling	54% female	Median = 25 (19–81)	No	Austria and Germany	40% students	23% tertiary education	Leadership = 0.28*** Entitlement and exhibitionism = 0.28*** Vulnerable = 0.21***	Primary = 0.40*** Secondary = 0.44***	0.27***	NE
Schade et al. (2021)	743	Cyber aggression	54% female	Median = 25 (19–81)	No	Austria and Germany	40% students	23% tertiary education	Leadership = 0.19*** Entitlement and exhibitionism = 0.21*** Vulnerable = 0.17***	Primary = 0.28*** Secondary = 0.30***	0.16***	
Nocera et al. (2022)	404	Cyberbullying	59% women	25.16 (18–29)	Yes	USA	45% enrolled in college	45% enrolled in college	NE	0.69–0.75 with four dimensions of cyberbullying	NE	0.74–0.82 with four dimensions of cyberbullying
Sánchez-Medina et al. (2020)	374	Sexual cyberbullying	NR	NR	No	Canary Islands (Spain)	Higher education students	Higher education students	0.461***	0.543***	0.608***	NE
Azami & Taremian (2021)	425	Cyberbullying	53.5% female	16.61	No	Iran	High school students	High school students	No relationship	No relationship	No relationship	NE
Afal et al. (2021)	200	Cyberbullying	NR	NR	No	Pakistan	Adolescents	Adolescents	A combined scale of Dark Triad −0.04			NE

Table 4.1 (*cont.*)

Study	Sample size	Type of behavior	Gender	Age (mean)	MTurk or similar	Country	Occupation	Education	Narcissists	Psychopathy	Machiavellianism	Sadism
							Sample characteristics			Correlations		
Giumetti et al. (2022)	317	Cyberbullying perpetration (Time 1)	80.1% female	21.24 (19–31)	No	USA	College students	College students	0.16*	0.36*	0.33*	NE
Giumetti et al. (2022)	317	Cyberbullying perpetration (Time 2)	80.1% female	21.24 (19–31)	No	USA	College students	College students	0.10	0.27*	0.25*	NE
Giumetti et al. (2022)	317	Traditional perpetration (Time 1)	80.1% female	21.24 (19–31)	No	USA	College students	College students	0.16*	0.40*	0.27*	NE
Giumetti et al. (2022)	317	Traditional perpetration (Time 2)	80.1% female	21.24 (19–31)	No	USA	College students	College students	0.18*	0.40*	0.27*	NE
March & Marrington (2023)	288	Antisocial online behavior	37.7% female	28.69	No	Australia (80.4%) and USA (9.4%)	NR	NR	0.31***	0.36***	0.34***	NE
Yuan et al. (2020a)	879	Cyberbullying	41.9% female	13.51	No	China	Junior high schools' students	Junior high schools' students	NE	NE	0.551***	NE
Antoniadou et al. (2019)	1,097	Online disinhibition	51% female	13.95 (12–17)	No	Greece	Junior high school students	Junior high school students	Only psychopathy was examined Grandiose-manipulative = 39***; callous-unemotional = 0.27***; Impulsive-irresponsible = 39***			NE
Goodboy & Martin (2015)	227	Cyberbullying (visual)	51.8% female	20.97 (18–40)	No	USA	Undergraduate students	Undergraduate students	19*	0.34***	0.26***	NE
Goodboy & Martin (2015)	227	Cyberbullying (text)	51.8% female	20.97 (18–40)	No	USA	Undergraduate students	Undergraduate students	0.27***	0.38***	0.30***	NE
Safaria et al. (2020)	2,407	Cyberbullying	50.1% female	13 (12–18)	No	Indonesia	School adolescents	School adolescents	0.126***	0.136***	0.175***	NE

Study	N	Construct	% Female	Age		Country	Setting 1	Setting 2				
Pabian et al. (2015)	324	Cyber aggression	63.0% female	16.05 (14–18)	No	Belgium	Adolescents from schools, scouting organizations & sports clubs	Adolescents from schools, scouting organizations & sports clubs	0.29***	0.43***	0.30***	NE
Wright et al. (2022)	683	Cyberbullying perpetration	46.7% female	13–16	No	China	School adolescents	School adolescents	NE	NE	Time 1 = 0.30* Time 2 = 0.31*	NE
Wright et al. (2022)	480	Cyberbullying perpetration	50.1% female	13–16	No	Cyprus	School adolescents	School adolescents	NE	NE	Time 1 = 0.26* Time 2 = 0.26*	NE
Wright et al. (2022)	480	Cyberbullying perpetration	46.5% female	13–16	No	India	School adolescents	School adolescents	NE	NE	Time 1 = 0.31* Time 2 = 0.31*	NE
Wright et al. (2022)	813	Cyberbullying perpetration	50.2% female	13–16	No	USA	School adolescents	School adolescents	NE	NE	Time 1 = 0.31* Time 2 = 0.31*	NE
Alavi et al. (2022)	323	Cyberbullying	53.56 female	18–26	No	Malaysia	NR	NR	SEM = significant relationship	SEM = significant relationship	SEM = no relationship	SEM = significant relationship
Gajda et al. (2022)	251	Cyberbullying	72.6% female	28.54 (18–60)	No	Poland	NR	Secondary, vocational, or higher education	0.192**	0.300***	0.273***	0.365***
Gajda et al. (2022)	251	Cyber victimization	72.6% female	28.54 (18–60)	No	Poland	NR	Secondary, vocational, or higher education	0.088	0.166**	0.142*	0.180**
Panatik et al. (2022)	400	Cyberbullying	70.8% female	18–37	No	Malaysia	Public universities students	Public universities students	0.274***	0.376***	0.417***	NE
Nocera & Dahlen (2017, 2020)	317	Cyberbullying perpetration	70% female	Median age = 20	No	USA	College student	College student	Pathological grandiosity = 0.24* Pathological vulnerability = 0.27*	0.42*	0.27*	0.50***
Nocera & Dahlen (2017, 2020)	317	Cyberbullying victimization	70% female	Median age = 20	No	USA	College student	College student	Pathological grandiosity = 0.21* Pathological vulnerability = 0.25*	0.37*	0.21*	0.47***

Table 4.1 *(cont.)*

Study	Sample size	Type of behavior	Gender	Age (mean)	MTurk or similar	Country	Occupation	Education	Narcissists	Psychopathy	Machiavellianism	Sadism
						Sample characteristics			Correlations			
Kircaburun et al. (2018a)	761	Cyberbullying	64% female	20.70	No	Turkey	Undergraduate students	Undergraduate students	0.30***	0.41***	0.46***	0.47***
Zhang et al. (2022)	501	Cyber aggression	49.10% female	14.01 (11–20)	No	China	Junior high school students	Junior high school students	0.22***	0.31***	0.32***	NE
Zerach (2016)	347	Cyberbullying victimization	58.2% female	NR	No	Israel	NR	NR	Vulnerability =0.19***; Grandiosity = 0.20**; Pathological = 0.20***	NE	NE	NE
Zerach (2016)	347	Cyberbullying offending	58.2% female	NR	No	Israel	NR	NR	Vulnerability = 0.10; Grandiosity = 0.08; Pathological = 0.10	NE	NE	NE
Pineda et al. (2022b)	393	Cyberbullying	46.3% female	14.18 (12–18)	No	Spain	High school students	High school students	0.05	0.13**	0.05	0.19**
Shahnawaz et al. (2020)	207	Cyber aggression	NR	16–19	No	India	Adolescents	Adolescents	NE	NE	NE	0.349**
Asih (2023)	292	Cyberbullying	70.89% female	Most of the sample = 25–27	WhatsApp	Indonesia	NR	29.11% graduate and post graduate; 58.9% diploma & undergraduate	0.1096	0.5329**	0.0014	NE
Cheng & Lee (2022)	162	Victimization	74.69% female	NR	No	Malaysia	Undergraduate student	Undergraduate student	0.07	0.30*	0.24**	
Kurek et al. (2019)	709	Cyber aggression	50.5% female	15.56 (13–17)	No	New Zealand	High school students	High school students	0.17**	0.05	NR	0.26**
Jin et al. (2022)	1,921	Online deviant behavior	40.45% female	15.03	No	China	Middle and high school students	Middle and high school students	0.29***	0.36***	0.32***	NE

							High school students	High school students	Path analysis results: no direct relationship	Path analysis results: no direct relationship	Path analysis results: direct relationship	NE
Sari & Adriani (2022)	943	Cyberbullying	60.44% female	NR	No	Indonesia	High school students	High school students	0.20**	0.41**	0.21**	NE
Demircioğlu & Köse (2022)	547	Cyberbullying	49.9% female	15.8	No	Turkey	High school students	High school students	0.183***	0.176****	0.330***	NE
Leite et al. (2023)	773	Online harassment total	60.4% female	27.39 (19–78)	No	Portugal	NR	Mean years of educative = 13.06				NE
Lai et al. (2023)	327	Rumor-sharing intention	52.9% female	30.66	No	China	NR	NR	0.1220*	0.276**	0.393**	NE
Huang et al. (2023)	571	Cyberbullying	40.6% female	14.53 (12–16)	No	China	Highschool students	Highschool students	0.17***	0.32***	0.36***	NE
Miran et al. (2023)	801	Cyberbullying	52.1% female	18 to 23	No	Pakistan	NR	NR	NE	0.66***	NE	NE
Pabian & Vandebosch (2023)	2,000	Online aggression perpetration	53.9% female	49.89 (19–79)	No	The Netherlands	NR	NR	0.19***	0.27***	0.15***	0.29***
Pabian & Vandebosch (2023)	2,000	Online moral disengagement	53.9% female	49.89 (19–79)	No	The Netherlands	NR	NR	0.32***	0.52***	0.39***	0.59***
Pabian & Vandebosch (2023)	2,000	Online aggression victimization	53.9% female	49.89 (19–79)	No	The Netherlands	NR	NR	0.17***	0.24***	0.09***	0.19***

Note: AT = Amazon Turk; NR = not reported; NE = not examined; GN = grandiose narcissism; VN = vulnerable narcissism; SNS = social network sites.
* $p < 0.05$; ** $p < 0.01$; *** $p < 0.001$.

CHAPTER 5

Dark Triad/Tetrad and Hate Behaviors
Cyberstalking and Trolling

A certain degree of overlap exists between *trolling* and *cyberstalking*, as both acts involve hateful behaviors that are repeated online and harmful. Yet differences can also be seen between the two. *Trolling* refers to deceptive, disruptive, and destructive acts in an online social setting with no apparent purpose. *Cyberstalking*, on the other hand, refers to the repeated targeting of a specific person via the Internet in a manner that causes the victim to experience distress or fear (similar to traditional offline stalking). Based on these definitions, trolls could sometimes be considered cyberstalkers and vice versa (McEwan, 2014). Unlike trolling, however, cyberstalking typically entails behaviors that are targeted toward a specific individual, often someone with whom the stalker is familiar (such as a former romantic partner), and that occur over an extended period of time (Swenson-Lepper & Kerby, 2019). Bhasin and Mehta (2019) contend that trolling is cyberstalking. Perhaps they mean to argue that both behaviors entail similar actions. Yet their victims differ greatly, as trolling targets a much larger population than cyberstalking. This chapter focuses on these two undesirable behaviors that share a similar activating source, that is, the Dark Tetrad. First, a range of aspects are addressed in relation to cyberstalking, followed by the addressing of these same aspects in relation to trolling.

5.1 Cyberstalking

The act of stalking relates to the willful, repeated, and malicious behavior of following or harassing another person. Most cases that are reported entail the stalking of a former, current, or desired intimate partner, are continuously on the rise, and could result in physical, psychological, or financial distress (Coleman, 1997). Gamache et al. (2021) present two dimensions of stalking: hyper-intimacy and domineering control. The former includes typical courtship activities that are taken to an extreme, as well as the invasion of personal boundaries and relationships; the latter includes behaviors that reflect hostile control and domination of the other, including overt threats and intimidation. Domineering control also comprises more intrusive forms of control and boundary violations (e.g., going through other people's voicemails, emails, or social media accounts) and even surveillance and spying. It should be noted that while both dimensions of stalking include behaviors that may correspond with cyberstalking, they differ in their online behaviors: the hyperintimacy dimension is greatly related to an ongoing search for closeness and intimacy, while the domineering control dimension is greatly based on aggressiveness and coercion (e.g., provoking an argument online or intruding on social media/applications).

The significant prevalence of technology in everyday life has led to increased access to the personal information of others – circumstances that greatly facilitate cyberstalking, thanks to the relative ease of stalking an intimate partner online (Smoker & March, 2017). Nevertheless, unlike the large corpus of research on more traditional, overt forms of stalking, the literature is lacking in studies on cyberstalking, particularly that of an intimate partner (Smoker & March, 2017). The National Centre for Cyberstalking Research in the United Kingdom defines cyberstalking as "A course of action that involves more than one incident perpetrated through or utilizing electronic means that causes distress, fear, or alarm" (Maple et al., 2011, p. 4). Although similarities can be seen in how *cyberstalking* is defined, definitions tend to differ in the aspects that they emphasize or overlook. For example, cyberstalking has been defined as the use of technology for repeatedly monitoring and/or harassing another person, and it is commonly directed toward current or former intimate partners, primarily to achieve or maintain a romantic connection (March et al., 2021a; Branković et al., 2022).

Indeed, cyberstalking relates to the stalking of others through electronic and communication means, including hidden webcams, global positioning systems (GPS), and spyware, that enable the monitoring of their victim's behaviors, while maintaining anonymity through fake online profiles (Smoker & March, 2017; March, 2022). Cyberstalking behaviors may include remote surveillance, persistent contact, and direct threats to the victim. According to Meloy (1998), the Internet provides four unique aspects for stalkers: (1) lack of social constraints and anxiety; (2) lack of sensory information from the target; (3) increased potential deception; and (4) the element of surprise when reality does not conform to the stalker's fantasized involvement with the target. Users may stalk their ex-partners via the Internet, obsessively following posts they publish to track their every move. They also tend to frequent their ex-partner's Facebook page, particularly if they did not instigate their breakup (Stiff, 2019).

The cyberstalking of an intimate partner can be employed to secretly gain information about the target, especially in the initiation stages of a relationship or in response to perceived relationship threats. Intimate partners are more common targets of cyberstalking than complete strangers (Branković et al., 2022). Online platforms, such as social media, provide an opportunity for covertly monitoring an intimate partner's activities with minimal risk of being detected. Given the public nature of most social media profiles, the online monitoring of an intimate partner could be justified as acceptable, unavoidable even, since the information is automatically fed onto personal newsfeeds. This discreet, more passive form of cyberstalking capitalizes on publicly available information that is obtained without invasion. The cyberstalking of an intimate partner could also be elevated to include more invasive, deceptive behaviors – ones that directly intrude on the victim's privacy, often violating it. For example, logging into an intimate partner's social media account to check for activities, accessing an intimate partner's (password-protected) emails, and creating fake social media profiles to overcome privacy controls such as being blocked (March et al., 2017, 2022).

March et al. (2022) examined behavioral methods that are employed in actively pursuing an intimate partner online, in an attempt to gain information about the target. Among other concepts, the researchers explored whether the Dark Tetrad also relates to the cyberstalking of an intimate partner. Such actions may be: (1) *passive*, capitalizing on information that is publicly available and can be obtained without invasion; (2) *invasive*, directly intruding on and even violating the victim's privacy, such as logging into their social media account to check their activities, accessing their emails, or creating fake social media profiles to overcome privacy controls; and (3) *duplicitous*, posing as someone else by using a fake email or social media account, to provide them with online access to their victim, or using location settings on their victim's mobile devices to track their whereabouts.

5.2   The Impact of Cyberstalking on Victims

Stalking may impact the victim's psychological, physical, and financial well-being. Indeed, the vast majority of cyberstalking victims report being significantly affected by their experiences: 61% experience health consequences, 51% experience social consequences, 48% experience work consequences, and 41% experience educational consequences. While victims of cyberstalking and victims of offline stalking may suffer similar outcomes, those who are subjected to both types of behaviors combined are three times more likely to experience negative consequences than those who are victims of just one of these deviant behaviors (Harewell et al., 2021).

The most researched elements of cyberstalking victim impact are the far-reaching emotional and psychological consequences that manifest in the form of poor mental well-being, and whereby the greater the period of the cyberstalking, the more exacerbated its effects. For example, victims are twice as likely to experience mental health consequences when cyberstalking continues for more than one week, compared to victimization that occurs over a shorter period of time. The most prevalent emotions experienced by victims include depression, anxiety, stress, anger, low self-esteem, self-harm, shame, and isolation, as well as fear – which is a significant consequence of cyberstalking (Smoker & March, 2017; Harewell et al., 2021). Intrinsically linked to psychological effects, cyberstalking victims also experience physical symptoms that impact their social activities and everyday lives. Such symptoms may include changes to weight and appetite, difficulty sleeping, panic attacks, headaches, fatigue, nausea, and, in extreme cases, even self-harm (Smoker & March, 2017; Harewell et al., 2021). In addition, victims report spending tens of thousands of dollars on dealing with legal action, vandalism, relocation, and therapy (Smoker & March, 2017).

5.3   Cyber Surveillance

Stiff (2019) addresses the concept of *cyber surveillance* (that is similar yet not identical to stalking) specifically in relation to Facebook. According to the researcher, this type of surveillance occurs when a user follows the Facebook profile of a so-called friend, in an attempt to benefit from such actions, but not for the good of the victim. As such, seeking information about another user in order to purchase a suitable gift for them, for example, would *not* be considered surveillance. Moreover, the Facebook platform actively encourages visitors to browse through their friends' pages, where the latter voluntarily display various personal activities for others to see. As such, to distinguish between normative Facebook behaviors and cyber surveillance ones, the researcher notes that the latter entails deliberate, covert, and targeted activities, where the perpetrator does not simply scroll through their victim's feed, yet purposefully leverages the platform as a means for accessing the victim's personal profile, in order to conduct deviant behaviors against them.

Despite similarities between *cyber surveillance* and *cyberstalking*, these two behaviors differ in three distinct ways: (1) with cyber surveillance, the target could be any Facebook user to whom the surveillant has access, rather than a former or desired partner. These are mainly the surveillant's Facebook friends, or perhaps a non-friend who has defined their Facebook account as being visible to the public; (2) with cyberstalking, examining a former partner's Facebook profile is usually motivated by a desire to reconcile, or possibly a need for support in the transition to a new one. With cyber (Facebook) surveillance, however, no such support is sought. Instead, the surveillant is simply gathering information about the victim; and (3) the surveillance process does not entail aversive aspects for the perpetrator (who is happy to conduct this surveillance), unlike cyberstalking of a former intimate partner who may have moved on to a new romantic relationship (Stiff, 2019).

With romantic relationships, the decision to monitor a partner often stems from feelings of anxiety, hurt, betrayal, or suspicion. Technological applications facilitate surveillance, through monitoring behaviors, keystrokes, text messages, or phone calls, and can be conducted in several ways, from passive actions, such as remotely tracking a partner's use of technology from afar, to active strategies, such as soliciting information via mutual online acquaintances. The anonymity that the Internet provides enables people to view account information, track people's locations via GPS, or track a romantic partner's behavior – all unbeknown to the victim. The emergence of Facebook has been tied to increased proclivity for investigating a romantic partner's profile. Moreover, such privacy violations are associated with adverse outcomes of a romantic relationship (Hertlein & van Dyck, 2020). According to Hughes and Samuels (2021), control – achieved via surveillance and threats – involves the monitoring of a romantic partner via social media, emails, or telephone calls while using threats to encourage the victim to accommodate the perpetrator's desires. The following sections of this chapter focus on associations between the Dark Tetrad and cyberstalking. First, conceptual explanations regarding this relationship are presented, followed by research findings on this topic.

5.4   The Dark Triad/Tetrad and Cyberstalking

March et al. (2022) contend that people with higher levels of dark traits have a greater tendency to engage in intimate-partner cyberstalking.

Furthermore, there is a rationale whereby Dark Tetrad is expected to be related to various behavioral forms of cyberstalking. For example, the perpetration of intimate-partner cyberstalking has previously been attributed to increased sensation-seeking tendencies. It is therefore plausible that dark traits, which are associated with increased thrill-seeking and risk-taking characteristics (e.g., psychopathy), could be related to riskier cyberstalking behaviors, such as the employing of invasive cyberstalking methods (Branković et al., 2022; Leite et al., 2023).

5.4.1 *Narcissism*

Individuals with high narcissistic traits often respond to threats to their ego by exhibiting increased aggression. This suggests that narcissism (anger and jealousy) is crucial in stalking behaviors. Narcissists have an inflated view of self, cannot understand why others do not share their viewpoint, and may feel justified in exploiting or stalking others as a means for gaining admiration. Narcissists may be more likely to stalk others, due to their need to seek self-enhancement from social relationships and their compromised capacity for emotional and self-regulation (Ménard & Pincus, 2012). Essentially, narcissism comprises two primary forms: grandiose narcissism and vulnerable narcissism. The former is characterized by grandiosity, superiority, and dominance, while the latter is characterized by insecurity and ego-defensiveness, negative self-image, feelings of inadequacy, and negative emotionality. Unlike grandiose narcissism, vulnerable narcissism has been found to be correlated with aggressive/violent intimate-partner behaviors, such as sexual aggression and relationship violence. As intimate-partner cyberstalking is considered a form of aggressive behavior – one that is targeted toward a current or past intimate partner – vulnerable narcissism could be a predictor of such cyberstalking (March et al., 2020b).

5.4.2 *Psychopathy*

Indications of psychopathy are only seen in a minority of stalking perpetrators, mainly those who are motivated by something other than a desire to establish an affectional relationship with the victim. Individuals with relatively high psychopathic traits have been found to exhibit escalated stalking – in terms of frequency, severity, and diversity. They also appear to be relatively remorseless of the effects of their actions and tend to select victims who are vulnerable due to financial or employment-related issues (Smoker & March, 2017; Storey et al., 2009). Such individuals are characterized by high risk-taking behaviors, particularly in the form of psychological or romantic game-playing with a former or desired intimate partner (March, 2022). Psychopaths are more likely to engage in predatory and instrumental aggression, rather than emotional aggression, exhibiting such behaviors toward those with whom they are/would like to be intimate. As such, individuals with high psychopathy traits may specifically develop an intimate relationship with their victims, in order to produce an unstable environment in which they can satisfy their need for impulsivity and stimulation. Cyberstalking thereby enables perpetrators with high psychopathic traits to participate in malevolent romantic game playing, while physically distancing themselves from the potential emotional harm that their victim may suffer due to their relationship (Smoker & March, 2017).

According to March et al. (2020b), psychopathy may be primary or secondary. While primary psychopathy is characterized by emotional and affective deficits, secondary psychopathy is characterized by hostility, impulsivity, and antisocial behaviors. Given the vital role of impulsivity in secondary psychopathy, combined with limited self-control that increases the likelihood of cyberstalking, secondary psychopathy could be a significant predictor of intimate-partner cyberstalking. Using secondary psychopathy to predict such cyberstalking, therefore, suggests that impulsivity and poor self-control are central characteristics in this behavior, and also hints at the possible addictiveness of cyberstalking.

5.4.3   Machiavellianism

In close relationships, individuals with high traits of Machiavellianism tend to engage in emotional manipulation and are likely to believe that they themselves are being manipulated. Since these individuals benefit from strategic and regulating mating strategies, they cultivate relationships to serve their own needs. Distrust in a romantic partner, combined with the manipulative, exploitative, and deceptive nature of Machiavellianism, could motivate online surveillance as a defense strategy against personal or relational threats. Indeed, the methodical and calculated nature of online stalking could be especially appealing to the strategic, manipulative Machiavellian (Smoker & March, 2017).

Associated with moral flexibility and a tendency to deceive, individuals with high Machiavellianism traits have a dispositional propensity to manipulate and take advantage of others. In intimate relationships, such perpetrators have been shown to engage in emotional manipulation against their partners. People with high Machiavellianism traits are also vigilant and meditative in their behavior, and appear to be aware of their antisocial actions, covertly acting out against perceived threats. As such, the deceptive and manipulative behavior of the Machiavellian could be considered synonymous with the covert, deceitful nature of the cyberstalker (Smoker & March, 2017).

5.4.4 *Sadism*

Sadism is directly related to stalking since the rationale is that the perpetrator identifies the victim as someone who is worth harming and who will not understand why they have been targeted. A stalker with high levels of sadism will strive to frighten or demoralize their victim. For example, the perpetrator may leave evidence of their having had contact with the victim's personal property, such as removing or reorganizing certain items in the victim's home (Smoker & March, 2017; Hughes & Samuels, 2021). Stalkers with high traits of sadism have been shown to derive pleasure from intimidating and tormenting their victims. As individuals with high traits of sadism are motivated by dominance over others, they may employ covert means of stalking to achieve such control in either an intimate relationship (Kircaburun et al., 2018a; Hughes & Samuels, 2021) or in a nonromantic one, where the victim is random and previously unknown to the perpetrator (Smoker & March, 2017).

Although empirical studies are scarce, preliminary findings suggest that all Dark Triads significantly predict cyberstalking (Smoker & March, 2017; Kircaburun et al., 2018a). In a recent literature review, Wilson, Sheridan, and Garratt-Reed (2022) conclude that all Dark Tetrads are significant positive predictors of perpetrating cyberstalking in an intimate relationship, for both males and females. Moreover, Dark Tetrad traits appear to share similarities with the motivation and intent of perpetuating stalking behaviors. Nevertheless, research on this topic is limited, and as such, using Dark Tetrad traits for predicting cyberstalking is yet to be established (Smoker & March, 2017).

5.5 The Dark Triad/Tetrad and Cyber Surveillance

5.5.1 *Narcissism*

Although narcissists may be skilled at manipulating their online profiles and posts to fulfill their goals of self-aggrandizement and validation, they tend to lack empathy toward others, resulting in their disinterest in the online presence of people other than themselves. As such, it is unlikely that those high in narcissistic traits will engage in Facebook surveillance, which entails more sociable, outward-facing components that do not help such individuals fulfill their narcissistic goals (Stiff, 2019).

5.5.2 Psychopathy

People with psychopathic traits tend to dislike uncertainty, and as such, are motivated to decrease these unpleasant feelings. One method of doing so is by gathering information about their surroundings, in an attempt to enhance their feelings of control. Moreover, the greater their discomfort with such uncertainty, the greater their motivation to engage in behaviors that reduce their distress. Therefore, they may conduct Facebook surveillance, which, rather than serving a normative recreational purpose, may satisfy their voyeuristic tendencies and need for power and control (Stiff, 2019; March, 2022).

5.5.3 Machiavellianism

As Machiavellianism is linked to manipulating and exploiting others, individuals with high traits of this disorder will be more likely to engage in Facebook surveillance, leveraging this online platform to increase the advantageous information they possess. These individuals also enjoy gossiping, although discussing absent third parties is often negatively perceived as merely constituting frivolous cheap talk. It may fill a vital social function, as it enables the transmission of important information about others within a group. As the tendency to positively perceive gossip increases, users may increasingly use the Facebook platform for gathering such information. Indeed, since gossip offers a means for gathering information about others for the benefit of the gossiper, individuals with high traits of Machiavellianism may also endorse the use of talking as a means for gathering such information (Stiff, 2019).

5.6 Research Findings

The following sections present research findings on *Western cultures, non-Western cultures,* and *the Dark Tetrad and cyberstalking and surveillance* – as a means for controlling the culture variable when discussing the Dark Tetrad and cyberstalking. The primary expectation is that Dark Tetrad traits may be differentially related to intimate-partner cyberstalking across relationship contexts (March et al., 2021a). For example, a meta-analysis of 29 studies found a modest yet significant relationship (r = 0.200) between dark personalities and cyberstalking among juveniles (Wissink et al., 2023).

5.6.1 Western Cultures

In a study on 405 participants in Australia, March et al. (2020b) found that only vulnerable narcissism was a predictive factor of intimate-partner cyberstalking. Individuals with vulnerable narcissistic traits are hypersensitive to perceived interpersonal rejection, that may be internalized as a threat to their ego, in turn resulting in aggressive responses. Such individuals may, therefore, be motivated to cyberstalk their intimate partner to monitor their relationship and prevent narcissistic hurt should the relationship end. The researchers also contend that although previous studies show grandiose narcissism to be a significant predictor of intimate-partner cyberstalking, their findings indicate that grandiose narcissism no longer predicts this behavior when also including the vulnerable narcissistic factor, that is more correlated with violent intimate-partner behaviors, such as sexual aggression or violence.

March et al. (2020b) found that contrary to predictions, Machiavellianism was not a significant predictor of intimate partner cyberstalking, nor was primary psychopathy. Secondary psychopathy, on the other hand, was found to be such a predictor, in line with findings whereby impulsivity and poor self-control (characteristics of secondary psychopathy) are associated with increased cyberstalking. When examining predictors by gender, March et al. (2020b) found that vulnerable narcissism was a significant predictor of intimate-partner cyberstalking among women, while secondary psychopathy was such a predictor among men. The researchers claim that such results indicate possible gender-specific motives for intimate-partner cyberstalking, that is thought to be primarily motivated by the perpetrator's emotional attachment to the victim. Compared to men, women tend to engage in intimate-partner cyberstalking as a means for obtaining feelings of intimacy, possibly by preserving or establishing a relationship.

Using the vulnerable narcissism factor for predicting intimate-partner cyberstalking among women suggests that this is a strategic relationship-related behavior. Specifically, such behaviors in women might be best attributed to insecurity and ego-defensiveness, with their high sensitivity to rejection leading them to engage in preventive behaviors. Similarly, using the secondary psychopathy factor for predicting such behaviors among men suggests that this is thrill-seeking behavior that is grounded in their lack self-control capabilities. Men's motivation to cyberstalk their intimate partners may best be ascribed to sensation-seeking, whereby they are drawn to the tabooed thrill of the act despite their knowing that the behavior is unacceptable.

In a study on 449 participants from the United States, March et al. (2021a) found that across long-term and short-term relationships, people who cyberstalked their intimate partners presented higher Dark Tetrad traits, except for narcissism, in the long-term context. In a study on 689 participants from Australia, Smoker and March (2017) found that traits of Machiavellianism, narcissism, psychopathy, and sadism were all found to be significant predictors of engaging in intimate-partner cyberstalking behaviors, whereby the higher the levels of these traits, the more likely they are to engage in cyberstalking behaviors.

March et al. (2022), who studied 515 participants from the United States, found that all Dark Triad traits were positively related to over-all intimate-partner cyberstalking. Although psychopathy was correlated with all three behavioral forms of such cyberstalking (i.e., passive, inva-sive, and duplicitous), this was not so for the remaining traits. Narcissism and Machiavellianism, for example, were not found to be associated with the invasive form, and Machiavellianism was not found to be correlated with the duplicitous one. According to March et al. (2022), these dif-ferential patterns of correlations further establish the multidimensional nature of intimate partner cyberstalking. Associations between fundamen-tal social motives and behavioral forms of intimate-partner cyberstalking were sparse. Yet higher motivation for status, power, and mate seeking, as well as lower motivation for safety seeking, were found to be related to increased duplicitous cyberstalking. Moreover, high motivation for avoid-ing pathogens was found to be related to increased passive cyberstalking.

Ménard and Pincus (2012) found a positive association between vulner-able narcissism and cyberstalking in male college students in the United States in a sample of undergraduate students. Individuals with high traits of narcissism are considered sensitive to rejection and are aggressive in response to shame and guilt provoked by ego threats. In addition, inti-mate relationships may also threaten individuals with high narcissistic traits, due to their partner's familiarity with these undesirable narcissis-tic flaws. As such, individuals with narcissistic traits may conduct inter-personal cyberstalking to maintain the upper hand in a relationship and prevent potential narcissistic wounds leading to relationship dissolution (Smoker & March, 2017). In a sample of 1,804 participants from Quebec,

Canada, Gamache et al. (2021) found that Machiavellianism, where a cold and strategic approach to interpersonal relationships is applied, showed the strongest correlation with cyberstalking. Blais et al. (2023) examined 1,724 adults in Canada and found that across all three traits, only the anti-social facet of psychopathy and grandiose narcissism were related to cyber-stalking behavior within the past year; Machiavellianism and vulnerable narcissism were unrelated to cyberstalking. Leite et al. (2023) found in a sample of 773 Internet users from Portugal a strong and positive relation-ship between the Dark Triad traits and dimensions of cyberstalking and online harassment.

5.6.2 Non-Western Cultures

In a sample of 232 participants from Serbia, Branković et al. (2022) found that all Dark Tetrads were correlated with cyberstalking, yet differences were seen in relation to traditional offline stalking. Thus, psychopathy and sadism were related to more direct and overt forms of stalking (i.e., aggravated stalking), while narcissism and Machiavellianism were linked to more indirect covert ones (i.e., surveillance). Their findings highlight that the tendency toward a certain form of stalking depends on the perpe-trator's specific dark traits. Considering the social risk of stalking, such as harming their reputation, people with high traits of Machiavellianism and narcissism have been found to use more subtle stalking tactics, ones that are more difficult to trace. On the other hand, considering their more anti-social behaviors, individuals with high traits of psychopathy and sadism tend to implement more severe, in-person forms of stalking, often even benefitting from their victims knowing that they are stalking them, which could reflect the need for dominance and control or gratification of their sadistic desires. No differences in cyberstalking have been found between genders.

In a sample of 761 students from Turkey, Kircaburun et al. (2018a) found sadism to be associated with cyber trolling, cyberbullying, and cyberstalk-ing, with the latter two behaviors leading to greater deviant behaviors via social media platforms. The researchers concluded that perhaps a small minority of participants could not fulfill their need for cruelty, and as such, they became obsessed with the targets they were stalking online, fan-tasizing about making them suffer. In addition, their findings show that Machiavellianism is indirectly associated with problematic social media use, seen in cyberbullying and cyberstalking – yet only in the male sample and in the total one (not in the female sample).

Kircaburun et al. (2018a) also found that psychopathy was directly associated with cyberbullying and cyber trolling. Their findings show that narcissism is not associated with cyberbullying or cyber trolling but is related to higher cyberstalking (among the total and female samples). The researchers explained that women with high traits of narcissism appear to be more obsessed with online stalking than men, as a means for pursuing past or present intimate partners or harassing someone that is not to their liking. Given the nature of such behavior, those who engage in higher cyberstalking may be driven by the fear of missing out on what has been shared or posted by the target. Alternatively, they may simply be attempting to convey to the victim that they are watching their every (online) move. Moreover, such women may be continuously striving to have the upper hand in the relationship by following online interactions with their intimate partners. Finally, in two studies (N = 467) conducted in Brazil, da Silva et al. (2021) found that intimate partner cyberstalking is positively correlated with narcissism, psychopathy, and Machiavellianism.

5.6.3   The Dark Triad/Tetrad and Cyber Surveillance

In a sample of 257 participants in the United Kingdom, Stiff (2019) found that Machiavellianism leads to greater Facebook surveillance, which appears to be driven by the endorsement of gossip. The finding was the same for both Facebook tracking and investigating. For individuals with high traits of psychopathy, Facebook investigating was linked to intolerance of uncertainty, yet Facebook tracking was not. According to the researcher, these findings may relate to the pleasurable component of gathering information about another person without their knowledge as indeed this kind of surveillance is a more recreational type of activity. As those high in traits of psychopathy strive to relish feelings of power and control, they may also be keen to observe the profiles of others, as a means for satisfying their voyeuristic tendencies. Finally, narcissism was not found to predict either kind of Facebook surveillance, thereby supporting the concept whereby people with narcissistic traits are keen to have other people react to their profiles yet lack any interest in the social presence of others.

5.7   Trolling

The act of trolling is an interpersonal and antisocial behavior prominent in the Internet culture worldwide. A form of online bullying and harassment, trolling typically includes the instigating of aggressive arguments and the posting of inflammatory, malicious messages in online comment sections – with the aim of provoking reactions, disrupting discussions, and upsetting others (Craker & March, 2016). Much research has been devoted to exploring the phenomenon of *online trolling*. Laypersons have used the term in popular media and academic research to describe various online social behaviors, ranging from verbal abuse to hostile and bullying behaviors against other online community members (Lee et al., 2021).

Trolling has become increasingly pervasive among users of online social networking platforms. According to Craker and March (2016), the appeal to being a troll and engaging in such misconduct is enormous. Studies suggest that about one-quarter of people in the United States, 33% in Malaysia, and 11% in Hungary admit to having committed malicious online activities against strangers; in Europe, about 3% had experienced some degree of online bullying, as seen in a review of victim surveys (Reep-van den Bergh & Junger, 2018). While trolling has become a widely known Internet phenomenon, its definition remains unclear due to the large variety of practices that it encompasses. Trolling activities range from mocking individuals to disrupting online communities. The picture becomes especially vague when attempting to understand trolls' intentions and desired outcomes, which include self-gratification, amusement, and enjoyment, as well as thrill-seeking and even revenge (Verbalyte, Keitel, & Howard, 2022).

Trolling could be defined as a deviant, malicious, or antisocial online behavior with a motive to disrupt conversations and trigger conflicts (Coles & West, 2016). Alternatively, trolling could be defined as deceptive or destructive behavior in an online social environment (March, 2022). Others have defined trolling as an intentionally disruptive behavior that occurs (a) in the context of Internet discourse and (b) among users that have no relationship in real life (Fichman & Sanfilippo, 2016; Buckels et al., 2019). Trolls have also been defined as Internet users who aim to disrupt online interactions, while provoking others into conducting pointless and time-consuming discussions (Brubaker et al., 2021). Moreover, trolling often results in significant conflicts, emotional reactions, and disrupted communications – all for the benefit of the troll.

Trolling behaviors include instigating arguments by posting provocative or malicious messages, in a deliberate attempt to cause disruption and upset. Whatever their end goals, one critical aspect of such behavior is the sense of accomplishment that trolls achieve by gaining attention from others (Navarro-Carrillo et al., 2021; March, 2022). Acting alone or in cooperation with others, trolls either randomly or selectively target others, including social groups, political parties, corporate entities, and so forth. In some cases, trolling is merely a simpleminded attempt to annoy others. In other instances, however, trolls demonstrate such a degree of skill, creativity, dedication, and perseverance that their behaviors may be likened to an art form (Buckels et al., 2019).

Trolling behaviors should, however, be distinguished from other forms of antisocial online misconduct (Hardaker, 2010; Craker & March, 2016). For example, although both cyberstalking and trolling share certain attributes of aggression, the former lacks the disruptive and deceptive aspects that are prominent in trolling (Sest & March, 2017). Moreover, trolls strive to disrupt *strangers*, unlike cyberstalkers who usually know their victims and even target them specifically (Gylfason et al., 2021; Kircaburun et al., 2018a).

Online trolling has no apparent instrumental purpose (March et al., 2017; Kircaburun et al., 2018a; Papapicco & Quatera, 2019); it entails deliberate attempts to create discussions or sow discord through negative comments, insults, or provocations, while prolonging the length of the discussion. Acting as a troll is like a game of false identity, performed without the consent of the other players. Trolls try to be accepted as legitimate users, negatively intervening for as long as possible, until they are recognized as such by the others, at which time they tend to decrease their display of undesirable behaviors (Papapicco & Quatera, 2019).

When examining behaviors related to *trolling*, it is also essential to address the distinct behavior of *gender-trolling*, where although the so-called regular and anticipated trolling behaviors are exhibited, they are specifically targeted toward *female victims* (Mantilla, 2013; Paananen & Reichl, 2019). Mantilla (2013) presents a range of characteristics that distinguish gender trolling from random trolling. First, gender trolls are almost always men who make great concerted or coordinated efforts. Gender trolling also involves specific gender-based insults, such as the use of pejorative terms against women, as well as hateful, vicious, and vile language. Moreover, gender-trolling includes a credible component of threats, such as threats of physical harm (rape, torture, and even death), "doxxing" (revealing the offline identity of a person's online presence), or posting the home or work address of the victim, while encouraging others to also behave menacingly toward them (threatening their physical or professional safety). In addition, gender trolling tends to persist over long periods of time, years even in some extreme cases. Finally, this form of trolling nearly always occurs following the female victims having spoken out against some form of sexism.

The uncivil behavior of trolling could be explained through *schaden-freude*, a German term that refers to taking joy in other people's misfortunes or wishing that others may suffer adverse outcomes. People with dark personalities exhibit greater *schadenfreude* for both legal and non-legal stimuli. For example, when presented with legal stimuli, they were found to smile more intensely than others, suggesting that they experience greater levels of *schadenfreude*. Such a relationship was seen specifically in people with traits of psychopathy, who were found to employ laughter (i.e., negative humor) as a means for harming others (Porter et al., 2014). *Schadenfreude* has also been linked to narcissism and downward social comparison, where online users with lower self-esteem and less favorable opinions about themselves are more likely to experience *schadenfreude* when they see others fail. Moreover, *Lulz*, where trolls enjoy watching others suffer, could also be considered *schadenfreude*, that is, experiencing feelings of pleasure that stem from *passively* observing the suffering of others rather than from actively making others suffer (Brubaker et al., 2021).

In general, online trolling, which is greatly dependent on the specific context and circumstances, encompasses the following three components: behavior, intention, and motivation. Nevertheless, while observers might perceive all online antisocial behaviors (such as online insults and expressions of aggression) as a form of trolling, this is not necessarily so. For example, while *flaming*, which has been historically studied as online hostility and aggression, could be employed as a trolling tactic, not all forms of online trolling are hostile or aggressive. In many cases, trolls may simply use disingenuous politeness, misplaced humor, and overly sarcastic comments to cause annoyance and disruption in an online community (Lee et al., 2021).

Furian and March (2023) argue that as trolling is characterized by aggression, the I3 Theory of Aggression could provide an appropriate framework for understanding such perpetration. According to this theory, aggressive behaviors emerge via three interrelated processes: (1) instigation (i.e., exposure to environmental stimuli that promote aggression); (2) impellance (i.e., dispositional and stable factors, such as personality, that increase the likelihood of an aggressive response); and (3) inhibition (i.e., dispositional and stable factors, such as personality, that reduce the likelihood of an aggressive response). The Dark Tetrad is represented in the *impellance* part of this model. According to these researchers, in addition to the I3 Theory of Aggression being applicable for explaining trolling behaviors, it may also be used to explore additional antisocial online behaviors, such as cyberbullying or cyberstalking.

5.8   Victims of Trolling

Preventing and stopping trolling is particularly important in light of its damaging psychological impact on the victim, which is even greater than that of cyberbullying and in-person harassment (Gylfason et al., 2021). According to Sorokowski et al. (2020), offensive behaviors, such as trolling, have long been identified as a significant social problem. It is not surprising, therefore, that along with the hugely increasing popularity of the Internet, an increase has been seen in online behaviors of hatred. Moreover, such hateful behaviors have been shown to increase negative emotions, death by suicide, and even the assassination of public figures. Interestingly, not only humans are affected by online hateful behaviors, with hate campaigns leading to the failure of large-budget movies, for example. Indeed, in light of the hugely increasing prevalence of online hate behavior, research on the causes, signs, outcomes, and solutions to such behavior has also greatly increased.

By intentionally attacking individuals, online trolls strive to anonymously create discord through deception across all pages of an online social community. The adverse outcomes of their behaviors include (a) posting inflammatory statements or hate language to aggravate users; (b) inhibiting the growth of an online community or attempting to divide it; (c) excluding or attacking new users; (d) encouraging polarization of beliefs and hostility in groups; and (e) tricking users into an aimless debate (Jeffrey, Peltier, & Vannest, 2020). Internet trolling deliberately makes others feel uncomfortable or frustrated or disrupts the community by directing aggressive, inflammatory, and destructive comments toward victims. As with antisocial face-to-face interactions, Internet trolling can cause severe outcomes for the victims, including depression and anxiety. Experiencing defamation on the Internet also increases negative emotions, such as sadness or despair, while inhibiting the development and maintenance of interpersonal relationships. Studies show that these adverse effects of being a victim of trolling may last more than three years (Masui, 2019). In some cases, victims even experience increased suicidal ideation and self-harm (March, 2022). Additional reactions to suffering at the hands of an online troll may include frustration, anger, depression, shame, humiliation, low self-esteem, paranoia, disempowerment, symptoms of post-traumatic stress disorder, substance abuse, and even online and offline social withdrawal (Jeffrey et al., 2020).

Individuals with a role of online responsibility, such as website moderators or those in charge of keeping the order on public message boards, also experience a range of adverse outcomes following the frequenting of trolls on these platforms, including depression, anxiety, and trauma-like symptoms, sometimes even after just a brief encounter. While the upsetting prevalence and intensity of trolling behaviors have prompted some members of online social media forums to seek online emotional support from others, formal therapeutic support groups for troll victims are lacking. In summary, although trolls strive to disrupt digital *collectives*, trolling attacks also take a heavy toll on individual users (Jeffrey et al., 2020).

5.9 Dark Triad/Tetrad and Trolling

Despite the ever-increasing popularity of online dating sites, including location-based-real-time dating (LBRTD) applications (such as Tinder), trolling on such platforms is yet to be addressed in academic research (March et al., 2017). In general, despite growing public awareness, there is little empirical research on the phenomenon of trolling (Buckels, Trapnell, & Paulhus, 2014). However, according to Craker and March (2016) although still in its infancy, areas of academic research have begun to explore predictors of online misconduct. Moreover, despite the growing literature on hate behaviors, little is known about the personal characteristics of people who routinely engage in such activities (Sorokowski et al., 2020). The literature even lacks consensus on the definition of Internet hate or Internet haters – terms that refer to a broad range of derogatory behaviors. In addition, few studies have examined the personality traits and environmental factors that may promote or inhibit aggressive behaviors that are associated with Internet trolling (Masui, 2019). Despite this void in the scholarly literature, studies have offered various explanations regarding the dominating Dark Tetrad personalities that are entailed in trolling.

According to Lee et al. (2021), due to its high prevalence, trolling as a subject of academic study should be further clarified, as researchers use a range of criteria to describe the same phenomenon and address a range of different motivations and underlying processes that could lead to the same observed behavior. For example, when an individual behaves in an unruly and aggressive manner in an online community, the question that arises is whether this person is an emotional activist, an agent of opposing interest groups, or simply a bored teenager. When an Internet user posts provocative messages on an online discussion forum, such as opposing a majority position on a given issue, the question that arises is whether that user is vigorously defending an unpopular minority viewpoint or simply seeking to disrupt the discussion and create friction among community members.

In light of the latest research, a prototype troll is a man with a high level of psychopathic traits, with a tendency to sadism and a defect in empathy. These features, combined with high intelligence and proficiency in using digital technology, mean that trolls are often masters in manipulating others because they can use their knowledge to inflict emotional and moral suffering on victims while distancing themselves emotionally from their behavior (Kircaburun et al., 2018a; Stiff, 2019; Jabłońska & Zajdel, 2020; Necula, 2020).

From a lay perspective, Internet trolls exhibit characteristics of the classic Joker villain: a modern variant of the Trickster archetype from ancient folklore. Much like the Joker, trolls operate as agents of chaos on the Internet, exploiting "hot-button issues" to make users appear overly emotional or foolish. Should an unfortunate community member fall into their trap, the trolling tends to intensify merely for the merciless entertainment of the troll. This is why novice Internet users are routinely admonished with the words, "Don't feed the trolls!" (Buckels et al., 2014).

Hardaker (2010) contends that deception is characteristically necessary for trolling behaviors, with people who engage in trolling often portraying themselves differently on their trolling profiles than on their real ones. Aggression is also often used as a tactic in trolling behaviors (Hardaker, 2010; Craker & March, 2016). By employing malicious taunts and provocative comments, trolls can annoy or provoke others into retaliating. In addition, individuals who engage in trolling tend to create meaningless disruptions in their strive to gain attention or reactions from others (Hardaker, 2010). By combining *deception, aggression,* and *disorder,* trolls are able to achieve *success.* Hardaker (2010) suggests that individuals who engage in this behavior are motivated by their success in deceiving, aggravating, and disrupting the communities that they troll. If such success is not achieved, with their provocative attempts being ignored or misplaced, trolling individuals may broaden their trolling attacks or alternatively move on to new opportunities (Craker & March, 2016).

Lee et al. (2021) use the term *online trolls* to refer to people who express a minority opinion for purposes of amusement and with malicious intentions; on the other hand, they apply the term *vocal minorities* to refer to people who also express a minority opinion, yet are driven by strong convictions and ideologies, speaking out to defend their true beliefs. Moreover, these researchers posit that trolls have higher levels of dark personalities than vocal minorities. According to Kircaburun et al. (2018a), individuals engage in cyber trolling to overcome boredom, seek attention, and execute revenge while urging others to inflict harm on community members – all depicting dark personality traits.

Empirical evidence suggests clear patterns between cyber trolling and Dark Tetrad traits, especially psychopathy (Owen et al., 2017; Kircaburun et al., 2018a; Leite et al., 2023). According to Craker and March (2016), although research on trolling behaviors is limited, recent studies have identified associations between the Dark Tetrad and trolling behaviors. As such, Buckels et al. (2014) emphasize the importance of studying Dark Tetrad personality traits to further understand and profile trolls.

Navarro-Carrillo et al. (2021) examined whether online trolling behaviors are related to humor-related dispositions, especially "darker" humor-related characteristics. The researchers explain that trolls are online users who leverage their anonymous online presence to generate conflicts by presenting destructive comments and creating scenarios in which their potential victims may appear foolish. Based on empirical evidence, the researchers also claim that Dark Tetrad personality traits are significantly correlated with online trolling behaviors and with a greater tendency to engage in online trolling – as seen on various Internet platforms, such as Facebook or LBRTD applications. Notably, there is also increased convergence that while all dark personality factors may be positively related to the individual's engagement in online trolling, those of *psychopathy* are the most predictive of online trolling behaviors.

According to Navarro-Carrillo et al. (2021), studies have yet to disentangle associations between humor as an individual differentiating variable and online trolling. However, humor-based differences have been found to be relevant for predicting other derogatory online behaviors, such as cyberbullying among adolescents. Hence, one might anticipate that these findings may be generalized for additional disruptive online behaviors (such as trolling) and for additional personality tendencies in relation to "darker" humor-related characteristics. Buckels et al. (2014) argue that while the Dark Tetrad traits are yet to be investigated in the trolling literature, their relevance is suggested in research that links these traits to adolescent and adult bullying or that highlights the increased use of the Facebook platform by people with narcissistic traits – thus indicating that dark personalities leave large digital footprints.

According to Volkmer et al. (2023), the relationship between the Dark Tetrad and trolling may be due to lower affective empathy, a tendency for moral disengagement, and reduced behavioral inhibition anxiety in these individuals. Moreover, all four facets are positively associated with dominance, and social dominance orientation is known to be associated with both past trolling and trolling acceptance. An additional explanatory factor for the relationship between the Dark Tetrad and trolling behavior could be *intrinsic enjoyment*, as traits of narcissism, psychopathy, Machiavellianism, and sadism have been found to be positively correlated with the individual's enjoyment when viewing violent stimuli. *Narcissism* is the dimension of antagonism that primarily drives aggressive behaviors. However, all narcissistic dimensions have been found to be related to such behaviors, at least to a certain degree. *Psychopathy* may also be related to trolling behaviors due to its association with impulsivity. With Machiavellianism, the fast and sometimes impulsive nature of trolling may not appeal to their controlled and calculating nature (Furian & March, 2023). Finally, *sadism* has been found to be related to experiencing great pleasure during aggressive encounters. Associations between sadism and aggressive behaviors may be enhanced when conducted online due to the anonymity that the Internet offers (Furian & March, 2023).

The following sections present theories and explanations regarding the motives of each Dark Tetrad in trolling.

5.9.1   Narcissism and Trolling

The literature provides few explanations about the relationship between narcissism and trolling, yet there is some consensus that narcissism is a mild predictor of trolling (Lopes & Yu, 2017). One possible reason for such low associations could be that narcissism is not significantly related to online disinhibition. Another possible explanation is that narcissism may be milder than the other three Dark Tetrad traits when correlated with antisocial online behaviors (Wu et al., 2022). The reason is that while research indicates that sadism, Machiavellianism and psychopathy are linked to fast-life speed and decreased consideration of future consequences, narcissism is associated with slow-life history and increased consideration of future consequences.

Alternatively, this lack of association could stem from people with narcissistic traits being more preoccupied with themselves than with others while perceiving themselves as superior to others and more popular than others - at least compared to less popular individuals (Lopes & Yu, 2017). As narcissism is associated with downward social comparison rather than with trolling, associations between narcissism and trolling will likely be lacking (Lopes & Yu, 2017; Manuoğlu & Öner-Özkan, 2022). March (2019) even reports a *negative* relationship between vulnerable narcissism and Internet trolling, explaining that unlike grandiose narcissism, vulnerable narcissism is considered more defensive, masks feelings of inadequacy, and is associated with higher interpersonal distress. The negative relationship between vulnerable narcissism and Internet trolling suggests that Internet trolls are not necessarily insecure or responding to threats to their egos. Rather, their self-worth is intact and is not contingent on the recognition of others. In summary, narcissism is not expected to have any profound relationship with trolling.

5.9.2 *Psychopathy and Trolling*

Psychopathy is expected to be associated with trolling since those who troll on online platforms such as Facebook are likely to be driven by a need to satisfy their predatory impulses while lacking a display of guilt for the distress they have caused others. Internet trolls may be less impulsive, neurotic, and emotionally reactive than individuals with secondary psychopathy, yet more callous, manipulative, and lacking in remorse, similar to individuals with primary psychopathy (Manuoğlu & Öner-Özkan, 2022; March, 2022; Marrington et al., 2023). Moreover, people with high levels of psychopathy are more prone to impulsive, violent, and antisocial behaviors yet are less empathetic toward others. Since a defining feature of online trolls is disregarding the harm that their actions may cause others, they will score higher on psychopathy scales than vocal minorities (Lee et al., 2021). According to March and Steele (2020), the thrill-seeking nature of individuals with high levels of psychopathy traits could enjoy the thrill of causing online social mayhem through trolling. Furthermore, the empathy deficits and deceitful interpersonal characteristics of psychopathy align with those of trolling and callous, unprovoked attacks on other online users (Manuoğlu & Öner-Özkan, 2022).

Finally, Lopes and Yu (2017) argue that psychopaths might have different motivations when trolling. On the one hand, they may want to prey on weaker victims by exploiting their weaknesses (such as low self-esteem and attention-seeking behaviors). Nevertheless, they may also be motivated to bully socially salient and famous people, either as a means for undermining their social status or simply for fun. In other words, the sadistic tendencies of psychopaths are what lead them to enjoy bullying people who are perceived as physically attractive, wealthy, or famous – simply because they are more socially salient and attract greater attention than others (Marrington et al., 2023).

5.9.3   Machiavellians and Trolling

Machiavellianism refers to an individual's tendency to manipulate others for personal gain. According to Lee et al. (2021), since they tend to deceive others while disrupting online discussions for their personal gain, trolls will exhibit higher signs of Machiavellianism than the vocal minority. Furthermore, since individuals with traits of Machiavellianism tend to control others, they may also want to persuade other individuals to adopt similar opinions and behaviors. Thus, people who score high on Machiavellianism traits will express their counternormative attitudes without hesitation when confronting other people with different views. Hence, Machiavellianism is a distinctive personality marker that can differentiate vocal minorities from other online users (Lee et al., 2021). However, associations between Machiavellianism and trolling will likely be modest (Manuoğlu & Öner-Özkan, 2022), perhaps since people with traits of Machiavellian are extremely calculated and cautious in their behavior, and trolling could expose them, rendering them more vulnerable.

5.9.4   Sadism and Trolling

Buckels et al. (2014) state that everyday sadism is the most relevant dark personality with regards to trolling, since the trolling culture embraces a concept that is virtually synonymous with sadistic pleasure, known as *Lulz*. There is undoubtedly some pleasure to be gained from a clever retort or jab at an irritating online target. For individuals with sadistic personality traits, such pleasure is sufficiently motivating for inflicting harm on undeserving targets. Cruel behavior is enabled by inhibiting empathy and downplaying repercussions. With increasing Internet access, sadists can easily indulge their appetite for cruelty. This combination of (heightened) appetitive and (diminished) avoidance processes may help explain why online trolls behave the way they do toward their targets (Buckels et al., 2019). In other words, trolling is an example of everyday sadism: fueled by sadistic pleasure, unleashed by rationalization (Buckels et al., 2019; Furian & March, 2023; Marrington et al., 2023; Volkmer et al., 2023).

The unfettered nature of this new social playground, namely trolling, has revealed (encouraged even) a sadistic subgroup of players. No longer limited to anecdotal reports, evidence from empirical research is fast accumulating, whereby online trolls enjoy being cruel to others. They are even dispositionally sensitive to the rewards afforded by interpersonal cruelty and the humiliation of others (Buckels et al., 2014, 2019; Furian & March, 2023; Marrington et al., 2023). According to March and Steele (2020), individuals with high traits of sadism derive enjoyment and pleasure from inflicting physical or emotional pain and humiliation onto others. As such, trolling manifests as online sadism, with trolls using the Internet as their virtual "playground" in which to derive enjoyment at the expense of other users. Buckels et al. (2014) further contend that sadists tend to troll simply because they enjoy it. In other words, both trolls and sadists feel sadistic glee at the distress of others.

Not only do individuals with high traits of sadism enjoy harming others, but they are also willing to endure personal strain and sacrifice – just for the opportunity to do so. This behavior is also characteristic of trolls, who invest significant time and energy in anonymously disrupting and destroying online spaces, where the cloak of anonymity allows trolls to act on normally inhibited sadistic impulses. As such, trolls use this online anonymity to inflict pain on others, deriving pleasure and enjoyment from their suffering. March and Steele (2020) further suggest that the combination of psychopathy and sadism paints the Internet troll as a callous individual who lacks empathy and enjoys causing harm to others.

An interesting study (Paananen & Reichl, 2019) that examined gender-trolling in the United States, India, and Canada, namely trolling against females, found a very strong relationship between three dimensions of sadism (verbal, physical, and vicarious sadism) and gender trolling. The researchers conclude that gender trolls, like random trolls, are prototypical everyday sadists motivated primarily by the sadistic pleasure of victimizing others.

5.10 Research Findings

As in Chapters 2 and 4, the following sections present research findings by *Western* and *non-Western* cultures to examine possible associations between the Dark Tetrad and trolling while controlling the culture variable.

5.10.1 Western Cultures

In two online samples in the United States (total N = 1,215), Buckels et al. (2014) found that of all personality measures, including the Dark Triad and the Big Five, sadism was most robustly associated with trolling. In fact, these associations were so strong that it could even be said that online trolls are prototypical everyday sadists. The authors also noted that Dark Tetrad associations were specific to trolling. The enjoyment of other online activities, such as chatting and debating, was unrelated to sadism. The subsequent analysis also confirmed that Dark Tetrad–sadism associations were mainly due to the overlap between trolling and sadism. When conducting multiple regression, only sadism was found to predict trolling.

When controlling for sadism and other Dark Tetrad measures, narcissism was found to be negatively associated with trolling enjoyment. Notably, the researchers found that when controlling for enjoyment, the impact of sadism on trolling decreased by nearly one-half; moreover, the indirect effect of sadism through enjoyment was substantial, even remaining significant when controlling for overlap with Dark Triad scores. These findings indicate how sadism fosters trolling behaviors (Buckels et al., 2014).

In a later study, Buckels et al. (2019) conducted two studies with a total of 1,715 participants in the United States. In Study 1, the participants were asked to view stimuli depicting emotional/physical suffering and provide ratings of (a) perceived pain intensity and (b) levels of pleasure while viewing the photos. In Study 2, an online trolling questionnaire was developed and validated. The researchers found that people who conduct trolling behaviors and those with sadistic traits both tend to minimize the harm caused by an aggressive act, compared to others who lack such traits, and they also react more positively (i.e., with greater joy and happiness) to harmful written scenarios compared to their normative counterparts. Notably, associations between trolling and sadism were uniquely significant and could not be explained by broader forms of antisociality (i.e., aggression traits, callous-unemotionality, and psychopathy scores).

In a study of 415 participants, mainly from Australia (48%) and the United States (18.6%), Sest and March (2017) found that psychopathy and sadism traits were significant positive predictors of trolling behaviors. They explained that as trait psychopathy is characterized by impulsivity and thrill-seeking behaviors, creating online mayhem may serve as a central motivator in trolling. Furthermore, as individuals with high levels of everyday sadism traits experience enjoyment from hurting others, trolls may be motivated to inflict cruelty online. The researchers also found that addressing cognitive empathy as a predicting variable of trolling behaviors is contingent on individual trait psychopathy; specifically, when levels of trait psychopathy are high, individuals with higher levels of cognitive empathy are more likely to engage in trolling behaviors. The researchers explained that psychopathy is commonly associated with deficits in *affective* empathy rather than cognitive empathy, which usually remains intact. However, speculative, higher cognitive empathy may allow trolls to determine when they have succeeded in emotionally manipulating their victim (e.g., causing embarrassment or anger). Thus, Sest and March (2017) conclude that trolls who are most likely to be experts at inflicting emotional suffering on their victims will be those with high-trait psychopathy and high cognitive empathy.

Brubaker et al. (2021) examined 438 Reddit users in the United States. This online social news aggregator and discussion platform allows people to discuss various issues with other communities of interested persons. A hugely popular website, in 2020, Reddit was ranked the 6th most visited website in the United States and 18th in web traffic worldwide. However, Reddit is not a typical news aggregator website; it has traditionally carried a reputation as an online forum with a "seedy underbelly" where users can (and do) engage in hateful conduct. Brubaker et al. (2021) applied a composite scale of the Dark Triad that combined all items of the three traits into one Dark Triad scale. The results reveal that malicious motives, particularly *schadenfreude*, mediate the Dark Triad's influence on trolling. Although individuals may exhibit darker personality traits – suggesting that they are more self-centered, cunning, and insensitive to the needs of others (i.e., the Dark Triad) – simply possessing these traits does not mean that one will necessarily engage in online trolling. However, those who exhibit traits of narcissism, Machiavellianism, and psychopathy are more likely to demonstrate trolling behaviors if they enjoy passively observing the suffering of others. Moreover, those who possess these traits require self-enhancement that spirals into downward social comparisons, which, as the findings suggest, could result in trolling behaviors.

Brubaker et al. (2021) also conclude that as *schadenfreude* motivation is necessary for people with Dark Triad traits to engage in trolling, individuals who frequently observe and obtain pleasure from the defects of others are more likely to engage in trolling behaviors. The researchers claim that motives for conducting online trolling behaviors on Reddit stem from a combination of maladjusted personality traits – mainly Machiavellianism, psychopathy, and narcissism – coupled with *schadenfreude*, which, when combined, serve as the impetus for trolling behaviors. Yet these personality traits alone do not directly predict trolling since they are primarily associated with the individual; in other words, even if the online user is cunning and evil, unstable and selfish, these traits alone will not necessarily be manifested through online interactions. The researchers, therefore, conclude that the instigating factor in trolling behaviors is the *desire* to derive pleasure by either observing or inflicting suffering on others.

In a survey of 396 adults in Australia, Craker and March (2016) did not find associations between narcissism or Machiavellianism and trolling behaviors on Facebook, yet they did find psychopathy and sadism to be positive predictors of such trolling. Thus, individuals who troll on Facebook are more likely to lack empathy, be driven by the satisfaction of predatory impulses, and show brazen disregard for the psychological distress caused to others (psychopathy). They are also more likely to be ruthless, emotionally cruel, and driven by the pleasure that they obtain through the pain and discomfort of others (sadism). The researchers conclude that trolls even leverage the Facebook platform to gratify their desire to achieve negative social power by creating social chaos and negative interpersonal interactions.

Gylfason et al. (2021), who conducted a study that included 139 participants in Iceland, found that sadism, psychopathy, and Machiavellianism are positively correlated with Facebook trolling behaviors, with sadism serving as the strongest predictor. A positive yet nonsignificant association was also seen between narcissism and trolling. Finally, Machiavellianism was found to be a unique predictor of trolling behavior, which is not surprising since manipulation is a crucial component of Machiavellianism. The researchers also found that enjoying trolling is positively connected with traits of sadism and Machiavellianism and that sadism, psychopathy, and Machiavellianism are related to the enjoyment that stems from conducting debates. In addition, narcissism was positively associated with enjoyment from chatting. When conducting mediation analysis, the researchers found that the enjoyment of trolling fully mediated the relationship between Machiavellianism and trolling behaviors. They, therefore, mention that it is possible that individuals with high levels of Machiavellianism traits may troll simply because they enjoy doing so. The motivation to troll for Machiavellian purposes (i.e., to control and manipulate others) could be understood as merely taking pleasure in this activity. Motivation may differ for the other variables connected with trolling. Finally, no differences were seen in their findings by gender.

Navarro-Carrillo et al. (2021), who conducted a study on 201 undergraduate students in Spain, found moderate-to-strong associations between online trolling and traits of sadism, Machiavellianism, and psychopathy. As in prior research, narcissistic tendencies seem less relevant for constructing a personality profile of trolls. However, these data offer a convincing generalization of the strong associations between dark personality traits and the perpetration of online trolling – in an alternative sociocultural context (i.e., Spain) where such links have not yet been examined. Furthermore, their findings suggest that "darker" humor-related characteristics, such as joy that stems from laughing at others, may complement the personality effects of the more general dark traits, such as sadism or psychopathy, on online trolling. As such, psychopathy emerges as the most relevant predictor of online trolling.

Navarro-Carrillo et al. (2021) found that the predictive utility of psychopathy regarding online trolling is contingent on katagelasticism (a psychological condition in which a person excessively enjoys laughing at others; see Katagelasticism, 2023). More specifically, only in cases of high levels of katagelasticism will individuals with higher levels of psychopathy be inclined to perpetrate trolling behaviors. The researchers even state that elevated joy from laughing at others could perhaps be construed as a psychopathic manifestation – one that is linked to ridicule and laughter – and that those (nonpathological) psychopaths most prone to this humorous tendency could be perceived as having a representative troll profile. In other words, online trolling would not only be associated with the pleasure of provoking and annoying others but also with the enjoyment derived from ridiculing and making fun of them. These ideas support the assertion that humorous motivation underlies online trolling.

Lee et al. (2021), who performed an experimental study among 599 English-speaking participants in the United States, found that trolls scored the highest on psychopathy and sadism traits – significantly higher than participants of the normative majority, the social conformers, and the silent minority groups. However, only sadism was found to be a distinctive marker that distinguishes trolls from vocal minorities. Contrary to their prediction, the vocal minority group scored the highest on Machiavellianism, significantly higher than the trolls, the normative majority, and the social conformers – an unexpected finding. As people with traits of Machiavellianism tend to manipulate others for their own personal gain, they may also wish to persuade others to take a similar stand. In other words, people with high levels of Machiavellianism may express their counternormative attitudes without hesitation when encountering people with different or contradicting views of their own. Hence, Machiavellianism is a distinctive personality marker that could differentiate vocal minorities from other online users.

March et al. (2017) examined trolling on dating applications among 357 adults in Australia. The researchers found that similar to previous findings, sadism and psychopathy are associated with trolling behaviors, with individuals who perform trolling behaviors on cyber applications seemingly enjoying the taunting and humiliating of others, seeking opportunities to do so (i.e., trait sadism) and satisfying their predatory impulsive goals with brazen disregard for the pain caused to others (i.e., trait psychopathy). Consistent with previous studies, the researchers found that traits of narcissism and Machiavellianism were not predictive of trolling behaviors. The researchers explain that the self-absorption of narcissism and the strategic, manipulative nature of Machiavellianism might work in contrast to the impulsive and disruptive nature of people who engage in trolling behaviors. Individuals who engage in such behaviors seem to enjoy inflicting psychological and emotional harm on others (i.e., trait sadism), combined with a tendency to act carelessly and impulsively (i.e., trait psychopathy). As with the online troll, the dating applications troll is sadistic, psychopathic, and dysfunctionally impulsive. However, no differences between genders were found regarding trolling behaviors on dating applications, and gender was not found to moderate associations between personality traits and trolling behaviors. The weak effect of gender seems to be a common finding for trolling.

Papapicco and Quatera. (2019) analyzed fake profiles on the most infamous online "hunting ground" platforms, such as social networks, to create a taxonomy using emotional analysis. In the study, four fake Facebook profiles were analyzed, which were unmasked by real users. In the interactions, they admitted to being false profiles with provocative intent, then troll profiles. Their aim was to enable polarity of the *diatexts* – demonstrating how real users react to trolling and other hostile communication contexts. First, they analyzed the four fake "unmasked" profiles through the semiotics of profile images. Next, the researchers gathered and analyzed interactions of the identified profiles using quantitative and qualitative methods. According to the researchers, emotional analysis provides insights into interactions between trolls and real users, including how they are emotionally colored and which strategies the latter uses to react to provocations made by the former. The researchers found strong positive associations between the frequency of online comments, trolling enjoyment, and the identity of the trolls. They found similar relationship patterns between trolling and Dark Tetrad, whereby trolling positively correlates with psychopathy and Machiavellianism and, most robustly, with sadism. Pleasure derived from other online activities, such as chatting and discussing, was not found to be related to sadism. As such, cyber trolling seems to be a manifestation of the Internet of daily sadism, with the troll character serving as a malevolent case of a virtual avatar that reflects their real personality and ideal self.

March (2019) performed a multinational study, with 733 participants from North-West Europe (30.1%), Oceania (29.6%), the United States (12.1%), South-East Asia (10.4%), South-East Europe (10.1%), and other regions (7.7%). Their findings show that Internet trolling is predicted by positive trait psychopathy and sadism, negative social potency scores, and negative affective empathy scores. Furthermore, the results show a significant positive relationship between cognitive empathy and Internet trolling when trait psychopathy scores are higher. As in most studies mentioned earlier, gender was not found to be a significant predictor of Internet trolling. More specifically, their findings show that primary psychopathy (yet not secondary psychopathy) significantly predicts Internet trolling – as the Internet troll is more callous, manipulative, and lacking in remorse (characteristics related to primary psychopathy), yet less impulsive, neurotic, and emotionally reactive (traits associated with secondary psychopathy). The findings also show that direct and vicarious sadism are significant positive predictors of trolling behaviors. This suggests that the Internet troll enjoys directly hurting/humiliating others and watching them be humiliated/hurt.

In a sample of 400 participants (43.3% Australians), March and Steele (2020) found that gender (male), trait psychopathy, and trait sadism are significant predictors of trolling; however, self-esteem has no additional value on top of trait psychopathy and sadism in explaining trolling. Furthermore, they found a significant interaction between trait sadism and self-esteem; with high levels of sadism, there is a significant positive relationship between self-esteem and trolling. Regarding trait sadism and trolling, individuals with high trait sadism derive pleasure from causing pain to others, thus reflecting the enjoyment that trolls experience when inflicting suffering and humiliation on their victims.

Lopes and Yu (2017) examined whether Dark Triad personalities exhibit different online behaviors toward people of different social statuses. More specifically, they explored associations between dark personality traits and the trolling of the Facebook profiles of popular vs. less popular people. The participants, 135 students from a United Kingdom university, were exposed to these two types of Facebook profiles, presented in random order. Next, they were asked to rate their level of agreement with trolling comments on those pages. Their findings show a greater association between psychopathy and the trolling of popular individuals, compared to the trolling of less popular ones. The researchers explain that people with traits of psychopathy show a propensity for the bullying of famous individuals.

On the one hand, they prey on victims they perceive as being weaker and with less self-esteem, yet they may also be curious about people they perceive to have a higher social status, therefore preying on them and bullying them. On the other hand, no associations were found between narcissism or Machiavellianism and trolling. In a sample of 212 Swedish social network users, Karlsson and Kajonius (2020) found that trolling in the form of malicious posting is significantly correlated with all four personality traits. Nevertheless, sadism and Machiavellianism are the strongest predictors of trolling.

Sorokowski et al. (2020) examined whether specific psychological characteristics predict the online posting of hate comments, hypothesizing that online haters might experience elevated levels of envy. In a survey of 94 participants from Poland, the researchers found that high levels of psychopathy significantly predict posting hate comments online, yet narcissism and Machiavellianism do not. These findings align with previous studies, whereby high levels of psychopathy are associated with negative online behaviors, including trolling, cyberbullying, and conveying hate speech. The researchers contend their results might not be surprising, as psychopathy is characterized by impulsivity and thrill-seeking behaviors. Hence, high levels of impulsivity may foster reckless behaviors, such as expressing a negative opinion about someone or something – one that is evaluative yet does not offer constructive criticism. According to these researchers, posting online hate comments is not associated with higher levels of other Dark Triad traits (i.e., narcissism and Machiavellianism).

In a sample of 444 participants from Australia and the United States, Furian and March (2023) found that people with high levels of psychopathy and sadism traits participated in trolling. The researchers explain that as individuals with high levels of psychopathy traits are often callous and impulsive, trolling may be an appealing and thrill-seeking activity that enables them to aggressively prey on other online users.

Furthermore, as those with high levels of sadism traits derive pleasure from harming others, social media likely provides such individuals with a platform on which to inflict pain on others. Machiavellianism did not emerge as a predictor in their model. As individuals with high levels of agentic narcissism may employ charm to achieve this desire, it follows that this facet may not predict trolling. Moreover, while antagonistic narcissism has a strong positive correlation with trolling, it is nonsignificant in the model with all other predictors. This finding contradicts their expectations, possibly because antagonistic narcissism is mainly captured through psychopathy and sadism. Lastly, the researchers also found that people with high levels of communal narcissism engage in trolling to a greater degree, as do those with high levels of neurotic narcissism.

Volkmer et al. (2023), in an experimental design based on 1,026 German-speaking participants, found that the Dark Tetrad is positively associated with global trolling behaviors, following significant positive correlations between Machiavellianism, narcissism, psychopathy, and sadism – and global trolling behaviors. Moreover, they found psychopathy and sadism, yet not Machiavellianism or narcissism, to be significant predictors of immediate trolling motivation. Finally, they explain that psychopathy and sadism are significant predictors of trolling when considering all facets of the Dark Tetrad. In contrast, Machiavellianism and narcissism probably do not explain any variance in immediate trolling motivation when controlling for psychopathy and sadism.

Marrington et al. (2023) found in a sample of 157 Australian adolescents a strong effect of sadism and psychopathy on trolling. March, McDonald, and Forsyth (2023) also found in a replication study of 163 participants, mainly from Australia, a strong effect of sadism and psychopathy on trolling. Leite et al. (2023) found in a sample of 773 Internet users from Portugal a strong and positive relationship between the Dark Triad traits and online trolling. It should be noted that sadism and psychopathy emerge as strong predictors of trolling in Australian samples, a finding to consider in future research regarding cross-national comparisons.

5.10.2   Non-Westernized Cultures

Masui (2019), in a sample of 513 participants in Japan, found significant associations between engagement in Internet trolling and Machiavellianism, psychopathy, and everyday sadism. Like in many of the studies conducted in Western cultures, no associations were seen between Internet trolling and narcissism. The researcher's findings also show that the facilitating effect of Machiavellianism or psychopathy on Internet trolling is only seen in participants with high levels of loneliness. On the other hand, the degree of Internet trolling behavior does not differ between participants with high levels of Machiavellianism or psychopathy and low loneliness and those with low Dark Triad personality traits. The researcher concludes that the subjective feeling of a lack of interpersonal relationships increases the likelihood of aggressive responses in online situations among individuals with high Dark Triad personality traits. No associations were seen between narcissism or sadism and loneliness.

In a sample of 1,303 college students from China, Wu et al. (2022) found that online trolling is linked to Machiavellianism and psychopathy, two traits that partially mediate associations between online disinhibition and trolling. Moreover, men were found to exhibit higher levels of Dark Triad traits and were more likely to engage in online trolling than women, unlike many studies in Western cultures, where no gender differences were found. Furthermore, gender was found to moderate associations between psychopathy and online trolling. Narcissism was not found to be associated with online trolling or serve as a mediating factor, as, in general, narcissism is not associated with online disinhibition. Moreover, narcissism may be milder than the other two Dark Triad traits when correlated with antisocial online behaviors. Once again, this finding demonstrates that narcissism has a weak effect on trolling.

In a sample of 809 students from universities in Turkey, Manuoğlu and Öner-Özkan (2022) found that psychopathy and Machiavellianism are strongly related to sarcastic trolling – far beyond the effects of overt and relational aggression. This suggests that psychopathy and Machiavellianism comprise features that are more relevant for predicting sarcastic trolling (such as deception, manipulation, and low empathy) yet are less incorporated in overt and relational aggression. Expressing statements that are contrary to facts and truths and insincere expressions aimed at hurting others are prototypical examples of sarcasm that seem to be associated with the features mentioned earlier of these two traits. Unlike sarcastic trolling, troll deviancy was found to be predicted by relational and overt aggression, yet not by dark personality traits. As expected, the findings of this study also indicate that Machiavellianism predicts sarcastic trolling. The researchers explain that Machiavellianism is commonly associated with deception and manipulation that make victims feel embarrassed or guilty. Sarcasm also includes counterfactual expressions used to convey disapproval or deceive individuals or groups. Thus, it is unsurprising that in this study, Machiavellianism predicted sarcastic trolling. However, narcissism was not found to predict trolling. Therefore, as with most Western studies presented earlier, narcissism seems less relevant for constructing the psychological profile of individuals who engage in trolling in general and in sarcastic trolling in particular. Finally, psychopathy was found to predict sarcastic trolling, which entails the disregard of others and the harm they endure – a dominant characteristic of psychopathy.

Hamarta, Akat, and Akbulut (2023) found in a sample of 516 participants from Turkey a significant relationship between an aggregated scale of the Dark Triad traits and trolling. The relationship between each of the specific dark personalities and trolling were weaker.

****

Table 5.1 presents a summary of the research findings presented in this chapter. It should be noted that most of the studies on cyberstalking and trolling were performed in Westernized cultures, which raises questions about the generalizability of these findings to non-Western cultures. However, the few studies that were conducted in non-Western cultures point to similar findings regarding a relatively strong effect of Machiavellianism. The table supports two essential findings. First, strong associations were seen between sadism, cyberstalking, and trolling. Psychopathy was also found to be a strong predictor of trolling, although less firmly than sadism. Second, Machiavellianism was found to be a moderate but consistent correlate of cyberstalking and trolling. Finally, in both Western and non-Western cultures, narcissism was found to have the weakest relationship with cyberstalking and trolling. Many scholars contend that people with narcissistic traits are not interested in this hate behavior, perhaps because they perceive themselves as above this behavior (Craker & March, 2016). In other words, trolling does not give them the exposure or enjoyment they seek. According to studies, narcissism does not contribute to cyberbullying or trolling alone. Other indirect factors coupled with narcissism lead to problematic social media usage (Olckers & Hattingh, 2022). However, the relatively high correlations between trolling and the other three traits exemplify how individuals with Dark Triad traits feel very comfortable with and take great pleasure in the devastating outcomes of trolling cyberstalking.

Table 5.1 *Summary of research findings of the relationship between the Dark Tetrad/Triad and cyberstalking and trolling*

Study	Sample size	Type of behavior	Gender	Age (mean)	MTurk or similar	Country	Occupation	Education	Narcissists	Psychopathy	Machiavellianism	Sadism
			Sample characteristics						Correlations			
Branković et al. (2022)	232	Cyberstalking	64.2% female	34.53	No	Serbia	NR	54.3% university degree 22.8% high school or college students or graduates	0.33**	0.38**	0.40**	0.32**
Branković et al. (2022)	232	Aggravated stalking	64.2% female	34.53	No	Serbia	NR	54.3% university degree 22.8% high school or college students or graduates	0.23**	0.48**	0.25**	0.38**
Branković et al. (2022)	232	Intrusive stalking	64.2% female	34.53	No	Serbia	NR	54.3% university degree 22.8% high school or college students or graduates	0.20**	0.25*	0.18**	0.15*
Branković et al. (2022)	232	Surveillance stalking	64.2% female	34.53	No	Serbia	NR	54.3% university degree 22.8% high school or college students or graduates	0.25**	0.21**	0.28**	0.19**
Smoker & March (2017)	689	Intimate-partner cyberstalking	70% female	26	No	Australia	NR	NR	0.23***	0.37***	0.37***	0.39***
Stiff (2019)	259	Facebook surveillance: Facebook tracking	57.9% female	20.49 (15–69)	"Prolific.ac"	United Kingdom	NR	NR	No relationship	Significant relationship	Strong positive relationship	NE

Study	N	Measure	% female	Age (range)	"Prolific.ac"	Country						
Stiff (2019)	259	Facebook surveillance: Facebook investigating	57.9% female	20.49 (15–69)	Yes	United Kingdom	NR	NR	No relationship	Significant relationship	Strong positive relationship	NE
March et al. (2021a)	449	Intimate-partner cyberstalking	49.9% female	41.19 (23–75)	Yes	USA	NR	NR	Significant relationship	Significant relationship	Significant relationship	Significant relationship
Kircaburun et al. (2018a)	761	Cyberstalking	64% female	20.70	No	Turkey	Undergraduate students	Undergraduate students	0.37***	0.25***	0.37***	0.34***
March et al. (2022)	449	Cyberstalking (total)	49.9% female	41.19 (23–75)	Yes	USA	NR	NR	0.13**	0.21*	0.16**	0.16**
March et al. (2022)	449	Cyberstalking; passive	49.9% female	41.19 (23–75)	Yes	USA	NR	NR	0.11**	0.15**	0.20**	0.16**
March et al. (2022)	449	Cyberstalking; invasive	49.9% female	41.19 (23–75)	Yes	USA	NR	NR	0.08	0.15**	0.05	0.08
March et al. (2022)	449	Cyberstalking; duplicitous	49.9% female	41.19 (23–75)	Yes	USA	NR	NR	0.10**	0.22**	0.07	0.11**
Gamache et al. (2021)	1804	Stalking & cyberstalking (total)	82.6% female	24.3 (18–30)	No	Quebec, Canada	52.1% students; 40.1% full-time or part-time workers	90.4% post-high school education; 44.1% university degree	0.27***	0.18***	0.35***	NE
Gamache et al. (2021)	1,804	Stalking & cyberstalking; hyper-intimacy	82.6% female	24.3 (18–30)	No	Quebec, Canada	52.1% students; 40.1% full-time or part-time workers	90.4% post-high school education; 44.1% university degree	0.25***	0.20***	0.32***	NE
Gamache et al. (2021)	1,804	Stalking & cyberstalking; dominating control	82.6% female	24.3 (18–30)	No	Quebec, Canada	52.1% students; 40.1% full-time or part-time workers	90.4% post-high school education; 44.1% university degree	0.20***	0.09**	0.29***	NE

Table 5.1 (*cont.*)

Study	Sample size	Type of behavior	Gender	Age (mean)	MTurk or similar	Country	Occupation	Education	Narcissists	Psychopathy	Machiavellianism	Sadism
						Sample characteristics			Correlations			
Kircaburun et al. (2018a)	761	Cyber trolling	64% female	20.70	No	Turkey	Undergraduate students	Undergraduate students	0.28***	0.38***	0.42***	0.39***
Alavi et al. (2022)	323	Cyber trolling	53.56 female	18–26	No	Malaysia	NR	NR	SEM = no relationship	SEM = significant relationship	SEM = no relationship	SEM = significant relationship
March et al. (2020b)	405	Intimate-partner cyberstalking	69.6% female	24.67	No	Australia	NR	NR	Grandiose = 0.14* Vulnerable = 0.25*	Primary = 0.20* Secondary = 0.28*	0.29*	Verbal = 0.31* Physical = 0.34* Vicarious = 0.09
Ménard & Pincus (2012)	1,741	Overt stalking	54% female	19.30	No	USA	Undergraduate students	Undergraduate students	Only for narcissism Grandiose (male) = 0.15***; grandiose (female) = 0.07*; Vulnerable (male) = 0.21***; vulnerable (female) = 0.08*			
Ménard & Pincus (2012)	1,741	Cyberstalking	54% female	19.30	No	USA	Undergraduate students	Undergraduate students	Only fore narcissism Grandiose (male) = 0.09*; grandiose (female) = 0.10**; Vulnerable (male) = 0.20***; vulnerable (female) = 0.14***			
Buckels et al. (2014)	207	Commenting frequency (h/day)	52% female	36.1	Yes	USA	NR	NR	0.27*	0.23*	0.33**	Sadism total = 0.43*** Direct sadism = 0.35**** Direct physical = 0.35*** Direct verbal = 0.32** Vicarious sadism = 0.39***

Study	N	Measure	% female	Mean age		Country		Education				Sadism
Buckels et al. (2014)	207	Commenting frequency (controlling for overall Internet use)	52% female	36.1	Yes	USA	NR	NR	0.30**	0.23*	0.33***	Sadism total = 0.40*** Direct sadism = 0.36*** Direct physical = 0.34** Direct verbal = 0.33** Vicarious sadism = 0.40***
Buckels et al. (2014)	609	Global assessment of Internet trolling	43% female	35.04	Yes	USA	NR	NR	0.18***	0.55***	0.34***	Sadism total = 0.68*** Direct sadism = 0.65*** Direct physical = 0.62*** Direct verbal = 0.56*** Vicarious sadism = 0.55***
Buckels et al. (2019)	304	Online trolling	51.8% female	34.4	Yes	USA	NR	14.8% high school students, 41.1% some college or university education; 36.2% undergraduates; 7.2% graduates	0.26***	0.63***	0.32***	0.71***
Buckels et al. (2019)	223	Online trolling	78% female	19 (95% under 25)	Yes	Canada	NR	NR	NE	0.43***	NE	44***
Buckels et al. (2019)	223	Trolling enjoyment	78% female	19 (95% under 25)	Yes	Canada	NR	NR	NE	NE	NE	0.38***
Buckels et al. (2019)	223	Trolling frequency	78% female	19 (95% under 25)	Yes	Canada	NR	NR	NE	NE	NE	0.30***
Buckels et al. (2019)	223	Trolling skill	78% female	19 (95% under 25)	Yes	Canada	NR	NR	NE	NE	NE	0.58***

Table 5.1 (*cont.*)

Study	Sample size	Type of behavior	Gender	Age (mean)	MTurk or similar	Country	Occupation	Education	Correlations			
									Narcissists	Psychopathy	Machiavellianism	Sadism
Wu et al. (2022)	1,303	Online trolling	49.9% Female	19.05 (17–26)	No	China	College students	College students	0.20***	0.49***	0.36***	NE
March (2019)	733	Internet trolling	70.5% female	23.53	No	Multinational	57.9% = currently studying	57.9% students	Vulnerable = 0.12**	Primary = 0.47** Secondary = 0.29***	NE	Direct = 0.50*** Vicarious = 0.39*** 0.59**
March & Steele (2020)	400	Internet trolling	67.5% female	24.97 (18–75)	No	43/3% Australian	73.7% currently employed	59.5% undergraduate students	NE	0.56**	NE	NE
Manuoğlu & Öner-Özkan (2022)	809	Sarcastic trolling	66.8% female	21.5	No	Turkey	Students from local universities	Local university students	0.12**	0.34**	0.25**	NE
Manuoğlu & Öner-Özkan (2022)	809	Troll Deviancy Scale	66.8% female	21.5	No	Turkey	Students from local universities	Local university students	0.10**	0.32**	0.18**	NE
Manuoğlu & Öner-Özkan (2022)	809	Global Assessment of Facebook Trolling	66.8% female	21.5	No	Turkey	Students from local universities	Local university students	0.05	0.29**	0.06	NE
Lopes & Yu (2017)	135	Agreement score to trolling comments toward the popular Facebook profile	83.7% female	20.45	No	United Kingdom	Students	Students	0.08	0.45***	0.16	NE

Study	N	Variable	Gender	Age		Country						
Lopes & Yu (2017)	135	Agreement score to trolling comments toward the less popular Facebook profile	83.7% female	20.45	No	United Kingdom	Students	Students	0.08	0.30***	0.22**	NE
Sorokowski et al. (2020)	94	Hating online comments	41% female	33.4 (15–71)	No	Poland	NR	NR	No significant effect (regression)	Significant positive effect (regression)	No significant effect (regression)	NE
Gylfason et al. (2021)	139	Facebook trolling behaviors	85.6% female	25.2% (under 25) 51.8% (25–34) 22.9% (above 34)	No	Iceland	NR	NR	0.105	0.285***	0.367***	0.449***
Gylfason et al. (2021)	139	Enjoyment of trolling	85.6% female	25.2% (under 25) 51.8% (25–34) 22.9% (above 34)	No	Iceland	NR	NR	0.045	0.052	0.340***	0.269**
Gylfason et al. (2021)	139	Commenting frequency (h/day)	85.6% female	25.2% (under 25) 51.8% (25–34) 22.9% (above 34)	No	Iceland	NR	NR	0.179*	0.186*	0.208*	0.175*

Table 5.1 (*cont.*)

Study	Sample size	Type of behavior	Sample characteristics						Correlations			
			Gender	Age (mean)	MTurk or similar	Country	Occupation	Education	Narcissists	Psychopathy	Machiavellianism	Sadism
Brubaker et al. (2021)	438	Comments per day on Reddit	44.6% female	NR	No	USA	NR	27.2% some college education; 37.3% 4-year college degree; 20.9% advanced degree		Composite scale 0.070		NE
Brubaker et al. (2021)	438	Schadenfreude	44.6% female	NR	No	USA	NR	27.2% some college education; 37.3% 4-year college degree; 20.9% advanced degree		Composite scale 0.492**		NE
Brubaker et al. (2021)	438	Trolling online	44.6% female	NR	No	USA	NR	27.2% some college education; 37.3% 4-year college degree; 20.9% advanced degree		Composite scale 0.086		NE
Brubaker et al. (2021)	438	Observed other Reddit users engaging in trolling	44.6% female	NR	No	USA	NR	27.2% some college education; 37.3% 4-year college degree; 20.9% advanced degree		Composite scale −0.070		NE

Study	N	Trolling measure	Gender	Age (range)	Online sample	Country	Sample description	Sample description				
Masui (2019)	513	Internet trolling	51.1% female	46.8 (20–69)	No	Japan	NR	NR	0.20***	0.30***	0.37***	0.39***
Craker & March (2016)	396	Facebook trolling	75–90% female	34.41 (18–77)	Survey Monkey	Australia	NR	NR	0.18***	0.39***	0.34***	0.35***
Navarro-Carrillo et al. (2021)	201	Online trolling	50.7% female	21.88 (18–42)	No	Spain	Undergraduate students	Undergraduate students	0.20** (partial correlation, controlling for gender)	0.43*** (partial correlation, controlling for gender)	0.30*** (partial correlation, controlling for gender)	0.32*** (partial correlation, controlling for gender)
Karlsson & Kajonius (2021)	212	Trolls (malicious posting)	73% female	38.36 (15–80)	No	Sweden	28% students; 52% working	28% students	0.17*	0.32***	0.42***	0.54***
Lee et al. (2021)	599	Online trolls	43.7% female	35.61	Yes	USA	NR	NR	NE	Trolls scored the highest on psychopathy and sadism	Unexpectedly, the vocal minority group scored the highest on Machiavellianism	Trolls scored the highest on psychopathy and sadism
March et al. (2017)	357	Trolling on Tinder* (and other dating applications)	71% female	22.50 (18–60)	No	Australia	NR	NR	0.11*	0.32***	0.20***	0.25***
Paananen & Reichl (2019)	347	Gender trolling	100% male	32.67	Yes. Also 4chan, Reddit	USA = 192; India = 107; Canada = 19	NR	NR	NE	NE	NE	Verbal = 0.47*** Physical = 0.61*** Vicarious = 0.41***
Paananen & Reichl. (2019)	347	Internet trolling	100% male	32.67	Yes. Also 4chan, Reddit	USA = 192; India = 107; Canada = 19	NR	NR	NE	NE	NE	Verbal = 0.57*** Physical = 0.63*** Vicarious = 0.51***
Furian & March (2023)	444	Internet trolling	66% female	34.95 (18–84)	154 from Cloud Research	59% Australia; 22% USA	32.2% are current students	32.2% are current students	Agentic 0.31** Communal 0.28** Antagonistic 0.53** Neurotic 0.29**	0.64**	0.42**	0.65**

Table 5.1 (cont.)

Study	Sample size	Type of behavior	Gender	Age (mean)	MTurk or similar	Country	Occupation	Education	Narcissists	Psychopathy	Machiavellianism	Sadism
						Sample characteristics			Correlations			
Volkmer et al. (2023)	1,026	Global trolling	77.2% female	26.46 (18–77)	No	Germany	German universities and a psychology website	German universities and a psychology website	0.34**	0.49**	0.31**	0.48**
Volkmer et al. (2023)		Immediate trolling motivation	77.2% female	26.46 (18–77)	No	Germany	German universities and a psychology website	German universities and a psychology website	0.23**	0.42**	0.24**	0.42**
Marrington et al. (2023)	157	Internet trolling	58% female	15.58 (13–18)	No	Australia	Adolescents	Adolescents	NE	0.43***	NE	0.39***
Hamarta et al. (2023)	516	Online trolling	71.6% female	21.09 (18–31)	No	Turkey	University students	University students	Dark Triad aggregated scale 0.41***			NE
March et al. (2023)	163	Internet trolling	50.3% female	27.36 (18–62)	No	63.8% Australian	NR	NR	NE	0.60***	NE	0.59***
Leite et al. (2023)	773	Cyberstalking total	60.4% female	27.39 (19–78)	No	Portugal	NR	Mean years of educative = 13.06	0.430***	0.241***	0.399***	NE
Leite et al. (2023)	773	Cyberstalking control	60.4% female	27.39 (19–78)	No	Portugal	NR	Mean years of educative = 13.06	0.327***	0.254***	0.307***	NE
Leite et al. (2023)	773	Cyberstalking justification	60.4% female	27.39 (19–78)	No	Portugal	NR	Mean years of educative = 13.06	0.383***	0.181***	0.343***	NE
Leite et al. (2023)	773	Cyberstalking time	60.4% female	27.39 (19–78)	No	Portugal	NR	Mean years of educative = 13.06	0.322***	0.150***	0.318***	NE

	N	Behavior	Gender	Age		Country		Education				
Leite et al. (2023)	773	Flaming total	60.4% female	27.39 (19–78)	No	Portugal	NR	Mean years of educative = 13.06	0.272***	0.343***	0.374***	NE
Leite et al. (2023)	773	Trolling total	60.4% female	27.39 (19–78)	No	Portugal	NR	Mean years of educative = 13.06	0.247***	0.278***	0.310***	NE
Resett & González Caíno (2023)	437	Internet trolling	61% female	28.4 (18–50)	No	Argentina	NR	18% – secondary studies 74% – some university studies and above	0.123**	0.233***	0.322***	NE
Blais et al. (2023)	1,724	Engagement in any cyberstalking	50.0% female	49.0 (19–80)	No	Canada	NR	27.2% completed high school 31% completed B.A. 27.3% technical or community college	Grandiose = 0.09** Vulnerable = 0.06**	Interpersonal manipulation = 0.11** Affective = 0.11** Lifestyle = 0.12** Antisocial = 0.18***	Antagonism = 0.07** Agency = -0.02 Planfulness = -0.07**	NE

Note: MTurk or similar = Amazon MTurk; NR = not reported; NE = not examined; GN = grandiose narcissism; VN = vulnerable narcissism; SNS = social network sites.
* $p < 0.05$; ** $p < 0.01$; *** $p < 0.001$.

CHAPTER 6

The Dark Triad/Tetrad Is above the Law
Cybercrime

As of 2022, the number of Internet users was estimated at 5.3 billion, an 8% increase over the previous year (Internet Live Stats, 2022). This figure – representing 66% of the global population – reflects the changing nature of human interaction. By eliminating spatial boundaries, it offers unlimited, permanently available access to programmed activities that can be undertaken independent of geographic location and over a network that is both cost- and time-efficient. However, access to the digital world also opens up new territory for criminal operations, a phenomenon known as cybercrime. Low input of resources and easy availability of specially designed software – such as crime-as-a-service programming – enhance the digital world's attractiveness for such nefarious activities (Selzer & Oelrich, 2021; Perenc, 2022).

While the opportunity to hide one's physical appearance grants permission to express oneself more freely and openly, it also allows people to hide or fabricate their personal data: their gender, educational level, financial situation, and so on. Taking advantage of the Internet to express "other selves" that are often fundamentally different from the ones that dominate their actual lives, also applies to pathological personalities and behaviors that differ from social norms. These, too, can be easily projected into cyberspace due to its free, unregulated environment. Since the structural and functional properties of the Internet favor anonymity, nonverbal interaction, asynchrony of interaction, and faintly defined standards, it becomes readily amenable to the commission of crime (Perenc, 2022). It allows people who are not even specialists in information technology to be able to carry out complex digital attacks (Selzer & Oelrich, 2021). The prevailing anonymity lowers the inhibition to commit such crimes, as does the more negligible risk of being sanctioned for doing so (Selzer & Oelrich, 2021). These advantages favor the shift of criminality from the physical to the digital sphere (Selzer & Oelrich, 2021). Moreover, as easily as cybercrime can be perpetrated by knowing individuals, it can also be utilized by organized crime groups (Perenc, 2022). Cybercrime, therefore, becomes a challenge not only for the economy but to society and government policymakers.

Escalating cyber threats and vulnerabilities has become a serious concern for large and small organizations, governments, and the general public. In 2023, Symantec, a data protection service, reported that the number of cyberattacks since the onset of the Russo-Ukrainian war reached an all-time high. Although the most targeted sectors were still education and research, attacks on the healthcare sector registered a 74% year-on-year increase. Overall, global cyberattacks increased in 2022 by 38% over 2021. Projecting into the future, Symantec contends that the ferreting out of the sources of ransomware operations and the tracking of threat actors will become even more challenging. Instead, its data protection focus will necessarily shift to data-wiping and exfiltration detection (Symantec, 2023). The boundaries between state cyber operations and hacktivism (hacktivism is the use of computer-based techniques such as hacking as a form of civil disobedience to promote a political agenda or social change) (Hacktivism, 2023) have also been blurred. The anonymity of the Internet enables undercover activity by nation-states just as it does by individuals and criminal organizations. In addition, nation-states can perpetrate crimes without fear of retaliation. According to Symantec, the number of attacks on cloud-based networks shot up by an astonishing 48% in 2022 as compared to 2021 (Symantec, 2023).

While there are various ways to categorize cybercrime, the most prominent is to distinguish between cyber-dependent and cyber-enabled crime. Cyber-dependent crimes are those that require the use of a computer, computer networks, or other forms of information and communication technology. Typical examples: the hacking of computer systems, websites, or online accounts, disseminating malware, and DDoS (distributed denial-of-service) attacks, malicious attempts to disrupt the traffic of targeted servers, services, or networks by overwhelming them or their supportive infrastructure with floods of Internet traffic. In a successful DDoS attack, the incoming flood of traffic originates from many different sources. This makes it impossible to stop by immediately blocking a single source that has been detected. Cyber-enabled crimes, by contrast, are traditional crimes wherein information and communication technology is used but is not mandatory. Typical examples of cyber-enabled crimes are online fraud, threats, stalking, child pornography, or online grooming (Selzer & Oelrich, 2021).

Deceptive or deviant activity is a necessary feature of hacker attacks that find entry to computer systems, networks, or organizations. "Phishing" or "spear phishing," common tactics in cyberattacks, essentially rely on tricking users into taking actions that run malware, reveal credentials, or allow unauthorized access. Sometimes, these actions are in the service of nationalism, moral outrage, or personal financial gain. Regardless of motive, there are myriads of ways to infiltrate a system. Cautious hackers, carefully extracting information using system tools, may proceed slowly in the desire to remain undetected for as long as possible. These hackers cover their tracks in order to mitigate possible legal troubles or maintain a presence on the network for future exploitation. More expedient hackers may force their way onto systems and networks with "noisy" tactics, executing quick "get-in-and-get-out" maneuvers that extract as much information as possible and leave expeditiously (Jones et al., 2021).

6.1   The Dark Triad/Tetrad and Cybercrime

In addition to uncovering the mechanisms underlying cybercrime, current research also focuses on the personality traits of perpetrators in the attempt to uncover proclivities for antisocial cyberspace behavior. The Dark Tetrad, one model of personality disorders of cybercrime perpetrators, includes four salient traits: psychopathy, Machiavellianism, narcissism, and sadism. The assumption is that individuals expressing this axial set of behaviors have a greater predisposition to cybercrime (Perenc, 2022).

The traits composing the Dark Tetrad are characterized by emotional coldness, lack of empathy, self-promotion, aggressiveness, and proclivity to unethical behavior. High scorers in these personality traits also exhibit motives for profit-seeking at the expense of others (Selzer & Oelrich, 2021). Psychopathy, considered the most malevolent of all the traits in the Dark Tetrad, is characterized by impulsivity and blatant disregard for the rights of others. This may factor into psychopathic personalities' viewing cybercrime as a valid means for achieving their goals. Psychopaths express overall approval of white-collar crime such as accounting fraud and insider trading. As the criminality of individuals scoring high in psychopathic tendencies has wide range, it can safely be assumed that those individuals could easily "digitize" their deviant behavior (Selzer & Oelrich, 2021).

In a sample of 53 students at a major German university, Selzer and Oelrich (2021) find that high scores in psychopathy and Machiavellianism correlate strongly with increased cybercriminal intentions. Machiavellian frames of mind are antecedents to perceiving cybercrime as "opportunities." As individuals with this personality type exhibit keen rationality, analytical skills, and strategic planning, their predispositions are easily honed into carrying out long-range cybercriminal projects. Furthermore, Machiavellian personalities are highly skilled in manipulation, so it is felt that the most prominent security risk to the general public is the innocence of the individuals seated behind the computer, not the penetration of software or hardware.

Narcissism does not seem to be a strong predictor of cybercriminality. Cybercrime, which is essentially clandestine, may not provide narcissists with the same self-enhancement and validation that traditional crime does, unless the hacking involves public recognition or admiration for their phenomenal skill. High scorers on the Dark Tetrad trait of narcissism may resort to cybercrime when they feel entitled to rewards that were denied them. Stephenson and Walter (2012) contend that those scoring high on the trait of sadism are rarely cybercriminals since obtaining satisfaction in the virtual world is more challenging than in the physical world. Nevertheless, hackers often obtain sadistic pleasure in discovering and penetrating system vulnerabilities.

Individuals scoring high in the Dark Tetrad employ different approaches to cybercrime. We now review the distinct kinds of cybercrime in relation to the personality types in the Dark Tetrad.

6.1.1 Hacking

Hacking, the premier crime of our cyber age, refers to the use of computers to gain unauthorized access to information systems by exploiting the vulnerabilities of digitized networks (Seigfried-Spellar et al., 2017). According to Wikipedia (Hacker, 2023), there are two types of hackers: Enthusiastic members of the computer programming subculture who specialize in developing advanced hardware and software technology and individuals who maliciously subvert computer security. Due to wholesale mass media adoption of the term "hacker," mainstream use of the term usually only connotes the computer criminals. However, within the hacker community itself, the term refers to individuals motivated by intellectual curiosity, while the pejorative term "cracker" (i.e., criminal hacker) identifies those computer-savvy individuals who use their skills with malicious intent (Matulessy & Humaira, 2016).

Although self-designated hobbyists are generally acknowledged and accepted by computer security professionals, the hacker community diminishes them as "script kiddies" though they are able to disrupt websites, crack passwords, deface websites, and carry out identity theft. Their modus operandi is to use programs written by others with little knowledge of how the programs actually work (Seigfried-Spellar et al., 2017; Hussain et al., 2022). Hackers involved in circumventing computer security are subgrouped into White-hats, Black-hats, and Gray-hats.

- Black-hat hackers
  Black-hat hackers, or "crackers," are typically motivated by the financial gain that can be procured by breaking into systems and stealing, exploiting, or selling the filched data. While most skilled crackers are motivated by profiteering and not the thrill of vandalizing protected property, there are also social mischief-makers in the cyberworld who do seek revenge or notoriety.
  Crackers often sell fixes for the system vulnerabilities they discover back to the system owners whose networks they hacked, or they sell their technological breakthroughs to other black-hat hackers who then steal information on their own.
- White-hat hackers
  White-hat hackers, sometimes called ethical hackers, assist system owners in detecting and fixing the security vulnerabilities in their computerized networks. Although White-hat hackers apply many of the same tools and methods used by Black-hat hackers, their work is not illegal because it is done with the consent of the system managers. White-hat hackers are typically well-paid for their service to ensure they do not go over to the dark side.
- Gray-hat hackers
  Gray-hat hackers are security experts who occasionally violate laws or organizational protocols but do so without malicious intent. Gray-hats include those whose ideological positions compel them to attack adversarial political positions. They are often referred to as "hacktivists." Gray-hat hackers can be White-hats by day and Gray-hats by night (Sabillon et al., 2016; Gaia et al., 2020; Hacker, 2023).

6.1.2 Insider Threats

The dark side of the abundance of personal information on the Internet is that legally protected information can be compromised by trusted insiders. These people are current or former employees, contractors, or business partners with access to an organization's network, system, or data (Gaia et al., 2020; Harms et al., 2022). As the 2022 Cost of Insider Threats: Global Report reveals, insider threat incidents have risen 44% over the past two years, with costs per incident up more than a third to $15.38 million (Bank Info Security, 2022). A substantial portion of insider-generated losses derive from embezzlement, pilfering of proprietary secrets, or theft of customer information. Incidents of fraud range from direct theft of company funds to complex arrangements wherein company services or data are illegitimately traded for financial gain. Intellectual property theft tends to be technically sophisticated, with insiders using their access to steal source code or customer information. Nefarious insider attacks include inserting malware (most commonly logic bombs) to tamper with and disrupt system hardware (Nurse et al., 2014). (A logic bomb is a code intentionally inserted into a software system to set off a malicious function when specified conditions are met.) (Logic bomb, 2023).

According to 88% of cybersecurity professionals, insider threats are especially concerning since an organization's defenses are arguably focused on external threats. This leads to inadequate bulwarks against attacks originating from sources with knowledge of and access to systems, security processes, and precious company secrets (Nurse et al., 2014). It has been estimated that 70% of organizational security breaches are not reported since doing so would jeopardize a company's reputation. Companies choose to avoid litigation that might lead to long-term customer loss (Gaia et al., 2020). The United States Cybersecurity and Infrastructure Security Agency cynically notes that there are only two types of organizations: Those whose workers have already stolen their intellectual property and those who simply do not know about it yet (Gaia et al., 2022). Nurse et al. (2014) contended that insiders pilfering company information have psychological traits that are high on the Dark Tetrad. In a narrative review, Marbut and Harms (2023) found that dark triad traits are risk factors that increase the likelihood of threat behavior or its efficacy.

6.1.2.1 Insider Threat and Rationalization Theory
The conventional market model assumes that cyber offenders are rational economic actors who balance expected returns against the

probability of getting caught (Gaia et al., 2022). It is posited that potential cybercrime can be deterred if the likelihood of punishment is imminent or the penalty is severe. From the viewpoint of cyber criminals, "rationalizations" for nefarious behavior are defense mechanisms. These "vocabularies of adjustment" are sometimes called neutralization techniques designed by individuals committed to the normative system (Padayachee, 2020, 2021).

Research shows that the use of neutralization techniques is anteced-ent to cybercrime (Padayachee, 2020, 2021). Padayachee mentions several common rationalizations used by Dark Tetrad personalities. The rationali-zation of "Denial of Responsibility" involves psychological alienation with individuals claiming that their behavior is beyond control. Some perpetra-tors claim ignorance of the organizational security policy. The rationaliza-tion of "Denial of Injury" involves disconnect from the act of maleficence and its consequences by asserting that the action taken is acceptable since no individual was harmed. The abstract nature of information resources gives this rationalization its credence.

Offenders often claim the "Defense of Necessity" wherein the act of maleficence is portrayed as imperative under the assumption that white-collar crime is nothing more than standard business practice. Violating respected protocols in order to meet a deadline is another example of such rationalizations. Neutralization of responsibility is often externalized by applying the rationalization of "Condemning the condemners" where blame for malicious activity is shifted to the accusers by smearing them as hypocritical, corrupt, or misguided.

Some neutralization techniques are based on taking "moral high ground." The rationalization of the "Appeal to Higher Loyalties" frames deviation from organizational protocols out of allegiance to higher interests where perpetrators claim that they violated company policy in order to meet a crit-ical deadline. In using the rationalization of the "Metaphor of the Ledger," perpetrators justify maleficence by counterbalancing acts of malevolence with acts of benevolence. Perpetrators feel that they have earned the right to small delinquencies because they are upstanding and deserve to "be cut some slack" for occasional missteps (Padayachee, 2020, 2021).

6.1.3   Cyberattacks

In 2021, 1 out of every 61 organizations was impacted by ransomware. Since companies that can afford to pay will continue to be targeted, threats from ransomware will only balloon and become more sophisticated. Hackers who work within victims' networks will be able to customize their real-time data exfiltration or extortion (Horowitz, 2021). Defenses such as reconfiguring a system, performing detailed inspections of computers, or taking a network offline do ameliorate the impact of such threats, but even minor actions such as restarts, software updating, and hard-drive image restorations are met with end-user resistance. When security precautions occur too frequently, users may simply ignore or block them. Skilled cyberattackers can penetrate control networks and then manipulate sensor readings or feedback signals so as to keep their actions undetected (Jones et al., 2021). Many intrusion detection algorithms only investigate the magnitude of attack residuals and cannot ward off sophisticated stealth (Hu et al., 2019).

Jones et al. (2021) maintain that cyber stealth varies along a continuum from short- to long-term. Mimicry Deception Theory, the model they conceived for long-term deception states that three interrelated components: complexity, slow extraction, and community/host integration are required for successful stealth attacks. These attacks are difficult to detect precisely because of the extensive analysis of system logs that capture attacker interactions with the system and correlate "unusual" events. As most systems overwrite or delete their logs when nearing storage capacity or after mandatory retention occurs, insufficient data often prevent discovering attackers "hiding in plain sight" who are adept at blending their encroachments into legitimate network traffic. Randomized port scanning, accompanied by a long wait-time before scanning the next port, renders stealthy reconnaissance of computer networks hard to detect (Jones et al., 2021).

6.2 The Dark Tetrad and Hacking

The illegal cyber incursions noted above necessitate more sophisticated research into the negative personality traits of hackers. Strategic approaches to system defense may rely upon analyses of the differing psychological profiles of hackers. The traits associated with the Dark Tetrad have been studied in subclinical populations where individuals have found ways to function in society without incurring severe punishment such as incarceration. Jones et al. (2021) employ the Trait Activation Theory to explain how individuals exhibiting high expressions of traits in the Dark Tetrad tend to encroach upon computer systems. They contend that both the situation and the hacker's personality must be examined when predicting criminal behavior. In this theory, a situation is relevant if it allows subversive traits to emerge. The researchers divide situations into "strong" and "weak" categories. A weak situation is one wherein unclear behavioral demands pertain: Outcomes or the paths to achieve them are uncertain, or there is little consensus on the company approach. The domain of cybersecurity can be considered a "weak" situation that amplifies different cybercriminal tendencies, suggesting that strategic decisions should trigger diverse actions that align with different cybercriminal personalities.

It has been noted that an insider's attachment to a workplace may mitigate cybercrime (Nurse et al., 2014). Yet the personality traits of the Dark Tetrad have not been formally labeled as constructs that explain insider behavior. Nevertheless, convicted insider attackers all have personal predispositions that could be considered precursors to cyber espionage and sabotage. These include a unique need for attention, a sense of entitlement, arrogance, impulsivity, lack of conscience, and lack of empathy (Maasberg et al., 2015, 2020). Research has examined the association between the techniques of neutralization mentioned earlier and insider cybercrime (Padayachee, 2020, 2021). The contention is that personality is indeed a mediating factor. Socially aversive traits such as psychopathy, Machiavellianism, narcissism, and possibly sadism enable the dissociation required to invoke these techniques (Padayachee, 2020, 2021).

Jones et al. (2021) assert that traits in the Dark Triad can be associated with different approaches to cybercrime. As in regular criminal activity, where most of the antisocial actions are undertaken by reckless individuals, so is cybercrime. Yet levels of impulsivity vary: Psychopaths are the most impulsive, while Machiavellian personalities are the most cautious. Individuals scoring high in psychopathy excel in short-term superficial deceptions, while the long-term strategies – those detailed in Mimicry Deception Theory – align more closely with Machiavellianism (Jones et al., 2021). Machiavellian traits have been associated with greater changes made to emails intended to deceive end-users. Individuals scoring high in psychopathy and narcissism make significantly fewer changes to their email lures. Finally, individuals scoring high in narcissism are more vulnerable to phishing, potentially due to their overconfidence. It has been observed that this effect is boosted when narcissistic attackers phish narcissistic end-users. However, it is still unclear whether the approaches to cyber deception associated with traits in the Dark Tetrad directly translate into the technical aspects of a cyberattack.

Traits in the Dark Tetrad seem to better represent characteristics of the personality of malicious individuals than do the personality traits of the Big Five (Openness, Conscientiousness, Extraversion, Agreeableness, and Neuroticism) (Cristescu, Ciuperca, & Cirnu, 2022). While characterizing large-scale personality traits may be less time-consuming than examining the motives of a single perpetrator, analysis of the social interactions in which personality traits are manifested is critical for understanding why a particular individual is inclined to behave in the way that they do (King et al., 2018). As all traits in the Dark Tetrad are characterized by "emotional coldness," it indicates that malicious intentions on the part of perpetrators can be disguised by manipulating how others perceive them. The question becomes how to identify malicious persons who are adept at hiding their true selves. Therefore, we must consider the context in which cybercriminals operate to assess whether a specific individual is likely to commit cybercrime (King et al., 2018).

6.2.1 Research Findings

Most studies on the relation of personality to cybercrime focus on traits in the Big Five. However, the research has primarily centered on individual proclivities to commit cybercrime rather than on how cybercrime is approached. Scant research has been undertaken on the relation of criminal personalities to approaches to hacking. The thrust of most of the research effort has been on socially engineered attacks such as phishing (Jones et al., 2021) (A social engineering attack is a malicious attack which typically involves some form of psychological manipulation, specifically fooling otherwise unsuspecting users or employees into handing over confidential or sensitive data) (De Groot, 2023).

As most companies are reluctant to reveal actual data on the cybercrimes they have experienced, researchers studying the relationship between cybercrime and pathological personalities have had to design experimental simulations in which they present participants whose psychological profiles they have identified with fictionalized hacking scenarios. The participants are asked to truthfully report their attitudes and behavioral intentions regarding the scenarios the researchers have devised.

Such a study of the neutralization techniques dark personalities use to justify malicious cyber behavior was undertaken by Padayachee (2020, 2021) in South Africa using 170 respondents. The findings indicate that different personality types in the Dark Triad use different neutralization techniques to justify their actions. Gender also plays a role. The rationalization of the "Defense of necessity" strongly correlates with psychopathy in males and with Machiavellian traits in females. Padayachee asserts that the personality patterns in the Dark Triad also have an on affect noncompliance with organizational protocols and moral beliefs.

Padayachee's study also finds a strong correlation between psychopathic males who evince little empathy for others and the rationalization of the "Metaphor of the ledger." The use of this rationalization is only moderate among psychopathic females. A moderate correlation also exists between this rationale and logically minded women with Machiavellian traits. This prompts Padayachee to propose a curvilinear relationship between morality, unreasonable/unclear policies, the "Metaphor of the ledger," and psychopathy in both females and males and Machiavellian-oriented females. Padayachee shows a strong relationship between psychopathy in males and the rationalization of "Denial of injury." A similarly strong relationship exists between this rationalization and Machiavellian traits in females.

The rationalization of the "Appeal to higher loyalties" strongly correlates with Machiavellian traits in females and with psychopathic traits in males. Padayachee notes that the behavioral patterns associated with Machiavellian tendencies vary across genders. Therefore, strategies devoted to the mitigation of cybercrime based upon the identification of these rationalizations in potential insider cybercriminals must take the role played by gender into consideration.

Both the rationalization of "Condemnation of condemners" and the rationalization of "Denial of responsibility" are strongly associated with psychopathic tendencies in males. Narcissism was found irrelevant to techniques of neutralization. The use of rationalizations to justify cybercrime intersects with opportunity and motivation. Padayachee hypothesizes that a male or female's position within an organization influences the actualization of their Dark Triad personality traits. The research suggests that interventions formulated to maintain information security are fertile ground for further inquiry (Padayachee, 2020, 2021).

Fagade et al. (2017) use a system dynamics model to uncover patterns in malicious insider attacks. By coupling actors' observable behavior and the technical footprints found in incident logs together with social profiles in the "Big Five" personality model, they conclusively state that intimate knowledge of the mentality of cybercriminals is essential for effective cybersecurity. They also assert that the less narcissistic an individual is, the less likely they are to be involved in cybersecurity intrusions.

In a large-scale survey of 439 American university undergraduates, Gaia et al. (2020, 2021) find that Machiavellianism, narcissism, and psychopathy are all predictors of attraction to White-hat hacking. Psychopathy and Machiavellianism were statistically strong predictors of attraction to Black and Gray-hat hacking.

Building on the data from Gaia et al.'s (2020, 2021) sample, Sanders et al. (2019) conclude that even if White-hat hackers possess Machiavellian and psychopathic tendencies, these traits are necessary to uncover the nefarious cyberactivity of their Black-hat counterparts. The analysis shows that Gray-hat hackers oppose authority, Black-hat hackers are thrill-seekers, and White-hat hackers tend to be narcissistic. Narcissism is insignificantly correlated to Gray- and Black-hat hacking. Seigfried-Spellar et al.'s (2017) 235-participant survey found a strong relationship between psychopathy and computer crime among their American respondents.

Jones et al. (2021) conducted two experimental simulations; in the first, 258 participants were enrolled, and in the second, 250 participants were enrolled (75% of whom were American men). In Study 1, stealth was defined by a series of steps that are part of established hacker practices. In Study 2, stealth was defined by several markers of intrusion into computer networks, including the types of ports scanned and the codes and scanning options used. The findings show that to a significantly greater extent, subjects with Machiavellian proclivities committed cyber intrusions whose stealth is based on long-term mimicry. Individuals with high narcissistic or psychopathic traits had less capacity for stealth. Since situations affect our perceptions, and the lack of established Internet security protocols for dealing with hackers turns cyberspace into a relatively "weak" situation in which cyber criminals are freer to operate. This makes the differential impacts of traits in the Dark Triad more pronounced, and it is also reflected in the type of cybercrime perpetrated. Nevertheless, the strong correspondence to the established behavior patterns associated with the Dark Triad prevails with strategic planning associated with Machiavellian traits, erratic/impulsive behavior with psychopathy, and overconfidence with narcissism. The understudied ecology of the Internet combined with Trait Activation Theory and the profiles of the personality types in the Dark Triad dovetail to predict malevolent activity in the cyber realm.

Curtis et al. (2021) designed a resource control game to probe the association between traits in the Dark Triad and performance. Their study contained 312 participants. The researchers modified the FlipIt game to maximize potential differences between strategic vs. aggressive attackers. The participants were the attackers. They played against random defenders and a game-theoretic algorithm. The findings show that only Machiavellian personality types played well overall. This finding supports the contention that Machiavellian personality types are highly adept at cheating, deceiving, and manipulation and are able to do so with caution and flexibility. Their strategic decision-making contrasts with the self-enhancing approaches employed by narcissists and with the aggressive/impulsive conduct of psychopaths, both of whom underperformed in the restricted resource-controlled game environment.

Although Curtis et al. (2021) demur from applying their research directly to cybersecurity, parallels do exist: Overconfident narcissists and impulsive psychopathic attackers were indeed disarmed by the controls in the resource game. So, in situations where organizations are able to make informed decisions about the personalities of insider attackers, appropriate strategic resource control tactics could provide a defense against cyberattacks. While Machiavellian attackers were more successful against these algorithms, the research findings form a foundation for more predictive modeling of the decision-making driving cyberattacks.

Carre, Curtis, and Jones (2018) examine consumer reactions to security breaches to determine the best approach for minimizing an organization's reputational damage when data breaches occur. Their study investigates how traits in the Dark Triad influence perceptions of the responsibility of and trust in a company after the occurrence of a data breach. In this experiment, 253 American participants reacted to lifelike scenarios presented by the researchers. The data indicate that those with high scores in narcissistic and psychopathic traits view employees as more responsible for data breaches and companies as less responsible. This suggests that people with these personality profiles do not expect companies to protect their data, and no psychological contract breach occurs when their data are stolen. In the regression analysis, Machiavellian personality traits positively correlate to perceptions of company responsibility.

Carre et al. find that all personality types rate a company that has experienced a data breach as generally less trustworthy, but the regression analysis reveals that those with high Machiavellian traits rate a company that apologizes for its data breach as more competent. Carre et al. contend that individuals do not react positively when responses to data breaches do not align with their own views on corporate responsibility. The researchers conclude that it is essential to consider consumer expectations when dealing with the effects of data breaches and how best to restore customer trust once breaches have occurred.

Gaia et al. (2022) examined the responses of 303 American participants. The research shows modest support among Machiavellian and psychopathic personality types for the contention that cybercriminals use a rational choice calculus as to whether to violate privacy laws. A critical assessment of new employees' personalities may be necessary to combat the deception of sophisticated insider attacks. However, this may not be feasible for ethical or practical reasons, as White-hat hackers also have Machiavellian and psychopathic personality traits.

Amon et al. (2023), in an experimental simulation containing 245 American respondents, find that although personality types in the Dark Triad have sufficient understanding of the principle of personal privacy, they deliberately disrespect it. The notoriety or the entertainment value achieved by publishing other people's personal photographs is more compelling. Individuals scoring high in psychopathic traits frequently share photos of strangers, while individuals with narcissist profiles frequently share photos of family, friends, or themselves. The latter aligns with the linkage between narcissistic traits and self-disclosure. The study concludes that while the relationship between personality type and sharing behavior may be complex, attention-seeking antisocial personality traits contribute to maladaptive attitudes to the rights of privacy.

Maasberg et al. (2020), in a large survey of 768 American professionals in technology, healthcare, manufacturing, finance, academics, and service-oriented fields, find significant correlations between each trait in the Dark Triad and intentions to engage in insider threats. The regression coefficients varied across traits, with psychopathy having the most robust relationship (β = 0.559, p < 0.001) and narcissism the least (β = 0.236, p < 0.001). Machiavellian traits were in the middle (β = 0.379, p < 0.001). This confirms previous research on the importance of each trait in the Dark Triad.

Laakasuo et al. (2021) designed a hypothetical cross-sectional experiment with 1,007 recruits from Finland. The researchers presented them with the implausible scenario of "mind upload," the making of digital copies of the human brain. Conceived as a paradigm relating to the trans-humanistic dream of eternal life and the elimination of suffering, it was introduced as a feature of artificial general intelligence (AGI). The research aimed to determine whether the presence of personality traits in the Dark Triad could predict acceptance of this futuristic paradigm. Given the knowledge that AGI is an untested technology whose power could be subverted by unscrupulous individuals for control of humankind, understanding whether the embrace of "mind upload" is associated with pathological antisocial personality traits is, for Laakasuo et al. (2021), a task of immediate urgency.

The study's findings show that approval of this technology weakly correlates with the psychopathic profile. However, it strongly correlates with the Machiavellian profile. The authors speculate that the egotistical, callous, cold, calculating attributes of this mental outlook combined with selfish motivation could make "mind upload" an appealing tool for grand-scale control of others. It is even conceivable that clever Machiavellian-oriented individuals would masquerade as utilitarian ethicists in order to promote their covert goal of world domination. Laakasuo et al. argued that this is the first study to establish an empirical link between morality and psychological dispositions. Noting the low correlation between psychopathy, approval of mind upload, and utilitarianism, Laakasuo et al. maintain that psychopathy is substantially correlated to various dimensions in the Machiavellian profile, and these items can load on a mutual factor. Although the researchers focus on psychopathy since this has become a hot topic in discussions of the safety of AIG, the impulsivity and need for immediate gratification inherent in the psychopathic personality type make it unlikely that psychopaths would engage with "mind upload." By contrast, the strategic, more calculated mindset of Machiavellian-oriented types would be able to encompass the long-term power implications of "mind upload." Laakasuo et al. (2021) conclude that the risk that this Dark Triad personality type presents to future developments in the field of AGI is not trivial.

6.3   Other forms of cybercrime

This section deals with the relation of personality types in the Dark Tetrad with other forms of cybercrime such as media piracy, phishing, and fraud.

6.3.1   Digital Media Piracy

Piracy of digital media is the act of uploading, downloading, or streaming nonpurchased music tracks, films, or any other media. Easy access to copying technology on the Internet makes digital piracy easy to accomplish. For example, MUSO, a company tracking digital media piracy, reports that in 2019, the last season of the popular TV show "Game of Thrones" was downloaded illegally over 66 million times in just one format alone (Satchell, Corr, & Latzman, 2022). Media piracy is part of a group of illegal activities going by the term "micro-crimes," illegal activities with low immediate interpersonal consequences are known to be implemented by many individuals in society who do not consider this transgressive. DataProt, an independent review site, presented some piracy statistics for 2023. Their statistics revealed that pirated video material gets over 230 billion views annually. More than 80% of global online piracy can be attributed to illegal streaming services. Digital video piracy costs the United States economy between $29.2 and $71 billion annually. In addition, 126.7 billion viewings worth of United States-produced TV episodes are pirated annually. Annual global revenue losses from digital piracy are between $40 and $97.1 billion in the movie industry. Illegal downloading of copyrighted materials takes up 24% of the global bandwidth (DataProt, 2023).

Despite the financial or moral implications of media piracy, there is little contemporary research on the personality traits of the individuals who engage in it. Empirical research on these behaviors might aid in developing targeted interventions to prevent this type of illegal activity. Not only does digital media piracy require little expertise, but it also has formidable prosocial implications – namely, the group bonding that is evidenced when many people view pirated television programs or films together. Satchell et al. find that the average participant has engaged in media piracy at least once, suggesting that this illegal behavior is more widespread than previous research suggests.

6.3.1.1 The Dark Triad/Tetrad and Digital Media Piracy

The responses in the sample of 351 international and 321 American participants in the Satchell et al. (2022) research show that psychopathy is not highly correlated to media piracy. Furthermore, the callousness and meanness associated with this personality type have a limited direct impact on the interpersonal nature of this micro-crime.

6.3.2 Phishing

Phishing, one of the more widespread forms of hacking, is a "form of social engineering in which attackers (known as phishers) attempt to retrieve confidential data from individuals by fraudulently mimicking automated electronic communications from seemingly trustworthy public organizations" (Myers, 2006, p. 1). Attackers collect private data (i.e., user account passwords, credit/debit card numbers) using phony emails or fake websites created by copying pages from legitimate websites and sending a fraudulent Internet address to targeted victims via spam messages, texts, or social networking (Basit et al., 2021). The phishing websites are common entry points for socially engineered fraud.

Phishing originates from obtaining unauthorized access to the network of a membership-based online service provider. As personal identity in virtual space becomes increasingly more valuable, attempts to steal and misuse user data only intensify. Based on technology developed in the mid-1990s, phishers are able to create false user accounts and fraudulently generate credit card numbers. They then send out messages prompting users to update their accounts or validate their profiles. In this way, they gain access to sensitive information and financial data (Lee & Paek, 2020).

Cybersecurity statistics indicate that there are 2,200 cyberattacks daily, with a cyber-attack happening every 39 seconds on average. In the United States, a data breach costs an average of $9.44M, and cybercrime is predicted to cost $8 trillion by 2023. About 300,000 new malware are created daily, 92% of which are delivered via email and have a detection period of 49 days. Statista reveals that the global Security as a Service market is projected to reach over $22 billion in 2026. In the first six months of 2022, 2.8 billion malware attacks and 255 million phishing attacks were reported. In 2022, 71% of businesses reported falling victim to ransomware attacks (James, 2023).

In 2018, over a third of phishing attacks were hosted on websites with https and secure sockets layer certificates (Lee & Paek, 2020). Phishing attempts have been aimed payment services (36%), software-as-a-service/webmail (21%), financial institutions (16%), file hosting or cloud storage (9%), and social media (4%). In addition, a technique known as spear phishing relies on deceiving recipients into opening malicious attachments or links. The programs activated at these "innocent" addresses then plant malware on the phones, tablets, and computers of the unsuspecting victims. This technique has been employed by 71% of organized groups. Research shows that consumers perceive privacy and security concerns as obstacles to online shopping. They also maintain negative views of unsolicited emails sent by online merchants. Other intrusions include online harassment, Internet snooping (unauthorized access to another person's or company's data), and other aggressive or intrusive behaviors (Lee & Paek, 2020).

Lee and Paek (2020) list several types of phishing:

Voice phishing: Phishers can subvert smartphones that have Internet access to gather information for their attack. In voice phishing (also known as vishing), scammers engage in direct conversation with victims following a predefined script. Using phone numbers that appear to be valid (i.e., the lure) and by answering questions from potential victims (i.e., the hook), fishers generate the trust they need to proceed with their scam operations.

Email-based phishing: Email phishing allows offenders to target many people simultaneously. Fraudsters send seemingly legitimate email messages (i.e., the lure), for instance, impersonating an employee in a company security department complete with the organization's email address signature and logo. Recipients are prompted to follow a link in the message asking for their personal data to resolve supposed issues with their accounts.

Spear phishing: Spear phishing is the selective targeting of a group of people who possess some commonality. In this type of phishing, offenders carefully research their targets in order to tailor their attack. Spear phishing attacks are delivered via phone calls, email, text messages, and social media. Phishing continues to evolve by adjusting to developing technologies and exploiting human error, unpredictability, and heuristics. Spam filters developed to detect and deter phishing campaigns are continually being made obsolete by sophisticated personalized emails that persuade people to respond (Curtis et al., 2018).

6.3.2.1 The Dark Triad/Tetrad and Phishing

According to Moody, Galletta, and Dunn (2017), understanding how personality traits in the Dark Tetrad affect Internet security could assist in the development of more accurate detection methods. Curtis et al. (2018) examined adjustments made to phishing emails by Dark Triad personalities. Curtis et al.'s experiment used two cohorts of American participants; the first 100 acted as attackers and the second 340 as end-users. The first set was charged with creating phishing emails and the second set was charged with reading them along with harmless emails. The findings show that individuals preponderantly high in psychopathic traits are more likely to send mass emails that require little effort. Their impulsiveness makes them poor at tasks involving attention to detail. They also tend to make minimal changes to the subject line of the phishing emails they send. Likewise, narcissists' overconfidence inhibits them from making alterations to their phishing strategy that might assist them in avoiding possible detection. Exaggerated belief in their own skill leads them to adopt less individualized techniques. By contrast, phishers high in Machiavellian traits do tend to calibrate phishing emails, carefully adjusting them to match specific characteristics of the recipients they intend to defraud.

While it might seem that individuals who score high in any of the personality traits in the Dark Triad would not be vulnerable to malicious email attacks due to their low willingness to consent to any proposal, Curtis et al. find that narcissists' overblown sense of invulnerability makes them susceptible to phishing. Curtis et al. also find that although high scores on the Dark Triad do not correlate with the effectiveness of the phishing emails, there is a marginally significant dyadic relationship between the phishing emails created by narcissistic attackers and narcissistic end-users. First, Curtis et al. deduce that narcissists' exaggerated belief in their own perspicuity may prevent them from detecting phishing attempts that come their way. Second, individuals high in narcissism are functionally impulsive and may pursue potentially interesting emails without considering the consequences. This is borne out by Sudzina and Pavlicek (2017), who, upon surveying 133 university students from the Czech Republic, conclude that narcissists are more likely to click on seemingly advantageous offers once led there by websites touting "good deals."

6.3.3   Fraud

Fraud, as defined by the Oxford American Dictionary, is "intentional deception or misrepresentation that could result in some unauthorized benefit to oneself" (Smith, Emerson & Mauldin, 2021, p. 1). Cressey (1953) created what is called the fraud triangle, whose three vertices represent opportunity, incentives, and rationalization. Opportunity is defined as advantageous circumstances for committing fraud: perhaps weak controls or a lax managerial, regulatory, or cultural environment. Incentives are defined as the pressure, either internal or external, driving someone to commit fraud. Finally, rationalization is defined as the need to justify doing something that is socially viewed as improper (Ramamoorti & Epstein, 2016). Since it is unusual to commit fraud without suffering some psychological distress from cognitive–affective dissonance, a typical fraudster tells himself: "Everybody is doing it, and I am no different from others who are overworked, underpaid, and deserve their ill-gotten gain." This enables perpetrators to assuage normal feelings of guilt (Cressey, 1953).

Wolfe and Hermanson (2004) augment Cressey's model by adding the factor of capability, which represents the specific traits and abilities that influence the decision to commit fraud. As Wolfe and Hermanson put it (pp. 38–39), "Opportunity opens the doorway to fraud, and incentive and rationalization can draw the person toward it. But the individual must also have the capability to recognize the open doorway ... and to take advantage of it by walking through [it]." Smith et al. (2021) state that the framework developed by Wolfe and Hermanson (2004) is an incremental modification of the theoretical model advanced by Cressey (1953).

By including capability in the model, the use of the Dark Tetrad can uncover a deeper dimension in the psychological dynamics of fraudulent behavior. As it turns out, while the incidence of deviant, abnormal personalities is relatively small in the general male population – 2% or less – on Wall Street and in corporate America, the incidence of traits in the Dark Tetrad seems to be in the 10–20% range. This figure includes those described as subclinical psychopaths ("almost psychopaths") (Ramamoorti & Epstein, 2016). With respect to the fraud triangle, the vertices of rationalization and incentives become irrelevant as conceiving of rationalizations does not concern anyone with little or no conscience, and pressure or incentive is endemic to this work environment. In such circumstances, the fraud triangle collapses into a singularity: opportunity. Personality types in the Dark Tetrad do "whatever it takes" to enrich themselves or to experience the high of "getting away with it." With such individuals, the likelihood of fraud is high. Once individuals with Dark Tetrad personalities have attained positions of power and influence, the possibility of eliminating potential opportunities is hardly guaranteed. Because of their dominance, these personality types may be able to override well-designed controls instituted against fraud and create opportunities that would not have existed otherwise (Ramamoorti & Epstein, 2016). According to Kramer and Seda (2017), individuals high in traits in the Dark Tetrad are more prevalent in corporate management, and they may become predators who actively search for opportunities to commit fraud over and over again.

There are several forms of fraud including insurance fraud and online consumer fraud.

6.3.3.1 Insurance Fraud

Most adults in the developed world maintain some form of insurance: Social insurance, health insurance, automobile insurance, home insurance, or insurance for valuable possessions. While it is impossible to estimate the exact extent of fraudulent insurance claims, the Coalition Against Insurance Fraud estimates that in 2006, about $80 billion was lost in the United States due to insurance fraud (Insurance Fraud, 2022). Moreover, recent data show that insurance fraud costs American consumers $308.6 billion annually in increased rates. The United States insurance fraud statistics reveal that, in 2021, fraud was suspected in 20% of insurance claims. Insurance fraud costs an average United States family between $400 and $700 annually through increased premiums. In 2020, the global identity theft insurance market amounted to around $570 million (Lazic, 2022).

Given the association of the traits in the Dark Tetrad with willful, deceitful, manipulative, and malevolent behavior, it is reasonable to presume that these personality traits would exist in those individuals who present fraudulent claims for deliberately broken items or for items that were broken while drunk or angry that are covered under household insurance (Modic et al., 2018).

6.3.3.2 Online Consumer Fraud

Specific characteristics of online consumer transactions make them especially prone to consumer fraud (Harrison et al., 2018). First, these transactions usually occur over commonly used communication channels such as emails and web pages. Second, the difficulty in validating identities in online transactions provides ample opportunity to commit fraud. Third, this wholesale abuse of information systems occurs due to the absence of adequate mechanisms of punishment or control. Finally, existing control systems are often fragmentary and quickly outdated due to technological advances. As a result, online consumer fraud has increasingly become systematic, enabling fraudsters to solicit easy victims.

6.3.4 The Dark Triad/Tetrad and Cyber Fraud

6.3.4.1 Narcissists and Cyber Fraud

The exaggerated self-view of narcissists indicates long-term psychological distress and dysfunction (Harrison et al., 2018). One nonmonetary motivation in committing fraud is ego gratification; the desire to be portrayed as superior in combination with exploitative socially inconsiderate attitudes toward others make narcissists more motivated to commit fraud.

6.3.4.2   *Machiavellianism and Cyber Fraud*

Since individuals with high levels of Machiavellian traits strongly distrust others – often manifesting in paranoia and cynicism – they tend to engage in fraud only when the risk of getting caught is low (Harrison et al., 2018). Keen awareness of their surroundings make them hesitant to engage in unethical activity that others could witness. Yet, their approval of manipulation as a valid mechanism for accomplishing their goals and good communication skills allow them to take pleasure in economic opportunism. Monetary rewards and the prestige of "getting away with it" are strong motivators for this personality type (Harrison et al., 2018).

6.3.4.3   *Psychopaths and Cyber Fraud*

As they believe that they are above the social, moral, and legal principles that govern society, those who rate high on a scale of psychopathic traits exhibit more amoral and antisocial behavior than individuals who do not. Psychopathic personalities rarely experience shame or remorse and are more likely to rationalize acts of fraud (Harrison et al., 2018). Individuals with these traits willingly dominate others with no sensitivity to the feelings of the people they hurt. Nor are they perturbed by the impact of their behavior on the emotional, financial, physical, social, or professional well-being of others. The superficial apologies of subclinical psychopaths fail to convey any sense of remorse.

Secondary psychopathy is associated with impulsive, short-term decision-making. Their acting because they "want to" has a narcissistic tone, although they prefer to characterize themselves as spontaneous free spirits. Situations that elicit anger or frustration may increase their propensity to commit fraudulent cyber behavior (March, 2022). So far, there is hardly any information about sadism and fraud.

6.3.5   *Research Findings*

Ansari (2020), in a study of American workers, found that different aspects of the personality types in the Dark Triad correlate with different dimensions of fraud. Their findings show that individuals scoring high in psychopathic traits are more willing to rationalize online fraud, and this tendency expedites their intention to commit it. High scores on Machiavellian traits in the Dark Triad correlate significantly with perceived opportunities to commit cyber fraud and the subsequent motivation to do so. Narcissism significantly affects capability, but narcissists may not be compelled to commit fraud because they fear that getting caught would affect their image.

Ansari concludes that individuals with high combinations of psychopathy, Machiavellianism, and narcissism possess both the mindset and the interpersonal behavior patterns that ultimately stimulate intent to commit fraud. Therefore, a deeper analysis of their psychological traits is imperative.

Modic et al. (2018) designed a two-part online study consisting of realistic online insurance claim scenarios to evaluate the behavior of individuals submitting insurance claims in relation to the Dark Triad. One part of the study, containing 344 respondents, included monetary incentives; the other, containing 699 respondents, did not. The two parts were performed consecutively. The authors hypothesize that whether analyzed separately or in combination, traits in the Dark Triad would positively correlate with exaggerated claim sizes and "fibbing," claiming fraudulent damages (like entering claims for items that were intentionally broken).

The findings show that while all traits in the Dark Triad positively predict "fibbing," the effects are strongest when all traits are taken together. In the study without monetary incentives, the link between psychopathy and "fibbing" was weak, confirming that these individuals require concrete goals as motivators. In the monetized study, this incentive emerges as the strongest predictor of "fibbing." The researchers conclude that all traits in the Dark Triad should be viewed as one construct since the multicollinearity of the variables might make the statistics unreliable. The study shows that the effect of the Dark Triad on willingness to commit insurance fraud is modulated by situational factors. Greater willingness to commit insurance fraud among individuals with high psychopathic tendencies occurs when the insured items are broken in anger rather than when the damage occurs accidentally or when the individual causing the damage was drunk.

Harrison et al. (2018) use a two-pronged experiment employing American college students to examine the relationship between traits in the Dark Triad and online consumer fraud. The data reveal that each element of the Dark Triad affects different aspects of the decision-making process, leading to commission of consumer fraud. Psychopathic and Machiavellian traits influence intentions to commit cyber fraud more substantially than narcissism, while narcissism significantly affects motivation and capabilities. Machiavellian propensities affect opportunity and motivation. Psychopathic traits affect rationalization substantively. Individuals who score high in psychopathy, narcissism, and Machiavellianism combined possess personality traits that activate every phase in the decision-making process of committing fraud. The study also indicates that deterrence mechanisms affect the psychological profiles differently.

Orhan and Collisson (2022) investigate how often people make false online claims to receive free food from restaurant take-out services and how acceptable they perceive this behavior to be. The study examines 197 adults in the United States. The data reveal that consumers of restaurant delivery services who score high in traits in the Dark Triad are more likely to submit false claims for refunds. They also find that consumers who score high in narcissism and psychopathy are most likely to have engaged in refund fraud and are most likely to do so in the future. These individuals are also most likely to perceive their behavior as socially acceptable.

The inherent challenge of validating subjective customer complaints makes restaurant take-out delivery a ripe source of exploitation by individuals with personality traits in the Dark Tetrad. Narcissists use their social adeptness by reporting food as missing, damaged, or mislabeled. When narcissists' over-the-top expectations of the food deliveries are not met, their complaints regarding restaurants that they once rated as "fine" may inadvertently be recorded as refund fraud. Given the popularity of take-out food (Yeo et al., 2017), the easy availability of instructions on how to defraud food delivery services on the Internet (McKenna, 2020; DarkOwl, 2021), and the difficulty of operationalizing food refund fraud in light of the perverted behavior of individuals in the Dark Triad, more research is needed on the connection between exploitative personalities, particularly narcissism and food expectations. Sadism, the willingness to hurt others, may also be a significant factor in giving restaurants and take-out services poor reviews (Orhan & Collisson, 2022).

Smith, Emerson, and Mauldin (2021, 2023) examine the relationship between Dark Triad personality traits and students' propensity to engage in online cheating. Smith et al. (2023) emphasized that in the online environment, students have greater opportunity to collaborate and access forbidden resources, while educators have a reduced capacity to monitor and enforce academic integrity. Cheating in cyberspace is easier and more convenient than ever, and instructors must be aware of students' strategies to circumvent the learning process. Using the conceptual model of the Fraud Diamond and its influence on specific traits in the Dark Triad, their first study (Smith et al., 2021) is based on the responses of 209 undergraduates in accounting at two universities in the United States. The research shows that each element of the Dark Triad impacts the ethical decision-making process involved in resorting to homework assistance websites.

The data show that narcissism correlates directly with capability but not with motivation. However, an indirect connection between narcissism and motivation exists through capability and opportunity. Narcissism has a significant indirect positive correlation with the intent to commit fraud and the act itself. However, those associations are relatively weak. Machiavellianism has significant indirect correlation with motivation. This is in opposition to most prior research, which indicates the minor influence of Machiavellianism on academic cheating. Psychopathy was the only trait that had a strong direct relationship with motivation, not unsurprisingly. Psychopathy was far more potent in predicting intention and action than any other element in the Dark Triad. The effect of psychopathy on intention was more than six times greater than that of narcissism and nearly four times greater than narcissism on execution. Machiavellianism seems only to impact opportunity (Smith et al., 2021).

The second study (Smith et al., 2023) examined 631 American university students. They found that rationalization was the culmination of academic misconduct and that one's capacity to rationalize the proposed action is directly associated with motivation, capability, and opportunity. Their findings also showed that rationalization was directly related to students' intentions to use unauthorized websites during online assessments and their actual use. Their results were generally consistent with those of Smith et al. (2021). Moreover, their findings of significant associations between opportunity, rationalization, narcissism, and motivation conformed with their respective theoretical foundations. Also, in line with their theoretical predictions, they found positive associations between psychopathy and both motivation and intention, as well as between rationalization and action, thereby replicating the results reported by Smith et al. (2021).

The two studies confirm that each element in the Dark Triad exerts a differential influence on the components of the Fraud Diamond and on individuals' intentions to commit and engage in academic fraud. Furthermore, it shows that the traits in the Dark Tetrad amplify each phase of the decision-making process.

*****

Table 6.1 summarizes the findings of the studies revealing the role of the Dark Tetrad in cybercrime. Psychopathy seems to have the strongest relationship, followed by Machiavellianism and then narcissism. It should be noted that very few studies examine the effect of sadism. This is a lack that needs to be addressed.

Table 6.1 *Summary of research findings of the relationship between the Dark Tetrad/Triad and cybercrime*

Study	Sample size	Type of behavior	Gender	Age (mean)	AT or similar	Country	Occupation	Education	Narcissists	Psychopathy	Machiavellianism	Sadism
						Sample characteristics			Correlations			
Gaia et al. (2020)	439	Black-hat hackers	28% female	Between 20 and 21	No	USA	Sophomore and junior undergraduate students	Sophomore and junior undergraduate students	No significant relationship	Significant relationship	Significant relationship	NE
Gaia et al. (2020)	439	White-hat hackers	28% female	Between 20 and 21	No	USA	Sophomore and junior undergraduate students	Sophomore and junior undergraduate students	Significant relationship	Strong relationship	Strong relationship	NE
Gaia et al. (2020)	439	Gray-hat hackers	28% female	Between 20 and 21	No	USA	Sophomore and junior undergraduate students	Sophomore and junior undergraduate students	No significant relationship	Significant relationship	Significant relationship	NE
Gaia et al. (2022)	303	White-hat hackers	NR	NR	NO	USA	Undergraduate students	Undergraduate students	No significant relationship	Significant relationship	Significant relationship	
Seigfried-Spellar et al. (2017)	235	Website defacement	65% female	72% (between 18 and 35)	Yes	USA	NR	NR	NE	0.24***	NE	NE
Seigfried-Spellar et al. (2017)	235	Identity theft/fraud	65% female	72% (between 18 and 35)	Yes	USA	NR	NR	NE	0.44***	NE	NE
Seigfried-Spellar et al. (2017)	235	Virus writer	65% female	72% (between 18and 35)	Yes	USA	NR	NR	NE	0.36***	NE	NE
Seigfried-Spellar et al. (2017)	235	Unauthorized access	65% female	72% (between 18 and 35)	Yes	USA	NR	NR	NE	0.31***	NE	NE

Table 6.1 (*cont.*)

Study	Sample size	Type of behavior	Gender	Age (mean)	AT or similar	Country	Occupation	Education	Correlations			
									Narcissists	Psychopathy	Machiavellianism	Sadism
Seigfried-Spellar et al. (2017)	235	Total number of different types of computer crime	65% female	72% (between 18 and 35)	Yes	USA	NR	NR	NE	0.46***	NE	NE
Jones et al. (2021)	258	Long- vs. short-term deception	41% female	33.88	Yes	USA	NR	NR	0.15*	0.07	0.44**	NE
Jones et al. (2021)	258	Hacking step: passive reconnaissance	41% female	33.88	Yes	USA	NR	NR	-0.01	-0.01	0.10	NE
Jones et al. (2021)	258	Hacking step: active reconnaissance	41% female	33.88	Yes	USA	NR	NR	-0.11	-0.09	0.09	NE
Jones et al. (2021)	258	Hacking step: exploitation	41% female	33.88	Yes	USA	NR	NR	-0.11	-0.18**	-0.11	NE
Jones et al. (2021)	258	Hacking step: elevation of privilege	41% female	33.88	Yes	USA	NR	NR	-0.13*	-0.10	0.04	NE
Jones et al. (2021)	258	Hacking step: establish persistence	41% female	33.88	Yes	USA	NR	NR	-0.16*	-0.14*	0.00	NE
Jones et al. (2021)	258	Hacking step: extracting data	41% female	33.88	Yes	USA	NR	NR	-0.12*	0.02	-0.07	NE
Jones et al. (2021)	258	Hacking step: covering up	41% female	33.88	Yes	USA	NR	NR	-0.02	-0.05	0.00	NE
Jones et al. (2021)	213	Hacking step: top ports	25% female	24.44	No	USA	NR	Students and staff members at a large university	-0.06	0.06	0.21**	NE

Jones et al. (2021)	213	Hacking step: ping count	25% female	24–44	No	USA	NR	Students and staff members at a large university	0.05	0.09	0.10	NE
Jones et al. (2021)	213	Hacking step: flags	25% female	24–44	No	USA	NR	Students and staff members at a large university	−0.08	−0.04	0.19**	NE
Jones et al. (2021)	213	Hacking step: command count	25% female	24–44	No	USA	NR	Students and staff members at a large university	0.01	0.06	0.21**	NE
Jones et al. (2021)	213	Hacking step: alerts raised	25% female	24–44	No	USA	NR	Students and staff members at a large university	−0.08	−0.06	0.05	NE
Jones et al. (2021)	213	Hacking step: subnetwork score	25% female	24–44	No	USA	NR	Students and staff members at a large university	0.04	0.15*	0.08	NE
Jones et al. (2021)	213	Long-term deception	25% female	24–44	No	USA	NR	Students and staff members at a large university	0.20**	0.18**	0.44**	NE
Jones et al. (2021)	213	Hacking knowledge	25% female	24–44	No	USA	NR	Students and staff members at a large university	0.011	−0.06	0.01	NE
Ansari (2020)	290	Intention to commit fraud	35% female	58% below 35 (18–70)	Yes	USA	48.6% earn 45,000 US$ and above	71.7% B.A. degree and above	0.037**	0.51**	0.44**	NE
Ansari (2020)	290	Perceived opportunity to commit fraud	35% female	58% below 35 (18–70)	Yes	USA	48.6% earn 45,000 US$ and above	71.7% B.A. degree and above	0.015**	0.28**	0.38**	NE
Ansari (2020)	290	Perceived capability to commit fraud	35% female	58% below 35 (18–70)	Yes	USA	48.6% earn 45,000 US$ and above	71.7% B.A. degree and above	0.34**	0.41**	0.49**	NE
Ansari (2020)	290	Willingness to rationalize online fraud	35% female	58% below 35 (18–70)	Yes	USA	48.6% earn 45,000 US$ and above	71.7% B.A. degree and above	0.54**	0.69**	0.55**	NE
Ansari (2020)	290	Motivation to commit online fraud	35% female	58% below 35 (18–70)	Yes	USA	48.6% earn 45,000 US$ and above	71.7% B.A. degree and above	0.14**	0.27**	0.42**	NE

Table 6.1 (*cont.*)

Study	Sample size	Type of behavior	Sample characteristics						Correlations			
			Gender	Age (mean)	AT or similar	Country	Occupation	Education	Narcissists	Psychopathy	Machiavellianism	Sadism
Selzer & Oelrich (2021)	53	Cybercrime intention	47.1% female	23.49 (19–29)	No	Germany	Students in a German university	Students in a German university	0.05	0.337*	0.30 (*p* < 0.1)	NE
Selzer & Oelrich (2021)	53	A positive attitude toward hacking	47.1% female	23.49 (19–29)	No	Germany	Students in a German university	Students in a German university	0.020	0.244	0.239	NE
Selzer & Oelrich (2021)	53	Positive subjective norm toward hacking	47.1% female	23.49 (19–29)	No	Germany	Students in a German university	Students in a German university	0.102	0.420*	0.328*	NE
Selzer & Oelrich (2021)	53	Perceived ability to hack	47.1% female	23.49 (19–29)	No	Germany	Students in a German university	Students in a German university	0.020	0.229	0.215	NE
Modic et al. (2018)	344	Insurance fraud: 0 = did not over-claim; 1 = over-claimed at least once	55.5% female	40 (18–75)	Yes	United Kingdom	NR	NR	0.13*	0.09	0.12*	NE
Harrison et al. (2018)	303	Motivation to commit online consumer fraud	NR	NR	No	USA	College students	College students	0.081	0.180	0.208**	NE
Harrison et al. (2018)	303	Perceived opportune to commit online consumer fraud	NR	NR	No	USA	College students	College students	0.085	–0.138**	–0.044	NE

Study	N	Variable	% female	Age		Country	Sample	Sample detail				NE
Harrison et al. (2018)	303	Perceived capabilities to commit online consumer fraud	NR	NR	No	USA	College students	College students	−0.213**	0.179	0.268**	NE
Harrison et al. (2018)	303	Willingness to rationalize committing seller fraud.	NR	NR	No	USA	College students	College students	−0.272**	0.697***	0.607***	NE
Harrison et al. (2018)	303	Intention to commit online consumer fraud	NR	NR	No	USA	College students	College students	−0.234	0.697***	0.569***	NE
Carre et al. (2018)	253	The company's responsibility to protect the data	61% female	37–56	Yes	USA	NR	NR	−0.138*	−0.314*	−0.104	NE
Carre et al. (2018)	253	Individual's responsibility for protecting data	61% female	37–56	Yes	USA	NR	NR	0.061	0.003	0.053	NE
Carre et al. (2018)	253	Company's responsibility for data breach	61% female	37–56	Yes	USA	NR	NR	−0.305*	−0.297*	−0.068	NE
Carre et al. (2018)	253	Individual's responsibility for data breach	61% female	37–56	Yes	USA	NR	NR	0.305*	0.338*	0.177*	NE
Maasberg et al. (2020)	768	Intentions to engage in insider threat behavior	42% female	34.7 (18–73)	Yes	USA	Working professionals from a variety of occupations	N.R.	β = 0.286, p < 0.001	β = 0.559, p < 0.001	β = 0.379, p < 0.001	NE
Smith et al. (2021)	209	Capability of online cheating	57.4% female	95% (between 19 and 24)	No	USA	Undergraduate students	9% freshmen, 18% sophomores, 33% juniors, 40% seniors	0.170	Morality = 0.046; impulsiveness = −0.032	0.055	NE

Table 6.1 (*cont.*)

			Sample characteristics							Correlations			
Study	Sample size	Type of behavior	Gender	Age (mean)	AT or similar	Country	Occupation	Education	Narcissists	Psychopathy	Machiavellianism	Sadism
Smith et al. (2021)	209	Rationalization for online cheating	57.4% female	95% (between 19 and 24)	No	USA	Undergraduate students	9% freshmen, 18% sophomores, 33% juniors, 40% seniors	0.345**	Morality = 0.311**; impulsiveness = 0.204	0.250	NE
Smith et al. (2021)	209	Opportunity for online cheating	57.4% female	95% (between 19 and 24)	No	USA	Undergraduate students	9% freshmen, 18% sophomores, 33% juniors, 40% seniors	0.166	Morality = 0.016; impulsiveness = 0.024	0.204	NE
Smith et al. (2021)	209	Intention to commit online cheating	57.4% female	95% (between 19 and 24)	No	USA	Undergraduate students	9% freshmen, 18% sophomores, 33% juniors, 40% seniors	0.350**	Morality = 0.400**; impulsiveness = 0.307**	0.261*	NE
Smith et al. (2021)	209	Online cheating	57.4% female	95% (between 19 and 24)	No	USA	Undergraduate students	9% freshmen, 18% sophomores, 33% juniors, 40% seniors	0.222	Morality = 0.157; impulsiveness = 0.114	0.184	NE
Laakasuo et al. (2021)	1007	Approval of mind upload	54% female	37.55	Prolific Academic	Finland	NR	60% had at least a Bachelor's degree or higher	−0.01	0.15***	0.18***	NE
Orhan & Collisson (2022)	197	Likeliness of engaging in fraud (food refund)	44.7% female	38.49 (19–69)	Yes	USA	97.9% employed/ self-employed	NR	0.74***	0.85***	0.83***	NE
Orhan & Collisson (2022)	197	Perceived acceptability of fraud (food refund)	44.7% female	38.49 (19–69)	Yes	USA	97.9% employed/ self-employed	NR	0.72***	0.83***	0.83***	NE
Orhan & Collisson (2022)	197	Refund fraud rationalization (food refund)	44.7% female	38.49 (19–69)	Yes	USA	97.9% employed/ self-employed	NR	0.8***	0.69***	0.66***	NE

Study	N	Variable	% female	Age	Platform	Country	Employment/expertise					
Orhan & Collisson (2022)	197	Previous refund fraud (No = 0, Yes = 1) (food refund)	44.7% female	38.49 (19–69)	Yes	USA	97.9% employed/ self-employed	NR	0.52***	0.63***	0.62***	NE
Orhan & Collisson (2022)	197	Food refund fraud frequency	44.7% female	38.49 (19–69)	Yes	USA	97.9% employed/ self-employed	NR	0.47***	0.59***	0.57***	NE
Padayachee (2020, 2021)	170	Neutralization (total)	24% female	28.8% = 35–44; 34.1% = 45–54;	LinkedIn	South Africa	44% – expertise in information technology (IT)	NR	0.133	0.487***	0.301**	NE
Padayachee (2020, 2021)	170	Intention for desirable security behavior	24% female	28.8% = 35–44; 34.1% = 45–54;	LinkedIn	South Africa	44% – expertise in IT	NR	0.020	−0.272**	−0.097	NE
Padayachee (2020, 2021)	170	Actual security behavior	24% female	28.8% = 35–44; 34.1% = 45–54;	LinkedIn	South Africa	44% – expertise in IT	NR	−0.014	−0.192*	−0.087	NE
Padayachee (2020, 2021)	170	Neutralization: denial of responsibility	24% female	28.8% = 35–44; 34.1% = 45–54;	LinkedIn	South Africa	44% – expertise in IT	NR	0.0025	0.394***	0.205*	NE
Padayachee (2020, 2021)	170	Condemnation of the condemners	24% female	28.8% = 35–44; 34.1% = 45–54;	LinkedIn	South Africa	44% – expertise in IT	NR	0.0092	0.408***	0.217**	NE
Padayachee (2020, 2021)	170	Appeal to higher loyalties	24% female	28.8% = 35–44; 34.1% = 45–54;	LinkedIn	South Africa	44% – expertise in IT	NR	0.0016	0.405***	0.234**	NE
Padayachee (2020, 2021)	170	Denial of injury	24% female	28.8% = 35–44; 34.1% = 45–54;	LinkedIn	South Africa	44% – expertise in IT	NR	0.188*	0.419***	0.345***	NE
Padayachee (2020, 2021)	170	Defense of necessity	24% female	28.8% = 35–44; 34.1% = 45–54;	LinkedIn	South Africa	44% – expertise in IT	NR	0.181*	0.448***	0.307**	NE
Padayachee (2020, 2021)	170	Metaphor of the ledger	24% female	28.8% = 34.1% – 45–54;	LinkedIn	South Africa	44% – expertise in IT	NR	0.432***	0.170*	0.319**	NE

Table 6.1 (cont.)

Study	Sample size	Type of behavior	Gender	Age (mean)	AT or similar	Country	Occupation	Education	Narcissists	Psychopathy	Machiavellianism	Sadism
									Sample characteristics → Correlations			
Smith et al. (2023)	631	Online cheating: capability	58.3% female	592 (below 24)	No	USA	University students	University students	0.241**	0.132	0.150*	NE
Smith et al. (2023)	631	Online cheating: opportunity	58.3% female	592 (below 24)	No	USA	University students	University students	0.249**	0.094	0.134	NE
Smith et al. (2023)	631	Online cheating: motivation	58.3% female	592 (below 24)	No	USA	University students	University students	0.285**	0.345**	0.315**	NE
Smith et al. (2023)	631	Online cheating: rationalization	58.3% female	592 (below 24)	No	USA	University students	University students	0.320**	0.346**	0.329**	NE
Smith et al. (2023)	631	Online cheating: intention	58.3% female	592 (below 24)	No	USA	University students	University students	0.322**	0.402	0.340**	NE
Smith et al. (2023)	631	Online cheating: action	58.3% female	592 (below 24)	No	USA	University students	University students	0.266**	0.175	0.200**	NE

Note: AT = Amazon Turk; NR = not reported; NE = not examined; GN = grandiose narcissism; VN = vulnerable narcissism; SNS = social network sites.
* $p < 0.05$; ** $p < 0.01$; *** $p < 0.001$.

CHAPTER 7

The Dark Triad/Tetrad and Romantic Relationships in Cyberspace

7.1 Intimate Relationships in Cyberspace

The Internet has become a significant field for social interactions. The growing number of users, together with developments such as email, chats, instant messaging, and video conferencing such as Microsoft Teams, Zoom, and FaceTime, has fostered the formation of a new category of interpersonal relationships, namely, that of the online relationship (Aviram & Amichai-Hamburger, 2005; Chamie, 2022). The increasing popularity of online dating in the past 20 years has come with a growth in both the number and revenue of online dating websites. Over 1,400 dating sites in North America alone are estimated to generate 2 to 4 billion dollars in revenue annually (Lamphere & Lucas, 2019). The popularity of online dating has also grown worldwide in recent years and is projected to continue. In 2022, there were over 366 million online dating service users. By 2027, it is estimated that there will be 440 million people seeking love through online platforms. Additionally, Internet dating generated 2.86 billion US dollars in 2022, with the market showing no signs of slowing down (Statista, 2023b).

Popular sites such as Match.com, eHarmony. com, Chemistry.com, OurTime.com, and OKCupid.com make it easy for individuals to meet potential online matches. While online dating sites provide an avenue for meeting people online, they also include the potential for these relationships to transition into offline face-to-face relationships. In addition to traditional websites, there are several popular online dating applications. Popular applications such as Tinder, Bumble, Coffee Meet Bagel, and Zoosk that users download to their phones make browsing easy for potential mates. Online dating is not limited to dating sites and applications; social networking sites such as Facebook, Instagram, Snapchat, and Twitter have created new ways of connecting with others who may share similar interests (Lamphere & Lucas, 2019). Mobile technology has increased the growth in the use of online dating sites. These innovative technologies provide a highly relevant platform for reaching out to men and women (Zerach, 2016; Olckers & Hattingh, 2022).

Cyber relationships are, in essence, virtual relationships or a form of communication between two people. Anonymity and privacy in relationships are something that is cherished by many. Virtual online friends win importance over time to real-life family and friends. People experiencing social phobia and anxiety can find a suitable outlet for their emotional needs. An affair in cyberspace is defined as a romantic and/or sexual relationship that is initiated via online contact and maintained predominantly through electronic conversations that occur through email and in virtual communities such as chat rooms, interactive games, or newsgroups (Young et al., 2000; Aviram & Amichai-Hamburger, 2005).

There are several differences between online and face-to-face interactions, called *real-life* relationships (Aviram & Amichai-Hamburger, 2005). First, the global nature of the Internet diminishes the requirement for physical proximity, which is essential in real-life relationships. Online users experience proximity by sharing the same cyberspace, which usually means sharing the same interests or social groups. Virtual or online communities allow strangers worldwide to meet instantly 24 hours per day, 7 days a week. Given the global nature of the Internet, online relationships can be culturally diverse and consequently seem more glamorous than the people one already knows in day-to-day living (Young et al., 2000; Aviram & Amichai-Hamburger, 2005).

Electronic communication allows at least some individuals to feel less inhibited. Consequently, such people might be likelier to be open, honest, and forthright in expressing their emotions and revealing personal truths (Young et al., 2000). Finally, the Internet allows users to maintain anonymity, thus fostering increased self-disclosure and creating a feeling of greater closeness, hyper-intimacy, and a hyper-personal effect (Amichai-Hamburger, 2005). As a result, the appearance of intimacy that might take months or years in an offline relationship may only take days or weeks online. This perceived sense of trust, intimacy, and acceptance has the potential to encourage online users to use these relationships as a primary source of companionship and comfort (Young et al., 2000).

For some people, an online relationship could progress into personal phone calls, letters, and offline meetings. Others prefer the distance and relative anonymity and control offered by the Internet and might prefer to confine the relationship to cyberspace. In either case, getting one's needs met through a romantic relationship in cyberspace might adversely impact an ongoing, long-term, face-to-face relationship and is likely to cause marital discord and separation and could ultimately lead to divorce. Clinicians increasingly see evidence of this as clients present concerns about how this new form of infidelity, the virtual affair, impacts their relationships. Thus, they must be aware of this trend as they assess couples and plan treatment strategies (Young et al., 2000).

Furthermore, once the person has begun to use online relationships to meet his or her needs, such online comfort can quickly turn into an erotic dialogue, often referred to as *cybersex*. Cybersex involves two online users engaging in private discourse about sexual fantasies. The dialogue is typically accompanied by sexual self-stimulation. Emotional intimacy can lead to cybersex, and the reverse is possible (Young et al., 2000). Those persons who are sexually compulsive may find the Internet an attractive venue to pursue these interests. For some, time online can quickly lead to talking with a cyberlover and/or various forms of cybersex (Young et al., 2000).

7.2 The Negative Outcomes of Cyber Relationships

While cyber relationships offer some advantages to normative people, they also attract dark personalities who perceive the nature of the cyber relationship as appealing for their malevolent intentions. Dark Tetrads use dating applications to hunt their predators. This is one of their preferred hunting grounds. Prior research on the greater degree of dark traits suggesting hostile masculinity found among dating application users may indicate that a relatively high percentage of violent predators use dating applications. These dating applications users can alter their profiles to appear likable and mild-mannered as a ruse to attract vulnerable potential victims. Once connected through dating applications, individuals with Dark Tetrads may manipulate individuals into trusting them and agreeing to an in-person meeting. Individuals with hostile masculinity traits are motivated by promiscuous and impersonal sex. Also, violent sexual perpetrators use dating applications as hunting grounds for vulnerable individuals (Valentine et al., 2023).

Virtual relationships have more than often devastated real lives. The popularity of mobile dating applications has increased reports of antisocial behavior. Antisocial behaviors can vary in intensity from unpleasant to violent and, whether intentional or not, result in a violation of social norms and a disregard for the recipient's right to feel safe and secure (Mayshak et al., 2020). Persons with criminal intentions are always in search of weak and unsuspecting minds. Dark personalities with exploited cyber relationships present fake profiles. These fake profiles are often created on social networking sites with vile intentions, and people are often tricked into false relationships. Robbery, thefts, kidnappings, blackmailing, and even murders have been the aftermath of such interactions. Many people have suffered irretrievable personal losses due to addiction to social networks (Bhattacharyya, 2015).

Catfishing, which can have a significant psychological impact, is a peculiar digital phenomenon that involves luring someone into a relationship by adopting a fictional online persona (Dey, 2022). Upon becoming aware of the deceit and scam, victims report experiencing depression, anxiety, paranoia, increased embarrassment, anger, and fear. Catfishing can also have a tremendous financial impact – for example, in 2020, Australian residents lost approximately $37 million (AUD) to catfishing, particularly romance scams (Lauder & March, 2023). In the United States in 2020, reported losses to romance scams reached a record $304 million, up about 50% from 2019. For an individual, that meant a median dollar loss of $2,500. From 2016 to 2020, reported total dollar losses increased more than fourfold, and the number of reports nearly tripled (Fletcher, 2021).

Cyber dating abuse can lead to adverse outcomes for the message receiver and possibly for the relationship. When people are hurt by a message from their partner, they typically try to distance themselves or may feel more distant. Relational distance impacts how partners feel toward one another and may lead to lower support, trust, and perceived relationship quality (Lancaster et al., 2019). In addition, there are mental health implications of cyber dating abuse victimization. Some studies suggest a link between cyber dating abuse victimization and depression. Cyber dating abuse was linked to depression even after accounting for psychological (non-cyber) violence by an intimate partner. In addition, cyber dating abuse has been linked to posttraumatic symptoms over and above any other form of intimate partner violence (Strickland, Love, & Kimmes, 2022). Experiencing cyber dating abuse is also associated with adverse psychological and physical outcomes, including weight change, sleep disturbances, and self-harm (Branson & March, 2021).

Another vulnerability of the victims of cyber relationships is revenge pornography. Like all acts of nonconsensual pornography, victimization by means of revenge pornography results in public shame and humiliation. Studies have shown that images posted on the most famous revenge pornography sites are viewed thousands of times. Revenge pornography can severely impact victims' mental health. Regarding broader public perceptions of revenge pornography, there is a general tendency to blame the victim, regardless of the perpetrator's sex or that of the victim. (Gavin & Scott, 2019). Victims of revenge pornography experience a loss of dignity, security, and respect from family and friends. The victims are perceived to be promiscuous, which leads to adverse subjective and social outcomes (Mckinlay & Lavis, 2020). They also reported experiencing humiliation, shame, embarrassment, and the ruin of their reputation; sexual shame and sexual problems; body image issues; education and employment disruptions; becoming paranoid and hyper-vigilant; having trust issues; and concerns for personal safety faced due to stalking, harassment, and threats of being gang-raped because their online and offline personal and professional information had also been published alongside the photos and text, which is also known as *doxing* (Hearn & Hall, 2022).

Experiencing sexual cyber abuse can have significant adverse effects, such as feelings of guilt, shame, and depression, often resulting in withdrawal from social networks and inflicting self-harm. Compared to other dating applications, Tinder is associated with short-term relationships, dangerous and often risky sexual behaviors, and acts of nonconsensual sex. In addition, compared to other dating applications, Tinder users may also experience more antisocial behavior, such as cybercrime and invasion of privacy (Duncan & March, 2019; Ciocca et al., 2020; Lyons et al., 2020; Linares et al., 2021).

Violence by an intimate partner can be another devastating experience for the victim of abuse in a cyber relationship. It is considered one of the most common types of violence and has been recognized as a public health problem in the last decade (World Health Organization, 2013). However, new technologies have introduced cyber dating with its new methods of abuse, which have devastating outcomes for victims. Mental health consequences related to intimate cyber partner violence victimization include depressive symptoms, anxiety, posttraumatic stress disorder, substance abuse including but not limited to alcohol and marijuana, aggressiveness or hostility, and suicidal ideation or attempts (Pineda et al., 2022a).

Finally, it should be noted that cyber dating abuse is challenging to detect. One of the reasons for this is that victims rarely contact law enforcement because of the embarrassment, shame, or harm that may result from reporting cybercrime victimization. Individuals are often targeted for romance scams, wherein a fraudster develops a romantic relationship with a person and gets the individual to send them money over time. Victims of these scams often feel substantial shame and embarrassment over their experience, not only because of the money lost but also because of the emotional trauma experienced by the betrayal of someone they thought loved them. Additionally, when they report their experiences to the police, they often report feeling blamed by the police because of their complicity in transferring funds to the fraudster (Holt et al., 2022).

Section 7.3 consists of three subsections. Section 7.3.1 reviews the behavior of Dark Tetrad personalities in dating applications, particularly Tinder. Tinder is among the most prevalent dating applications (Rochat et al., 2023). Therefore, it is not surprising that it has attracted the attention of Dark Tetrad personalities and has become one of their primary hunting grounds. There are other popular dating applications, such as Bumble. However, a significant amount of research on dating applications and Dark Tetrad personalities focuses on using Tinder to hunt their victims. Other dating application studies regarding dark personalities will also be reviewed.

Section 7.3.2 focuses on the nature of the relationship between Dark Tetrads and their victims. This relationship can be defined as toxic, and the foremost essential features of these relationships are reviewed in this section. These include *catfishing*, which occurs at the start of the relationship, an abusive intimate relationship in the more advanced stages, and *ghosting*, which may occur at the termination stage of relationships. For example, Dark Tetrad personalities who do not accept the end of the relationship may use revenge pornography to cause more profound destruction to their victims.

Section 7.3.3 focuses on darker aspects of the relationship between Dark Tetrad personalities and their victims, such as sexuality, pornography, nonconsensual sexual images and messages, cyberflashing, grooming, and child pornography. Few studies have examined the relationship between these disturbing behaviors and Dark Tetrad personalities. Studies relevant to these issues are presented in this subsection.

7.3   Dark Triad/Tetrad, Tinder, and Other Online Dating Applications

7.3.1   *The Motives of Dark Triad/Tetrad*

Online dating has created a new mating environment that differs from traditional mating. As a technological dating environment, Tinder is the flagship of online dating. Tinder users exhibit personality differences and other kinds of individual differences compared to nonusers (Sevi, 2019). Tinder, a location-based real-time dating (LBRTD) application, uses a global positioning system to 'match' users within similar proximity (Duncan & March, 2019; March et al., 2020a, 2020b). Tinder, well-known for its 'swipe right, swipe left' concept, has become an online-dating behemoth. It was the most downloaded dating application in 2022, with 64 million worldwide downloads. Additionally, more than any other region, Tinder was downloaded in North America and Latin America. In the United States, 84% of online daters were aware of Tinder, and 37% used the platform. Not only is it widely known by singles looking for love, but Tinder is the most prominent dating service in the United States, followed by Match and eHarmony (Statista, 2023b).

With 10 million active daily users, Tinder is the leading online dating application (Sevi, 2019; March et al., 2017). Its popularity has been corroborated in research, reporting that 92% of their participants had previously used Tinder. Such popularity statistics highlight the importance of Tinder receiving a particular research focus compared to other LBRTD applications (March et al., 2017; Duncan & March, 2019). Research has also found that Tinder is often used as a tool for users to engage in extradyadic sexual relationships (Timmermans, De Caluwe, & Alexopoulos, 2018; Lyons et al., 2020). The reason for using Tinder cited most often by the media is short-term relationships; the dating application is often referred to as a *hook-up application* (Lyons et al., 2022a). According to Timmermans et al. (2018), 18–25% of Tinder users are in a committed relationship while on Tinder. Tinder users who are not single may use this application to satisfy their curiosity or assess their value as potential dating partners. Tinder infidelity is sometimes restricted to forming an online-only bond with another user through online conversations (i.e., online emotional infidelity). However, it could also lead to face-to-face meetings and sexual intercourse with other users (i.e., offline sexual infidelity). While several findings show that some people use Tinder to be unfaithful, this is not necessarily the case for everyone (Timmermans et al., 2018).

Jonason and Bulyk (2019) noted that Tinder might be a compensatory mating strategy. Accordingly, they expect that people would prefer meeting their partners in their day-to-day lives, but when this is not possible, they may use Tinder to find the relationships and sex they want. However, face-to-face meetings have indeed characterized the evolution of human mating. There might be biases in mate selection mechanisms that require specific inputs – such as voice and physical attractiveness – which Tinder dating fails to provide. In addition, Tinder dating may also come with new costs, such as ghosting, that people need to be equipped with to deal with in their dating lives. According to March et al. (2020a), Tinder use could be motivated by the desire for sex, relationships, socializing, belongingness, and social approval, as well as practicing flirting and developing social skills, to meet people while traveling, passing the time, getting to know people with the same sexual orientation, and to cope with the end of a relationship.

Personality differences may influence the use of Tinder, as Tinder users were shown to be more extroverted and open to new experiences than nonusers. The Dark Tetrad could be another possible difference between Tinder users and nonusers (Ciocca et al., 2020). In addition, research has begun to uncover motivations for using Tinder, demonstrating that relationship initiation and hookups for casual sex are not the only objectives. These motivations also depend on individual differences, such as age, sex, disgust sensitivity, and personality. Due to the unprecedented popularity of Tinder in online dating and the consequences of such behavior, it is vital to investigate how individuals differ in their motivations to use the application. Beyond the Big Five paradigm and fundamental individual differences (e.g., sex and age), socially malevolent traits such as the Dark Tetrad are particularly interesting in understanding the motivations for using online dating applications (Lyons et al., 2020).

Sevi (2019) contended that according to sexual strategies theory, humans possess two types of mating strategies: long-term and short-term. Short-term mating is indexed by *sociosexuality,* an individual's inclination to engage in uncommitted sexual relations. People may have long-lasting relationships, such as life-long marriages, but other forms of mating exist. Some mating relationships can be short durations, weeks, days, or even hours. This variability in sexual strategy provides a rich repertoire of mechanisms that solve possible adaptive problems related to mating. Different adaptive problems may emerge in various contexts; according to sexual strategies theory, some mate preference adaptations are context dependent. Online dating applications have introduced a new context to the world of mating. It is, therefore, essential to study how this evolutionary theory of sexual strategies operates in this context.

Tinder allows individuals with Dark Tetrad personality traits to pursue short-term mating strategies (Tsoukas & March, 2018; Sevi, 2019; Lyons et al., 2022a). Particularly in mating, individuals high on Dark Tetrad have more intimate sexual fantasies, have more sex partners, and have lower standards when choosing short-term mates, which increases the probability of finding a mate. This suggests that those with high levels of Dark Tetrad utilize short-term mating strategies (Sevi, 2019; Lyons et al., 2022a). Dark Tetrad personality traits influence both romantic and sexual relationships in terms of mating behavior. Thus, it could be argued that Tinder provides a mating context similar to a traditional context where the main effects of the relations between Dark Tetrads and sexual strategies can be seen. However, it can also have dissimilarities stemming from its nature that makes it a different mating context and possibly lead to differences in moderating effects like sex on the relation between Dark Tetrad and sexual strategies (March et al., 2017; Timmermans et al., 2018; Sevi, 2019).

Narcissism (e.g., vanity and self-centeredness), Machiavellianism (e.g., manipulation and cynicism), psychopathy (e.g., callous social attitudes and amorality), and sadism (i.e., a person who enjoys inflicting psychological and emotional harm on others) are linked to attitudes and behaviors related to casual sex. Those persons with Dark Tetrad personality traits are willing to lower their standards of their sex partners and have promiscuous sociosexual attitudes, suggesting they may be present on Tinder if joining is at least partially motivated by casual sex (March et al., 2017; Jonason & Bulyk, 2019). Another reason to expect those Tinder users to be high on the Dark Tetrad is that these traits are linked to various manifestations of aggression, including coercive online sexual behavior and cyberbullying (Duncan & March, 2019). Like most dating applications, the nature of the Tinder application unintentionally promotes the active exploitation and abuse of others with features such as limited feedback during and after interactions. The veil of anonymity may make this online niche particularly appealing to those set on abusing and taking advantage of others. Those fundamental aspects of the personalities of Dark Tetrad may enable them to be simultaneously aggressive and sexual toward others (Jonason & Bulyk, 2019).

The specific motivations of each Dark Tetrad for using Tinder will be presented in the following.

7.3.1.1 Narcissism and Tinder

There is no clear evidence that narcissists use Tinder more than the other three dark personalities. However, there is much interest in narcissists' interpretation and motivation for using Tinder. According to March et al. (2020a), it is possible and indeed likely that the effect of narcissism on Tinder behaviors depends on contextual factors. Therefore, it would be helpful to consider the role of context grounded in the appropriate theory to understand how narcissism plays out in antisocial behaviors on Tinder. Narcissists use Tinder to improve flirting and social skills only. They display a sense of superiority and entitlement, for example, believing themselves to be more desirable than their romantic partners. The relationship between narcissism and this motivation may, therefore, reflect the tendency of narcissists to believe that they already excel in this field and do not need to develop their flirting or social skills (Lyons et al., 2020).

Online dating sites also represent an exciting arena to study associations between narcissism and cyberbullying as an enabling venue for anonymity, excessive self-promotion and regulation of self-esteem, and the potential deception of others. Social networking sites are also one of the best reflections of narcissism due to opportunities for narcissistic self-imaging. Narcissists often engage in ludic love, characterized by game-playing, fear of commitment, desire for alternatives, and deception (Zerach, 2016). Narcissists are likely to pursue short-term mating as they lack empathy, possess unrealistic fantasies concerning romantic relationships, and behave exploitatively in interpersonal relationships (Tucaković, Bojić, & Nikolić, 2022). Timmermans et al. (2018) contended that narcissistic individuals tend to be less committed to their romantic partners than less narcissistic individuals and prefer casual sexual interactions as they do not like to have sex with someone they feel emotionally close to. Moreover, while in a committed relationship, people with high narcissism tend to be attentive to alternative dating partners and are more likely to cheat on their partners.

As for the link to online infidelity, narcissists have higher chances of reporting extradyadic online affairs, and narcissism positively influences Tinder users' motives related to traveling (e.g., meeting new people when traveling) and self-validation, for example, to use Tinder to get an ego-boosting (March, 2022). Furthermore, narcissism has been associated with a more opportunistic than exploitative mating style (Duncan & March, 2019). Finally, there are indications that narcissism is the most influential trait in predicting prior experience of infidelity, intentions to engage in infidelity, and perceived susceptibility to a partner's infidelity (Timmermans et al., 2018).

Trait narcissism has been conceptualized as comprising two primary forms: grandiose and vulnerable (Branson & March, 2021). Grandiose narcissism is characterized by grandiosity, arrogance, interpersonal aggression, dominance, and manipulation. By contrast, vulnerable narcissism is characterized by insecurity and feelings of inadequacy and incompetency, which are defensively obscured by narcissistic behaviors. Very few studies have explored the relationship between dual-factor narcissism and cyber dating abuse. The relationship between the two forms of narcissism and cyber dating abuse may be attributed to the online environment facilitating behaviors less appropriate in face-to-face courtship, such as aggression, grandiosity, and exploitation, all behaviors characteristic of narcissistic traits (Branson & March, 2021).

7.3.1.2 Psychopathy and Tinder

Individuals with high levels of trait psychopathy are more likely to express a short-term mating orientation as they pursue an exploitative, impulsive, and aggressive mating strategy (Tucaković et al., 2022). Those with higher levels of trait psychopathy may be attracted to Tinder as the application offers the potential for opportunistic predatory behavior and to satisfy their desire for short-term, impulsive relationships (March, 2022). Psychopathy is associated with sexual coercion, predatory sexual behavior, and impulsive, aggressive, and short relationships (Duncan & March, 2019). Individuals with high levels of psychopathy seek multiple potential partners to satisfy their unrestricted sexuality and self-interest. As such, the more opportunities on Tinder for sexual encounters, the more likely individuals with high levels of psychopathy (single or non-single) will use this application (March, 2022). Additionally, Tinder may appeal to the individual with high psychopathy, as the application offers anonymous sexual coercion and predatory sexual behavior (Duncan & March, 2019).

Trait psychopathy is characterized by remorselessness, shallow emotion, callousness, violation of social norms, and interpersonal manipulation. Like narcissism, psychopathy comprises two main forms: *primary psychopathy* and *secondary psychopathy*. There are indications that secondary psychopathy is the most influential trait in predicting prior experience of infidelity, intentions to engage in infidelity, and perceived susceptibility to a partner's infidelity (Timmermans et al., 2018). Affective and interpersonal deficits, including callousness and grandiosity, characterize primary psychopathy. By contrast, secondary psychopathy is characterized by disturbed emotional conscience, impulsivity, and antisocial proclivity, and both forms have been associated with the perpetration of offline intimate partner violence. Therefore, researchers recommend conceptualizing psychopathy as a dual factor, particularly when exploring intimate partner violence-related behavior. This may be especially important for online behavior research, as the dimensions of psychopathy have produced differential predictive utility. By examining psychopathy multidimensionally, the unique utility of primary and secondary psychopathy to predict cyber dating abuse may be explored (Branson & March, 2021).

7.3.1.3   Machiavellianism and Tinder

Machiavellian individuals may be more prone to short-term mating. They are emotionally detached from other people and are therefore reluctant to engage in committed intimate relationships (Tucaković et al., 2022). In addition, Machiavellianism predicts the use of sexual deception – including the avoidance of confrontation – within committed romantic relationships (Timmermans et al., 2018). Also, Machiavellianism predicts sending unsolicited explicit images, and psychopathy is associated with trolling behavior on dating applications (Timmermans et al., 2018). Finally, Machiavellianism has been associated with strategic and manipulative behaviors in intimate relationships (Duncan & March, 2019). As Tinder offers the potential for deceptive dating tactics to enhance sexual activities, this may appeal to individuals with higher levels of Machiavellianism (Duncan & March, 2019).

7.3.1.4   Sadism and Tinder

Sadistic individuals might use online dating websites and applications to facilitate engaging in short-term sadistic sexual interactions (Tucaković et al., 2022). Those high in sadism may use Tinder to satisfy their antisocial needs (Lyons et al., 2022a). They might be attracted to Tinder to facilitate sadistic sexual interactions, such as the option of sending unsolicited sexual images (Duncan & March, 2019). Sadists may enjoy taunting and humiliating others and seek opportunities to do so (March et al., 2017).

7.3.2   Research Findings

In a sample of 271 participants from the United States, Sevi (2019) found that Tinder users have higher levels of Dark Triad personality traits (i.e., Machiavellianism, narcissism, and psychopathy) than nonusers. Considering that the most mentioned reason for using Tinder is for short-term mating and that the application is called the *hook-up* application, this difference between Tinder users and nonusers supports the contention that dark personalities are associated with short-term mating strategies. Furthermore, correlation analyses between the Dark Triad traits and Tinder-user motivation have demonstrated that Tinder users with higher scores of Dark Triad traits exhibited greater motivation to use Tinder for short-term mating (Sevi, 2019). By contrast, no significant relation existed between the Dark Triad traits and motivation to use Tinder for long-term mating. The findings of Sevi's (2019) study support the argument that the Dark Triad would promote the motivation to use Tinder for short-term mating (Sevi, 2019; Ciocca et al., 2020), while the motivation for long-term mating would not be expected. The possible moderating effect of gender was also explored in this study, and no significant effect was found.

In a study of a total of 587 Australian undergraduates and high school students, Duncan and March (2019) found that narcissism, Machiavellianism, psychopathy, and sadism were significant positive predictors of antisocial-general use of Tinder. According to them, individuals with high levels of these dark traits may be attracted to Tinder for several reasons. First, those with high-trait narcissism may use the anonymity of Tinder in order to exploit potential romantic partners purely to fulfill their own narcissistic needs. Second, Machiavellians may artificially use the application to enhance their reputations and manipulate social relationships. Third, individuals with high-trait psychopathy could use Tinder to satisfy their desire for short-term, impulsive, and aggressive relationships. Finally, individuals with high-trait sadism might be attracted to Tinder as a mechanism to facilitate sadistic sexual interactions. Their findings also showed that gender (specifically women) and higher levels of trait Machiavellianism were significant predictors of antisocial sexual behavior. Finally, Duncan and March (2019) concluded that given the significance of trait Machiavellianism in predicting the use of Tinder for esteem purposes, individuals with higher levels of trait Machiavellianism might be more inclined to use Tinder to increase their ego and self-worth strategically.

Finally, gender (specifically, men) and higher levels of trait Machiavellianism, psychopathy, and sadism were significant predictors of antisocial sexual behavior. Duncan and March (2019) explained that as Tinder offers the potential for deceptive dating tactics to enhance sexual activities, this may appeal to individuals with higher levels of trait Machiavellianism. In addition, Tinder may appeal to the individual with high-trait psychopathy, as the application offers the opportunity for anonymous sexual coercion and predatory sexual behavior. Finally, it is unsurprising that individuals with higher trait sadism would use Tinder for antisocial-sexual purposes, as trait sadism is predictive of sexual assault and violence. According to Duncan and March (2019), their results indicate different explanatory variables for different antisocial behaviors on Tinder. Notably, the results suggest that antisocial online behavior is not unidimensional, and an approach examining individual differences would be appropriate to facilitate an understanding of online behaviors.

In a study of two samples of American participants (299 participants in Study 1; 282 participants in Study 2), Jonason and Bulyk (2019) found that the Dark Triad of psychopathy, narcissism, and (slightly) Machiavellianism was higher among Tinder users than nonusers. This finding supports their assumption that Tinder usage is partially related to casual sex because traits that enable casual sex behavior, like the Dark Triad, are higher in Tinder users. Similar findings were presented by Lyons et al. (2022a) in a sample of men (n = 67) and women (n = 149), current or former Tinder users from the United Kingdom, United States, and Canada. They found a significant effect of the Dark Triad for using Tinder. For psychopathy, they found that those high in psychopathy were more likely to use Tinder to gain sexual experience. The high sex drive and short-term mating orientation associated with psychopathy translate into using online dating applications for sexual gratification. Another significant finding about psychopathy was using Tinder to distract oneself from other tasks. Lyons et al. (2022a) explained that perhaps high psychopathy individuals procrastinate by focusing on more intrinsically motivating tasks, such as finding short-term sexual partners online. The associations between psychopathy, distraction, and sexual experience motivations could have links with highly psychopathic individuals' overall impulsive, hedonistic, and procrastinating lifestyles.

The motivations for using Tinder were evident in Machiavellianism's long-term strategic and flexible nature. Lyons et al. (2022a) found that Machiavellianism had a positive correlation with using Tinder for social approval (i.e., to get validation from others about one's attractiveness), when traveling, as a consequence of peer pressure, to pass the time or for entertainment, and to practice social skills and flirting. Machiavellian individuals may have a more utilitarian approach to entertainment and use tools that provide real-life benefits (e.g., acquiring a partner). All motivations could reflect using the social and online environment to reach long-term objectives. Lyons et al. further argued that their findings extend self-presentation to the dating environment. Using Tinder for social approval and conforming to peer pressure could all be part of a façade that makes Machiavellian individuals more socially desirable partners (Lyons et al., 2022a).

Based on two large samples (sample 1 = 1,616; sample 2 = 1,795) from the Netherlands, Timmermans et al. (2018) showed that Machiavellianism positively correlates with social approval and sexual experience. Furthermore, narcissism is positively associated with social approval, passing time/entertainment, and distraction. Finally, psychopathy is positively associated with the sexual motive. Their findings also showed that Machiavellianism and narcissism in non-single Tinder users were positively associated with the social approval motive (Timmermans et al., 2018). Also, non-single Tinder users scored higher on psychopathy compared to non-single nonusers. In turn, psychopathy in this group of non-single Tinder users was associated with the sexual experience motive for using Tinder. Timmermans et al. (2018) state that a psychopath is likelier to use Tinder to create a target-rich mating environment. This logic is confirmed by their results that show that non-single Tinder users who scored high on psychopathy reported significantly more one-night stands (Timmermans et al., 2018).

March et al. (2020a) examined anger as a moderator of the relationship between grandiose exhibitionism and entitlement, exploitative narcissism, and aggressive and harassing behaviors on Tinder. For a sample of 1,001 Australian Tinder users, March et al. (2020a) found that the relationship between narcissism facets and aggression and harassment was only (positively) significant at medium and high levels of anger, indicating that anger plays a crucial role in the relationship between narcissism and antisocial behavior on Tinder. According to them, individuals with high-trait narcissism are more aggressive than others when provoked by ego threats. Furthermore, this ego threat played out as anger when an individual did not respond to their romantic advances. Based on these results, March et al. (2020a) concluded that narcissism alone is limited to explaining antisocial behavior on Tinder.

In a sample of 358 university students from Turkey, Demircioğlu and Köse (2023) found that narcissism was a significant predictor of using social networking sites to find partners, with risk-taking fully mediating the link between narcissism and face-to-face dating a partner who had been met via social networking sites. Narcissistic individuals were more likely to use social networking sites to find partners. They were also likely to engage in risky behaviors, which, in turn, were positively associated with face-to-face dating with individuals met via social networking sites. Demircioğlu and Köse also found that the positive relationship between psychopathy and using social networking sites to find partners was fully mediated by impulsivity. The possibility of having amusing and exciting conversations online with a stranger may motivate a psychopath to fulfill their expectations without delay.

Demircioğlu and Köse (2023) also found that the relationship between Machiavellianism and using social networking sites to find partners was fully mediated by impulsivity. In addition, the direct association between Machiavellianism and face-to-face dating with a partner met via social networking sites was insignificant. Demircioğlu and Köse contended that it could be speculated that this association may be moderated by such variables as the degree of perceived benefits of face-to-face dating a specific person who had been met via social networking sites. According to Demircioğlu and Köse (2023), Machiavellians may date a partner meeting via social networking sites only when assured of their physical or psychological satisfaction.

7.4   Dark Triad/Tetrad and Toxic Relationship

7.4.1   Cyber Dating and Relationship Abuse

The rise of new technologies has raised new social issues. Among these problems are new methods of aggression between romantic partners (Pineda et al., 2022a). As a result, there has been an increase in technology-facilitated abuse in romantic relationships. People use digital mediums such as mobile phones and social media to control, threaten, or harass their partners (Bhogal & Wallace, 2022). Cyber dating abuse is a contemporary form of intimate partner violence involving electronic communication technology to direct abuse toward a romantic partner. It has been defined as the control, harassment, stalking, and abuse of one's dating partner via technology and social media (Zweig et al., 2014).

Cyber dating abuse has been conceptualized as multidimensional, including psychological control and monitoring behaviors, such as surveilling a partner's social media without consent, and psychological and verbal aggression, such as sending threats and insults electronically (Branson & March, 2021). There are specific forms of online intimate partner violence ranging from insults, threats, humiliations, dissemination of private information, harassment, stalking, forcing partners to delete former romantic partners on social media, limiting social media posts, controlling online interactions with friends/family, monitoring a partner's online whereabouts, and controlling behaviors and monitoring of the romantic partner invading their privacy. Online intimate partner violence also includes using new phone applications to track their partner's location (Pineda et al., 2022a). Cyber dating abuse has devastating outcomes and is related to depression and suicidal ideation, showing the importance of researching cyber dating abuse and the factors that drive its perpetration (Bhogal & Wallace, 2022).

The components of direct aggression are related to deliberate behaviors that aim to cause harm, such as threats or insults. On the other hand, the control components include behaviors that aim at surveillance or invasion of privacy, either by the partner or a former partner. Since this type of behavior is directed to cause the partner suffering by showing no respect or consideration for his or her consent and deliberation when sharing or controlling specific content, it is possible to perceive the existence of a lack of concern with the feelings of the other as well as a lack of affection and empathy toward the other. In this sense, it is vital to understand which aspects of the personality may be involved in the occurrence of this type of abuse (Zweig et al., 2014; Linares et al., 2021; de Jesus Costa et al., 2023).

Social networking sites provide Dark Tetrads with a platform that allows them to present themselves in ways that accommodate their propensity for manipulation and deceit. Specifically, social networking sites may provide such individuals with opportunities to build and maintain interpersonal connections that best suit them, namely superficial relationships devoid of intimacy. Thus, in line with the motivations associated with each trait, social networking sites might serve as a beneficial mechanism for narcissists to self-enhance, for psychopaths to act out impulsively without real-world consequences, for Machiavellians to develop strategic allies, deceive others for gain, and build positive reputations (Vander Molen et al., 2018), and for sadists to derive enjoyment from the victims' suffering of the victims (March et al., 2017). The relation seems clear: Elevated scores in the Dark Tetrad should be related to higher cyber intimate partner violence levels. However, very little research studies the relationship between the dark side of personality and cyber intimate partner violence (Pineda et al., 2022a).

Cyber dating abuse has been conceptualized as an online form of intimate partner violence. Longitudinal analyses demonstrate a positive, co-occurring relationship between the two forms (Branson & March, 2021). The evolutionary theory could clarify the involvement of Dark Tetrad in cyber dating and relationship abuse. Evolutionary scientists suggest that cyber dating abuse is a form of mate retention that evolved to increase mating success and keep a relationship intact (Bhogal & Wallace, 2022). According to Branson and March (2021), the evolutionary perspective could also explain cyber dating abuse as a mate retention behavior motivated by jealousy.

The general aggression model can explain cyber dating abuse as an aggressive response influenced by inputs (i.e., personality traits, such as dark personalities) and routes (i.e., jealousy). The general aggression model posits that aggression results from a process comprising inputs, routes, and appraisals. Inputs (i.e., person or situation factors) influence routes (i.e., cognitions, affect, and arousal), leading to an appraisal, decision process, and aggressive response. Regarding inputs, certain personal factors, such as aggressive or hostile personality traits, could influence the inclination toward aggressive emotions and attitudes. Given that jealousy is characterized by cognitive and affective components, the general aggression model also allows for jealousy as a route (Branson & March, 2021).

The following review of cyber dating and relationship abuse is divided into several subsections, each representing specific processes in abusive relationships. Therefore, the presentation is organized according to the timeline during which each of these destructive behaviors might appear. The starting point of this section is the beginning of the toxic relationship, namely, catfishing. Subsequently, the relationship of Dark Tetrads with their intimate partner, including dating abuse and toxic relationships, is reviewed. Finally, this section discusses the last stage of the relationship that characterizes Dark Tetrad, ghosting, and revenge pornography.

7.4.1.1   Catfishing and Breadcrumbing

The early stage of a cyber relationship is essential and often determines the nature of the future relationship. At this early stage, users of online dating sites are expected to provide details such as interests, hobbies, likes, and dislikes. Algorithms then run through the databases containing this information to match people with similar details. Most users believe that online dating has considerable risk since one is only sometimes sure that the other person is sincere. Catfish misrepresent themselves as more desirable and attractive to attract potential partners (Olckers & Hattingh, 2022; Lauder & March, 2023).

Catfishing, in terms of online dating, is the intentional misrepresentation of various aspects of a person to pursue an exclusively online relationship (Mosley et al., 2020). Catfishing refers to a form of online deception and fraud whereby an individual steals another person's identity or creates a fake identity and uses this stolen/fake identity as their own. Catfishing is performed to trick someone into developing an online relationship, making the act distinct from impersonation alone. Catfishing is underreported due to people not knowing they have been catfished or because the catfish do not want to reveal their identity (Olckers & Hattingh, 2022; Lauder & March, 2023).

As of early 2022, around 1 in 10 adults in the United States said they had interacted with a catfish online. Moreover, 8% of United States men said they had sent money to a catfish as of January 2022 (Statista, 2023b). Experiencing catfishing can have a significant psychological impact. Upon becoming aware of the deceit and scam, victims report experiencing depression, anxiety, paranoia, increased embarrassment, anger, and fear. Catfishing can also have a tremendous financial impact (Lauder & March, 2023). The effect of dark traits on online dating has attracted recent interest and is relevant to the probable identity of many catfishers (Moor & Anderson, 2019; Jonason et al., 2021). Adult attachment is a factor contributing to the dark side use of social media in catfishing. Fearful or preoccupied attachment has been found to be a significant predictor of being a catfish (Mosley et al., 2020). These individuals misrepresent themselves as likable, like this fear of abandonment and withdrawal when placed under emotional distress. An in-person relationship does not appeal to them, but an online-only relationship does. To find a partner to cater to their relationship needs, these individuals will misrepresent themselves to make connections more easily. Catfishers may create a fake online identity that may refer to actual events or places to make their profile more believable (Olckers & Hattingh, 2022).

Jonason et al. (2009) found that the dark personality scores were positively correlated with having more sex partners, an unrestricted sociosexuality, and a greater preference for short-term mates. They contended that the association between the dark personality composite was correlated with short-term mating beyond the effects of the participant's age, sex, and extraversion. The connection between dark traits and short-term mating drives users toward dating applications in terms of the number of installed applications and average daily use time (Freyth & Batinic, 2021).

From an evolutionary perspective, personality traits are adaptive and naturally selected. An evolutionary psychology perspective, specifically the cheater strategy hypothesis, provides a practical, theoretical framework to understand the link between Dark Tetrad traits and catfishing (Fox & Rooney, 2015; Lauder & March, 2023). According to this perspective, those high on Dark Tetrad traits may employ social networking sites to execute "cheater strategies" that help them attract friends and achieve their interpersonal and social goals despite their antisocial personality traits (Lauder & March, 2023). In an experimental design, Drouvelis et al. (2022) found that individuals high in some Dark Triad traits were likelier to misrepresent themselves if given the opportunity. This was found for psychopaths and narcissists but less for Machiavellians.

Narcissists use social networking sites for self-promotion to project a positive self-image and acquire many so-called friends. They are also likely to engage in catfishing behaviors. People with high narcissism deceive others by editing their online profiles to gain more attention and attract potential partners. This deceptive online self-portrayal is a crucial characteristic of catfishing behavior. People with high narcissism seek ego boosts to inflate their self-esteem. As such, although speculative, they may catfish for specific targets (i.e., those with high status and physical attractiveness) because attracting and deceiving high-status individuals provides them with an ego boost (Lauder & March, 2023). People who scored high on narcissism had more online friends and uploaded more photos than those who had low scores on narcissism. They are likelier to update their status for self-presentation than social media users who scored low on narcissism. Narcissistic individuals usually use their social media accounts to exhibit wealth, success, and attractiveness, which would satisfy their needs for self-promotion. In addition, people who have narcissistic tendencies present themselves more favorably to attract others and build their ideal selves on social media. People who scored high on narcissistic personality features also used self-regulatory strategies, such as relationship management, to feel more special. Consequently, narcissists are expected to be more enthusiastic about initiating relationships through online social networks (Demircioğlu & Köse, 2023).

Machiavellianism predicts self-oriented goal pursuit on Facebook and predicts more self-monitoring and self-promoting Facebook behavior in men. Persons with Machiavellian traits have also been shown to be more likely to use the site to manipulate their romantic partners (Fox & Rooney, 2015). Machiavellianism is often linked to deceptive behavior, and deception is a crucial characteristic of catfishing (Lauder & March, 2023). However, there is another approach regarding Machiavellian and social network relationships. According to this approach, individuals with high scores on Machiavellianism tend to manipulate others to reach their goals. They are expected to use all communication tools to reach their aims and satisfy their needs. People who scored high on Machiavellianism prefer face-to-face interaction with other parties. Therefore, it can be expected that individuals who score high on Machiavellianism would be more likely to date partners they met via social networking sites face-to-face than those who score low on Machiavellianism.

People with higher levels of psychopathy perpetrated more catfishing behaviors. Although psychopathy has not previously been explored concerning catfishing, it has been found to predict other antisocial online behaviors such as trolling, cyberstalking, and online fraud. It is possible that due to the impulsive, destructive, and unremorseful characteristics of psychopathy, those with high levels of psychopathy engage in catfishing as they are attracted to the opportunity to anonymously exploit others online with a blatant disregard for the pain they are causing (Lauder & March, 2023). The relationship between psychopathy and using social networking sites to find partners could be mediated by impulsivity. Individuals with high impulsivity levels are more prone to participate in dangerous sexual activities, such as having intercourse with strangers than those with low impulsivity levels. As a result, individuals may use social networking sites to find partners to satisfy their urges faster and effortlessly. Furthermore, impulsivity was positively related to inappropriate online sexual activity. For a psychopath, the possibility of having amusing and exciting conversations online with a stranger may motivate impulsive individuals to meet their expectations without delay (Demircioğlu & Köse, 2023).

Those with high sadism also perpetrated more catfishing behaviors. Individuals with high sadism are callous and experience satisfaction when hurting others. The manipulation these individuals often display is performed to inflict harm. Like the relationships observed between sadism, trolling, and grief, those with high sadism whom catfish may perpetrate the act because they enjoy ridiculing, embarrassing, and harming others through an anonymous platform (Lauder & March, 2023).

Breadcrumbing is a manipulative behavior defined as leading on a romantic or former romantic interest intermittently engaging in flirtatious contact without any intention of progressing in the relationship (Navarro et al., 2020). Hardly any research has examined whether people with Dark Tetrad traits are more likely to engage in breadcrumbing. Willis, Cliver, and March (2023) conducted the first study to show that those who indicated that they had breadcrumbed someone had significantly greater vulnerable narcissism and Machiavellianism views than those who had not. Given that those who have high scores on Machiavellianism endorse the view that human beings are selfish and untrustworthy, they may be more likely to breadcrumb someone as they believe it to be acceptable and normal. Considering that those with vulnerable narcissistic traits desire social approval, they may be more likely to breadcrumb someone as it satisfies their need for attention and approval rather than terminating the relationship. All other Dark Triad dimensional traits were greater for those who had ghosted someone breadcrumbed, and these differences approached significance in the direction predicted.

7.4.1.2 Research Findings

Lauder and March (2023) examined the relationship between Dark Tetrads and catfishing in a sample of 664 English-speaking participants from Australia, the United States, and Canada. Their findings showed that psychopathy, narcissism, and sadism had a strong positive and significant association with catfishing. Conversely, Machiavellianism was not a significant, positive predictor of the perpetration of catfishing. One of their explanations for the lack of effect of Machiavellianism on catfishing is that the traits of Machiavellianism and psychopathy are considered to overlap, and psychopathy may subsume variance explained by Machiavellianism when deceptive mating strategies are explored. Given that psychopathy was a significant predictor in catfishing perpetration, it is possible that due to the overlap between psychopathy and Machiavellianism, Machiavellianism did not emerge as a significant predictor. Lauder and March (2023) also explored interactions between gender and Dark Tetrad traits in predicting catfishing perpetration, and no interaction reached statistical significance.

In a sample of 313 participants from the United Kingdom (70.9%), United States (28.4%), and Australia (0.6%), Willis et al. (2023) found that while vulnerable narcissism, secondary psychopathy, and Machiavellianism tactics were significantly positively correlated with inauthentic online dating self-presentation, only vulnerable narcissism emerged as a significant predictor in their model. Neither primary psychopathy, secondary psychopathy, nor either dimension of Machiavellianism were significant predictors of inauthentic online dating self-presentation. Their findings showed that vulnerable narcissism predicts inauthentic self-presentation across Facebook, Instagram, and online dating.

Aviram and Amichai-Hamburger (2005) examined whether the desire for an act of online infidelity is based on personality and relationship-related factors, similar to real-life infidelity. According to Aviram and Amichai-Hamburger, among the personality factors that contribute to the development of a desire for an online affair, narcissism seems to play a pivotal role. They surveyed 200 participants who indicated they were involved in a real-life relationship during the study. The sample included 76 Israelis, 74 Americans, and 28 individuals of other nationalities (Europeans and Asians). Their measure of narcissism identified four components: vanity and attention-seeking, authority and control, self-sufficiency, and manipulation and exhibitionism.

Their findings showed that among the narcissistic personality dimensions included in their study, the manipulation and exhibitionism component contributed significantly to predicting higher Internet relationship expectations. Apart from its significant link to actual infidelity, narcissism is relevant to online communication. The Internet love story can be described as a narcissistic accelerator, enabling people with narcissistic tendencies to meet online and create a familiar tale that flatters their grandiosity. An online relationship constitutes a self-object unit for the two parties engaged in the cyber dialogue. The concept of self-object refers to using another person as an extension or continuation of the self for mirroring and self-idealization. The view of the Internet relationship as a self-object unit comports with the view of Internet dialogue as a solipsistic introjection, in which the individuals forming the online relationship feel as if their mind has merged with the mind of their online companion and the online companion becomes a character within their intrapsychic world (Aviram & Amichai-Hamburger, 2005).

7.4.1.3 Abusive/Toxic Relationship

Cyber dating abuse involves control, manipulation, and surveillance via information communication technology, and those who possess Dark Tetrad traits tend to control and manipulate behaviors toward a romantic partner. In addition, those high in the traits are more likely to display derogatory behaviors toward others and attempt to induce jealousy in a romantic partner. These behaviors are parallel to those shown in cyber dating abuse. The dark traits are beneficial to attracting mates, particularly as those high in these traits have multiple sexual partners, are opportunistic, and adopt an exploitative mating style once in a romantic relationship. There are parallels between cyber dating abuse and the Dark Tetrad, as both involve manipulation, control, and exploitation (Mayshak et al., 2020; Bhogal & Wallace, 2022).

According to Bui and Pasalich (2021), psychopathic traits may play unique roles in underpinning the perpetration of psychological abuse in romantic relationships despite some overlap in the symptomatic presentation of these personality pathologies (e.g., impulsive and manipulative behavior). Bui and Pasalich (2021) argued that maladaptive personality functioning is another critical risk factor for committing violent behavior in romantic relationships. Individuals high on psychopathic traits demonstrate empathy deficits and coercive behavior that may be related to their increased risk for committing different forms of intimate partner violence, including psychological abuse. Bui and Pasalich (2021) contended that maladaptive mental representations of self and others are fundamental to understanding the emergence and maintenance of personality pathology. From this standpoint, maladaptive personality traits – those reflecting symptoms of psychopathy – may be one potential mechanism for more distal effects of insecure attachment on the perpetration of psychological abuse in intimate relationships.

Importantly, Bui and Pasalich (2021) found parallel indirect pathways from insecure attachment to the perpetration of psychological abuse via psychopathic traits, suggesting that these maladaptive personality features may be implicated in distinct developmental and/or maintenance processes underpinning relationship violence. According to Bui and Pasalich (2021), individuals high on attachment avoidance might engage in psychological abuse due to elevated psychopathic traits. By contrast, individuals high on attachment anxiety may perpetrate psychological abuse underpinned by deficits associated with psychopathic traits. Bui and Pasalich (2021) have proposed specific accounts for why individuals with these different maladaptive personality traits may engage in intimate partner violation. Individuals with psychopathic traits exhibit unique deficits in interpersonal affective functioning, particularly callousness and emotional detachment, which may explain their motives for psychological abuse. These individuals may lack remorse associated with their abusive behavior and focus on the control and power that the psychological abuse provides them in the relationship, which can often be planned but also impulsive if activated by intense anger.

7.4.1.4   Research Findings

In a sample of 1,189 participants in Spain, Pineda et al. (2022a) found that psychopathy is more related to cyber intimate partner violence direct aggression than to cyber intimate partner violence control. This finding converges with the aggressive nature of people with high scores in psychopathy, who tend to use aggression for instrumental purposes. Machiavellianism was the only Dark Tetrad trait that positively correlated with intimate cyber partner violence victimization and perpetration but did not predict it due to an inverse relation with cyber intimate partner violence. The negative results between in-person intimate partner violence and cyber intimate partner violence may be explained by the inherent Machiavellian aggressive tendencies, where the risk of getting caught while perpetrating aggressive behaviors is greater in virtual media than in person.

The results showed a weak relationship between narcissism and intimate cyber partner violence perpetration and victimization. This weak relationship may be due to a narcissist's propensity to directly aggress only when their ego or personal position is threatened. Specifically, narcissism is primarily related to cybercontrolling, presumably because these people feel entitled to monitor or dominate their partner's behavior. Finally, sadistic personalities reported more victimization at the same time as perpetration. This finding shows cyber intimate partner violence as a two-way relationship where individuals with a prominent sadistic trait tend to suffer direct abuse behaviors while they perpetrate them. Likewise, sadism is related to being victimized by cybercontrolling behaviors. Thus, this sadistic trait is dangerous for those exhibiting it prominently and their intimate partners (Pineda et al., 2022a). Pineda et al. (2022a) concluded that there is an established connection between the different traits of the Dark Tetrad and cyber intimate partner violence.

Bui and Pasalich (2021) examined whether maladaptive personality traits account for the indirect association between attachment insecurity and the perpetration of cyber psychological abuse. They examined a community sample of 200 participants in Australia. Bui and Pasalich (2021) found significant associations between more frequent perpetration of face-to-face and cyber psychological abuse, higher levels of attachment anxiety and avoidance, and elevated scores for psychopathic traits. Results from mediation analysis helped clarify the nature of these interrelationships. Psychopathic traits accounted for the indirect effects of attachment anxiety on in-person and cyber psychological abuse. Furthermore, psychopathic traits accounted for the indirect effects of attachment avoidance on both forms of psychological abuse. Together, their findings support the conjecture that insecure attachment may underpin maladaptive personality traits, which appear to be linked to the perpetration of psychological abuse in the cyberworld.

Bui and Pasalich (2021) further concluded that their results support this theoretical model. Psychopathological traits accounted significantly for indirect associations between anxious and/or avoidant attachment and psychological abuse perpetrated via electronic devices. Bui and Pasalich's (2021) findings may help inform intervention efforts to reduce the risk of engagement in intimate partner violation. They found that maladaptive personality traits had direct effects, whereas insecure attachment only evinced indirect effects on the perpetration of psychological abuse. Their results suggest assessing for and targeting symptoms of personality pathology, particularly psychopathic traits, in interventions for psychological abuse.

Duffy, March, and Jonason (2023) examined 278 participants from the United Kingdom. Their findings showed a strong relationship between vulnerable narcissism and intimate partner cyberstalking. They contended that those who cyberstalk intimate partners might be more neurotic, insecure, and jealous. Furthermore, the relationship between secondary psychopathy and intimate partner cyberstalking was also positive and robust, suggesting that those who cyberstalk intimate partners may have lower self-control and higher impulsivity.

March et al. (2021b) examined the relationship between vulnerable narcissism and cyber dating abuse among 415 Australian participants. They found that men and women with high levels of vulnerable narcissism reported perpetrating cyber dating abuse. They explained that the contingent nature of self-esteem within vulnerable narcissism explains their results; the feelings of inadequacy associated with vulnerable narcissism and the vulnerable narcissist's potential preoccupation with fears of abandonment and rejection may drive online monitoring/abusive behaviors regardless of the perpetrator's gender.

In their study, Branson and March (2021) replicate and extend cyber dating abuse research by exploring the utility of narcissism and psychopathy to predict behavior. Branson and March (2021) examined 817 participants, mostly Australians (81.3%). Their findings showed strong associations between hostility and vulnerable narcissism and secondary psychopathy, more so than grandiose and primary psychopathy. The findings also demonstrated that only vulnerable narcissism emerged as a significant (positive) predictor of cyber dating abuse.

Their results indicate that cyber dating abuse is better associated with narcissism characterized by insecurity, emotional reactivity, and feelings of inadequacy (i.e., vulnerable narcissism), compared to grandiose callousness and instrumental aggression (i.e., grandiose narcissism). Further, the utility of vulnerable narcissism to predict cyber dating abuse supports an evolutionary framework. Specifically, as vulnerable narcissism is characterized by feelings of insecurity, inadequacy, and incompetence, such individuals may perceive themselves as the inferior mate within a relationship (i.e., with lower mate value). As disparate value between mates may increase the likelihood of infidelity, mate poaching, and relationship termination, the mate of lower value may employ mate retention behaviors, which include perpetrating cyber dating abuse. Incidentally, the lack of utility of grandiose narcissism to predict cyber dating abuse also supports an evolutionary framework, as it is less likely that the grandiose narcissist, who has an inflated ego and sense of self-grandiosity, would experience feelings of insecurity and lower mate value (Branson & March, 2021).

Branson and March (2021) expected that primary psychopathy and secondary psychopathy would explain the additional, significant (positive) variance of cyber dating abuse. Their results partially supported this expectation, with only secondary psychopathy emerging as a significant (positive) predictor. They explained that the perpetration of cyber dating abuse might be better associated with psychopathy characterized by impulsivity and reactivity (i.e., secondary psychopathy) than manipulation and callousness (i.e., primary psychopathy). Their results are aligned with the theoretical framework of the general aggression model, according to which personality traits characterized by aggression are predictive of aggressive behavior, and jealousy as a route may also contribute to an aggressive response. In particular, the utility of psychopathy may be especially relevant to the appraisal process in the general aggression model. Here, an individual appraises the situation and decides on an immediate aggressive response or delayed thoughtful action. Primary psychopathy and secondary psychopathy are associated with different forms of appraisal and decision-making. As individuals with high secondary psychopathy are considered impulsive and reactive, they may be more likely to select an immediate, aggressive response, such as cyber dating abuse. By contrast, individuals high in primary psychopathy may be more likely to choose a delayed aggressive response due to their increased proactive aggression and reduced impulsivity (Branson & March, 2021).

Branson and March (2021) concluded that individuals more prone to relationship jealousy have high-trait vulnerable narcissism, and high-trait secondary psychopathy is more prone to cyber dating abuse. Whereas offline intimate partner violence perpetration has been broadly connected to each predictor in their study, their findings indicate that online abuse may be characterized differently. For example, the perpetrator of cyber dating abuse may not be characterized by grandiosity and arrogance (grandiose narcissism) or proactive, instrumental callousness (primary psychopathy) and is more likely to be characterized by jealousy, insecurity, emotionality (vulnerable narcissism), impulsivity, and antisocial tendencies (secondary psychopathy).

Mayshak et al. (2020) took a different perspective and examined Dark Tetrads as victims. More specifically, they examined the presence of Dark Tetrad traits in perpetrators and victims of antisocial and coercive controlling behaviors across different dating mediums. Their sample consisted of 1,009 Australian adults. They found that females and those higher in sadism were more likely to report the experience of antisocial behaviors; face-to-face dating and grandiose narcissism were associated with the perpetration of antisocial behaviors; and users of other online dating (websites, social media, but not applications) and those high in psychopathy were more likely to report experiences of coercive control.

Mayshak et al. (2020) contended that the concept of the sadist as a victim requires further investigation. Due to their tendency to look for opportunities to inflict harm, sadists are more likely to engage in antisocial behaviors and, therefore, perhaps experience more acts of retaliation. Only grandiose narcissism was associated with perpetuating antisocial behaviors; however, this only applied to the face-to-face dating group and not across other dating mediums. Mayshak et al. (2020) explained that as grandiose narcissism is associated with self-affirmation, a sense of entitlement, and more reactive aggression, it may be that the immediacy of the face-to-face environment resulted in reactivity for having entitlement expectations thwarted. Furthermore, grandiose narcissists are more likely to succeed in dating and face-to-face interactions due to their charming, confident nature; thus, they may have more opportunities to perpetrate antisocial behaviors.

Additionally, although psychopathy was associated with coercive control experiences, other Dark Tetrad traits, including grandiose narcissism, were not. Grandiose narcissism was expected to be associated with experiences of coercive control due to previous research suggesting that those who assess their mate value as higher perceived partners as controlling. As psychopathy is associated with externally orientated thinking, it is more likely that those scoring high on psychopathy may look to other sources (e.g., partners) to explain feelings of unhappiness or confinement (Mayshak et al., 2020).

A similar study was conducted by de Jesus Costa et al. (2023), who examined the associations between psychopathic traits (e.g., interpersonal manipulation, callous affect, erratic lifestyle, and criminal tendencies) and cyber dating abuse among 249 students at Portuguese universities. The study also examined the mediating effect of Internet addiction on this relationship. The results demonstrated that almost all psychopathic traits were related to direct aggression and control. The findings on cyber dating abuse perpetration were that the traits of erratic lifestyle and criminal tendencies are positively associated with the perpetration of cyber dating abuse in the form of direct aggression. Furthermore, it was found that psychopathic traits positively predict Internet addiction, victimization, and the perpetration of cyber dating abuse. Internet addiction positively predicts both victimization and the perpetration of cyber dating abuse. Concerning cyber dating abuse, psychopathic traits positively predict dating violence.

Regarding the relationship between psychopathic traits and both victimization and the perpetration of cyber dating abuse, the findings revealed a partial mediation exercised by Internet addiction in those dimensions of cyber dating abuse. The results showed that cyber abuse is perpetrated online and that psychopathic traits are associated with such abuse. According to de Jesus Costa et al. (2023), psychopathic traits leave individuals more vulnerable to excessive Internet use, increasing their antisocial behavior in their interpersonal relationships and victimization, thus making it possible to observe mediation in both. de Jesus Costa et al. (2023)

concluded that Internet addiction strongly influences certain personality factors that increase the likelihood of online abuse, in this case, dating. Furthermore, they highlighted the mutual association between victimization and perpetration, showing that one person can be both a victim and an aggressor.

Bhogal and Wallace (2022) conducted a study of two samples from the United Kingdom of participants who were in a relationship when they participated. One sample consisted of 132 heterosexuals, while the second sample consisted of 124 heterosexuals people. The study found that those higher in the Dark Triad traits did not engage in more cyber dating abuse behaviors. They defined this finding as unexpected since one would expect those with traits associated with antisocial behavior to also engage in cyber dating abuse behaviors, also considered a form of antisocial behavior. On the other hand, their finding that Machiavellianism does not predict cyber dating abuse is somewhat consistent with previous literature.

Bhogal and Wallace (2022) advanced several explanations for their findings. First, those high in Machiavellianism can manipulate and deceive, suggesting they are good at concealing their true motives. Therefore, those who are high in this trait may be underreported. Second, those high in narcissism have a high sense of grandiosity, demonstrating that they are likelier to present themselves favorably. Therefore, those high in narcissism may have been less likely to report higher levels of cyber dating abuse as this is consistent with socially undesirable behaviors. Third, individuals high in psychopathy may be likelier to engage in alternative antisocial online behaviors such as revenge porn and cyberbullying than cyber dating abuse.

Zerach (2016) examined 347 Israeli adult participants divided into four groups: *homosexual men* (*n* = 110) and *homosexual women* (*n* = 114), *heterosexual men* (*n* = 35), and *heterosexual women* (*n* = 88). The findings indicate that for the general sample, both narcissism vulnerability and grandiosity were positively related to cyberbullying victimization but not to offend, as well as to cyberbullying dating victimization and offending. Interestingly, while narcissism vulnerability was positively related to cyberbullying victimization and offending among homosexual men, narcissism grandiosity was positively related to cyberbullying victimization and offending among homosexual women. No associations between these variables were found among heterosexual groups. Notably, the group (homosexual male vs. other groups) moderated the association between narcissism vulnerability and cyberbullying victimization.

Zerach (2016) concluded that the study's findings provide substantial evidence that homosexual men and women on online dating sites are more likely to be cyberbullying victims than their heterosexual counterparts and are, therefore, vulnerable populations. The heightened levels of victimization among homosexual men and women may be explained by internalized homophobic attitudes related to sexual prejudice, dominance-promoting behavior, and stronger traditional masculine norms. These attitudes may have developed earlier than homosexual sexual identity formation. Another possible explanation stems from the victim-victimizer link in which homosexuals bullied over the years in different settings may find Internet anonymity appealing for transgressive conduct (Zerach, 2016).

Takezawa, Matsui, and Kawasaki (2023) examined the relationship between grandiose and vulnerable narcissism and cyber dating abuse among 603 adults in Japan. They focused on gender differences. Their findings showed a significant relationship between grandiose narcissism and cyber dating abuse, mainly in men. However, there was no significant relationship between the dimensions of narcissism and the dimensions of cyber dating abuse for females. The findings showed that men with a high grandiose narcissism tend to engage in harassment and invasive behavior when their relationship anxiety is high. However, grandiose narcissism is not associated with cyber dating abuse under low relationship anxiety. Takezawa et al. (2023) concluded that examining the association between narcissism and cyber dating abuse is insufficient when examining narcissism as a risk factor for cyber dating abuse. The association between narcissism and cyber dating abuse will become more apparent if the type of narcissism and the presence or absence of threats to self-evaluation are considered. However, it should be noted that no association was found between narcissism and cyber dating abuse perpetration in women.

One important note to the previous findings is that most studies were performed in Western cultures. Therefore, there is a need for much more studies in non-Western cultures to allow the generalization of the findings.

7.4.2   Dark Triad/Tetrad, Ghosting, and Revenge Pornography

7.4.2.1   Ghosting

While researchers have extensively explored the early and middle stages of romantic and sexual relationships for Dark Tetrads, they have generally failed to address the termination stage of relationships (Jonason et al., 2021). Ghosting is a relatively common and indirect form of relationship termination where one person stops communicating with the other and often *unfriends* and *unmatches* them on social media. Ghosting may be a particularly appealing way to terminate relationships for those characterized by dark traits because they tend to lack the empathy that might suppress this style of ending a relationship and are mainly motivated to seek casual sex. Ghosting is callous and passive-aggressive, allowing the perpetrator to avoid the undesirable or punishing aspects of relationship termination. Those characterized by dark traits have low levels of empathy and prefer reward-seeking behaviors, which may be traits that make ghosting appealing to such persons (Jonason et al., 2021). More specifically, the grandiosity and pride of narcissists may be unwilling to admit to a "mating mistake" (i.e., delusions of grandeur) or to have a confrontation in which they may be revealed to be wrong. Their ghosting behavior constitutes avoidant conflict management. In addition, the overt duplicity of those who are Machiavellian may also promote ghosting, given that those open and honest breakups may run contra to their deceptive and pragmatic approach to the world and relationships (Jonason et al., 2021).

Life history theory provides a theoretical framework for understanding the relationship between dark traits and ghosting. Although humans are generally characterized by using slower life history strategies compared to most other species, some might prefer short-term over long-term gains in some circumstances. Life history strategies could be considered as individual differences. Fast-life history strategists are often more selfishly motivated and impose externalities on others for their benefit. In some circumstances, they might be preferred over striving for long-term gains. Therefore, given the fast life history strategies of those high in-the-dark traits, ghosting could be expected to appeal more to them (Jonason et al., 2021).

7.4.2.2 *Revenge Pornography*

Another aspect concerning the termination of an abused relationship and Dark Tetrads is revenge pornography. Pina et al. (2017) contended that one of the ways dark personalities might react to the termination of a relationship by their partner is through revenge pornography. Revenge pornography is the act of distributing sexually explicit images or videos of another individual without their consent, with the intent of causing humiliation or distress (GOV United Kingdom 2015; Chandler & Munday, 2019; Rood & Schriner, 2021; Karasavva & Forth, 2022). Revenge pornography is a type of cyber harassment that often directly impacts the workplace and one's job prospects. Once an image is uploaded to web platforms, it is often impossible to remove it. The area of revenge pornography is akin to *doxxing*, that is, having one's personal information leaked to websites or forums, which is also profoundly unsettling (Rood & Schriner, 2021).

According to Thomason-Darch (2021), with the COVID-19 pandemic and lockdown measures within the United Kingdom, cases of revenge pornography increased notably. The Revenge Porn Helpline (2021) supported over 3,000 people in 2020, an increase of 87% compared to 2019. More people were isolated in their homes and initiated and maintained relationships online, making revenge pornography more apparent. With 90% of adults online and the sharing of sexually explicit images more widespread than ever, these provide increased opportunities for harassment and exploitation online, increasing victimization. Before the pandemic, studies reported that 61% of respondents had shared nude photos of themselves, and one in eight social media users were victims of revenge pornography. Thus, the pandemic only exacerbated this growing issue (Thomason-Darch, 2021).

Revenge pornography is perhaps the most well-known and widely discussed nonconsensual sexual image offense within the general population and in popular media outlets. Indeed, the seminal qualitative review on reasons behind this behavior (Harper, Fido, & Petronzi, 2021) documented multiple instances of perpetrators wanting 'revenge' for an ex-partner halting or ending a relationship and/or because of their misdeeds or sexual shortcomings. These kinds of explanations may have some grounding in the available evidence on engagement with revenge pornography, with reports on how such material received more views and comments when the reason for posting accompanied it (Harper et al., 2021; Karasavva & Forth, 2022; Karasavva et al., 2023a).

Certain personality traits may influence revenge pornography, including the Dark Tetrad (Karasavva & Forth, 2022; Karasavva et al., 2023a, 2023b). These subclinical personality traits have distinct characteristics, with a few key common features, including social manipulation, aggressiveness, and placing their interests above others. However, it is unclear if and how dark traits are associated with revenge pornography. According to Karasavva et al. (2023a), research findings related to the Dark Tetrad and the tendency to engage in revenge pornography. However, the primary argument seems to be that their fundamental malevolent nature drives them to use revenge pornography against their intimate partner when the relationship has been terminated.

7.4.2.3 Research Findings

In their study of 341 volunteers in the United States, Jonason et al. (2021) found that those participants with high-in-the-Dark Triad traits found ghosting acceptable, but this was only in the context of short-term relationships. They also found this pattern to be more robust in men than women for narcissism and (slightly so) psychopathy. Jonason et al. (2021) contend that these results are consistent with a life history approach to the Dark Triad traits and romantic relationships. Ghosting may be a way for people high on psychopathy and narcissism – especially men – to engage in ghosting as an efficient, low-cost way of divesting themselves of one casual sex partner to pursue other opportunities or avoid unwanted commitments.

Their findings also showed that those who had ghosted others in the past were more Machiavellian and more psychopathic (but not narcissistic) than those who had not ghosted anyone. A possible explanation is that while the difference in Machiavellianism may be explained by shared variance with psychopathy, the effect of psychopathy may be a lack of empathy. The results seem to confirm that narcissistic people's repertoire may include a greater degree of understanding the pain of others to more effectively get what they want from them as part of the relationship instead of ending it like Machiavellians and psychopaths. Jonason et al. (2021) concluded that a life history framework might be an excellent paradigm for understanding the relationship termination behaviors of people with high levels of the Dark Triad.

In a sample of 313 participants from the United Kingdom (70.9%), United States (28.4%), and Australia (0.6%), Willis et al. (2023) found that those who had ghosted someone had significantly greater vulnerable narcissism and secondary psychopathy than those who had not ghosted someone. No other significant relationships were found between antisocial dating behaviors and Dark Triad traits.

Using a sample of 722 participants from the United Kingdom, Brewer et al. (2023) examined the relationship between the Dark Triad traits and seven primary breakup strategies adopted to terminate a romantic relationship. These strategies were avoidance/withdrawal (e.g., avoiding contact or closeness), positive tone/self-blame (e.g., taking the blame for the breakup to avoid hurting the partner), open confrontation (e.g., clearly explaining the reasons for the breakup), cost escalation (e.g., making the relationship increasingly unpleasant), manipulation (e.g., promoting new relationships to the partner), distant/mediated communication (e.g., terminating the relationships via text or email), and de-escalation (e.g., delaying the breakup or suggesting that the breakup is temporary).

Their results demonstrated that Machiavellianism and psychopathy predicted greater cost escalation/manipulation breakup strategy use and lower engagement in open confrontation. Moreover, Machiavellianism predicted greater avoidance/withdrawal and de-escalation when terminating a romantic relationship, while psychopathy predicted greater distant/mediated communication and lower use of a positive tone/self-blame. Narcissism predicted only one breakup strategy: a greater open confrontation with romantic partners. Finally, they concluded that when terminating romantic relationships, those high on Dark Triad traits are likelier to engage in manipulative breakup strategies and are less likely to use breakup strategies characterized by empathy or compassion.

Pina et al. (2017) examined the behavioral propensity to engage in revenge porn and associated perpetrator characteristics. More specifically, participants were asked whether, after their partner ended the relationship with them, going through photos on their phone, they came across a nude photo of their now ex-partner sent them during the relationship. Participants were asked whether they would decide to upload this photo to the Internet and what their reactions would be if they did this. In a sample of 100 participants in the United Kingdom, their results demonstrated that higher levels of Machiavellianism, narcissism, and psychopathy were correlated with a greater likelihood of perpetrating revenge porn. Pina et al. (2017) explained that this finding suggests that the trait of interpersonal manipulation motivated by a general callous affect, a characteristic of the Dark Triad, is essential in perpetuating revenge porn. Only psychopathy retained independent significance in predicting revenge porn proclivity. This suggests that endorsing psychopathic traits, such as a deficit in empathy, is more influenced by a proclivity for revenge porn than the unique traits of narcissism and Machiavellianism. This finding showed that, aside from the Dark Triad, only psychopathy was an independent predictor of committing romantic revenge.

Pina et al. (2017) also demonstrated that only Machiavellianism retained a significant independent predictor of revenge porn proclivity. This suggests that Machiavellian traits, such as a strategic orientation and ruthless manipulation, were of more significant influence in predicting a proclivity for revenge porn. Unexpectedly, psychopathy retained no significant relationship with either approval or enjoyment of revenge porn. This was somewhat surprising as approval and enjoyment of revenge porn were positively correlated with a proclivity for revenge porn, with which psychopathy demonstrated a positive correlation. Instead, Machiavellianism was found to be positively correlated with revenge porn approval. Higher endorsement of these traits was correlated with a more significant approval of revenge porn being committed. However, only Machiavellianism was found to retain independent prediction of revenge porn approval. It could be surmised that the deceitful and strategic orientation in Machiavellian behavior and revenge porn explains this relationship.

By contrast, while narcissism and Machiavellianism yielded positive correlations with revenge porn enjoyment, only narcissism was an independent predictor. This suggests that narcissistic traits significantly influence the likelihood of enjoying revenge porn (i.e., experiencing greater control, excitement, and amusement) compared to traits unique to Machiavellianism. Pina et al. (2017) assumed that perhaps engaging in revenge, porn fulfills a narcissistic individual's notion of entitlement, grandiosity, and need for ego reinforcement, all potentially prevalent needs after a relationship breakup. Surprisingly, sadistic tendencies yielded no significant relationship with revenge porn proclivity, approval, and enjoyment. This finding contradicts recent research that implicates sadism alongside the Dark Triad in perpetuating sexual assault and online sexual violence. However, Pina et al. (2017) explained that this inconsistency might be because the study sample consisted of only female participants.

Thomason-Darch (2021) examined 306 participants in the United Kingdom and found that the Dark Tetrad positively correlated with the approval of revenge porn, suggesting that increased levels of these traits are associated with this behavior. These traits were also positively correlated with revenge porn enjoyment, except for narcissism, in which no significant correlation was demonstrated. This is surprising as narcissism was correlated with revenge porn proclivity and approval, which correlate with enjoyment. However, only sadism was a significant predictor in the regression analysis. Thomason-Darch (2021) concluded that sadism better predicts antisocial online behaviors compared to the Dark Triad, as sadistic pleasure appears to motivate this behavior. However, other findings suggest that other dark traits are also related to revenge porn.

In a sample of 810 Canadian students, Karasavva and Forth (2022) found that narcissism, psychopathy, and sadism, but not Machiavellianism, were positively correlated with revenge pornography perpetration. They also found that higher psychopathy and narcissism scores significantly predicted revenge pornography perpetration. According to them, this finding suggests that specific characteristics associated with psychopathy and/or narcissism are essential in explaining the motivations associated with revenge pornography perpetration. In addition, a higher endorsement of sadistic tendencies was predictive of revenge pornography victimization.

They explained this finding by a higher tendency of those with sadistic traits to engage in sexually risky online behaviors, such as sexting or cyberflashing, thus rendering them vulnerable to future victimization.

For the same sample of 810 Canadians, Karasavva et al. (2023a) found that none of the Dark Tetrads explained revenge pornography proclivity. Psychopathy and sadism were significantly related to revenge pornography enjoyment, while narcissism and Machiavellianism were unrelated to this behavior. Sadism was the only dark personality that was related to revenge pornography approval. Karasavva et al. (2023b) also found that cyberflashing was positively correlated with higher scores in narcissism and psychopathy but not Machiavellianism or sadism.

It should also be noted that most studies on ghosting and revenge porn were conducted in Western societies. Therefore, any generalization of the abovementioned studies should be restricted to these societies. It is possible that many non-Western societies may be too conservative to allow studies on ghosting and revenge porn to be conducted.

7.4.3   Dark Triad/Tetrad, Pornography, and Nonconsensual Sexual Images and Texts

7.4.3.1   Pornography

Individuals with high Dark Tetrad traits have a strong interest and desire for sex and sexual situations. People with Dark Tetrad traits have more sexual fantasies, a high frequency of sexual dreams, slight sexual disgust, prefer one-night stands and relationships termed *friends-with-benefits*, are unfaithful in romantic relationships, use various tools, such as Tinder, engage in casual sex, and engage in sexting activities. Individuals high on the Dark Tetrad can be expected to endorse the reasons for watching pornography more strongly (Burtăverde et al., 2021). One theoretical framework often used to consider the relationship between Dark Tetrad and pornography is the uses and gratifications perspective (Paul, 2009). The perspective theory focuses on how individuals use media to satisfy their needs and aims to discover the underlying motives for various types of media use.

According to Paul (2009), some scholars have argued that specific antisocial personality characteristics will likely result in people seeking sexually explicit content featuring depictions of more extreme and less socially acceptable behaviors. One view suggests that antisocial personality characteristics encourage some individuals to seek sexually explicit materials from others on the Internet. It is speculated that the goodness of fit of antisocial personality characteristics with antisocial sexual content promotes a tremendous depth of involvement in antisocial sexual stimuli. A desire to experience greater levels of depth of involvement (and possibly greater levels of resulting arousal) may, therefore, specifically attract individuals with higher levels of antisocial personality characteristics to such content (Fisher & Barak, 2001).

As with other media content, persons with higher levels of psychopathy are expected to rely on Internet pornography to obtain optimal arousal levels. Psychopathy is associated with antisocial entertainment activities, such as watching aggressive films, playing violent video games, and searching the Internet for extreme forms of pornography (Shim, Lee, & Paul, 2007). If pornographic materials represent an opportunity to fulfill a need for arousal, those higher in psychopathy are more likely to use and be aroused by Internet pornography (Paul, 2009). Due to psychopathic characteristics of seeking high arousal and stimulation, individuals with high levels of psychopathy are likely to seek more sexually bizarre, aggressive, and potentially violent pornography. Therefore, they would be likely to respond favorably to unsolicited Internet pornography. Such individuals require intense stimuli to experience arousal and are not concerned with societal norms. Given the novelty and sensation-seeking characteristics of psychopathy, this potentially leads such individuals to pursue unsolicited sexual content online. They are likely to experience some level of affective satisfaction from experiencing unsolicited Internet pornography, such as by mistyping a web address and arriving at a pornography website (March, 2022).

On the other hand, psychopathy is negatively correlated with romance, family-oriented films, and nonviolent sports. Because psychopaths are not satisfied with moderate levels of stimulation, they might pursue particularly aggressive, violent, or sexually bizarre content on the Internet that other people would probably avoid. If links to Internet pornographic messages fit their arousal needs, those high in psychopathy are likelier to respond to such Internet pornography. Overall, psychopathic personality traits indicate that those with a strong antisocial disposition seek more intense stimuli, including popular and deviant content. Given that most unsolicited Internet pornography includes a variety of sexual behaviors, it is reasonable to expect that those with a high antisocial disposition are more likely to pursue exposure to unsolicited Internet pornographic material than those with a low antisocial disposition (Shim et al., 2007).

According to Muris et al. (2020), it has been demonstrated that in the domain of sexuality, narcissism, Machiavellianism, and (especially) psychopathy are positively associated with feelings of sexual desire, deviant sexual fantasies and behaviors, infidelity and cheating, and exploitative and coercive behaviors. All are characteristics of short-term mating (i.e., showing less commitment and investment in a relationship with one person but placing greater emphasis on sexual activity with multiple partners) and a fast life strategy (i.e., a lifestyle prioritizing current reproduction, facilitating short-term relationships, and seeking immediate benefits). People with antisocial personality traits display higher levels of cravings for pornography. They are more inclined to access deviant pornographic materials on the Internet, consistent with empirical evidence demonstrating that these persons have a fast life strategy flavored by sexually deviating and morally inappropriate actions. Individuals characterized by short-term mating may choose to watch pornography to satisfy their increased sex drive in contexts and situations when they cannot engage in casual sex. As such, the increased sex drive dimension of reasons for watching pornography should not be understood as an adaptation but as a by-product that clusters around adaptations such as a short-term mating orientation (Burtăverde et al., 2021).

Intrasexual competition is another explanation that could explain the Dark Tetrad consumption of pornography. Intrasexual competition is a common sexual strategy that increases access to new partners and supports maintaining existing relationships. In humans, there is considerable within-sex variation in how competitive individuals are and how people compete (Lyons, Gillies, & Brewer, 2019). Social networking sites are also used as a forum for intrasexual. Social comparison and self-promotion are essential features of social networking sites, especially among younger or more intense users. Aggressive behavior, such as cyberbullying and relational aggression, is also commonplace. Therefore, exposure to online promotion, comparison, and aggression may encourage intrasexual competition. It is also plausible that those with an elevated drive for competition spend more time using these sites (Lyons et al., 2019).

Narcissism is positively associated with more unrestricted socio-sexuality and less relationship commitment, which were associated with more engagement in online sexual activities. Furthermore, narcissistic individuals may seek out idealized forms of sexual images and behaviors and, therefore, engage more frequently in the consumption of Internet pornography. Cyberspace provides more potential partners and activities, allowing narcissistic individuals to select idealized sexual partners and engage in idealized sexual activities. Thus, narcissism influences engagement in multiple dimensions of online sexual activities, such as seeking sexual partners and cybersex (Liu & Zheng, 2020).

Grubbs et al. (2023) applied a multidimensional approach to narcissism (Narcissistic Antagonism, Agentic Extraversion, and Narcissistic Neuroticism) to explain the relationship between narcissism and cyber pornography use. According to them, it is reasonable to assume that the component of narcissism most associated with entitlement (i.e., narcissistic antagonism) would similarly be related to pornography-related outcomes. The relationship between the two other dimensions and cyber pornography use is expected to be weaker because the two dimensions are not strongly associated with entitlement.

Specific aspects of narcissism have been linked to sexuality and are described as *sexual narcissism*. A sexual narcissist is preoccupied with sex and sexual interaction (Kasper et al., 2015). Widman and McNulty (2010) defined sexual narcissism as sexual entitlement, sexual exploitation, low sexual empathy, and an inflated sense of sexual skill. According to Liu and Zheng (2020), sexual narcissism refers to an egocentric pattern of sexual interaction and is expected to be more strongly associated with online sexual activities than general narcissism. Sexual narcissism is a domain-specific measure of narcissism assessing the activated cognitive components of narcissism in sexual situations (Widman & McNulty, 2010).

Given the sexual issues associated with narcissism, Internet pornography may be another aspect of the Internet that is appealing to a narcissist. Narcissistic individuals may seek out idealized forms of sexual images and behaviors. It seems that these individuals may form an intense attachment to Internet pornography, as it portrays these idealized images and scenarios. This idealized attachment may be related to self-seeking pleasure and intense sexual gratification when a narcissist consumes Internet pornography (Kasper et al., 2015). For example, narcissists focus on sexual object choice (i.e., sexual images, thoughts, or representations of a person). The more control narcissists have over their sex object, the more gratifying the object becomes to them. The consumption of Internet pornography offers this control. Internet pornography consumers can maneuver through the Internet to seek the ideal sex image. In this way, the Internet is a narcissistic medium that allows individuals to act out sexual impulses of fantasy and grandiosity (Kasper et al., 2015).

There is very little research linking pornography and sadism. Moreover, there is hardly any theory on this relationship. Sexual sadism is a paraphilia whereby an individual derives sexual excitement from another person's physical or psychological suffering (DeLisi et al., 2017). Sexual sadism disorder includes a preoccupation with pornography involving sadistic violence (Liu et al., 2022).

7.4.3.2 Sexting and Cyberflashing

7.4.3.2.1 *Sexting* Sexting has generated significant interest among the public, media, and research communities. Sexting is a sexual communication characterized by sexts, that is, text messages, photos, and/or videos with sexually explicit or provocative content that are sent or received via technological devices (Clancy, Klettkeand, & Hallford, 2019; Morelli et al., 2021). According to Hernández et al. (2021), broadly defined, sexting (which combines the words *sex* and *texting*) is the sharing of personal text messages with sexual-erotic content or sexually attractive, provocative, or nude photographs or videos using information and communication technologies. In their study, sexting refers specifically to sending personal and sexually provocative pictures, considering the sexual intensity of the published content. They distinguish between erotic sexting (sending seductive, erotic, or sexy photographs) and pornographic sexting (sending nude or semi-nude photographs or videos), both active and direct forms of sexting, increasing the risk of online victimization and risky sexual.

Sexting is increasingly considered normative sexual behavior in adolescence and early adulthood and part of the repertoire of interpersonal sexual communication. Sexting behavior is highly prevalent, particularly for young adults, with 48.56% having sent and 56.01% having received image-based sexts. Hernández et al. (2021) noted that about 33% of young males and females send their partners nude to near-nude photos. However, dissemination or sharing of sexts with others represents a specific and potentially problematic subset of sexting behaviors, mainly when it is nonconsensual. Consequently, much discussion around sext dissemination and associated harms has focused on the perpetration of nonconsensual sext dissemination, which has been associated with severe legal, personal, and emotional consequences. (Clancy et al., 2019, 2020; Sparks, Stephens & Trendell, 2023).

Victims of nonconsensual sext dissemination may experience mental health consequences such as distress, anxiety, and reduced self-esteem. Victims have also reported losing employment, and in the context of images being distributed for revenge purposes, some report post-traumatic stress symptoms and suicidal ideation. Given these severe consequences, it is critical to consider the role of consent underlying this behavior. Previous research has assumed that sext dissemination occurs against the original sender's consent, using terms such as revenge pornography, involuntary or nonconsensual pornography, electronically mediated sexual violence, or image-based sexual abuse (Clancy et al., 2019, 2020).

The psychological consequences of sexting are serious for both the receivers and the senders of sexts. For instance, receiving nonconsensual or unwanted sexts and sending sexts under coercion have been identified as predictors of mental health problems such as higher anxiety, depression, stress, and reduced self-esteem. Furthermore, sexting has been associated with lower psychological well-being levels and less confidence in social skills. Moreover, nude self-portraits have severe stigmatizing consequences for young people. The dissemination of nonconsensual sexts has been explained partially based on normalizing that sexts are usually resending or seen by others and a positive attitude toward disseminating sexts as being funny. This suggests that disseminating sexts may reinforce normalizing online aggression (Hernández et al., 2021).

Considering the proposed deviance of sexting, personality traits associated with the perpetration of deviant behaviors could be expected to predict that the individual might send unsolicited explicit images. The personality traits of a Dark Tetrad are considered socially aversive and are associated with antisocial behavior. Furthermore, these dark personality traits have been associated with more deviant sexual tendencies, including coercion, positive attitudes toward rape, and repeated sexual advances. In particular, psychopathy has been strongly associated with the perpetration of sexually deviant behavior (March & Wagstaff, 2017). Morelli et al. (2021) mentioned two main reasons the Dark Triad expects to affect different sexting behaviors. First, previous research has shown that aspects related to maladaptive personality traits of narcissism and psychopathy, such as exhibitionism and lack of empathy, frequently emerge in the online context. Second, certain maladaptive personality dispositions may lead individuals to behave more negatively, affecting online sexual communication, and are more likely to lead to problematic sexting behaviors and subsequent negative consequences.

However, because the study of the Dark Tetrad is relatively new, there is currently little published research on how it relates to sexting behaviors. Moreover, the specific relationship between personality traits and sexting among adolescents and young adults has been scarcely investigated (Morelli et al., 2021). Nevertheless, the Dark Triad concept may constitute an alternate explanation for the nonconsensual dissemination of sexts (Clancy et al., 2019). According to March and Wagstaff (2017), the positive association between dark personality traits and sexually exploitative behavior could extend to sending unsolicited explicit images, previously defined as online sexual harassment. Thus, if sending unsolicited explicit images is a sexually deviant behavior, one could expect that individuals with higher levels of dark personality traits (particularly psychopathy) would be more inclined to engage in this behavior.

Hernández et al. (2021) focused on narcissism and its relationship to sexting and grooming. According to Hernández et al. (2021), the narcissistic content in selfies reflects the sociocultural models of body image promoted by social media. These aspects of self-presentation are related to sexting behaviors and sexual motivations. Narcissism predicts exhibitionist and uninhibited behavior, over and above extraversion and the drive for entertainment. Moreover, the relationship between sexual narcissism and lack of sexual empathy is evident, and both contribute to online sexual activities, including sexting and online grooming victimization (Hernández et al., 2021).

7.4.3.2.2 *Cyberflashing* Cyberflashing means sharing sexually explicit images via digital technologies (e.g., text messaging, instant social media) to unsuspecting or nonconsenting recipients (Harper et al., 2021). Cyberflashing encompasses several behaviors, from sending self-produced sexual media to the nonconsensual transfer of pornographic media via digital technologies such as Bluetooth or Apple's AirDrop feature. That is, sending these stimuli may be related to sexual grooming and represent the stage at which the individual sending the media attempts to desensitize a potential partner to engage in sexual activity. However, it is essential to note that cyberflashing does not include consensual sexting behavior within established personal or romantic relationships. Cyberflashing appears to be a gendered form of violence, with half of women having received at least one unsolicited sexual image compared to only one-quarter of men (Sparks et al., 2023).

The key feature of cyberflashing that dictates whether a behavior falls under the umbrella of nonconsensual sexual images is that the media is shared in a nonconsensual or intrusive manner. Though likely to evoke distress in the receiver, one mechanism of cyberflashing may be to garner the possibility of short-term mating, particularly in the current fast-paced context of dating applications and so-called hook-up culture. It could be that cyberflashing is a modern method of initiating this contact without the necessity of making oneself vulnerable in a physical way, which would be consistent with emerging research on young people's emerging preference to form and maintain relationships in online settings (Harper et al., 2021).

However, little psychological research has suggested a coherent paradigm for studying this phenomenon. Given the increasing prevalence of online dating, establishing theoretical models for the motivations underpinning a range of cyberflashing behaviors and possible ways to prevent further victimization should become a priority in this area of research (Harper et al., 2021). The possible relationship between the Dark Tetrad and cyberflashing could be explained by the lack of empathy, propensity for risk-taking, selfishness, and interpersonal hostility emblematic of the Dark Tetrad (Karasavva et al., 2023b). Although these subclinical personality traits share some vital common features, they are distinct, as described in Chapter 1. In the context of cyberflashing as a deviant sexual behavior, it is possible that individuals with dark personality traits could be more likely to engage in this behavior. However, the relationship between dark personality traits and the reasons that motivate cyberflashing remains unclear (Karasavva et al., 2023b) and requires theoretical and empirical work.

7.4.3.3 *Grooming and Online Child Pornography*

Internet child pornography is a remarkably prolific criminal and social concern. Offenders download, collect, and circulate child pornography online. In comparison to contact sex offenders toward children, little research has explored Internet-facilitated sex offending targeting children. Given the potential for individual differences to manage and prevent behavior, such studies could provide vital information regarding managing Internet child pornography offenses. However, challenging hurdles must be overcome to assess the consumption of Internet child pornography, including mandatory reporting and socially biased responses (March, 2022).

Online grooming is a relationship based on trust between minors and adults who use information and communication technologies to seduce and abuse minors for sexual purposes. A potential adult abuser befriends a child to gain the child's trust, which allows the abuser to obtain the child's consent to engage in inappropriate sexual or exhibitionist behavior, increasing the likelihood of future sexual abuse of the minor. This process of online grooming requires sexting activities and often starts with the adult sending text messages and photographs with sexual-erotic content before becoming an abusive relationship. Groomers are often cybercriminals whose computer activities focus on pedophilia (Hernández et al., 2021). Grooming also has adverse consequences. Sexting as a form of online victimization and other sexual victimization behaviors such as online grooming are related to mental health symptoms, such as depression and increased emotional distress, sleep problems, low frustration tolerance, feelings of inability to resolve difficulties, suicidal thoughts, increased impulsiveness, and symptoms of post-traumatic stress (Hernández et al., 2021).

7.4.4   Research Findings

7.4.4.1   Pornography

Burtăverde et al. (2021) examined the relationship between dimensions of pornography consumption and the Dark Triad in a sample of 276 Romanian undergraduate psychology students. They found that those watching pornography to increase their sex drive had high levels of the Dark Triad traits and were more interested in casual sex. Burtăverde et al. (2021) also found that those high on the second dimension of the reasons for watching pornography – namely, enhancing sexual performance – had higher scores on the Dark Triad traits. They explained that besides reflecting a short-term mating orientation, watching pornography might be viewed as a tactic that enhances the probability of attracting a mate and, implicitly, the probability of reproduction.

The third dimension of pornography consumption was for "social and instrumental reasons." Their findings were that individuals with high scores on this dimension also had high levels of Machiavellianism and psychopathy but not narcissism. According to Burtăverde et al. (2021), this category of reasons for watching pornography reflects reasons that refer to watching pornography mainly because of seeking the acceptance of social groups, such as friends. This category may be explained by the fact that watching pornography is a common habit. Furthermore, it is well known that young people place greater importance on their reputation and social acceptance than older people. Therefore, watching pornography may facilitate social approval among peers, especially college-aged ones.

The fourth reason for pornography consumption is a lack of relational and emotional skills. People high on this dimension had lower scores on Machiavellianism and psychopathy but not narcissism. The reasons encompassed by this factor suggest that individuals who score high on them watch pornography to regulate their mood and deal with negative emotions. People seem to use pornography to alleviate negative emotions, which may be explained by the fact that pornography consumption induces psychological moods and emotions such as pleasure and satisfaction evoked during casual sex and sexual intercourse (Burtăverde et al., 2021).

Burtăverde et al. (2021) also demonstrated that psychopathy mediated the relationship between sex and the reasons for consuming pornography, except for the dimension of enhancing sexual performance, for which there were no sex differences. This may be because men are more interested in casual sex than women, have a more comprehensive array of sexual fantasies, and men high on psychopathy have frequent sexual fantasies. Consequently, they may use pornography to satisfy this need. Therefore, psychopathy represents an explicative mechanism of the indirect relationship between sex and the reasons for consuming pornography.

Muris et al. (2020) examined 121 participants from the Netherlands and found that Dark Triad traits, especially psychopathy and narcissism, were positively related to the craving for pornography and deviant pornography consumption. However, follow-up analyses suggested that these relationships were only present in men and not in women. According to Muris et al. (2020), this gender difference supports the contention that men are more strongly inclined to engage in short-term mating behavior – a fast life strategy – and morally condemnable actions than women.

In a sample of 377 students from the United States, Paul (2009) found that men (n = 179) with more antisocial personality dispositions appear likelier to use all forms of online pornographic content. However, they are more likely to be aroused than others if that content is perceived as particularly intense, out of the mainstream, or potentially more socially inappropriate. According to Paul (2009), this makes sense in that those higher in psychopathy are expected to need more intense stimuli to experience arousal and to care less about the consequences of behaving counter to societal norms. The findings regarding impulsive thrill-seeking and antisocial behavior support this explanation. For women (n = 158), it seems that, like male respondents, women with higher levels of antisocial personality are more drawn toward all forms of pornographic content. Like men, however, women with higher levels of psychopathy are only more aroused by such content if it is particularly intense or alternative.

In a sample of 337 students from the United States, the findings in a study by Shim et al. (2007) support their expectation that psychopathy is an important predictor of one's response to unsolicited Internet pornographic content. A higher score suggests that respondents are more willing to be exposed to Internet pornography when encountering such material. Their study also found an interaction between sexual disposition and psychopathy and one's responsiveness to unsolicited Internet pornography. Individuals with high sexual disposition and high psychopathy appear particularly inclined to consume unwanted Internet pornography. Their findings clearly show that psychopathy should be considered an essential factor in studying the effects of unsolicited Internet pornography.

Grubbs et al. (2023) examined the relationship between three dimensions of narcissism (Narcissistic Antagonism, Agentic Extraversion, and Narcissistic Neuroticism) in five samples, four of them in the United States and one in English-speaking students in Malaysia. Across all samples, they found consistent, robust associations between narcissistic antagonism and perceived addiction to pornography. Narcissistic neuroticism and narcissistic extraversion demonstrated inconsistent relationships with both pornography use frequency and perceived addiction, with significant-but-small positive associations between these factors of narcissism and pornography-related variables evident in some samples, nonsignificant associations evident in other samples, and significant-but-small negative associations in other samples. Grubbs et al. (2023) concluded that narcissistic antagonism is the most consistently and strongly related to perceived addiction.

Some empirical research provides evidence for the link between sexual narcissism and online sexual activities. For instance, Kasper et al. (2015) found in a sample of 257 participants from the United States that those high on the Narcissistic Personality Inventory and Index of Sexual Narcissism endorsed a greater frequency of Internet pornography use. More notably, individuals who use Internet pornography seem to have higher levels of both general narcissistic characteristics and sexual narcissism. In a sample of 339 Chinese participants, Liu and Zheng (2020) found that narcissism was related to engaging in multiple dimensions of online sexual activities, which extended the previous finding that narcissism was correlated with Internet pornography use (Kasper et al., 2015). Based on their study, Liu and Zheng (2020) contended that a positive association between narcissism and online sexual activities might be attributable to the fact that narcissists' desire for idealized images and partners is satisfied through frequent engagement in online sexual activities. Moreover, narcissists may be more familiar with the Internet and thus engage in online sexual activities more frequently. In a sample of 185 American individuals recruited voluntarily through online platforms such as social media and college class forums, Calvert et al. (2021) found that those with higher levels of narcissism and sexual narcissism were more likely to engage in pornography consumption.

7.4.4.2 *Sexting and Grooming*

A meta-analysis of 19 independent samples found a small but significant effect ($r = 0.148$) of dark personalities on sexting among juveniles (Wissnik et al., 2023). Morelli et al. (2021) investigated how specific maladaptive personality traits related to different kinds of sexting among adolescents and young adults across 11 countries spanning four continents (Europe, Asia, Africa, and North America). The main goal was to identify specific relationships between the Dark Triad traits and different sexting behaviors. They found that narcissism and Machiavellianism emerged as positive predictors of sharing sexts. Individuals with high narcissism generally display more online behaviors geared toward self-presentation. They use pictures and words to communicate about themselves more frequently and do so mostly positively. It is worth noting that psychopathy showed no main effect on sharing one's sexts. However, this relationship appears to have been conditioned by age. Specifically, the relationship between psychopathy and sharing one's sexts was stronger for older participants.

Both risky sexting (i.e., sexting during substance and alcohol use and sharing sexts with strangers) and aggravated sexting (i.e., nonconsensual sexting and sexting under pressure) were positively predicted by Machiavellianism and psychopathy. Machiavellianism emerged as a positive predictor of risky sexting. The possible explanation for this empirical evidence can be found in some aspects of the Machiavellian trait, characterized by the manipulation and deception of others, combined with a lack of emotionality and disregard for morality. Morelli et al. (2021) findings showed that risky sexting was also positively predicted by psychopathy. People with high levels of psychopathy are more inclined to unrestricted attitudes toward promiscuity, especially a lack of attachment. Thus, they may consider it to be appropriate to share sexts with strangers they meet online. Moreover, people with higher psychopathy levels are very impulsive, exhibiting low levels of fear and self-control. They are very likely to engage in sexting during substance and alcohol use (Morelli et al., 2021).

Machiavellianism positively predicted nonconsensual sexting. Machiavellian people are emotionally detached and have low empathy and a willingness to exploit others. Moreover, they adopt strategies with a long-term orientation in making decisions and planning behaviors to achieve their purposes. Thus, they may act by planning a strategy to obtain and post sexts by a partner or an acquaintance without their consent. Psychopathy also emerged as a positive predictor of nonconsensual sexting. People with high psychopathy have little empathy for others or concern for socially unacceptable behaviors. Individuals high in psychopathy can also indulge in nonconsensual sexting as they do not care about inflicting harm or causing distress. This trait often represents the best predictor of romantic revenge (Morelli et al., 2021).

Machiavellianism and psychopathy positively predicted sexting under pressure. Individuals high in Machiavellianism are primarily concerned about maintaining a positive image within the group. Thus, they may be involved in sexting under pressure, thinking that this behavior would maintain their popularity within the group. Concerning psychopathy, the research found that, conversely to Machiavellians, people high in psychopathy tend to act instinctively and without worrying about their reputation. Furthermore, the relationship between psychopathy and both forms of aggravated sexting (i.e., nonconsensual sexting and sexting under pressure) was more robust for boys than girls. Morelli et al. (2021) concluded that not all Dark Triad traits are equally related to sexting behaviors. Sharing one's sexts was predicted by narcissism and Machiavellianism, whereas risky sexting, nonconsensual sexting, and sexting under pressure were related to psychopathy and Machiavellianism. Narcissism did not appear to be related to a more damaging form of sexting, which was instead predicted by psychopathy. Ultimately, Machiavellianism represented a significant predictor of all forms of sexting behaviors.

In a sample of 240 Australian adults, March and Wagstaff (2017) found a strong effect of Machiavellianism in predicting attitudes toward and the perpetration of sending unsolicited explicit images of one's genitals to others. Based on the utility of Machiavellianism in independently predicting attitudes toward and the perpetration of sending unsolicited explicit images and the mediating nature of Machiavellianism and all other dark personality traits, these explicit images may be an aggressive mating strategy rather than a manifestation of evil personality traits. More so than the other dark personality traits, individuals with high levels of Machiavellianism are apt behavioral strategists, effectively (and charmingly) exploiting situations and others for their benefit. Thus, unlike the need for admiration associated with narcissism, the callous nature associated with psychopathy, and the enjoyment of inflicting suffering associated with the trait sadism, it appears that the trait that best predicts sending unsolicited explicit images is that associated with the strategic manipulation of others and situations (March & Wagstaff, 2017).

In their sample of 505 adults from Australia, Clancy et al. (2019) found that all three Dark Triad traits were significantly associated with sext dissemination, with the most substantial relationship for Machiavellianism. This finding is similar to that of March and Wagstaff (2017). However, Clancy et al. (2019) noted that effect sizes were small in their study in all cases. Dark Triad traits did not independently predict dissemination after controlling for motivations for dissemination. This may have been because finding dissemination funny or not a big deal may be a proxy behavior for the Dark Triad traits and may account for this variance. Motivations such as these for disseminating sexts seem congruent with a lack of empathy and consideration of others, mainly because there was a strong awareness of the negative consequences that can occur (Clancy et al., 2019).

In another study of 691 adults in English-speaking countries, Clancy et al. (2020) expected sext dissemination to be associated with higher Dark Triad traits. Instead, their study found sext dissemination "as a joke" associated with Machiavellianism but not psychopathy or narcissism. Notably, despite associations between sext dissemination and all Dark Triad traits, few participants endorsed motivations of revenge, spite, or getting the recipient into trouble. Again, this suggests that few young adults endorse explicitly pernicious motivations for sext dissemination, and it is not synonymous with revenge pornography or image-based abuse. However, socially undesirable motivations such as these are prone to underreporting. Moreover, individuals sharing these Dark Triad traits may perceive their behaviors and intentions as less problematic than those they may impact.

Pina et al. (2021) examined the relationship between image-based sexual abuse, defined as the creation, distribution, and/or threat of distributing intimate images of another person online without their consent, and the Dark Triad. They examined 126 English-speaking participants from the United Kingdom recruited via social media. Machiavellianism and psychopathy were found to predict image-based sexual abuse proclivity, while narcissism predicted greater feelings of excitement and amusement toward image-based sexual abuse. They concluded that their findings suggest a distinct personality profile of perpetrators of image-based sexual abuse and that moral disengagement mechanisms play a role in facilitating and reinforcing this behavior.

Pineda et al. (2023) examined the relationship between Dark Tetrad and online sexual victimization and the perpetration of online sexual victimization behaviors. They examined 1,988 participants from Spain (90.96%), Latin America (7.84%), and other countries or regions (1.20%). They found that the personality trait that best predicts the perpetration of online sexual victimization behaviors is sadism, followed by narcissism. On the other hand, the dark trait that most predicted online sexual victimization was sadism. According to Pineda et al. (2023), this finding shows that while people with high scores in sadism perpetrate more online sexual victimization behaviors, they also tend to suffer more from such behaviors. This relationship might be explained by the pleasure those people with elevated rates of this trait get from victimizing others, causing them not to consider the possibility of being victimized by the same behaviors.

For both online sexual victimization and the perpetration of online sexual victimization behaviors, psychopathy was a very weak predictor, even presenting negative connections with being victimized by it. This finding is surprising, and Pineda et al. tried to explain it by invoking the construct overlaps between sadism and psychopathy, both cruel traits related to a general tendency to exploit others. They concluded that their findings might be better explained by the sadistic tendencies of feeling pleasure from others' suffering rather than the psychopathic impulsiveness, lack of emotionality, and conscientiousness, among other more psychopathy-related characteristics.

Pineda et al. (2023) noted that among participants who indicated that they had suffered from online sexual victimization behaviors, the perpetrator was someone they knew from a previous face-to-face relationship rather than someone they only knew from the Internet or someone they did not know at all. Notwithstanding, no differences were observed among the four traits attending to whom people high on each of them tend to victimize. This means that people with high scores for sadism (as well as for the other three traits) victimize others regardless of whether they previously knew them. Furthermore, at a descriptive level, these online sexual victimization contacts were made via messaging applications and social media, as expected nowadays, since its use is normalized and accessible to nearly everybody.

In an online qualitative and quantitative survey of 480 adults from Australia, Mayshak et al. (2023) reached similar conclusions to Pineda et al. (2023). Regarding negative experiences, they found that individuals with elevated Dark Tetrad traits, especially women, reported many online and offline dating victimization, expressed frustration and concerns about deliberate misrepresentation on the part of their dating partners, and revealed a high sensitivity to rejection. Respondents with elevated Dark Tetrad traits also noted many difficulties managing close relationships. Mayshak et al. concluded that their study contributes to the current knowledge by illustrating that people with elevated Dark Tetrad traits, especially women, are prone to dating abuse and victimization.

Lyons et al. (2022b) explored the influence of exposure to sexist social media content on rape cognitions and whether this differed depending on the presence of socially aversive personality traits. In a sample of 180, mostly United Kingdom citizens, Lyons et al. found that although sexist tweets were rated less acceptable, exposure to sexist social media did not affect rape-supportive attitudes, victim blame, or hostile masculinity. Their findings showed that while all three Dark Triad traits correlated positively with rating the sexist tweets acceptable and humorous, the prime condition (exposure to sexist or neutral tweets) did not impact the outcome variables. Psychopathy was the strongest predictor of proclivity to sexual violence. According to Lyons et al. (2022a), one of their interesting findings is the positive relationship between the Dark Triad traits and perceptions of sexist tweets as acceptable and funny. They contended that it is possible that perceptions of sexist humor as funny perpetuate rape cognitions in those who have higher levels of Dark Triad traits.

Resett et al. (2022) examined 728 Argentinian adolescents between 11 and 18 years of age. Using a structural model to predict sexting and grooming, they found that high levels of dark personality, lower levels of anxiety, and high depression scores – albeit marginally – were the significant predictors. For grooming, only higher sexting and depression scores explained the variance. They concluded that dark personality scores and problems are significant predictors of sexting and grooming and that sexting is a predictor of grooming. It should be noted that their findings demonstrated that of the three dark personalities, only psychopathy was a significant predictor of sexting for males but not for females. The findings regarding the Dark Triad and grooming were even weaker. More studies in similar cultures are required to clarify the abovementioned findings further.

In a sample of 1,763 adolescent participants aged between 12 and 16 years from Spain, Hernández et al. (2021) found that adolescents who are more extraverted, narcissistic, disinhibited, and less empathic are at greater risk of sexting and online grooming victimization. According to them, narcissism is a relevant element of the personality profile that characterizes adolescents who engage in sexual-erotic risks, such as sexting and online grooming. The intention in both cases is to present themselves according to an ideal self, how they would like to be, or how they would like others to perceive them. Narcissists endeavor to be desired by someone else. Therefore, sharing their pictures on the Internet or social media arouses others' sexual-erotic desire. Narcissistic individuals crave admiration and approval; thus, receiving likes is an expression of positive social feedback, experiencing positive emotional affect, which may reinforce their narcissistic complacency.

Furthermore, narcissists are excessively interested in demonstrating their physical attractiveness, which increases sexting activity. The urge to send erotic sexts and enhanced self-presentations balances or regulates the perceived social rejection and the desire to compensate for that rejection. This need for secondary positive reinforcement has been highlighted by previous research as facilitating operant conditioning and encouraging adolescents to continue posting more pictures.

In two independent samples in the United Kingdom (Study 1; n = 290, Study 2; n = 364), Fido et al. (2022) examined whether judgments of deep faking (the use of widely accessible artificial intelligence to dynamically transpose one image, or a series of similar images, onto a secondary source such as a still photograph or a motion picture; which creates an indistinguishable illusion that the target individual is engaging in sexual behavior) differed as a function of victim status (celebrity or noncelebrity), victim and participant demographics, and image use while controlling for the potential effect of dimensions of psychopathy and beliefs about a just world. Their findings showed that both the interpersonal and antisocial facets of psychopathy predicted a proclivity to generate and share deep fakes across both samples, with the antisocial facet predicting more significant victim blame and reduced criminality and victim harm. They explained that the precise mechanism underpinning this association is likely to be a function of those scoring higher on psychopathy having reduced empathy for the impact of others and gaining pleasure from inflicting emotional distress on others through their actions.

Sparks et al.'s (2023) findings, in a sample of 541 Canadian students, implicated Dark Triad traits as potential risk factors for perpetuating non-consensual dissemination and cyberflashing. Sparks et al. explained that the more prominent effect of narcissism on cyberflashing suggests one of two possibilities: (1) Cyberflashing may not be done to harm but under the assumption that the recipient may want to see such an image, or (2) cyberflashing may be being used as a means of approval-seeking to compensate for their fragile self-esteem.

****

Table 7.1 summarizes research findings relevant to the topics covered in this chapter. Most of the studies are based on samples outside the United States. The average age of most participants is up to 20 years or younger. More data regarding the participants' occupations and work experience are required. The size of the correlations is relatively moderate, although it is higher than in Chapters 2 and 4–6. This indicates that some possible moderators and mediators affect the relationship between Dark Tetrads and intimate cyber relationships. Finally, more studies on the sadism trait are needed. Many scholars are still examining the Dark Triad traits. There is a need to reach a consensus on whether sadism is part of dark personalities. As it is, it is very confusing to remain in a situation where not all scholars practically consider sadism as the fourth dark trait.

Table 7.1 *Summary of research findings of the relationship between the Dark Tetrad/Triad and romantic relationships in cyberspace*

Study	Sample size	Type of behavior	Gender	Age (mean)	AT or similar	Country	Occupation	Education	Correlations			
									Narcissists	Psychopathy	Machiavellianism	Sadism
Pineda et al. (2022a)	1,189	Cyber dating abuse – control victimization	78% female	29.36 (18–65)	No	Spain	NR	61.8% university studies 17.3% vocational training 20.9% high school and lower	0.085**	0.096**	0.045	0.143**
Pineda et al. (2022a)	1,189	Cyber dating abuse – direct aggression victimization	78% female	29.36 (18–65)	No	Spain	NR	61.8% university studies 17.3% vocational training 20.9% high school and lower	0.113**	0.137*	0.072*	0.211**
Pineda et al. (2022a)	1,189	Cyber dating abuse – control perpetration	78% female	29.36 (18–65)	No	Spain	NR	61.8% university studies 17.3% vocational training 20.9% high school and lower	0.124**	0.141**	0.122**	0.132**
Pineda et al. (2022a)	1,189	Cyber dating abuse – direct aggression perpetration	78% female	29.36 (18–65)	No	Spain	NR	61.8% university studies 17.3% vocational training 20.9% high school and lower	0.234**	0.144**	0.145**	0.265**
Thomason-Darch (2021)	306	Revenge porn proclivity	75.8% female	28.26 (18–77)	No	United Kingdom	NR	NR	0.11*	0.17**	0.12*	0.20**
Thomason-Darch (2021)	306	Revenge porn enjoyment	75.8% female	28.26 (18–77)	No	United Kingdom	NR	NR	0.07	0.18**	0.15*	0.21**

Table 7.1 (cont.)

Study	Sample size	Type of behavior	Gender	Age (mean)	AT or similar	Country	Occupation	Education	Narcissists	Psychopathy	Machiavellianism	Sadism
										Correlations		
						Sample characteristics						
Thomason-Darch (2021)	306	Revenge porn approval	75.8% female	28.26 (18–77)	No	United Kingdom	NR	NR	0.14**	0.23**	0.31**	0.17**
Sevi (2019)	271	Tinder for long-term relationship	53.5% female	30.78 (18–73)	Yes	USA	NR	NR	−0.03	−0.11	0.04	NE
Sevi (2019)	271	Tinder for a short-term relationship	53.5% female	30.78 (18–73)	Yes	USA	NR	NR	0.32***	0.60***	0.34***	NE
Duncan & March (2019)	587	Antisocial use of Tinder – general	79% female	23.75	No	Australia	NR	50.9% undergraduate students; 45.9% high school education	0.21***	0.42***	0.33***	0.42***
Duncan & March (2019)	587	Antisocial use of Tinder – esteem	79% female	23.75	No	Australia	NR	50.9% undergraduate students; 45.9% high school education	0.12**	0.17***	0.23***	0.12**
Duncan & March (2019)	587	Antisocial use of Tinder – sexual	79% female	23.75	No	Australia	NR	50.9% undergraduate students; 45.9% high school education	0.20***	0.49***	0.35***	0.36***
Jonason & Bulyk (2019)	299	Tinder users and nonusers	45% female	32.56 (18–61)	Yes	USA	NR	NR	Medium level among users (N = 68)	Lowest level among users (N = 68)	Highest level among users (N = 68)	NE
Lyons et al. (2020)	216	Motives for using Tinder: social approval	69% female	22.87 (18–56)	No	United Kingdom (n = 164) or USA & Canada (n = 32)	First-year psychology students	First-year psychology students	0.10 for female 0.24* for male	0.25** for female 0.19 for male	0.29** for female 0.24* for male	0.15 for female 0.24 for male
Lyons et al. (2020)	216	Motives for using Tinder: relationship seeking	69% female	22.87 (18–56)	No	United Kingdom (n = 164) or USA & Canada (n = 32)	First-year psychology students	First-year psychology students	−0.03 for female −0.09 for male	−0.02 for female −0.09 for male	0.19* for female 0.36** for male	0.09 for female −0.09 for male

Study	N	Variable	% female	Age M (range)		Country	Sample	Sample	Corr 1	Corr 2	Corr 3	Corr 4
Lyons et al. (2020)	216	Motives for using Tinder: sexual experience	69% female	22.87 (18–56)	No	United Kingdom (n = 164) or USA & Canada (n = 32)	First-year psychology students	First-year psychology students	0.22** for female / 0.28** for male	0.40** for female / 0.53** for male	0.29** for female / 0.24* for male	0.24** for female / 0.35** for male
Lyons et al. (2020)	216	Motives for using Tinder: flirting/social skills	69% female	22.87 (18–56)	No	United Kingdom (n = 164) or USA & Canada (n = 32)	First-year psychology students	First-year psychology students	−0.04 for female / −0.07 for male	0.14 for female / −.05 for male	0.27** for female / 0.14 for male	0.02 for female / 0.02 for male
Lyons et al. (2020)	216	Motives for using Tinder: traveling	69% female	22.87 (18–56)	No	United Kingdom (n = 164) or USA & Canada (n = 32)	First-year psychology students	First-year psychology students	0.19* for female / 0.07 for male	0.22** for female / 0.18 for male	0.24** for female / 0.19 for male	0.21** for female / 0.07 for male
Lyons et al. (2020)	216	Motives for using Tinder: ex	69% female	22.87 (18–56)	No	United Kingdom (n = 164) or USA & Canada (n = 32)	First-year psychology students	First-year psychology students	−0.03 for female / 0.14 for male	0.13 for female / 0.21 for male	0.15 for female / 0.15 for male	−0.03 for female / 0.16 for male
Lyons et al. (2020)	216	Motives for using Tinder: belonging	69% female	22.87 (18–56)	No	United Kingdom (n = 164) or USA & Canada (n = 32)	First-year psychology students	First-year psychology students	0.13 for female / 0.15 for male	0.12 for female / 0.17 for male	0.21* for female / 0.15 for male	−0.03 for female / 0.06 for male
Lyons et al. (2020)	216	Motives for using Tinder: peer pressure	69% female	22.87 (18–56)	No	United Kingdom (n = 164) or USA & Canada (n = 32)	First-year psychology students	First-year psychology students	0.17* for female / −0.13 for male	0.10 for female / −0.08 for male	0.21* for female / 0.17 for male	0.04 for female / 0.04 for male
Lyons et al. (2020)	216	Motives for using Tinder: socializing	69% female	22.87 (18–56)	No	United Kingdom (n = 164) or USA & Canada (n = 32)	First-year psychology students	First-year psychology students	0.02 for female / 0.01 for male	0.12 for female / 0.06 for male	0.14 for female / 0.14 for male	0.14 for female / 0.06 for male
Lyons et al. (2020)	216	Motives for using Tinder: sexual orientation	69% female	22.87 (18–56)	No	United Kingdom (n = 164) or USA & Canada (n = 32)	First-year psychology students	First-year psychology students	0.10 for female / 0.19 for male	0.10 for female / 0.30* for male	0.13 for female / 0.25* for male	−0.06 for female / 0.20 for male

Table 7.1 (cont.)

Study	Sample size	Type of behavior	Gender	Age (mean)	AT or similar	Country	Occupation	Education	Correlations			
						Sample characteristics			Narcissists	Psychopathy	Machiavellianism	Sadism
Lyons et al. (2020)	216	Motives for using Tinder: pass time	69% female	22.87 (18–56)	No	United Kingdom (n = 164) or USA & Canada (n = 32)	First-year psychology students	First-year psychology students	0.14 for female 0.27* for male	0.23* for female 0.13 for male	0.33* for female 0.14 for male	−0.01 for female 0.19 for male
Lyons et al. (2020)	216	Motives for using Tinder: distraction	69% female	22.87 (18–56)	No	United Kingdom (n = 164) or USA & Canada (n = 32)	First-year psychology students	First-year psychology students	0.11 for female 0.18 for male	0.24** for female 0.33** for male	0.17* for female 0.30* for male	0.01 for female 0.36** for male
Lyons et al. (2020)	216	Motives for using Tinder: curiosity	69% female	22.87 (18–56)	No	United Kingdom (n = 164) or USA & Canada (n = 32)	First-year psychology students	First-year psychology students	0.07 for female −0.11 for male	0.01 female −0.01 for male	0.19* for female 0.05 for male	−0.11 for female −0.07 for male
March et al. (2020a)	1,001	Tinder behavior: anger on Tinder	53.7% female	22.42	No	Australia	NR	NR	Grandiose = 0.11** Entitlement = 0.17**	NE	NE	NE
March et al. (2020a)	1,001	Tinder behavior: aggression on Tinder	53.7% female	22.42	No	Australia	NR	NR	Grandiose = 12** Entitlement = 0.13*	NE	NE	NE
March et al. (2020a)	1,001	Tinder behavior: harassment on Tinder	53.7% female	22.42	No	Australia	NR	NR	Grandiose = 10** Entitlement = 0.22**	NE	NE	NE
Timmermans et al. (2018)	471	Motives for using Tinder: social approval	72.8% female	22.89 (18–58)	No	The Netherlands	NR	78.6% students	N = 81 non-single Tinder users = 0.30**	N = 81 non-single Tinder users = 0.14	N = 81 non-single Tinder users = 0.28*	NE
Timmermans et al. (2018)	471	Motives for using Tinder: pass time/ entertainment	72.8% female	22.89 (18–58)	No	The Netherlands	NR	78.6% students	N = 81 non-single Tinder users = 0.22*	N = 81 non-single Tinder users = −0.02	N = 81 non-single Tinder users = 0.15	NE
Timmermans et al. (2018)	471	Motives for using Tinder: traveling	72.8% female	22.89 (18–58)	No	The Netherlands	NR	78.6% students	N = 81 non-single Tinder users = 0.10	N = 81 non-single Tinder users = −0.02	N = 81 non-single Tinder users = −0.11	NE

Study	N	Variable	% female	Age (range)		Country		Sample	r	r	r	
Timmermans et al. (2018)	471	Motives for using Tinder: sexual experience	72.8% female	22.89 (18–58)	No	The Netherlands	NR	78.6% students	N = 81 non-single Tinder users = 0.16	N = 81 non-single Tinder users = 0.31**	N = 81 non-single Tinder users = 0.27*	NE
Timmermans et al. (2018)	471	Motives for using Tinder: ex	72.8% female	22.89 (18–58)	No	The Netherlands	NR	78.6% students	N = 81 non-single Tinder users = 0.06	N = 81 non-single Tinder users = 0.03	N = 81 non-single Tinder users = −0.10	NE
Timmermans et al. (2018)	471	Motives for using Tinder: belongingness	72.8% female	22.89 (18–58)	No	The Netherlands	NR	78.6% students	N = 81 non-single Tinder users = 0.14	N = 81 non-single Tinder users = 0.08	N = 81 non-single Tinder users = 0.08	NE
Timmermans et al. (2018)	471	Motives for using Tinder: relationship seeking	72.8% female	22.89 (18–58)	No	The Netherlands	NR	78.6% students	N = 81 non-single Tinder users = −0.09	N = 81 non-single Tinder users = 0.07	N = 81 non-single Tinder users = −0.06	NE
Timmermans et al. (2018)	471	Motives for using Tinder: flirting/ social skills	72.8% female	22.89 (18–58)	No	The Netherlands	NR	78.6% students	N = 81 non-single Tinder users = −0.15	N = 81 non-single Tinder users = 0.04	N = 81 non-single Tinder users = 0.09	NE
Timmermans et al. (2018)	471	Motives for using Tinder: sexual orientation	72.8% female	22.89 (18–58)	No	The Netherlands	NR	78.6% students	N = 81 non-single Tinder users = 0.06	N = 81 non-single Tinder users = 0.16	N = 81 non-single Tinder users = 0.09	NE
Timmermans et al. (2018)	471	Motives for using Tinder: socializing	72.8% female	22.89 (18–58)	No	The Netherlands	NR	78.6% students	N = 81 non-single Tinder users = −0.15	N = 81 non-single Tinder users = −0.09	N = 81 non-single Tinder users = −0.11	NE
Timmermans et al. (2018)	471	Motives for using Tinder: peer pressure	72.8% female	22.89 (18–58)	No	The Netherlands	NR	78.6% students	N = 81 non-single Tinder users = 0.05	N = 81 non-single Tinder users = 0.14	N = 81 non-single Tinder users = 0.09	NE
Timmermans et al. (2018)	471	Motives for using Tinder: distraction	72.8% female	22.89 (18–58)	No	The Netherlands	NR	78.6% students	N = 81 non-single Tinder users = 0.26*	N = 81 non-single Tinder users = 0.08	N = 81 non-single Tinder users = 0.03	NE
Timmermans et al. (2018)	471	Motives for using Tinder: curiosity	72.8% female	22.89 (18–58)	No	The Netherlands	NR	78.6% students	N = 81 non-single Tinder users = 0.11	N = 81 non-single Tinder users = −0.11	N = 81 non-single Tinder users = 0.03	NE
Freyth & Batinic (2021)	555	Motive for using dating application: love	41.8% female	43.09	No	Germany	NR	NR	0.07	0.04	0.06	NE
Freyth & Batinic (2021)	555	Motive for using dating application: sex	41.8% female	43.09	No	Germany	NR	NR	0.06	0.17**	0.14**	NE

Table 7.1 (cont.)

Study	Sample size	Type of behavior	Gender	Age (mean)	AT or similar	Country	Occupation	Education	Narcissists	Psychopathy	Machiavellianism	Sadism
						Sample characteristics				Correlations		
de Jesus Costa et al. (2023)	249	Victimization direct aggression	82.7% female	21.38 (17–49)	No	Portugal	University students	University students	NE	Interpersonal manipulation = .198* Callous affect = 0.127* Erratic lifestyle = 0.192** Criminal tendencies = 0.236**	NE	NE
de Jesus Costa et al. (2023)	249	Victimization control	82.7% female	21.38 (17–49)	No	Portugal	University students	University students	NE	Interpersonal manipulation = 0.149* Callous affect = 0.108 Erratic lifestyle = 0.164** Criminal tendencies = 0.163*	NE	NE
de Jesus Costa et al. (2023)	249	Perpetration direct aggression	82.7% female	21.38 (17–49)	No	Portugal	University students	University students	NE	Interpersonal manipulation = 0.117 Callous affect = 0.084 Erratic lifestyle = 0.139** Criminal tendencies = 0.190*	NE	NE

de Jesus Costa et al. (2023)	249	Perpetration control	82.7% female	21.38 (17–49)	No	Portugal	University students	University students	NE	Interpersonal manipulation = 0.208** Callous affect = 0.094 Erratic lifestyle = 0.196** Criminal tendencies = 0.173**	NE	NE	NE
Branson & March (2021)	817	Cyber dating abuse	78.2% female	28.16 (18–73)	No	Mostly Australians (81.3%)	NR	NR	Vulnerable = 0.24*** Grandiose = 0.14***	Primary = 0.25*** Secondary = 0.28***	NE	NE	NE
March et al. (2021b)	415	Cyber aggression in relationships	51% female	32.68 (18–74)	No	Australia	NR	NR	Vulnerable = 0.47***	NE	NE	NE	NE
Bui & Pasalich (2021)	200	Face-to-face relationship psychological abuse	73.5% female	22.3 (18–70)	No	Australia	NR	NR	NE	47***	NE	NE	NE
Bui & Pasalich (2021)	200	Cyber relationship psychological abuse	73.5% female	22.3 (18–70)	No	Australia	NR	NR	NE	36***	NE	NE	NE
Bhogal & Wallace (2022)	124	Cyber dating abuse	79% female	30.68	No	United Kingdom	63.7% members of the public 36.3% students	NR	−0.05	08	0.15	NE	NE
Zerach (2016)	347	Cyberbullying dating victimization	58.2% female	NR	No	Israel	NR	NR	Vulnerability = 0.18** Grandiosity = 0.24*** Pathological = 0.21***	NE	NE	NE	NE
Zerach (2016)	347	Cyberbullying dating offending	58.2% female	NR	No	Israel	NR	NR	Vulnerability = 0.18** Grandiosity = 0.17*** Pathological = 0.20***	NE	NE	NE	NE
Pina et al. (2017)	100	Revenge porn proclivity	83.7% female	25.81 (18–54)	No	British (87%)	NR	NR	0.29*	0.36**	0.32**	0.16	
Pina et al. (2017)	100	Revenge porn approval	83.7% female	25.81 (18–54)	No	British (87%)	NR	NR	0.09	0.13	0.34**	0.02	
Pina et al. (2017)	100	Revenge porn enjoyment	83.7% female	25.81 (18–54)	No	British (87%)	NR	NR	0.26**	0.16	0.19	0.06	

Table 7.1 (*cont.*)

Study	Sample size	Type of behavior	Sample characteristics						Correlations			
			Gender	Age (mean)	AT or similar	Country	Occupation	Education	Narcissists	Psychopathy	Machiavellianism	Sadism
Jonason et al. (2021)	341	Short-term relationships ghosting	76.4% female	29.12 (18–72)	No	USA	NR	42.1% undergraduate students	0.16*	0.17*	0.17*	NE
Jonason et al. (2021)	341	Long-term relationships ghosting	76.4% female	29.12 (18–72)	No	USA	NR	42.1% undergraduate students	0.02	0.02	0.09	
Resett et al. (2022)	728	Sexting	62% female	14.27 (11–18)	No	Argentina	High school students	High school students	No significant effect	Significant effect for males in structural model for males	No significant effect	NE
Resett et al. (2022)	728	Grooming	62% female	14.27 (11–18)	No	Argentina	High school students	High school students	No significant effect	No significant effect for males	No significant effect	NE
Harper et al. (2022)	511	Belief about revenge porn: victims as promiscuous	56% female	30.5	No	United Kingdom	NR	NR	0.24***	0.39***	0.30***	0.34***
Harper et al. (2022)	511	Belief about revenge porn: victim harm	56% female	30.5	No	United Kingdom	NR	NR	-0.13**	-0.26***	-0.13**	-0.14**
Harper et al. (2022)	511	Belief about revenge porn: avoiding vulnerable behaviors	56% female	30.5	No	United Kingdom	NR	NR	0.13**	0.24***	0.36***	0.27***
Harper et al. (2022)	511	Belief about revenge porn: offense minimization	56% female	30.5	No	United Kingdom	NR	NR	-0.12**	-0.01	-0.13***	-0.10*
Harper et al. (2022)	227	Belief about revenge porn: victims as promiscuous	56% female	29.92	No	United Kingdom	NR	NR	0.31***	0.51***	0.29***	0.43***

Study	N	Measure	% Female	Age		Country						
Harper et al. (2022)	227	Belief about revenge porn: victim harm	56% female	29.92	No	United Kingdom	NR	NR	−0.20**	−0.34***	−0.19**	−0.28***
Harper et al. (2022)	227	Belief about revenge porn: avoiding vulnerable behaviors	56% female	29.92	No	United Kingdom	NR	NR	0.18**	0.26***	0.35***	0.23***
Harper et al. (2022)	227	Belief about revenge porn: offense minimization	56% female	29.92	No	United Kingdom	NR	NR	0.06	0.22***	0.33***	0.22***
Harper et al. (2022)	227	Revenge porn: direct proclivity	56% female	29.92	No	United Kingdom	NR	NR	0.21**	0.45***	0.11	0.43***
Harper et al. (2022)	227	Revenge porn: enjoyment proclivity	56% female	29.92	No	United Kingdom	NR	NR	0.20**	0.45***	0.17*	0.46***
Harper et al. (2022)	227	Revenge porn: approval proclivity	56% female	29.92	No	United Kingdom	NR	NR	−0.25***	−0.40***	−0.17*	−0.32***
Harper et al. (2022)	232	Belief about revenge porn: victims as promiscuous	55% female	30.64	No	United Kingdom	NR	NR	0.17**	0.28***	0.30***	0.26***
Harper et al. (2022)	232	Belief about revenge porn: victim harm	55% female	30.64	No	United Kingdom	NR	NR	−0.07	−0.18**	−0.04	−0.03
Harper et al. (2022)	232	Belief about revenge porn: avoiding vulnerable behaviors	55% female	30.64	No	United Kingdom	NR	NR	0.10	0.23***	0.37***	0.31***
Harper et al. (2022)	232	Belief about revenge porn: offense minimization	55% female	30.64	No	United Kingdom	NR	NR	0.04	0.13*	0.15*	0.11

Table 7.1 (cont.)

Study	Sample size	Type of behavior	Sample characteristics						Correlations			
			Gender	Age (mean)	AT or similar	Country	Occupation	Education	Narcissists	Psychopathy	Machiavellianism	Sadism
Harper et al. (2022)	232	Revenge porn judgment scale: victim blaming	55% female	30.64	No	United Kingdom	NR	NR	0.15*	0.30***	0.29***	0.28***
Harper et al. (2022)	232	Revenge porn judgment scale: perceived criminality	55% female	30.64	No	United Kingdom	NR	NR	0.02	−0.16*	−0.13	−0.14*
Harper et al. (2022)	232	Revenge porn judgment scale: perceived harm	55% female	30.64	No	United Kingdom	NR	NR	−0.01	−0.17*	−0.01	−0.09
Karasavva et al. (2023b)	816	Cyberflashing	72.0% female	20.08 (16–60)	No	Canada	Undergraduate students	Undergraduate students	0.07*	0.08*	0.03	0.01
Karasavva & Forth (2022)	810	Revenge pornography: victimization	72.0% female	20.08 (16–60)	No	Canada	Undergraduate students	Undergraduate students	0.09*	0.17***	0.03	0.17***
Karasavva & Forth (2022)	810	Revenge pornography: perpetration	72.0% female	20.08 (16–60)	No	Canada	Undergraduate students	Undergraduate students	0.16**	0.19***	0.05	0.18***
Karasavva et al. (2023a)	810	Revenge pornography: enjoyment	72.0% female	20.08 (16–60)	No	Canada	Undergraduate students	Undergraduate students	0.25***	0.32***	0.24***	0.35***
Karasavva et al. (2023a)	810	Revenge pornography: approval	72.0% female	20.08 (16–60)	No	Canada	Undergraduate students	Undergraduate students	0.001	0.02	−0.06	0.01
Karasavva et al. (2023a)	810	Revenge pornography: proclivity	72.0% female	20.08 (16–60)	No	Canada	Undergraduate students	Undergraduate students	0.11**	0.11***	0.08*	0.10**
Clancy et al. (2019)	505	Sext dissemination	66.9% female	20.6 (18–55)	No	92.1% Australians	NR	NR	Positive meaningful relationship	Positive meaningful relationship	Strongest relationship	NE

Study	N	Measure	% female	Age (range)		Country	Sample	Sample				NE
Morelli et al. (2021)	6,093	Own sext (consensual exchange of own sexts)	60.4% female	20.35 (13–30)	No	Belgium, China, Czech Republic, Ireland, Italy, Malaysia, Poland, Russia, Turkey, Uganda, USA	High school and university students	High school and university students.	0.11**	0.11**	0.17**	NE
Morelli et al. (2021)	6,093	Risky sexting (sexting during substance and alcohol use; sexting with strangers on line)	60.4% female	20.35 (13–30)	No	Belgium, China, Czech Republic, Ireland, Italy, Malaysia, Poland, Russia, Turkey, Uganda, USA	High school and university students	High school and university students.	0.15**	0.22**	0.28**	NE
Morelli et al. (2021)	6,093	Nonconsensual sexting (to a partner or an acquaintance without his/her consent)	60.4% female	20.35 (13–30)	No	Belgium, China, Czech Republic, Ireland, Italy, Malaysia, Poland, Russia, Turkey, Uganda, USA	High school and university students	High school and university students.	0.05**	0.16**	0.12**	NE
Morelli et al. (2021)	6,093	Sexting under pressure of a partner or friends	60.4% female	20.35 (13–30)	No	Belgium, China, Czech Republic, Ireland, Italy, Malaysia, Poland, Russia, Turkey, Uganda, USA	High school and university students	High school and university students	0.10**	0.19**	0.17**	NE
Pina et al. (2021)	126	Image-based sexual abuse: proclivity	74.3% female	25.51 (18–63)	No	United Kingdom	NR	NR	0.11	0.18*	0.14	0.32**
Pina et al. (2021)	126	Image-based sexual abuse: victim blame	74.3% female	25.51 (18–63)	No	United Kingdom	NR	NR	−0.07	0.30**	0.24**	0.28**
March & Wagstaff (2017)	240	Sending unsolicited explicit images	72% female	23.96	No	Australia	NR	NR	0.23***	0.19***	0.26***	0.22***

Table 7.1 (*cont.*)

Study	Sample size	Type of behavior	Gender	Age (mean)	AT or similar	Country	Occupation	Education	Correlations			
									Narcissists	Psychopathy	Machiavellianism	Sadism
Clancy et al. (2020)	691	Sext dissemination frequency	52.8% female	22.43 (18–35)	Yes – 312 participans	English-speaking countries: USA (69.0%), Australia (17.4%), United Kingdom (8.4%), Canada (5.2%)	NR	NR	0.071	0.049	0.085	NE
Burtăverde et al. (2021)	322	Reasons for watching pornography: increased sex drive	83.6% female	21.14	No	Romania	Undergraduate students	Undergraduate students	0.21*	0.31**	0.22**	NE
Burtăverde et al. (2021)	322	Reasons for watching pornography: enhancing sexual performance	83.6% female	21.14	No	Romania	Undergraduate students	Undergraduate students	0.22**	0.22**	0.28**	NE
Burtăverde et al. (2021)	322	Reasons for watching pornography: social and instrumental reason	83.6% female	21.14	No	Romania	Undergraduate students	Undergraduate students	0.10	0.24**	0.12*	NE
Burtăverde et al. (2021)	322	Reasons for watching pornography: lack of relational and emotional skills	83.6% female	21.14	No	Romania	Undergraduate students	Undergraduate students	−0.01	−0.25**	−0.24**	NE

Study	N	Variable	% female	Age (range)		Country				Positive significant relationship		
Shin et al. (2007)	337	Responses to unsolicited Internet pornography	53.1% female	20	No	USA	Undergraduate students	Undergraduate students	NE	NE	NE	NE
Hernández et al. (2021)	1,763	Erotic sexting	50.99% female	14.56 (12–16)	No	Spain	Students in secondary education	Students in secondary education	0.31**	NE	NE	NE
Hernández et al. (2021)	1,763	Pornographic sexting	50.99% female	14.56 (12–16)	No	Spain	Students in secondary education	Students in secondary education	0.16**	NE	NE	NE
Hernández et al. (2021)	1,763	Grooming	50.99% female	14.56 (12–16)	No	Spain	Students in secondary education	Students in secondary education	0.23**	NE	NE	NE
Lauder & March (2023)	664	Catfishing	40.3% female	28.84 (18–77)	No	Australia (49.9%), USA (28.4%), Canada (4.2%)	NR	NR	0.40***	0.54***	0.41***	0.77***
Tucaković et al. (2022)	216	Short-term mating orientation	74.1% female	29.05 (20–56)	No	Serbia	NR	NR	0.18**	0.20**	0.11	0.28**
Tucaković et al. (2022)	216	Long-term mating orientation	74.1% female	29.05 (20–56)	No	Serbia	NR	NR	−0.08	−0.15*	0.01	−0.16*
Pineda et al. (2023)	1,988	Online sexual victimization	79.00% female	29.37 (18–74)	No	Spanish (90.96%), Latin American (7.84%), other nationalities (1.20%)	NR	62.50% university degree; 18.60% vocational training; 18.9% high school or lower,	0.029	0.088***	0.073*	0.150**
Pineda et al. (2023)	1,988	Perpetration of online sexual victimization behaviors	79.00% female	29.37 (18–74)	No	Spanish (90.96%), Latin American (7.84%), other nationalities (1.20%)	NR	62.50% university degree; 18.60% vocational training; 18.9% high school or lower,	0.158**	0.213**	0.113**	0.262*

Table 7.1 (cont.)

Study	Sample size	Type of behavior	Gender	Age (mean)	AT or similar	Country	Occupation	Education	Narcissists	Psychopathy	Machiavellianism	Sadism
						Sample characteristics			Correlations			
Muris et al. (2020)	121	Pornography craving	62% female	25.16 (18–65)	No	Netherlands	NR	73.6% B.A. and above 24.6% high school or equivalent	0.39***	0.39***	0.29**	NE
Muris et al. (2020)	121	Pornography use Frequency	62% female	25.16 (18–65)	No	Netherlands	NR	73.6% B.A. and above 24.6% high school or equivalent	0.16	0.25**	0.25**	NE
Schokkenbroek et al. (2022)	1,144	Cyber dating abuse	51.3% female	47.66	No	Belgium	NR	NR	Significant correlation	Significant correlation	Significant correlation	NE
Farooq & Ashraf (2022)	100	Online deception in TikTok users	54% female	21.13	No	Pakistan	NR	The majority had B.Sc. level education	0.52**	0.69**	0.45**	0.77**
Bhogal & Wallace (2022)	124	Cyber dating abuse	79% female	30.68	No	United Kingdom	45% students; 79% members of the public	45% students; 79% members of the public	−0.05	0.08	0.15	NE
Duffy et al. (2023)	278	Intimate partner cyberstalking	58% female	35.78 (21–67)	No	Australia	24.8% are currently students	24.8% are currently students	Vulnerable = 0.85***	Secondary = 0.76***	NE	NE
Demircioglu & Köse (2023)	358	Using social networking sites to find partners	62.3% female	22.68 (18–49)	No	Turkey	University students	University students	0.16**	0.16**	0.10	NE
Demircioglu & Köse (2023)	358	Face-to-face dating with a partner met via social networking sites	62.3% female	22.68 (18–49)	No	Turkey	University students	University students	0.15**	0.11*	0.12*	NE

Study	N	Behavior / measure	Gender	Age		Country	Sample	Sample				
Takezawa et al. (2023)	603	Cyber dating abuse: harassment	71% female	25–29, 63,7%	No	Japan	36% company employee 18% university students	36% company employee 18% university students	Grandiose (male) = 0.18* Vulnerable (male) = 0.12	NE	NE	NE
Takezawa et al. (2023)	603	Cyber dating abuse: intrusive behavior	71% female	25–29, 63,7%	No	Japan	36% company employee 18% university students	36% company employee 18% university students	Grandiose (male) = 0.20* Vulnerable (male) = 0.09	NE	NE	NE
Takezawa et al. (2023)	603	Cyber dating abuse: surveillance	71% female	25–29, 63,7%	No	Japan	36% company employee 18% university students	36% company employee 18% university students	Grandiose (male) = 0.09 Vulnerable (male) = 0.09	NE	NE	NE
Takezawa et al. (2023)	603	Cyber dating abuse: harassment	71% female	25–29, 63,7%	No	Japan	36% company employee 18% university students	36% company employee 18% university students	Grandiose (female) = −0.01 Vulnerable (female) = 0.04	NE	NE	NE
Takezawa et al. (2023)	603	Cyber dating abuse: intrusive behavior	71% female	25–29, 63,7%	No	Japan	36% company employee 18% university students	36% company employee 18% university students	Grandiose (female) = 0.11 Vulnerable (female) = 0.07	NE	NE	NE
Takezawa et al. (2023)	603	Cyber dating abuse: surveillance	71% female	25–29, 63,7%	No	Japan	36% company employee 18% university students	36% company employee 18% university students	Grandiose (female) = 0.06 Vulnerable (female) = 0.04	NE	NE	NE
Paul (2009)	377	Pornography use: male-focused content	53.11% female	20	No	USA	University Students	University students	NE	Impulsive thrill-seeking = 0.28*** (for male) Antisocial behavior = 0.12 (for male) Interpersonal manipulation = 0.31*** (for male) Cold affect = 0.08 (for male)	NE	NE

Table 7.1 *(cont.)*

Study	Sample size	Type of behavior	Gender	Age (mean)	AT or similar	Country	Occupation	Education	Narcissists	Psychopathy	Machiavellianism	Sadism
											Correlations	
						Sample characteristics						
Paul (2009)	377	Pornography use: standard fare content	53.11% female	20	No	USA	University students	University students	NE	Impulsive thrill-seeking = 0.29*** (for male) Antisocial behavior = 0.29*** (for male) Interpersonal manipulation = 0.16 (for male) Cold affect = 0.01 (for male)	NE	NE
Paul (2009)	377	Pornography use: specialized content	53.11% female	20	No	USA	University Students	University students	NE	Impulsive thrill-seeking = 0.30*** (for male) Antisocial behavior = 0.24*** (for male) Interpersonal manipulation = 0.26*** (for male) Cold affect = 0.06 (for male)	NE	NE
Paul (2009)	377	Pornography use: standard fare content	53.11% female	20	No	USA	University Students	University students	NE	Impulsive thrill-seeking = 0.30*** (for female) Antisocial behavior = 0.35*** (for female) Interpersonal manipulation = 0.16 (for female) Cold affect = 0.05 (for female)	NE	NE

Study	N	Behaviour	% female	Age	Platform	Country	Sample	Sample/education				
Paul (2009)	377	Pornography use: specialized content	53.11% female	20	No	USA	University Students	University students	NE	Impulsive thrill-seeking = 0.24***(for female) Antisocial behavior = 0.24***(for female) Interpersonal manipulation = 0.26***(for female) Cold affect = 0.02 (for female)	NE	NE
Scholz et al. (2023)	705	Intimate partner cyberstalking	47% female	46.3	No	Germany	NR	NR	0.18*	0.32***	0.32***	0.28***
Scholz et al. (2023)	705	Revenge porn	47% female	46.3	No	Germany	NR	NR	0.13*	0.24**	0.20**	0.29***
Willis et al. (2023)	313	Inauthentic self-presentation	55.91% female	27.54 (18–40)	Prolific	United Kingdom- 70.9%, USA-28.4%, Australia—0.6%	NR	48.9% – bachelor's degree; 20.8% – high school; 11.2% – undergraduates	Vulnerable – 0.27*** Grandiose – 0.10	Primary – 0.08 Secondary – 0.19***	Views – 0.09 Tactics – 0.13*	NE
Willis et al. (2023)	313	Breadcrumbing	55.91% female	27.54 (18–40)	Prolific	United Kingdom- 70.9%, USA-28.4%, Australia—0.6%	NR	48.9% – bachelor's degree; 20.8% – high school; 11.2% – undergraduates	Vulnerable – 0.16** Grandiose – 0.11	Primary – 0.10 Secondary – 0.13*	Views – 0.16* Tactics – 0.11*	NE
Willis et al. (2023)	313	Ghosting	55.91% female	27.54 (18–40)	Prolific	United Kingdom- 70.9%, USA-28.4%, Australia—0.6%	NR	48.9% – bachelor's degree; 20.8% – high school; 11.2% – undergraduates	Vulnerable – 0.16** Grandiose -0.10	Primary – 0.11 Secondary – 0.16**	Views – 0.05 Tactics – 0.07	NE
Brewer et al. (2023)	722	Breakup strategies with a romantic partner: avoidance/ withdrawal	80.33% female	24.70 (18–75)	No	United Kingdom	NR	NR	-0.04	-0.06	0.17*	NE

Table 7.1 (cont.)

Study	Sample size	Type of behavior	Sample characteristics						Correlations			
			Gender	Age (mean)	AT or similar	Country	Occupation	Education	Narcissists	Psychopathy	Machiavellianism	Sadism
Brewer et al. (2023)	722	Breakup strategies with a romantic partner: positive tone/self-blame	80.33% female	24.70 (18–75)	No	United Kingdom	NR	NR	−0.11*	−0.25*	−0.05	NE
Brewer et al. (2023)	722	Breakup strategies with a romantic partner: open confrontation	80.33% female	24.70 (18–75)	No	United Kingdom	NR	NR	0.05	0.16*	−0.16*	NE
Brewer et al. (2023)	722	Breakup strategies with a romantic partner: cost escalation / manipulation	80.33% female	24.70 (18–75)	No	United Kingdom	NR	NR	0.16*	0.32*	0.37*	NE
Brewer et al. (2023)	722	Breakup strategies with a romantic partner: distant/ mediated communication	80.33% female	24.70 (18–75)	No	United Kingdom	NR	NR	0.09	0.20*	0.17*	NE
Brewer et al. (2023)	722	Breakup strategies with a romantic partner: de-escalation	80.33% female	24.70 (18–75)	No	United Kingdom	NR	NR	0.06	0.17*	0.24*	NE
Grubbs et al. (2023)	630	Cyber pornography use	73.78% female	19.37	No	USA	Undergraduate students	Undergraduate students	Antagonism = 0.25** Extraversion = 0.08 Neuroticism = 0.04	NE	NE	NE
Grubbs et al. (2023)	377	Cyber pornography use	74.0% female	20.81	No	Malaysia (English speaking)	Undergraduate students	Undergraduate students	Antagonism = 0.17** Extraversion = 0.05 Neuroticism = 0.08	NE	NE	NE

Grubbs et al. (2023)	Cyber pornography use	1,063	49.8% female	48.20	Cloud Research panels	USA	NR	NR	NR	Antagonism = 0.48** Extraversion = 0.27** Neuroticism = 0.11**	NE	NE	NE
Grubbs et al. (2023)	Cyber pornography use	2,519	55% female	49.97	YouGov opinion polling	USA	NR	NR	NR	Antagonism = 0.52** Extraversion = 0.25** Neuroticism = 0.14**	NE	NE	NE
Grubbs et al. (2023)	Cyber pornography use	1,998	30.5% female	47.5	YouGov opinion polling	USA	NR	NR	NR	Antagonism = 0.45** Extraversion = 0.21** Neuroticism = 0.17**	NE	NE	NE

Note: AT = Amazon Turk; NR = not reported; NE = not examined; GN = grandiose narcissism; VN = vulnerable narcissism; SNS = social network sites.

* $p < 0.05$; ** $p < 0.01$; *** $p < 0.001$.

CHAPTER 8

The Dark Triad/Tetrad and Workplace Cyber Deviance

8.1 Workplace Cyber Deviance

In today's technology-driven organizations, communication technology is present on every desktop at every level of the organizational ladder (Vranjes et al., 2017), a phenomenon that radically alters how people within organizations communicate (Zhang & Leidner, 2014). Former face-to-face interaction is now increasingly mediated by email and the Internet.

Nevertheless, unchecked and unregulated cyber communication can facilitate workplace harassment (Zhang & Leidner, 2014; Keskin et al., 2016; Kowalski & Robbins, 2021). Whereas 20 years ago, workers might have been excluded from conversations at the copier or the water fountain, now they are blocked from internal electronic memos. Moreover, customers, fellow employees, or supervisors can be subjected to criticism via email or on company websites, which leads to public shaming, decreased worker productivity, decreased job satisfaction, and higher worker turnover (Kowalski & Robbins, 2021).

Recognizing that online employee activity using corporate software or public and private social media can negatively affect any organization, managers now attempt to monitor employee use of social media and other digital communication platforms (Kallis & Meluch, 2021). Yet, an organization's information technology departments cannot control all online worker behavior (Zhang & Leidner, 2014), especially since new avenues of aggression are constantly being devised, directly impacting productivity at the workplace and the organizational climate (Madan, 2014). Karthikeyan (2020) argued that cyberbullying in the workplace is viewed as an inappropriate and unwanted social exchange of behaviors initiated by any perpetrator online or any digital technology-supported equipment. This is now an epidemic across the world that is impacting productivity across the world. Moreover, it is rapidly spreading across the globe.

Organizations are paying close attention to how their employees use social media and other digital communication platforms. Specifically, organizations recognize that their employees' online actions using corporate software and public and private social media pages can live on and negatively affect the organization (Kallis & Meluch, 2021). Whereas counterproductive work behavior, as a general concept, has been featured in the literature for some time (see Cohen, 2018), research uniquely on cyber deviance is still in its relative beginning (Charlier et al., 2017). Nevertheless, it is clear from the existing body of cyber deviance research that the cyber deviance construct, while overlapping in some ways with counterproductive work behavior, encompasses a broader range of behaviors and focuses more explicitly on the role of technology in enabling deviant behavior. Cyber deviance can be described as behavior facilitated by communication technology, such as email or text messaging, that violates workplace norms or harms individual employees or the organization as a whole (Charlier et al., 2017).

Weatherbee (2010) defines cyber deviance as "voluntary behavior using information and communications systems which either threaten or results in harm to an organization, its members, or stakeholders" (p. 39). Charlier et al. (2017) distinguish between cyber-deviant behavior directed at individuals (CD-I) (e.g., cyber smearing, slander, insider threats, gossip, confidentiality breaching, or identity theft) and cyber-deviant behavior directed at the organization itself (CD-O) (e.g., cyber aggression, E-Harassment, E-Politics, hacking, computer abuse, piracy/theft, online job searching, or pornography).

Cyber deviance can take many forms. One is seemingly innocuous cyberloafing – broadly construed as using technology at work for personal purposes. According to Charlier et al. (2017), cyberloafing includes behaviors focused within an individual or intrapersonally (e.g., Web surfing, online shopping, personal email, online banking, online gaming, and social media). Over 80% of employed adults report having engaged in cyberloafing. A second more aggressive misuse of company technology is cyberbullying. Most working adults report having experienced this form of abuse (Ford, 2013; Karthikeyan, 2022). In turn, these cyber-deviant behaviors can be costly to organizations. They may lead to increased employee withdrawal and reduced individual and organizational performance (Charlier et al., 2017).

According to Karthikeyan (2020), workplace cyberbullying has three forms: (1) flaming: victimizing using inappropriate or vulgar language to attack or terrorize. (2) Harassing: sending inappropriate, hateful, and hurtful messages to victims to damage victims' morale and cause embarrassment. (3) Outing: purposefully leaving someone out or sharing their secrets or personal information in a public forum to damage the victim's reputation. The mode may be regular blackmail or sexual harassment.

The resulting phenomenon of workplace cyberbullying is accepted as an elevating and urgent problem faced by employees and employers (Keskin et al., 2016). Workplace cyberbullying occurs when an employee is systematically exposed to repeated adverse treatment from supervisors, colleagues, or subordinates in situations where the perpetrator has superior power over the victim. Workplace cyberbullying is hard for targets to avoid as they must receive email or text messages as part of their work. It may happen at any time of the day or in any place and persists even when victims are not at work. Some forms of cyberbullying, such as posting inappropriate pictures on social media, can reach large audiences because of the ripple effect of online sharing (Keskin et al., 2016).

8.1.1   Theories for Workplace Cyber Deviance

8.1.1.1   Neutralization Theory

Zhang and Leidner (2014) apply Sykes and Matza's (1957) neutralization theory to explain the rationale behind workplace cyberbullying: Lawbreakers are able to maintain their noncriminal image by portraying delinquent behavior as acceptable. While they may ostensibly support the ethos of a law-abiding society, they adhere to a subset of values that invert those of the general community. This subset defines these offenses as unreproachable; therefore, no embarrassment or disgrace attaches to perpetrators once this behavior is discovered. Although perpetrators may acknowledge that cyberbullying is socially unacceptable, they still do it because their subsystem of values provides the weapons with which to defend themselves. These weapons are referred to as neutralization techniques. They are denial of responsibility, denial of injury, denial of the victim, condemnation of the condemners, and appeal to higher loyalties, with "the metaphor of the ledger" added to neutralization theory later on. Perpetrators legitimize their bullying by claiming that the anticyberbullying policies in companies are untenable (Sykes & Matza, 1957; Zhang & Leidner, 2014).

8.1.1.2   Rational Choice Theory of Corporate Crime

This theory of corporate crime explains the perpetration of corporate crime as a rational choice: the weighing of a violation's perceived costs against its benefits (Zhang & Leidner, 2014). Two effect levels are included in the rational choice theory of corporate crime. The benefits and costs directed against firms are named firm-level effects, while the benefits and individual-level effects costs directed against individuals are called individual-level effects, although firm-level effects may also entail costs to individuals. In a simplified model that contains only individual-level cost effects, the disincentives of individual corporate delinquent behaviors include formal sanctions, informal sanctions, shame, and moral inhibitions.

Delinquent corporate behavior may be deterred by threats of sanctions: Formal, informal, and shaming. Formal sanctions are punishments meted out by specifically authorized officials. Informal sanctions refer to disapproval by managers and/or coworkers. Shame is a self-imposed sanction generating feelings of personal dissonance when delinquents' socially unacceptable behavior comes to light (Zhang & Leidner, 2014).

In some cases, an employee may decide not to commit a crime because of their moral repulsion toward such an act. More precisely, the employee may decide not to act, not because the perceived costs outweigh the benefits of the behavior but because s/he believes that it is immoral to conduct such behavior. Two crucial implications can be drawn from the description of moral inhibitions. First of all, moral rules are internalized. Specifically, external sanctions do not influence them (e.g., formal, informal, shame). Although certain criminal behaviors are deterred by fear of punishment, decisions based on one's sense of morality are not affected by notions of benefits and costs. Second, moral rules create a line among delinquent behaviors. Moral rules inhibit some criminal behaviors, while external sanctions may deter others from workplace cyberbullying. Within organizations, sanctions and moral inhibitions lose their efficacy: perpetrators know there is retribution for cyberbullying and may understand that it is immoral (Zhang & Leidner, 2014).

8.2 Cyberbullying and Cyber Aggression in the Workplace

Cyberbullying is based on power dynamics. Harassment occurs because of power imbalances (Vranjes et al., 2017). Workplace cyberbullying is different from workplace bullying in that information and communication technologies blur employee work–life boundaries, thereby extending the reach of cyberbullying to the home domain, a situation seldom seen in non-cyber forms of workplace bullying. Moreover, information and communication technologies enable a variety of new means of cyberbullying. Due to perceived invisibility, asynchrony, or anonymity embedded in workplace communication technology, barriers inhibiting cyberbullying have been weakened (Zhang et al., 2022). The concreteness and permanence of cyberbullying make its repercussions challenging to escape or endure. Workplace cyberbullying can include one-off behaviors, in contrast to workplace bullying, which consists of frequent, persistent harmful acts perpetrated by the same individual against the same victim. Indeed, many one-off acts of cyberbullying (i.e., unfairly blaming a subordinate's work using a public network) often result in injury from constant sharing (Zhang et al., 2022).

According to Vranjes et al. (2017), an established definition of cyberbullying applied to the specific work context is still absent from the literature. They defined workplace cyberbullying as all negative behavior stemming from the work context and occurring through the use of computer-mediated communication, which is either (a) carried out repeatedly and over a period of time or (b) conducted at least once but forms an intrusion into someone's private life (potentially), exposing it to a wide online audience. Zhang and Leidner (2014) defined workplace cyberbullying as instances where an employee is systematically exposed to repeated adverse treatment from supervisors, colleagues, or subordinates by electronic forms of contact over a long time, in a situation where the perpetrator has more power than the target. Workplace cyberbullying leaves targets feeling helpless and unable to defend themselves. Some examples of this behavior are gossiping online, insulting someone via online messages, purposely deleting someone's work files, forwarding someone's emails to third parties to harm them, and ignoring someone's work-related emails (Heatherington & Coyne, 2014).

Compared to the literature on traditional workplace bullying, systematic empirical research exploring cyberbullying within working contexts is initial. However, scholars are directing increasing attention to this research topic, and there is no doubt that our knowledge of cyberbullying at work will expand rapidly in the near future (Coyne & Farley, 2018). Organizations have taken notice of these negative behaviors and the implications that they have on organizational productivity and well-being. Cyberbullying and online harassment can threaten corporate image. As the lines between work and social media become blurred, communication that traditionally took place only at the workplace now has the potential to go online and cause organizational harm. How the public perceives individuals who post on social media – and, by extension, the organizations they are affiliated with – has potentially adverse outcomes for those organizations (Kallis & Meluch, 2021).

According to Karthikeyan (2022), cyberbullying is now classified as a hate crime since it has criminal intent. The need to analyze the criminal intent of the perpetrator that damages the working population and the organizational culture has become a pertinent area of research. The criminal intent devastates the conditions of the victim. The perpetrator's criminal intent negatively impacts the entire working environment, with destructive factors impacting productivity and enjoyment of working life in an organization. Intent to harm is not a defining criterion of workplace cyberbullying. Some perpetrators of workplace cyberbullying intending to increase worker productivity might not even recognize their behavior as bullying, such as when a supervisor publicly berates a subordinate in order to spur them to increase their output. Certain specific laws also exist to protect specific classes of persons against harassment if cyberbullying is based on age, gender, sexual orientation, or race.

8.2.1   Specific Forms of Cyberbullying

8.2.1.1   Academic Cyberbullying

According to Noakes and Noakes (2021), the shift of academic discourse to an online space without imposing protective guidelines allows academic cyberbullies to harass susceptible recipients. Despite the dangers it poses to academic free speech, academic cyberbullying is often overlooked. Without an adequate definition of online academic bullying (OAB), its targets cannot readily gauge its severity or confidently report that they are its victims. Nor do attackers have a reference point for understanding or correcting their incivility.

Noakes and Noakes (2021) claim that OAB is a drawn-out, excessive, one-sided online critique that goes beyond typical scholarly debate. They base this definition on extant conceptualizations of academic bullying focused on aggression and incivility among faculty members. Academic bullying among faculty is a form of common workplace bullying, although not as extensively researched as other types of bullying. With the expansion of social media, academics often interact in legitimate informal online debates. However, to our knowledge, research on digital intellectual harassment by academic cyberbullies is nonexistent. Noakes and Noakes (2021) assert that academics who espouse contrarian views are likely to utilize online mechanisms to share ideas that might have been suppressed in conventional academic fora. However, this contains risks as academic cyberbullies may readily justify their harassment as acceptable responses to unconventional ideas. Moreover, university policies and online guidelines may not protect these controversial scholars, giving the impression that cyber harassment in the university is tacitly endorsed. Academic bullying and abuse by Dark Triad personalities have been discussed by Cohen and Baruch (2022).

8.2.1.2   *Image-Based Sexual Abuse (IBSA) in the Workplace*

There is little academic research on IBSA in the workplace. One major concern is that private images can be easily uploaded and anonymously shared so often that it is difficult to find all the perpetrators. Disinhibition online typifies this cyber mob mentality, which can be attributed to anonymity in cyber forums or collective identity within private chat groups. The inability to be identified can help individuals with anxiety open up to strangers in online communities, yet perceived anonymity can also lead to toxic deinvidualization and hurting others (Rood & Schriner, 2021).

8.2.2   *Cyber Incivility at Work*

Giumetti et al. (2012) advance cyber incivility as one of the most frequently occurring forms of interpersonal mistreatment in the workplace. It is measured by asking individuals to report how frequently they experience rude and discourteous behavior. With the increasing Internet use and email communication at work, uncivil behaviors are spilling into online activities. According to Giumetti et al. (2012), with the rising rate of Internet use at work, the ease with which individuals can intentionally or unintentionally engage in incivility has likely increased. In addition, certain features of the Internet and other information and communication technologies make it easier for individuals to misinterpret the meaning behind messages and engage in deviant behavior. Specifically, online communication, as opposed to face-to-face communication, is text-based and can be addressed to multiple people and redistributed easily (Giumetti et al., 2012). Because this technology lacks many communication cues such as pitch, tone, rate of speech, and body language that are always present in face-to-face communication, subtleties can be missed, and possibilities for misinterpretation increase. Even if a message is not intended to be harmful, it may be perceived as such.

Additionally, many forms of information and communication technologies have a key feature that differs from face-to-face communications–perceived anonymity. In many ways, information and communication technologies provide the perfect venue in which deviant individuals might act since they are physically removed from the target, the consequences are less apparent and immediate, and there is an assumption of anonymity in some contexts (e.g., posts to online forums). Thus, engaging in cyber incivility may be easier than engaging in face-to-face incivility, likely increasing the prevalence of such behaviors (Giumetti et al., 2012).

8.3 Cyberloafing

Very little research has been done on social networking addiction in the workplace. The universal presence of the Internet in the workspace provides employees with a platform for cyberloafing, which organizations generally consider to be counterproductive (Lim & Teo, 2022). The intentional use of the Internet and mobile technologies for nonproductive work is known as cyberloafing (Rahman & Muldoon, 2020). Although the nature of social networking site addiction differs from other addicts, employees' use of surfing social networking sites at work has become a big issue at most companies. Because of the advent of social networking sites, several problems at work seem to exist (Choi et al., 2019). Recent studies suggest that people may feel they should maintain an online social network. This can cause social networking sites to be overused in some situations, including the workplace.

Cyberloafing has been referred to by several as a growing phenomenon that represents the problematic use of digital technology and deserves further research attention (Mihelič, Lim, & Culiberg, 2022). It is mentioned in the literature by several terms: cyberslacking, nonwork-related computer use, personal web use, problematic Internet use, personal email use, and so on. It frequently appears in the workplace (Charlier et al., 2017). Since the widespread use of the Internet and computer technology, misuse of these resources in the workplace has become a growing challenge for organizations (Rahman & Muldoon, 2020). Sometimes, it is portrayed as a threat to organizations' information security due to the widespread use of mobile and cloud technology. Cyberloafing not only wastes valuable time but also acts as a deterrence for efficient and successful goal achievement (Rahman & Muldoon, 2020).

One of the earlier definitions of cyberloafing was advanced by Lim (2002), who defined it as using an organization or company's Internet for personal work. Nevertheless, with the rise of social media, electronic commerce, and digital media, cyberloafing behavior has now broadened to use of any technology (Internet, computer, mobile device, etc.) (Rahman & Muldoon, 2020). Therefore, Lim (2002) operationalized the concept of cyberloafing to refer to personal emailing and browsing activities that an employee voluntarily undertakes during work hours. Extending this conceptualization, Henle and Blanchard (2008) propose that cyberloafing includes minor infractions of browsing, emailing, or online shopping, plus major ones of blogging, gaming, gambling, and pornography surfing. This classification is based on the legal liabilities incurred by organizations for the illicit activities of their employees.

Cyberloafing threatens nearly all organizations since most employees can engage in these detrimental behaviors on various information technology devices. Valli (2004), one of the few studies empirically measuring cyberloafing's effects at the organizational level, investigates nonbusiness-related Internet use on multiple sites. Internet logs from employee computers in three organizations were analyzed, and all online activities were classified as either business-related or nonbusiness-related according to the type of website accessed. The amount of improper Internet usage as a percentage of all Internet usage at these organizations ranged from 20.6% at a medium-sized state government agency to 74.6% at a large university department.

8.3.1   Consequences of Workplace Cyber Deviance

8.3.1.1   The Consequences of Workplace Cyberbullying

As mentioned earlier, workplace cyberbullying is distinguished from traditional workplace bullying in that perpetrators do not have to colocate with their targets. In workplace cyberbullying, victims are threatened via email, Facebook, WhatsApp, and so forth. Since it is arguably easier to cyberbully than to bully someone in person, one would expect to find even higher rates of cyberbullying than noncyberbullying. Perpetrators may not be fully aware of the scale of the suffering they cause because they do not directly witness their victims' pain (Zhang & Leidner, 2014). Zhang and Leidner (2014), calling it "an invisible fist," assert that cyberbullying is a major workplace stressor. It has been linked to anxiety, depression, panic attacks, substance abuse, insomnia, post-traumatic stress disorder, and suicide. Physical symptoms such as weight loss, exhaustion, headaches, trembling, and cardiovascular syndromes also appear (Vranjes et al., 2017; Baheer et al., 2023).

Because of these stress-related health issues, victims of cyberbullying generate more sick days, which become a prime source of organizational absenteeism. Cyberbullying also demotivates employees to put forth maximum effort in their work. The resulting decrease in productivity affects the entire business. Talent retention may also become an issue, increasing recruitment costs (Karthikeyan, 2020). For victims of workplace cyberbullying, the potential negative consequences are many, including mental anxiety and depression, low job satisfaction, counterproductive work behaviors, and the intention to quit (Vranjes et al., 2017).

Consequences of workplace cyberbullying can be as severe for witnesses as they are for victims, with coworkers feeling powerless to speak out if the cyberbully is their superior (Zhang & Leidner, 2014). Cyberbullying bystanders or witnesses who feel powerless against the perpetrator to help their coworker may be as affected as the victim. Witnessing bullying in the workplace may also severely affect the psychological well-being of employees, eventually causing a decrease in staff morale, job satisfaction, and commitment levels. Organizations do not treat workplace cyberbullying as a corporate crime, but violating respected organizational norms can result in a hostile work climate and violate organizational policies and norms. The impact of workplace bullying on the organizational level is an elevated rate of absenteeism, which will negatively impact profitability, productivity, and efficiency. Therefore, expecting workplace cyberbullying to have similar impacts would be appropriate. In addition, low workplace morale may result in high staff turnover rates and even quitting, which will necessitate the recruitment of new employees and training processes that are costly and time-consuming. Therefore, traditional bullying is more contained spatially as an intraorganizational issue. On the other hand, cyberbullying permeates beyond organizational boundaries. As corporate cyberbullying becomes public, it damages corporate reputations (Keskin et al., 2016).

8.3.1.2 Consequences of Cyberloafing

According to the International Data Corporation, 30%–40% of employees use their organizations' Internet for nonwork-related tasks. Between 60% and 80% of employees spend time on the Internet in nonwork-related activity. About 6 out of 10 people acknowledge that they check their social media accounts at work, while two-thirds say that reading items on Facebook is the most prevalent intrusion. Other studies find that 60% of online purchases were made during office hours (Chavan et al., 2021).

Studies show that on average, United States workers spend about 10% of their workday surfing the Internet, emailing friends, or shopping online (Rahman & Muldoon, 2020). This costs employers up to $85 billion annually (Andel, 2020; Lim & Teo, 2022). A survey of 3,200 Americans found that the average loss due to nonwork-related online activity is on the high side over two work hours per day and generates a $4,500 annual loss per employee. For a company with 1,000 employees, cyberloafing costs almost $600,000 per year (Alqahtani et al., 2022; Miech, 2022). Charlier et al. (2017) point out that cyberloafing correlates negatively with performance ratings given by supervisors. This conclusion is confirmed in workers' self-reports. The authors conclude that cyberloafing does not improve work–life balance.

8.4   The Dark Triad/Tetrad and Workplace Cyber Deviance

8.4.1   Cyberbullying

While workplace cyberbullying has become a hot topic in the media and has triggered much discussion in enterprises, research into workplace cyberbullying is still nascent. As mentioned earlier, working with information and communication technologies can expose employees to harmful online activities. It is, therefore, surprising that, to date, there have not been many contributions in the field of workplace cyberbullying, especially given the many adverse outcomes related to online misconduct (Zhang & Leidner, 2014; Vranjes et al., 2017). In addition, few studies have examined the causes of cyberbullying in the workplace.

Recent research has shown that traits in the Dark Triad are predictors of workplace bullying (Maasberg et al., 2015, 2020). The exploitative nature, ferociousness, lack of compassion, impulsivity, and ethical disengagement inherent in these traits indicate a proclivity toward cyberbullying. The few studies on the relationship between the Dark Triad traits and cyber deviance in the workplace found that the three dark personalities are related positively to organizational maltreatment and other forms of bullying, affecting employees' mental health and satisfaction with their jobs. Scholars also show that dark personalities are utterly unsympathetic to the suffering or the rights of others and are more voluntary towards bullying behavior than others, affecting the victim's well-being (Baheer et al., 2023). Scarduzio and Adams (2022) contend that Dark Triad personality traits are more likely to harass their coworkers online sexually. It should be noted that while most studies examine only the three personality defects of the Dark Triad, future research should include sadism as another dark trait.

While each trait in the Dark Triad is associated with specific motivators for cyberbullying, psychopathy is the most active cause of bullying behavior due to its lack of empathy for the victim. Corporate managers with psychopathic tendencies tend to use their overwhelming authority to implement "divide-and-conquer" schemas wherein bullying plays an integral part. Having climbed to high positions in the organization, these managers can poison the corporate climate with their unethical behavior (Daderman & Ragnestål-Impola, 2019). Corporate psychopaths use bullying to further the goals of promotion and power due to causing a divide and rule in place. Psychopaths are more likely to engage in bullying, crime, and drug use than others. Personalities who score more regarding psychopathy personality traits have been recognized to display spontaneous work performances, for example, offensive administration and workplace violence. When individuals high in psychopathy expose bullying behavior towards others, they do so with reduced empathic concern, affecting the victim's mental health. It is contended that cyberbullying consequently leads to several mental health issues that have a debilitating effect on employees (Baheer et al., 2023).

According to Baheer et al. (2023), bullies with Machiavellian personalities implement their personal agendas by exploiting others and successfully manipulating social and interpersonal interactions to create strategic alliances. They callously parade their immoral behavior before coworkers, causing social damage. Their attitude towards coworkers significantly affects turnover ratios. Individuals who score high in Machiavellianism effectively plan bullying tactics as opposed to psychopaths who act impulsively. Striving to maintain a good reputation, their covert cyberbullying is not always visible to others, especially since victims tend to suffer in silence (Daderman & Ragnestål-Impola, 2019). Therefore, cyberbullying might be a preferred strategy for them because it decreases their chances of being detected and exposed. Machiavellianism is associated with counterproductive treatment of associates, alexithymia, and the inability to read the feelings of others (Baheer et al., 2023).

People with narcissistic traits also have a positive relationship with bullying and are indirectly involved in tactics such as withholding information, spreading gossip, or constant carping on others' mistakes. Narcissists, highly satisfied by their bullying, manipulate and intimidate in order to acquire preferred job status. They take more recognition for their accomplishments than is due, and when they fail at an assigned task, they make sure that the responsibility falls on their coworkers, not themselves. They exhibit characteristics of self-importance, visualize enthusiastically regarding victory and supremacy, undertake resilient wisdom of inimitability and low sympathy, and habitually abuse or take advantage of their coordinates; they use their fragile self-esteem to get advantages from other organizations (Baheer et al., 2023). Since narcissists mainly concentrate on their own personas, their cyberbullying in the workplace is not more pronounced than that of individuals with high Machiavellian or psychopathic traits (Daderman & Ragnestål-Impola, 2019).

Min et al. (2019) assert that sadism is the most significant predictor of interpersonal incivility and workplace cyberbullying. Although similar to the other exploitative and vengeful traits in the Dark Triad, sadism is unique because it involves cruelty solely for cruelty's sake. Sadists positively enjoy their victim's pain as distinct from the other dark traits. Sadists pursue short-term rewards for hurting colleagues regardless of the long-term damage to their social relationships.

Given the severity of its consequences, more research into the rationale driving Dark Tetrads' workplace cyberbullying is imperative (Keskin et al., 2016; Charlier et al., 2017; Zhang et al., 2022).

8.4.2   Cyberloafing

Much research has been done on the impact of Dark Triad personality traits on adverse decision-making in work settings (Cohen, 2018). Attention now focuses on understanding the formation of cyberloafing behavior (Charlier et al., 2017). Much of the research in cyberloafing is focused on organizational aspects where several organizational factors are investigated to find their influences on this defiant behavior. Very few studies have tried to empirically understand and study the impact of individual traits on cyberloafing behavior. In addition, the study of the interaction between personality and situational characteristics is also relatively rare. Thus, there is a lack of research in understanding the issue of the cyberloafing phenomenon from individual traits perspective (Rahman & Muldoon, 2020). Most of the existing personality trait research in technology adaptation uses the Five-Factor model (Rahman & Muldoon, 2020).

A potential relationship between the Dark Triad and a technology-based form of counterproductive behavior is intuitive. However, according to Lowe-Calverley and Grieve (2017), previous research has also implicated an individual's perceived ability to deceive in the likelihood that they will engage in counterproductive behaviors in the workplace. Lowe-Calverley and Grieve (2017) defined the perceived ability to deceive as the perception of the extent to which one can successfully deceive others without such deception being detected. Interestingly, the perceived ability to deceive to predict counterproductive work behaviors was incremental to that of personality predictors typically associated with counterproductive work behaviors. Consistent with the link between the perceived ability to deceive and counterproductive workplace behaviors, perceptions of the ability to "get away with" cyberloafing are associated with intentions of cyberloafing. Notably, the Dark Triad relates to the perceived ability to deceive (Lowe-Calverley & Grieve, 2017). Lowe-Calverley and Grieve (2017) contended that the mechanisms at play might be different for each dark trait.

Psychopaths are predatory and decisive and violate social norms. Thus, individuals with this personality are prone to untruthful behavior and do not hesitate to use dishonesty for personal gain. Psychopaths, given their deceitful interpersonal style, it is unsurprising that individuals demonstrating higher levels of psychopathy also demonstrate a more remarkable perceived ability to deceive. Presumably, this would be associated with greater counterproductive workplace behaviors. However, their deficient affective processing and irresponsible behavioral style, combined with a lack of concern for social norms, suggest that they will act regardless of their perceived ability to deceive (Lowe-Calverley & Grieve, 2017; Rahman & Muldoon, 2020).

Individuals with Machiavellian personality traits are prone to untruthful behavior and do not hesitate to use dishonesty for power or personal gain. Lowe-Calverley and Grieve (2017) state that Machiavellianism is characterized by deception and manipulation. Based on this premise, and given the perceived ability to deceive, it seems possible that Machiavellians consider their ability to deceive prior to engaging in undesirable behavior and cyberloaf when they believe they can away with it. As mentioned in Chapter 2, Machiavellianism correlates strongly with problematic Internet use. It has a strong association with online gambling and sex, as well as with cyberstalking and cyberbullying.

Narcissism has been linked to deception due to the narcissist's need for self-enhancement. The narcissist's sense of entitlement also facilitates an attitude of "not having to play by the rules," which can result in lying. Narcissists' grandiose perception of their abilities may influence the belief that they can deceive. Moreover, their attitude that rules do not apply to them and their need for self-enhancement may also bolster the belief that they can deceive through lying; therefore, they might engage in undesirable cyberloafing behavior if they believe they can get away with it and can lie to maintain a positive reputation (Lowe-Calverley & Grieve, 2017; Kristinsdottir et al., 2021). This personality trait has been linked to more frequent use of Facebook, more intense use of social networking sites, and more extensive online networks, all known as antisocial behavior. Because narcissists tend to be exploitative, socially aversive, and antisocial characteristics while believing in short-term gain and would engage in technology for antisocial activities, it is reasonable to expect that individuals high in narcissism are more likely to engage themselves in cyberloafing behavior (Rahman & Muldoon, 2020).

8.5   Research Findings

8.5.1   Cyberbullying

Research on workplace cyberbullying is relatively scarce. Most of the research on cyberbullying aims to identify the antecedents and consequences of both victimization and perpetration. As most of it is conceptual, there is a need for empirical studies to shed light on this uprising phenomenon. Moreover, there is a need for more studies on the relationship between Dark Tetrad and cyberbullying in the workplace. Min et al. (2019) examined the frequency of workplace cyberbullying among individuals exhibiting Dark Tetrad traits in 376 American workers. Controlling for other Dark Triad traits, they show that sadism followed by psychopathy are significant predictors of cyberbullying.

Tripathi and Lim (2014) examine the moderating effects of Machiavellianism and perceived similarity to supervisors on the relationship between cyber incivility and revenge and avoidance. Based on a survey of 192 employees in Singapore, their results show that cyber incivility is positively related to both direct and indirect revenge. High Machiavellians seek both direct and indirect revenge against their supervisors, while low Machiavellians use avoidance as a coping strategy against cyber incivility. As mentioned earlier, there is a need for more research on this important relationship across cultures, occupations, and organizational types.

Most of the research on cyberbullying aims to identify the antecedents and consequences of victimization. Since this type of analysis is mainly conceptual, there is a need for empirical studies to confirm this phenomenon.

8.5.2   Cyberloafing

The findings of Lowe-Calverley and Grieve (2017) on a 273-person sample of currently or previously employed workers in Australia show that individuals possessing high levels of Dark Triad personality traits are more likely to engage in cyberloafing if they find they are able to do so without being discovered. There are significant correlations between primary psychopathy, Machiavellianism, and cyberloafing. By contrast, the relationship between narcissism and cyberloafing was significant, though moderate. Structural equation modeling shows that only psychopathy directly relates to cyberloafing. The two other Dark Triad traits have indirect relationships to the perceived ability to deceive, which, as mentioned earlier, is a significant factor in cyberloafing.

In a sample of 974 students from two major universities in the United States, Rahman and Muldoon (2020) find that among Dark Triad personality traits, narcissism is the most significant predictor of cyberloafing, followed by Machiavellianism. The results do not show a significant influence of psychopathy. The researchers find that narcissism is an essential mediator between psychopathy and cyberloafing, with individuals scoring high in psychopathy also scoring high in narcissism: This is the factor that causes them to engage in cyberloafing.

Choi (2018) examines the impact of narcissism on social media addiction in the workplace and how job satisfaction and organizational commitment are influenced by it. Sampling 285 office workers in South Korea, the study measures social media addiction along six parameters: salience, conflict, mood modification, withdrawal, tolerance, and relapse. The findings show that narcissism increases mood modification, withdrawal, and tolerance among social media addicts. They also examined the effect of the interaction between narcissism and perceived organizational support. They found that perceived organizational support negatively affects the relationship between narcissism and mood modification, narcissism and withdrawal, and narcissism and tolerance. They contended that based on their results, narcissism has a weaker impact on social media addiction when people have higher perceived organizational support in the workplace.

Choi (2018) concluded that narcissism increases mood modification, withdrawal, and tolerance among the subfactors of social media addiction in the workplace. Furthermore, according to Choi (2018), withdrawal and tolerance among social media addiction in the workplace subfactors mediate between narcissism and each relevant factor of job satisfaction/organizational commitment. Finally, perceived organizational support decreases the effect of narcissism on mood modification, withdrawal, and tolerance among the subfactors of social media addiction in the workplace.

***

Table 8.1 presents the major findings of the empirical research on the relationship between the Dark Tetrad/Triad and workplace cyberbullying and cyberloafing. As mentioned earlier, there is relatively little research on this topic, and most researchers call for more study of this critical issue.

Table 8.1 *Summary of research findings of the relationship between the Dark Tetrad/Triad workplace cyber deviance*

| | | | Sample characteristics | | | | | | Correlations | | | |
Study	Sample size	Type of behavior	Gender	Age (mean)	AT or similar	Country	Occupation	Education	Narcissists	Psychopathy	Machiavellianism	Sadism
Baheer et al. (2023)	410	Cyberbullying	43% female	52% (between 31–40)	No	Pakistan	Banking sector employees	55.1% Master's degree 28.8% Bachelor's degree	0.546***	0.535***	0.316***	NE
Lowe-Calverley & Grieve (2017)	273	Perceived ability to deceive	80% female	28.12	No	Australia	Variety of occupations 40.7% fulltime; 37.3% casual basis; 18.3% part-time	22% professionals	0.30***	0.40***	0.42***	NE
Lowe-Calverley & Grieve (2017)	273	Cyberloafing	80% female	28.12	No	Australia	Variety of occupations 40.7% fulltime; 37.3% casual basis; 18.3% part-time	22% professionals	0.13*	0.19**	0.15*	NE
Rahman & Muldoon (2020)	974	Cyberloafing	44% female	83.4% (20–24) 10.4% ≤ 19	No	USA	University students	University students – 58% juniors, 26% seniors	0.200***	0.104*	0.195***	NE
Choi (2018)	285	Social media addiction in the workplace: Salience	53.7% female	24.6% 20s; 27.4% 30s; 22.4% 40s	No	South Korea	28.8% manufacturing 32.2% service 10.2% construction	52.9% university undergraduates 20.8% community college 15.8% high school	−0.041 Regression coefficient	NE	NE	NE
Choi (2018)	285	Social media addiction in the workplace: conflict	53.7% female	24.6% 20s; 27.4% 30s; 22.4% 40s	No	South Korea	28.8% manufacturing 32.2% service 10.2% construction	52.9% university undergraduates 20.8% community college 15.8% high school	0.119 Regression coefficient	NE	NE	NE

Study	N	Outcome	% female	Age	Clinical sample	Country	Industry	Education	GN	VN		
Choi (2018)	285	Social media addiction in the workplace: mood modification	53.7% female	24.6% 20s; 27.4% 30s; 22.4% 40s	No	South Korea	28.8% manufacturing 32.2% service 10.2% construction	52.9% university undergraduates 20.8% community college 15.8% high school	181** Regression coefficient	NE	NE	NE
Choi (2018)	285	Social media addiction in the workplace: withdrawal	53.7% female	24.6% 20s; 27.4% 30s; 22.4% 40s	No	South Korea	28.8% manufacturing 32.2% service 10.2% construction	52.9% university undergraduates 20.8% community college 15.8% high school	0.081** Regression coefficient	NE	NE	NE
Choi (2018)	285	Social media addiction in the workplace: tolerance	53.7% female	24.6% 20s; 27.4% 30s; 22.4% 40s	No	South Korea	28.8% manufacturing 32.2% service 10.2% construction	52.9% university undergraduates 20.8% community college 15.8% high school	0.024** Regression coefficient	NE	NE	NE
Choi (2018)	285	Social media addiction in the workplace: relapse	53.7% female	24.6% 20s; 27.4% 30s; 22.4% 40s	No	South Korea	28.8% manufacturing 32.2% service 10.2% construction	52.9% university undergraduates 20.8% community college 15.8% high school	−0.109 Regression coefficient	NE	NE	NE
Min et al. (2019)	376	Cyberbullying frequency	46% female	40.08	Yes	USA	NR	NR	0.12*	0.32**	0.13*	0.43**
Min et al. (2019)	376	Disciplinary work actions	46% female	40.08	Yes	USA	NR	NR	0.15**	0.01	0.05	0.05

Note: AT = Amazon Turk; NR = not reported; NE = not examined; GN = grandiose narcissism; VN = vulnerable narcissism; SNS = social network sites.

* $p < 0.05$; ** $p < 0.01$; *** $p < 0.001$.

CHAPTER 9

Conceptual and Practical Implications

9.1 The Future of Cybercrime and Cyber Deviance

At the start of 2023, 5.16 billion people – the equivalent of 64.4% of the world's population – were on the Internet. The latest data show that the connected population grew by nearly 100 million just during 2022. In addition, today there are 5.44 billion unique mobile phone users (DataReportal, 2023). Facebook alone had 2.963 billion users as of January 2023, making it the world's most active social media platform. Moreover, the number of people on Facebook increased by roughly 5 million (+0.2%) in just the last three months of 2022, signifying that roughly 37% of all the world's people use Facebook and that figure does not include adolescents below the age of 13, which makes the statistic even more startling (Kemp, 2023).

However, our growing dependency on new technology has its dark side, as demonstrated by the increase in the adverse outcomes of this technology. According to the FBI, a minimum of 422 million individuals were impacted by cybercrime, with 800,944 complaints logged in 2022 alone. Nearly 33 billion accounts will be breached by the end of 2023 at a predicted cost of $8 trillion. Losses due to cybercrime are projected to rise from $6 trillion in 2022 to $10.5 trillion by 2025. Eighty percent of all reported cybercrime is attributable to phishing. Thirty-three billion accounts will be breached in 2023, which translates into 2,328 cybercrimes per day; close to 8,00,000 cyberattacks have already been recorded, an average of one every 39 seconds. Cybercrime affects 43% of small businesses annually. Cybersecurity ventures predicts that crypto crime will cost the world $30 billion annually by 2025 (Nividita, 2023).

In light of these statistics, society must find a way to deal with deviant cyber activity. Focusing on the salient personality traits in the Dark Tetrad: Self-aggrandizement and grandiosity, callous manipulativeness, impulsive antisocial behavior, and taking pleasure in the suffering of others (Martin et al., 2022), this book details the misuse of social networking sites by malevolent personalities. It is logical that individuals with personality traits on the Dark Tetrad would embrace social networking as a tool for achieving their nefarious goals as the anonymity of social networking platforms provides cover for social deviants and makes it nearly impossible to apprehend them. The assumption underlying this book is that growing awareness of the link between dark personality types and cybercrime will assist in mitigating the growing pandemic.

9.2 Conceptual and Practical Implications

9.2.1 *Social Media Addiction*

Future research needs to distinguish between passive and active use of social networks. In passive use, individuals browse for information only and do not participate in direct exchanges with others, while in active use, individuals communicate with each other, posting status updates and commenting on the posts of others. Active social network use is often associated with increased life satisfaction while passive social network use is a predictor of depression and low self-esteem. Hence, future studies correlating social network use and personality traits should distinguish between these two types of social network use (Kong et al., 2021). An interesting expansion was advanced by Akdeniz, Budak, and Ahçi (2022), who developed a scale for narcissism in social media. Akdeniz et al. reported good psychometric properties for their scale, and perhaps this should encourage scholars to develop similar scales for the other dark traits.

Personality traits in the Dark Tetrad indirectly contribute to social network addiction. Since changing one's personality is hard and limiting access to Facebook or Instagram is nearly impossible, uncovering the mediating roles that these factors play in social network addiction assumes vital importance. Trainings to inform the general public of the risks of Internet use and class discussions with young adults to familiarize them with measures to prevent social media addiction (Nikbin et al., 2022) could be the most effective ways to curb overuse of social networks. Raising awareness of the dangers of cyber dating abuse is, of course, essential for all communities and age groups (de Jesus Costa et al., 2023).

Psychologists, social scientists, organizations, and policymakers should all be involved in elucidating the factors driving social media addiction. It is imperative to create proactive prevention and intervention programs directed at psychopathic traits. These programs must promote behavior that fosters empathy and mutual respect (De Jesus Costa et al., 2022).

9.2.2 Facebook and Other Social Media Platforms

Early studies of Facebook focused on the effect Facebook was having on individuals and society as well as factors in individual personalities that influence the use of Facebook. Researchers are analyzing how user behavior on social networks reveals information about users' interests and personalities (Shiau, Dwivedi, & Lai, 2018). In a study of tweets on Twitter, Sumner et al. (2012) find that even if users post content with care, the words they use reveal a great deal more about their personalities than they might wish. This points to the need to raise awareness among users to prevent the misuse of information derived from online activity and the possible need for regulatory control.

Future research should identify the scope of the cheating strategies employed by social network users with Dark Tetrad personality traits. For example, individuals with Machiavellian profiles may strategically "friend" users they wish to exploit, or psychopaths may impulsively initiate friend requests to strangers only to act belligerently toward them. Individuals scoring high in Dark Tetrad traits may use online dating sites to identify and deceive potential short-term mates (Fox & Rooney, 2015). Stiff (2019) suggests that Facebook users should protect themselves from surveillance by people with high Dark Tetrad traits by becoming more circumspect about posting details of their lives online. They should be aware that other users may be actively seeking information that they consider valuable rather than passively consuming whatever their Facebook feed presents to them.

9.2.3 Hate Speech on Digital Platforms

Twitter, Instagram, and Facebook are among the top five platforms with high levels of cyberbullying which affects almost 41% of United States adults. Cyberbullying is even more prevalent among teenagers with 46% of Americans ages 13–17 having experienced at least one of its six types during 2020–2021. A Statista (2023a) survey notes that name calling is the most common form of cyberbullying. A recent 30-country United Nations–sponsored survey of nearly 170,000 youths up to 24 years of age reports that 33% of its participants had experienced cyberbullying (Aboujaoude & Savage, 2023).

As social media platforms such as Twitter and Facebook become more and more integrated into our lives, its platform features can analyze posts and comments to obtain insights into user personalities that can be employed to improve the detection of cyberbullying (Balakrishnan et al., 2019). Preventive strategies such as timeouts for posts containing offensive language can be updated by artificial intelligence.

Sorokowski et al. (2020), calling for more study of online haters, predict that incidences of online hate speech will only intensify (Schoenherr, Lilja-Lolax, & Gioe, 2022). Giumetti et al. (2022) assert that identifying perpetrators and providing interventions may deter this destructive behavior. As research links cyberbullying with deviant behavior, the authors advocate for early identification and counseling in order to guard the mental health of the wide range of social network users. Identifying risk factors and conscientiously working to reduce them may minimize cyberbullying, which in turn may curb the anxiety and depression prevalent among today's youth. Safaria et al. (2020) state that intervention to prevent the development of Dark Tetrad personality traits in adolescents might be essential for decreasing cyberbullying. Interventions should teach youth healthy cyber etiquette and the necessity to express empathy for others.

Correlations between individuals with Dark Tetrad personality traits and cyberstalking have predictive value, which may be important in understanding cyberstalking between partners. On an individual level, identification of what constitutes stalking may contribute to the self-understanding of potential perpetrators (Smoker & March, 2017). Blais et al. (2023) concluded that if researchers continue to examine the relationship between the Dark Tetrad and cyberstalking, they should draw on the separate literature for each trait to make sound theoretical arguments for why and how the traits matter for cyberstalking.

While online trolling is inherently harmful and antisocial, it can be carried out in nonhostile or even friendly ways. In light of the fact that almost all conceptualizations of online trolling emphasize its mischievous antisocial intentions, Lee et al. (2021) maintain that any conceptualization of trolling must preclude the normative valence of good vs. evil. Most empirical research focuses on acts of trolling instead of the actors who often deliberately disguise themselves and their intentions. Studies of specific social contexts in which online trolling occurs eliminate the generalizability of the research.

Obviously, dissenting attitudes, beliefs, and opinions that oppose the dominant view must be protected. However, online trolls often disguise themselves as legitimate vocal minorities in order to damage the cohesiveness of online communities. How do we distinguish these two kinds of objectors? Casual observers may find themselves incapable of knowing, and this ambiguity erodes public trust. Differentiating between the

two types of trolls requires markers that reveal the writers' true dispositions (Lee et al., 2021). Interventions to decrease harmful trolling could
include blocking trolls from websites or preventing users from responding
to them, while savvy Internet users could report trolls to website moderators (Gylfason et al., 2021). In order for research on trolling behavior to be
less ambiguous, it needs to control for Dark Tetrad personality traits and
not only for the Big Five (Schoenherr et al., 2022).

Ménard and Pincus (2012) maintain that education against stalking
must target males and females differently. While treatment should focus
on childhood trauma for all stalkers, it should focus on males' narcissistic vulnerability and its associated dysregulation and on females' insecure
attachment and alcohol expectancies.

Users should be forced by law to provide correct personal details in
their online profiles. Social media companies need procedures to confirm
the accuracy of the information users supply about themselves (Olckers &
Hattingh, 2022). Due to their very real insecurities, it may be difficult to
prevent individuals from misrepresent themselves online; so society should
encourage everyone to love themselves and not judge their supposed inadequacies. Online companies should only be allowed to have one company
profile and not be allowed to create fake profiles for the purpose of data
mining. Bots should be banned from social media entirely (Olckers &
Hattingh, 2022).

9.2.4   Cybercrime and Cyber Fraud

Seigfried-Spellar et al. (2017) point out computer crime is correlated to
both violent and nonviolent antisocial behavior, and not only to Dark
Tetrad traits. The authors suggest categorizing cybercrime as one part
of a higher-order antisocial behavior construct so as to weave more
complex relationships between psychopathic personality disorders and
cybercrime. Sociodemographic characteristics of age, gender, and social
background also play a role. Future research needs to focus on multiple elements in the framework not just one, which would enable psychologists, educators, and judicial officers to develop more sophisticated
computer crime-fighting strategies. As the situation is just as much a
product of exploitation of advanced technology as it is about the mindset of deviant individuals, future research should also focus on perfecting
cybersecurity (Perenc, 2022).

Still, IT professionals must be aware of the tendencies toward harmful behavior associated with Dark Tetrad personality traits to institute

more comprehensive risk management strategies (Maasberg et al., 2020). In the context of real-world audits, Ramamoorti and Epstein (2016) emphasize the challenge of utilizing existing psychological instruments to identify malicious behavior traits. While administrative procedures to mitigate potential insider harm exist, there is still a great need to sharpen policy tools, technical monitoring, and training and awareness programs. Identifying high-risk individuals through preemployment screening and multiple interviews might weed out "superstars" with malevolent intentions. Human Resource managers should adopt the impeccable credo of the medical community: "First, do no harm," and actively prevent selection of high-risk insiders no matter their brilliance (Maasberg et al., 2020; Marbut & Harms, 2023).

Yet, even the most stringent hiring practices may not eliminate malicious individuals from joining an organization's staff. Therefore, well-designed risk management plans should assume that high-risk insiders are present in the organization. In seeking to identify such individuals, it is vital that legal privacy protections not be transgressed. Balancing prudence with discriminatory profiling requires careful planning, along with involvement of legal and human resource specialists. Issue-specific security policies that are devised must be integrated into the overall risk-mitigation plan.

Most organizations have formal procedures to deal with insider threats. If an organization's staff is well trained, behavioral patterns associated with threats from heightened dark personality traits can be recognized sooner and formal risk-management processes triggered (Maasberg et al., 2020). In addition, sound leadership practices may help mitigate risk. If, for example, psychopathic or Machiavellian individuals perceive that high-level managers are breaking the rules, it may encourage them to do so as well. Unmaterialized promises of bonuses, raises, or promotions may trigger their adverse behavior. The motivation may be even stronger when a promised benefit is granted to another employee (Maasberg et al., 2020).

Managers often face a trade-off between their responsibility to protect the organization from cybercrime and the right to privacy of current employees and candidates being considered for employment (Maasberg et al., 2020). Maasberg et al. recommend using standard personality trait screening for monitoring employee behavior since these assessments have been accepted for use in normal populations and there is no reason to assume ipso facto that employees or job candidates are clinically impaired.

More comprehensive solutions might involve noting the frequencies of malicious violations and nonmalicious accidents that are of concern within specific job types and then measuring employee distributions for the risk and protective factors reviewed that are most closely related to them. Reward systems, protocols, motivational speeches from top management, and training could then be targeted toward resolving those problems in a manner informed by data on the organization's human capital. Additionally, this human capital data may facilitate the identification of further behavioral risks (or strengths) based on known worst (or best) outcomes associated with the types of employees in each job (Marbut & Harms, 2023).

9.2.5 Intimate Partner Cyber Relationships

When investigating antisocial online dating practices, researchers should employ multidimensional definitions of gender and use equal numbers of each sex in their research. Future research could explore antisocial behavior on popular sites such as Tinder by assessing both active and nonactive users and whether individuals with intensive Tinder use commit more antisocial behavior. A survey requesting that participants reveal how often they use the application could assess such trends. Given the uptick in "catfishing" and consequent victimization, more research is needed to prevent these occurrences (Lauder & March, 2023). A more comprehensive database is needed to analyze the reasons that users reject dating applications (Duncan & March, 2019).

Mayshak et al. (2020) find that although not all Dark Tetrad traits are associated with antisocial behavior or coercive control, sadism and psychopathy definitely are. Research into possible perpetrator–victim paradigms could lead to a more complex analysis of connections between the Dark Tetrad and antisocial behavior. With the rapid growth of online dating and proximity dating applications, greater attention needs to be paid to user safety (Mayshak et al., 2020). Fostering awareness of the specific risks of online dating needs to be promoted.

More studies are necessary to develop a comprehensive understanding of abuser typologies in order to glean insight for more effective intervention (Branson & March, 2021). To that end, online dating sites could use questionnaires to screen out jealous or hostile individuals. Since these sites must be open to all individuals, regardless of high Dark Tetrad scores, individuals with psychopathic or narcissistic tendencies could be flagged if complaints are lodged against them. Clinicians specializing in couples therapy might routinely assess jealous or aggressive personality traits in order to ward off relational abuse or violence. Clinical treatments could be created specifically for cyber dating abuse, say, as a reaction to being rejected by one's online suitor. In raising awareness in young adults about the dimensions of cyber dating, it is necessary to provide tools to identify and deal with risky dating situations. Sex education classes must directly and explicitly discuss issues related to abuse and the proper attitude toward it. Providing adequate information about the resources available to victims is also essential. Finally, creating specific prevention and intervention programs for the young adult and adolescent population (and even those who are younger) is mandatory – even if it requires instigating behavioral and emotional modifications in young people exhibiting psychopathic traits (de Jesus Costa et al., 2023).

Takezawa et al. (2023) assert that personality traits and gender should be considered when addressing cyber dating abuse. Men with grandiose narcissism are more likely to become aggressive when their relationships do not go as expected. Relationship anxiety may be a factor in their manifestations of controlling behavior. It may be necessary to stipulate clinical anxiety reduction programs while simultaneously informing dating partners of these dynamics.

Young individuals may not fully know the dangers of online flirting. Seemingly innocent exchanges of videos or photographs can be maliciously abused. Training and dissemination of strategies for safe use of romantic social networking sites need to emphasize careful decision-making, especially for "at-risk" adolescents (Demircioğlu & Köse, 2023). For their own mental well-being, children need to be made aware of untoward adult behaviors that are to be rejected out-of-hand (de Jesus Costa et al., 2023).

9.2.6 Workplace Cyber Deviance

Targets of cyberbullying in the workplace are often the most valued, skilled, and popular employees, individuals with a desire to help, teach, develop, and nurture others. It is precisely because of these traits that individuals with lesser social skills try to intimidate them (Workplace Bullying Institute, 2012). When organizations do not implement trainings or interventions to put an end to bullying, targeted individual often develop stress-related health problems and are very likely to become less productive (Herron, 2021).

With the goal of maintaining employee peak performance, Baheer et al. (2023) suggest organizational strategies that create diversions for those employees whose high scores in psychopathy would most likely create an adverse work environment. Managers should develop plans for these specific workers. While Human Resource managers need to identify employees who possess personality traits on the Dark Triad, it would be far better to tighten the organization's selection procedures to prevent these people from getting hired in the first place. We believe that some variant of personality testing that identifies traits in the Dark Tetrad should become part of the executive search process at least for public companies.

From a practical viewpoint, identifying situations that might trigger expressions of dark personality traits at work is essential. Human Resource professionals must design evidence-based interventions to prevent these employees from expressing their short- or long-term dark proclivities. This may include job design and selective placements as well as training and coaching in order to sensitize these individuals to potentially dangerous situations so as to better manage their dark impulses. Increasing other employees' abilities to cope with co-workers' dark behavior is another approach. This not only facilitates better work relationships but will also boost the work ethic in the organization (Nübold et al., 2017). The most effective remedy against the malevolence perpetrated by Dark Tetrad personalities within an organization is to ensure that such people do not accede to positions of power. Effective damage control requires that individuals exhibiting egregious behavior be removed from the system. This should be part of the risk assessment phase of audit planning. Controls over financial reporting should be strengthened and physical assets safeguarded (Ramamoorti & Epstein, 2016).

According to Sánchez-Medina et al. (2020), organizations need to care about and become involved in the psychosocial health of the workplace. Ensuring a culture of zero tolerance for harassment, bullying, and cyberbullying must be an essential feature of corporate social responsibility. Preventive management of sexual and cyberbullying must include information campaigns and training to raise awareness of the need for workplace safety. Moreover, junior managers with Dark Tetrad profiles who may one day become middle- or top managers must be schooled to ensure that their face-to-face and electronic interactions with staff are impeccable. Otherwise, cyberbullying or sexual harassment from people in authority could even lead to an employee's suicide (Sánchez-Medina et al., 2020).

9.2.6.1 *Cyberloafing*

Every organization needs stringent policies both to promote healthy Internet use and to prevent overuse and addiction. At present, there is minimal understanding of how personality traits such as Machiavellianism and narcissism contribute to cyberloafing (Tandon et al., 2021). Future research should include cross-cultural investigations of these personality traits in order to develop more accurate profiles of employees who are psychologically predisposed to cyberloafing as formal monitoring may not be sufficient to detect it. A nuanced study of these traits could form a knowledge base for identifying individuals who are prone to engage in such behavior. As it is not possible to overlook social media addiction in the workplace, Tandon et al. (2021) recommend extensive psychological screening of job applicants in order to uncover predispositions to cyberloafing, which may be a gratifying substrate for narcissistic traits that ultimately decrease job satisfaction and organizational commitment (Choi, 2018).

9.3 Limitations of Current Studies and Directions for Future Research

This book reviews the literature correlating the Dark Tetrad with various forms of cyber deviance and cybercrime. While most studies show significant consistent relationships between cybercrime and the Dark Tetrad or the Dark Triad (in cases where sadism was not examined), the effect, though stable is modest in many of the cases. This suggests that moderators or mediators strongly affect the relationship between Dark Tetrad and cyber deviance and crime (Cohen, 2016; Nübold et al., 2017). At present, little investigation has been conducted on this line of reasoning. Possible moderating variables might be online disinhibition, social support, or moral disengagement. In the predominant view, the Dark Tetrad consists of stable traits; hence, situational cues eliciting dark behavior have not been a major concern (Nübold et al., 2017), although they should be. Many studies inquire into cyberbullying via social media rather than examining specific venues such as Facebook, Instagram, or Twitter or else, they examine cyberbullying on only one platform in isolation from all the others. Research is needed to compare prevalence, predictors, and outcomes of cyberbullying across multiple social media platforms (Giumetti & Kowalski, 2022).

Giumetti and Kowalski (2022) further note that many studies are cross-sectional and based on self-reports, which not only introduces bias but also limits the ability to conclude that cyberbullying via social media is a direct cause of reduced well-being of the targets. Additional longitudinal and experimental research is needed using methodologies that measure actual behavior and not only self-reports. In addition, there is some disproportion in the amount of research on forms of cyber deviance. There are many studies on social network addiction and much less research on cyber deviance in the workplace. Future research should consider performing studies on all forms of cyber deviance and crime, not focusing only on specific ones.

Another problem is that most empirical research uses students from a single country as subjects. However, evidence suggests that cyberbullying via social media is also prevalent among working adults and that there may be cross-cultural variability. Therefore, research across cultures and age groups is needed. Another limitation is that most studies report only the prevalence of cyberbullying via social media or examine bivariate relationships with well-being. Little is known about the reasons for cyberbullying. Possible mediators might be empathy, rumination, or self-esteem (Giumetti & Kowalski, 2022). March et al. (2022) point out that even the definition of the term cyberstalking lacks consistency. There is also minimal research on cyberstalking in intimate relationships.

Another problem is the lack of consistency in the use of sadism as the fourth dark trait. In 1987, the American Psychiatric Association ruled that sadism is not a personality disorder. Craker and March (2016), Koban et al. (2018), and Pechorro et al. (2023) advocate for its inclusion in the list of personality disorders even though Blötner and Mokros (2023) find that measures of sadism and psychopathy indicate that the two constructs refer to the same phenomena and that in some cases psychopathy is an even better predictor of the behaviors ascribed to sadism.

The impasse concerning the correct terminology – whether it be Dark Triad or Dark Tetrad – is at present unresolved. Some researchers examine Dark Triad while others examine Dark Tetrad. No theory guides any of these ascriptions and this prevents definitive conclusions about the effect of dark personalities on cybercrime and cyber deviance. The high correlation between psychopathy and sadism strongly suggests that sadism is a dimension of psychopathy and not an independent personality trait. If future studies continue to show high positive correlation between psychopathy and sadism, it would be appropriate to only use the term Dark Triad as the current confusion slows down advances in research in this area.

Another limitation pointed out by Moor and Anderson (2019) is that there is little research with participants outside of Australia, Europe, North America, and Turkey. Thus, conclusions about the relationship between dark traits and antisocial online behavior cannot be generalized beyond those geolocations. All the studies have been conducted within the last 10 years and typically use young people as subjects. More research should be conducted on older populations. More research should also be conducted to understand how cultural values and social hierarchies affect adolescents with Dark Tetrad personality traits and their tendency to bully and be aggressive (Wright et al., 2020).

The intersection of cybercrime and deviance is also related to cyberterrorism, which emerged in the mid-1990s. Although there is no accepted definition of cyberterrorism, many recognize it as use of digital technology to generate social disruption with the goal of compelling social change based on ideological or political beliefs. Although cyberterrorism over the last two decades has targeted sensitive information, computer systems, and worldwide networks, criminals also attack these same targets. So, how do we distinguish between cyberterrorism and cybercrime (Holt et al., 2022)? In addition, swatting and doxing, relatively new forms of cyber deviance, have been derived from cyberterrorism.

Social networks, the Internet, and mobile phones are all tools with which dark personalities can utilize to realize their nefarious goals, whether they be power, money, status, or enjoyment of the persecution of others (Nübold et al., 2017). To cope with the increase in cyber deviance, we must better understand the motives, behaviors, and tactics of dark personalities who operate in the cyber realm. Only then will society be able to develop tools and structures to overcome the damage done to organizations and individuals. Research on the relationship between dark personalities and cyber deviance and cybercrime is needed to train individuals and organizations to better cope with the threat. This book is one step in that direction. While we cannot prevent dark personalities from committing cybercrime, we should be able to restrain them and slow them down.

References

Abell, L., & Brewer, G. (2014). Machiavellianism, self-monitoring, self-promotion and relational aggression on Facebook. *Computers in Human Behavior, 36*, 258–262. https://doi.org/10.1016/j.chb.2014.03.076

Aboujaoude, E., & Savage, M. W. (2023). Cyberbullying: Next-generation research. *World Psychiatry, 22*(1), 45–46. https://doi.org/10.1002/wps.21040

Achuthan, K., Nair, V. K., Kowalski, R., Ramanathan, S., & Raman, R. (2022). Cyberbullying research – Alignment to sustainable development and impact of COVID-19: Bibliometrics and science mapping analysis. *Computers in Human Behavior.* https://doi.org/10.1016/j.chb.2022.107566

Afzal, W., Latif, S., & Siddique, A. (2021). Dark Triad, cyberbullying and psychological distress among adolescents. *Education Sciences & Psychology, 59*(2), 71–76.

Ahmad, H., Arif, A., Khattak, A. M., Habib, A., Asghar, M. Z., & Shah, B. (2020). Applying deep neural networks for predicting Dark Triad personality trait of online users. 2020 *International Conference on Information Networking (ICOIN)*, 102–105.

Akat, M., Arslan, C., & Hamarta, E. (2022). Dark Triad personality and phubbing: The mediator role of Fomo. *Psychological Reports.* https://doi.org/10.1177/00332941221109119

Akdeniz, S., Budak, H., & Ah21çi, Z. G. (2022). Development of a scale of narcissism in social media and investigation of its psychometric characteristics. *International Education Studies, 15*(1), 200–209. https://doi.org/10.5539/ies.v15n1p200

Akhter, S., Islam, M. H., Haider, S. K. U., Ferdous, R., & Runa, A. S. (2022). Moderating effects of gender and passive Facebook use on the relationship between social interaction anxiety and preference for online social interaction. *Journal of Human Behavior in the Social Environment, 32*(6), 719–737. https://doi.org/10.1080/10911359.2021.1955801

Alavi, M., Latif, A. A., Ramayah, T., & Tan, J. Y. (2022). Dark tetrad of personality, cyberbullying, and cybertrolling among young adults. *Current Psychology*, 1–11. https://doi.org/10.1007/s12144-022-03892-4

Alipan, A., Skues, J., Theiler, S., & Wise, L. (2015). Defining cyberbullying: A multiple perspectives approach. In *Annual Review of Cybertherapy and Telemedicine: Virtual Reality in Healthcare: Medical Simulation and Experiential Interface* (Vol. 219, pp. 9–13). https://doi.org/10.3233/978-1-61499-595-1-9

Alotaibi, F. M., Asghar, M. Z., & Ahmad, S. (2021). A hybrid CNN-LSTM model for psychopathic class detection from tweeter users. *Cognitive Computation*, *13*(3), 709–723.

Alqahtani, N., Innab, A., Alammar, K., Alkhateeb, R., Kerari, A., & Alharbi, M. (2022). Cyberloafing behaviours in nursing: The role of nursing stressors. *International Journal of Nursing Practice*, Early view, 1–10 https://doi.org/10.1111/ijn.13079

Aluja, A., Garcia, L. F., Rossier, J., Ostendorf, F., Glicksohn, J., Oumar, B., ... & Hansenne, M. (2022). Dark triad traits, social position, and personality: A cross-cultural study. *Journal of Cross-Cultural Psychology*, *53*(3–4), 380–402. https://doi.org/10.1177/00220221211072816

American Psychiatric Association. (1987). *Diagnostic and Statistical Manual of Mental Disorders* (3rd ed., Revised (DSM-III-R)). Washington, DC: American Psychiatric Press.

American Psychiatric Association. (2000). *Diagnostic and Statistical Manual of Mental Disorders* (4th ed., text revision). Washington, DC: American Psychiatric Association.

American Psychiatric Association. (2013). *Diagnostic and Statistical Manual of Mental Disorders* (DSM-5). Retrieved from www.psi.uba.ar/academica/carrerasdegrado/psicologia/sitioscatedras/practicas_profesionales/820_clinica_tr_personalidad_psicosis/material/dsm.Pdf

Amichai-Hamburger, Y. (2005). Personality and the Internet. In Amichai-Hamburger, Y. (Ed.), *The Social Net: Human Behavior in Cyberspace* (pp. 27–55). Oxford University Press.

Amon, M. J., Necaise, A., Kartvelishvili, N., Williams, A., Solihin, Y., & Kapadia, A. (2023). Modeling user characteristics associated with interdependent privacy perceptions on social media. *ACM Transactions on Computer-Human Interaction*. http://dx.doi.org/10.1145/3577014

Andel, S. (January 2020). Why bosses should let employees surf the web at work. *The Conversation*. Retrieved from https://theconversation.com/why-bosses-should-let-employees-surf-the-web-at-work-128444

Andreassen, C. S. (2015). Online social network site addiction: A comprehensive review. *Current Addiction Reports*, *2*(2), 175–184. https://doi.org/10 1007/s40429-015-0056-9

Andreassen C. S., & Pallesen S. (2014). Social network site addiction – An overview. *Current Pharmaceutical Design*, *20*, 4053–4061.

Andreassen, C. S., Pallesen, S., & Griffiths, M. D. (2017). The relationship between addictive use of social media, narcissism, and self-esteem: Findings from a large national survey. *Addictive Behaviors*, *64*, 287–293. https://doi.org/10.1016/j.addbeh.2016.03.006

Ansari, S. (2020). *From the scammer perspective: Predispositions towards online fraud motivation and rationalization*. Doctoral dissertation, Purdue University Graduate School.

Antoniadou, N., Kokkinos, C. M., & Markos, A. (2019). Psychopathic traits and social anxiety in cyber-space: A context-dependent theoretical framework explaining online disinhibition. *Computers in Human Behavior*, *99*, 228–234.

Aplin-Houtz, M. J., Leahy, S., Willey, S., Lane, E. K., Sharma, S., & Meriac, J. (2023). Tales from the dark side of technology acceptance: The Dark Triad and the technology acceptance model. *Employee Responsibilities and Rights Journal*, 1–33. https://doi.org/10.1007/s10672-023-09453-6

Asghar, J., Akbar, S., Asghar. M. Z., Ahmad, B., Al-Rakhami, M. S., & Gumaei, A. (2021) Detection and classification of psychopathic personality trait from social media text using deep learning model. *Computational and Mathematical Methods in Medicine*, 5512241. https://doi.org/10.1155/2021/5512241

Asih, S. R. (2023). The Dark Triad personality in relation to cyberbullying: The role of self-esteem as a mediator [Hubungan Kepribadian Dark Triad dan Cyberbullying: Peran Self-Esteem Sebagai Mediator]. *ANIMA Indonesian Psychological Journal*, *38*(1), 038104. https://doi.org/10.24123/aipj.v38i1.4113

Aviram, I., & Amichai-Hamburger, Y. (2005). Online infidelity: Aspects of dyadic satisfaction, self-disclosure, and narcissism. *Journal of Computer-Mediated Communication*, *10*(3), JCMC1037. https://doi.org/10.1111/j.1083-6101.2005.tb00249.x

Azami, M. S., & Taremian, F. (2021). Risk factors associated with cyberbullying, cyber victimization, and cyberbullying-victimization in Iran's high school students. *Iranian Journal of Psychiatry*, *16*(3), 343–352. https://doi.org/10.18502/ijps.v16i3.6261

Azzahra, K. A., & Sihwi, S. W. (August 2022). Dark Triad personality traits prediction through Twitter analysis using support vector machine method. In *2022 1st International Conference on Smart Technology, Applied Informatics, and Engineering (APICS)* (pp. 102–107). IEEE.

Babiak, P., & Hare, R. D. (2006). *Snakes in Suits: When Psychopaths Go to Work*. New York: Regan Books.

Baheer, R., Khan, K. I., Rafiq, Z., & Rashid, T. (2023). Impact of Dark Triad personality traits on turnover intention and mental health of employees through cyberbullying. *Cogent Business & Management*, *10*(1), 2191777. https://doi.org/10.1080/23311975.2023.2191777

Balakrishnan, V., Khan, S., & Arabnia, H. R. (2020). Improving cyberbullying detection using Twitter users' psychological features and machine learning. *Computers & Security*, *90*, 101710. https://doi.org/10.1016/j.cose.2019.101710

Balakrishnan, J., & Griffiths, M. D. (2018). An exploratory study of "Selfitis" and the development of the Selfitis behavior scale. *International Journal of Mental Health Addiction*, *16*(3), 722–736. https://doi.org/10.1007/s11469-017-9844-x

Balakrishnan, V., Khan, S., Fernandez, T., & Arabnia, H. R. (2019). Cyberbullying detection on twitter using big five and Dark Triad features. *Personality and Individual Differences*, *141*, 252–257. https://doi.org/10.1016/j.paid.2019.01.024

Balcerowska, J. M., Sawicki, A., Brailovskaia, J., & Zajenkowski, M. (2023). Different aspects of narcissism and social networking sites addiction in Poland and Germany: The mediating role of positive and negative reinforcement expectancies. *Personality and Individual Differences*, *207*, 112172. https://doi.org/10.1016/j.paid.2023.112172

Balcerowska, J. M., & Sawicki, A. J. (2022). Which aspects of narcissism are related to social networking sties addiction? The role of self-enhancement and self-protection. *Personality and Individual Differences*, *190*, 111530. https://doi.org/10.1016/j.paid.2022.111530

Balta, S., Jonason, P., Denes, A., Emirtekin, E., Tosuntaş, Ş. B., Kircaburun, K., & Griffiths, M. D. (2019). Dark personality traits and problematic smartphone use: The mediating role of fearful attachment. *Personality and Individual Differences*, *149*, 214–219. https://doi.org/10.1016/j.paid.2019.06.005

Bańka, A., & Orłowski, K. (2012). The structure of the teacher Machiavellianism model in social interactions in a school environment. *Polish Psychological Bulletin*, *43*(4), 215–222. https://doi.org/10.2478/v10059-012-0024-3

Bank Info Security. (August 24, 2022). 2022 Ponemon cost of insider threats global report. Retrieved from www.bankinfosecurity.com/whitepapers/2022-ponemon-cost-of-insider-threats-global-report-w-10798

Barber, N. (1998). Sex differences in disposition towards kin, security of adult attachment, and sociosexuality as a function of parental divorce. *Evolution and Human Behaviour*, *19*(2), 125–132. https://doi.org/10.1016/S1090-5138(98)00004-X

Barberis, N., Sanchez-Ruiz, M. J., Cannavò, M., Calaresi, D., Verrastro, V. (2023). The Dark Triad and trait emotional intelligence as predictors of problematic social media use and engagement: The mediating role of the fear of missing out. *Clinical Neuropsychiatry*, *20*(2), 129–140. https://doi.org/10.36131/cnfioritieditore20230205

Barry, C. T., & Kauten, R. L. (2014). Nonpathological and pathological narcissism: Which self-reported characteristics are most problematic in adolescents? *Journal of Personality Assessment*, *96*(2), 212–219. https://doi.org/10.1080/00223891.2013.830264

Basit, A., Zafar, M., Liu, X., Javed, A. R., Jalil, Z., & Kifayat, K. (2021). A comprehensive survey of AI-enabled phishing attacks detection techniques. *Telecommunication Systems*, *76*, 139–154. https://doi.org/10.1007/s11235-020-00733-2

Baughman, H.M., Dearing, S., Giammarco, E., & Vernon, P.A. (2012). Relationships between bullying behaviors and the Dark Triad: A study with adults. *Personality and Individual Differences*, *52*, 571–75. https://doi.org/10.1016/j.paid.2011.11.020

Bergman, S. M., Fearrington, M. E., Davenport, S. W., & Bergman, J. Z. (2011). Millennials, narcissism, and social networking: What narcissists do on social networking sites and why. *Personality and Individual Differences*, *50*(5), 706–711. https://doi.org/10.1016/j.paid.2010.12.022

Bernat, F. P., & Makin, D. (2014). Cybercrime theory and discerning if there is a crime: The case of digital piracy. *International Review of Modern Sociology*, 99–119. www.jstor.org/stable/43499904

Bertl, B., Pietschnig, J., Tran, U. S., Stieger, S., & Voracek, M. (2017). More or less than the sum of its parts? Mapping the Dark Triad of personality onto a single Dark Core. *Personality and Individual Differences*, *114*, 140–144. https://doi.org/10.1016/j.paid.2017.04.002

Bhasin, D., & Mehta, A. (2019). Cyber stalking: New age terror. *International Journal of Law Management Humanities*, *2*, 320–328. www.brainyquote.com/quotes/willowbay_531432

Bhattacharyya, R. (2015). Addiction to modern gadgets and technologies across generations. *Eastern Journal of Psychiatry, 18*(2), 27–37.

Bhogal, M. S., & Wallace, D. (2022). Cost-inflicting mate retention tactics predict the perpetration of cyber dating abuse. *Evolutionary Psychological Science, 8*, 1–9. https://doi.org/10.1007/s40806-021-00307-8

Bilal, A., Nadeem, A., & Saleem, M. (2022). Cyber-psychopathy trait as predictor of cybersex addiction among university students. *Pakistan Journal of Humanities and Social Sciences, 10*(1), 20–28. https://doi.org/10.52131/pjhss.2022.1001.0170

Björkqvist, K., Lagerspetz, K. M., & Kaukiainen, A. (1992). Do girls manipulate and boys fight? Developmental trends in regard to direct and indirect aggression. *Aggressive Behavior, 18*(2), 117–127. https://doi.org/10.1002/1098-2337(1992)18:2<117::AID-AB2480180205>3.0.CO;2-3

Błachnio, A., Przepiorka, A., Cudo, A., Sękowski, A., & Pantic, I. (2023). The role of Machiavellianism and interdependent agency in Facebook intrusion. *Psychological Reports.* https://doi-org.ezproxy.haifa.ac.il/10.1177/00332941231153321

Blain, M. (2022). Political victimage ritual and evil. In Dryjanska, L., & Pacifici, G. (Eds.), *Evil in the Modern World.* Cham: Springer. https://doi-org.ezproxy .haifa.ac.il/10.1007/978-3-030-91888-0_8

Blais, J., Aelick, C. A., Scully, J. M., & Pruysers, S. (2023). Antisocial personality traits as potential risk factors for cyberstalking: Not all Dark Triad traits matter. *SSRN.* https://ssrn.com/abstract=4546645 or https://dx.doi.org/10.2139/ ssrn.4546645

Blickle, G., & Schütte, N. (2017). Trait psychopathy, task performance, and counterproductive work behavior directed toward the organization. *Personality and Individual Differences, 109*, 225–231. https://doi.org/10.1016/j.paid.2017.01.006

Blötner, C., & Beisemann, M. (2022). The Dark Triad is dead, long live the Dark Triad: An item-response theoretical examination of the Short Dark Tetrad. *Personality and Individual Differences, 199*, 111858. https://doi.org/10.1016/j .paid.2022.111858

Blötner, C., & Mokros, A. (2023). The next distinction without a difference: Do psychopathy and sadism scales assess the same construct? *Personality and Individual Differences, 205*, 112102. https://doi-org.ezproxy.haifa.ac.il/10.1016/j.paid.2023.112102

Board, B. J., & Fritzon, K. (2005). Disordered personalities at work. *Psychology, Crime & Law, 11*(1), 17–32. https://doi.org/10.1080/10683160310001634304

Boddy, C. (2011). *Corporate Psychopaths: Organizational Destroyers.* London: Palgrave Macmillan. https://doi.org/10.1108/09534811211214008

Bogolyubova, O., Panicheva, P., Tikhonov, R., Ivanov, V., & Ledovaya, Y. (2018). Dark personalities on Facebook: Harmful online behaviors and language. *Computers in Human Behavior, 78*, 151–159. https://doi.org/10.1016/j .chb.2017.09.032

Bohns, V. (February 22, 2022). How scammers like Anna Delvey and the Tinder Swindler exploit a core feature of human nature. *The Conversation.* Retrieved from https://interaksyon.philstar.com/trends-spotlights/2022/02/22/211224/ how-scammers-like-anna-delvey-and-the-tinder-swindler-exploit-a-core-feature-of-human-nature/

Bonfá-Araujo, B., Lima-Costa, A. R., Hauck-Filho, N., & Jonason, P. K. (2022). Considering sadism in the shadow of the Dark Triad traits: A meta-analytic review of the Dark Tetrad. *Personality and Individual Differences, 197,* 111767. https://doi.org/10.1016/j.paid.2022.111767

Boyd, D. M., & Ellison, N. B. (2007). Social network sites: Definition, history and scholarship. *Journal of Computer-Mediated Communication, 13*(1), 210–230. https://doi.org/10.1111/j.1083-6101.2007.00393.x

Brailovskaia, J., Margraf, J., & Köllner, V. (2019). Addicted to Facebook? Relationship between Facebook addiction disorder, duration of Facebook use and narcissism in an inpatient sample. *Psychiatry Research, 273,* 52–57. https://doi.org/10.1016/j.psychres.2019.01.016

Brailovskaia, J., Ozimek, P., Rohmann, E., & Bierhoff, H. W. (2023). Vulnerable narcissism, fear of missing out (FoMO) and addictive social media use: A gender comparison from Germany. *Computers in Human Behavior, 144,* 107725. https://doi.org/10.1016/j.chb.2023.107725

Brand, M., Wegmann, E., Stark, R., Müller, A., Wölfling, K., Robbins, T. W., & Potenza, M. N. (2019). The Interaction of Person-Affect-Cognition-Execution (I-PACE) model for addictive behaviors: Update, generalization to addictive behaviors beyond internet-use disorders, and specification of the process character of addictive behaviors. *Neuroscience & Biobehavioral Reviews, 104,* 1–10. https://doi.org/10.1016/j.neubiorev.2019.06.032

Branković, I., Dinić, B. M., & Jonason, P. K. (2022). How traditional stalking and cyberstalking correlate with the Dark Tetrad traits? *Current Psychology,* 1–5. https://doi-org.ezproxy.haifa.ac.il/10.1007/s12144-022-03681-z

Branson, M., & March, E. (2021). Dangerous dating in the digital age: Jealousy, hostility, narcissism, and psychopathy as predictors of Cyber Dating Abuse. *Computers in Human Behavior, 119,* 106711. https://doi.org/10.1016/j.chb.2021.106711

Brewer, G., Parkinson, M., Pickles, A., Anson, J., & Mulinder, G. (2023). Dark Triad traits and relationship dissolution. *Personality and Individual Differences, 204,* 112045. https://doi.org/10.1016/j.paid.2022.112045

Brod, C. (1984). *Technostress: The Human Cost of the Computer Revolution.* Reading, MA: Addison-Wesley, 1984.

Brown, W. M., Hazraty, S., & Palasinski, M. (2019). Examining the Dark Tetrad and its links to cyberbullying. *Cyberpsychology, Behavior, and Social Networking, 22*(8), 552–557. https://doi.org/10.1089/cyber.2019.0172

Broz, M. (2023). Photutorial, How many pictures are there (2023): Statistics, trends, and forecasts. Retrieved from https://photutorial.com/photos-statistics/

Brubaker, P. J., Montez, D., & Church, S. H. (2021). The power of schadenfreude: predicting behaviors and perceptions of trolling among Reddit users. *Social Media + Society, 7*(2), 20563051211021382. https://doi.org/10.1177/20563051211021382

Brunell, A. B., Gentry, W. A., Campbell, W. K., Hoffman, B. J., Kuhnert, K. W., & DeMarree, K. G. (2008). Leader emergence: The case of the narcissistic leader. *Personality and Social Psychology Bulletin, 34*(12), 1663–1676. https://doi.org/10.1177/0146167208324101

Buckels, E. E., Jones, D. N., & Paulhus, D. L. (2013). Behavioral confirmation of everyday sadism. *Psychological Science, 24*(11), 2201–2209. https://doi.org/10.1177/0956797613490749

Buckels, E. E., Trapnell, P. D., Andjelovic, T., & Paulhus, D. L. (2019). Internet trolling and everyday sadism: Parallel effects on pain perception and moral judgment. *Journal of Personality, 87*(2), 328–340. https://doi-org.ezproxy.haifa.ac.il/10.1111/jopy.12393

Buckels, E. E., Trapnell, P. D., & Paulhus, D. L. (2014). Trolls just want to have fun. *Personality and Individual Differences, 67*, 97–102. https://doi.org/10.1016/j.paid.2014.01.016

Buffardi, L. E., & Campbell, W. K. (2008). Narcissism and social networking web sites. *Personality and Social Psychology Bulletin, 34*(10), 1303–1314. https://doi.org/10.1177/0146167208320061

Bui, N. H., & Pasalich, D. S. (2021). Insecure attachment, maladaptive personality traits, and the perpetration of in-person and cyber psychological abuse. *Journal of Interpersonal Violence, 36*(5–6), 2117–2139. https://doi.org/10.1177/0886260518760332

Burtăverde, V., Jonason, P. K., Giosan, C., & Ene, C. (2021). Why do people watch porn? An evolutionary perspective on the reasons for pornography consumption. *Evolutionary Psychology, 19*(2), 14747049211028798. https://doi.org/10.1177/14747049211028798

Calvert, M., Linden, M., Kyser, K., Zeinert, K., & Foust, M. S. (2021). Personality correlates of gaming and pornography use. *Psi Beta Journal of Research, 1*(1), 34–40. https://doi.org/10.54581/JPWV2620

Campbell, K. (March 15, 2022). The science behind the tinder swindler catfishing, romance scams, and how to protect yourself. *Psychology Today*. Retrieved from www.psychologytoday.com/intl/blog/more-chemistry/202203/the-science-behind-the-tinder-swindler

Campbell, W. K., Bonacci, A. M., Shelton, J., Exline, J. J., & Bushman, B. J. (2004). Psychological entitlement: Interpersonal consequences and validation of a self-report measure. *Journal of Personality Assessment, 83*(1), 29–45. https://doi.org/10.1207/s15327752jpa8301_04

Campbell, W. K., Hoffman, B. J., Campbell, S. M., & Marchisio, G. (2011). Narcissism in organizational contexts. *Human Resource Management Review, 21*(4), 268–284. https://doi.org/10.1016/j.hrmr.2010.10.007

Carpenter, C. J. (2012). Narcissism on Facebook: Self-promotional and anti-social behavior. *Personality and Individual Differences, 52*(4), 482–486. https://doi.org/10.1016/j.paid.2011.11.011

Carre, J. R., Curtis, S. R., & Jones, D. N. (2018). Ascribing responsibility for online security and data breaches. *Managerial Auditing Journal, 33*(4), 436–446. https://doi.org/10.1108/MAJ-11-2017-1693

Casale, S., & Banchi, V. (2020). Narcissism and problematic social media use: A systematic literature review. *Addictive Behaviors Reports, 11*, 100252. https://doi.org/10.1016/j.abrep.2020.100252

Casale, S., & Fioravanti, G. (2018). Why narcissists are at risk for developing Facebook addiction: The need to be admired and the need to belong. *Addictive Behaviors*, *76*, 312–318. https://doi.org/10.1016/j.addbeh.2017.08.038

Chabrol, H., Van Leeuwen, N., Rodgers, R., & Séjourné, N. (2009). Contributions of psychopathic, narcissistic, Machiavellian, and sadistic personality traits to juvenile delinquency. *Personality and Individual Differences*, *47*(7), 734–739.

Chamie, J. (2022). Dating in a changing America. In *Population Levels, Trends, and Differentials*. Cham: Springer. https://doi.org/10.1007/978-3-031-22479-9_44

Chandler, D., & Munday, R. (2019). Revenge porn. Dictionary of Social Media. Oxford University Press. Retrieved from www.oxfordreference.com/view/10.1093/acref/9780191803093.001.0001/acref-9780191803093-e-1231

Charlier, S. D., Giumetti, G. W., Reeves, C. J., & Greco, L. M. (2017). Workplace cyberdeviance. In Hertel, G., Stone, D. L., Johnson, R. D., & Passmore, J. (Eds.), *Wiley Blackwell Handbooks in Organizational Psychology. The Wiley Blackwell Handbook of the Psychology of the Internet at Work* (pp. 131–156). Wiley-Blackwell. https://doi.org/10.1002/9781119256151.ch7

Charalampous, K., Ioannou, M., Georgiou, S., & Stavrinides, P. (2021). Cyberbullying, psychopathic traits, moral disengagement, and school climate: The role of self-reported psychopathic levels and gender. *Educational Psychology*, *41*(3), 282–301. https://doi.org/10.1080/01443410.2020.1742874

Chavan, M., Galperin, B. L., Ostle, A., & Behl, A. (2021). Millennial's perception on cyberloafing: Workplace deviance or cultural norm? *Behaviour & Information Technology*, 1–18. https://doi.org/10.1080/0144929X.2021.1956588

Chen, J. (November 2020). Second World. *Investopedia*. Retrieved from www.investopedia.com/terms/s/second-world.asp

Cheng, Z. W., & Lee, S. L. (2022). Victimizing the psychopaths and Machiavellians online, but not the charming narcissists: The insignificance of powerlessness. *Journal of Social and Educational Research*, *1*(1), 1–13. www.journalser.com/jser/article/view/6

Cheng, C., & Li, A. Y. L. (2014). Internet addiction prevalence and quality of (real) life: A meta-analysis of 31 nations across seven world regions. *Cyberpsychology, Behavior, and Social Networking*, *17*(12), 755–760. https://doi.org/10.1089/cyber.2014.0317

Choi, Y. (2018). Narcissism and social media addiction in workplace. *Journal of Asian Finance, Economics and Business*, *5*(2), 95–104. https://doi.org/10.13106/jafeb.2018.vol5.no2.95

Choi, Y., Chu, K., & Choi, E. J. (2019). Social network services addiction in the workplace. *The Journal of Asian Finance, Economics and Business*, *6*(1), 249–259. http://doi.org/10.13106/jafeb.2019.vol6.no1.249

Choi, W. H., Son, J. W., Kim, Y. R., Lee, S. I., Shin, C. J., Kim, S. K., & Ju, G. W. (2011). A study of covert narcissism in adolescent Internet addiction: Relationship to anonymity, presence, interactivity, and achievement motivation. *Journal of the Korean Academy of Child and Adolescent Psychiatry*, *22*(2), 103–111. https://doi.org/10.5765/jkacap.2011.22.2.103

Christie, R., & Geis, F. L. (1970). *Studies in Machiavellianism.* New York, NY: Academic Press.

Christensen, L. (2022). How to protect yourself from the Tinder Swindler and similar psychopaths. *Mental Health Matters, 9*(1), 8–9.

Chung, K. L., Morshidi, I., Yoong, L. C., & Thian, K. N. (2019). The role of the Dark Tetrad and impulsivity in social media addiction: Findings from Malaysia. *Personality and Individual Differences, 143*, 62–67. https://doi.org/10.1016/j.paid.2019.02.016

Ciocca, G., Robilotta, A., Fontanesi, L., Sansone, A., D'Antuono, L., Limoncin, E., ... & Jannini, E. A. (2020). Sexological aspects related to Tinder use: A comprehensive review of the literature. *Sexual Medicine Reviews, 8*(3), 367–378. https://doi.org/10.1016/j.sxmr.2019.12.004

Clancy, E. M., Klettke, B., & Hallford, D. J. (2019). The dark side of sexting – factors predicting the dissemination of sexts. *Computers in Human Behavior, 92*, 266–272. https://doi.org/10.1016/j.chb.2018.11.023

Clancy, E. M., Klettke, B., Hallford, D. J., Crossman, A. M., Maas, M. K., & Toumbourou, J. W. (2020). Sharing is not always caring: Understanding motivations and behavioural associations with sext dissemination. *Computers in Human Behavior, 112*, 106460. https://doi.org/10.1016/j.chb.2020.106460

Cleckley, H. (1941/1988). *The Mask of Sanity (5th ed.), Private Printing for Educational Use by Emily Cleckley 1988* (Formerly first published by C.V. Mosley Co.in 1941). Georgia: Augusta.

Cohen, A. (2016). Are they among us? A conceptual framework of the relationship between the Dark Triad personality and counterproductive work behaviors (CWBs). *Human Resource Management Review, 26*(1), 69–85. https://doi.org/10.1016/j.hrmr.2015.07.003

Cohen, A. (2018). *Counterproductive Work Behaviors: Understanding the Dark Side of Personalities in Organizational Life.* New York: Routledge. https://doi.org/10.4324/9781315454818

Cohen, A., & Baruch, Y. (2022). Abuse and exploitation of doctoral students: A conceptual model for traversing a long and winding road to academia. *Journal of Business Ethics, 180*(2), 505–522. https://doi-org.ezproxy.haifa.ac.il/10.1007/s10551-021-04905-1

Coleman, F. L. (1997). Stalking behavior and the cycle of domestic violence. *Journal of Interpersonal Violence, 12*(3), 420–432. https://doi.org/10.1177/088626097012003007

Coles, B. A., & West, M. (2016). Trolling the trolls: Online forum users constructions of the nature and properties of trolling. *Computers in Human Behavior, 60*, 233–244. https://doi.org/10.1016/j.chb.2016.02.070

Cooke, D. J., & Michie, C. (2001). Refining the construct of psychopathy: Towards a hierarchical model. *Psychological Assessment, 13*(2), 171–188. https://doi.org/10.1037/1040-3590.13.2.171

Coyne, I., & Farley, S. (2018). Cyberbullying within working contexts. In Cassidy, W., Faucher, C., & Jackson, M. (Eds.), *Cyberbullying at University in International Contexts*, (1st Edition, pp. 80–96). Abingdon, UK: Routledge.

Craker, N., & March, E. (2016). The dark side of Facebook: The Dark Tetrad, negative social potency, and trolling behaviours. *Personality and Individual Differences, 102*, 79–84. https://doi.org/10.1016/j.paid.2016.06.043

Cressey, D. R. (1953). *Other People's Money*. Montclair, NJ: Patterson Smith.

Cristescu, I., Ciuperca, E. M., & Cirnu, C. E. (2022). Exploiting personality traits in social engineering attacks. *Romanian Journal of Information Technology & Automatic Control/Revista Română de Informatică și Automatică, 32*(1), 113–122.

Curtis, S. R., Basak, A., Carre, J. R., Bošanský, B., Černý, J., BenAsher, N., Gutierrez, M., Jones, D. N., & Kiekintveld, C. (2021). The Dark Triad and strategic resource control in a competitive computer game. *Personality and Individual Differences, 168*, 110343. https://doi.org/10.1016/j.paid.2020.110343

Curtis, S. R., & Jones, D. N. (2020). Understanding what makes dark traits "vulnerable": A distinction between indifference and hostility. *Personality and Individual Differences, 160*, 109941. https://doi.org/10.1016/j.paid.2020.109941

Curtis, S. R., Rajivan, P., Jones, D. N., & Gonzalez, C. (2018). Phishing attempts among the Dark Triad: Patterns of attack and vulnerability. *Computers in Human Behavior, 87*, 174–182. https://doi.org/10.1016/j.chb.2018.05.037

Daderman, A. M., & Ragnestål-Impola, C. (2019). Workplace bullies, not their victims, score high on the Dark Triad and Extraversion, and low on Agreeableness and Honesty-Humility. *Heliyon, 5*(10), 1–9. https://doi.org/10.1016/j.heliyon.2019. e02609

DarkOwl. (2021). Increased threat to food delivery services on the Darknet. Retrieved from www.darkowl.com/blog-content/increased-threat-to-food-delivery-services-on-the-darknet

DataProt. (May 5, 2023). Piracy is back: Piracy statistics for 2023. Retrieved from https://dataprot.net/statistics/piracy-statistics/

da Silva, P. G. N., da Fonseca, P. N., de Medeiros, E. D., Couto, R. N., & Pereira, R. S. (2021). Intimate Partner Cyberstalking Scale (IPCS): Evidências Psicométricas no Brasil. *Revista Iberoamericana de Diagnóstico y Evaluación Psicológica, 2*(59), 5–17.

DataReportal. (2023). Digital around the world. Retrieved from https://datareportal.com/global-digital-overview

Davidson, G., Higgleton, E., Sargeant, H., & Seaton, A. (eds.), (1994). *Chambers Pocket Dictionary*. Edinburgh: Chambers.

DeAndrea, D. C. (2014). Advancing warranting theory. *Communication Theory 24*(2), 186–204. https://doi.org/10.1111/comt.12033

De Groot, J. (May 6, 2023). What are social engineering attacks? (Types & Definition). *Digital Guardian*. Retrieved from www.digitalguardian.com/blog/social-engineering-attacks-common-techniques-how-prevent-attack

de Jesus Costa, B., Simões, A. M., & Relva, I. C. (2023). Psychopathic traits and cyber dating abuse: Mediating effect of internet addiction in a university student sample. *Journal of Forensic Psychology Research and Practice, 23*(2), 113–135. https://doi.org/10.1080/24732850.2021.2016116

DeLisi, M., Drury, A., Elbert, M., Tahja, K., Caropreso, D., & Heinrichs, T. (2017). Sexual sadism and criminal versatility: Does sexual sadism spillover into nonsexual crimes? *Journal of Aggression, Conflict and Peace Research, 9*(1), 2–12. https://doi.org/10.1108/JACPR-05-2016-0229

Demircioğlu Z. I., & Çıkan, F. (2021). *Effects of the Dark Triad Personality Traits on Cyberbullying: A Meta-Analysis.* Presented at the International Congress of Psychology, Praha, Çek Cumhuriyeti, 2021. Accessed on July 23, 2021. Retrieved from https://hdl.handle.net/11511/93430

Demircioğlu, Z. I., & Köse, A. G. (2021). Effects of attachment styles, Dark Triad, rejection sensitivity, and relationship satisfaction on social media addiction: A mediated model. *Current Psychology, 40,* 414–428.

Demircioğlu, Z. I., & Köse, A. G. (2022). Antecedents of problematic social media use and cyberbullying among adolescents: Attachment, the Dark Triad and rejection sensitivity. *Current Psychology.* https://doi.org/10.1007/s12144-022-04127-2

Demircioğlu, Z. I., & Köse, A. G. (2023). Mediating roles of impulsivity and risk-taking in the links of the Dark Triad with flirting and dating via social media. *Psikoloji Çalışmaları, 42*(3), 643–665. https://doi.org/10.26650/SP2021-1018862

Dey, D. (2022). Perception/Deception: Fictional Selves and the Peculiarly Digital Phenomenon of Catfishing. *Asiascape: Digital Asia, 9*(1–2), 95–118. https://doi-org.ezproxy.haifa.ac.il/10.1163/22142312-bja10029

Djuraskovic, O. (2023). Top Instagram statistics for 2023. https://firstsiteguide.com/instagram-stats/

Dow, G. T. (2023). The Dark Tetrad and malevolent creativity. In Kapoor, H., & Kaufman, J. C. (Eds.), *Creativity and Morality* (pp. 69–80). Academic Press. https://doi.org/10.1016/B978-0-323-85667-6.00010-4

Drouvelis, M., Gerson, J., Powdthavee, N., & Riyanto, Y. E. (2022). Identity misrepresentation in cyberspace erodes human cooperation. *SSRN.* https://doi.org/10.2139/ssrn.4014880

Duffy, A., March, E., & Jonason, P. K. (2023). Intimate partner cyberstalking: Exploring vulnerable narcissism, secondary psychopathy, borderline traits, and rejection sensitivity. *Cyberpsychology, Behavior, and Social Networking, 26*(3), 147–152. https://doi-org.ezproxy.haifa.ac.il/10.1089/cyber.2022.0167

Duncan, Z., & March, E. (2019). Using Tinder to start a fire: Predicting antisocial use of Tinder® with gender and the Dark Tetrad. *Personality and Individual Differences, 145,* 9–14. https://doi.org/10.1016/j.paid.2019.03.014

Ehman, A. C., & Gross, A. M. (2019). Sexual cyberbullying: Review, critique, & future directions. *Aggression and Violent Behavior, 44,* 80–87. https://doi.org/10.1016/j.avb.2018.11.001

Eksi, F. (2012). Examination of narcissistic personality traits' predicting level of internet addiction and cyber bullying through path analysis. *Educational Sciences: Theory and Practice, 12*(3), 1694–1706.

El Keshky, M. E. S., Al-Qarni, M. S., & Khayat, A. H. (2022). Adaptation and psychometric properties of an Arabic version of the smartphone addiction scale (SAS) in the context of Saudi Arabia. *Addictive Behaviors, 131,* 107335. https://doi.org/10.1016/j.addbeh.2022.107335

Facebook. (2019). Statistics. http://newsroom.fb.com/company-info/

Fagade, T., Spyridopoulos, T., Albishry, N., & Tryfonas, T. (July 2017). System dynamics approach to malicious insider cyber-threat modelling and analysis. In *International Conference on Human Aspects of Information Security, Privacy, and Trust* (pp. 309–321). Cham: Springer.

Fan, C. Y., Chu, X. W., Zhang, M., & Zhou, Z. K. (2019). Are narcissists more likely to be involved in cyberbullying? Examining the mediating role of self-esteem. *Journal of Interpersonal Violence*, *34*(15), 3127–3150.

Farooq, R., & Ashraf, R. (2022). Dark trait tetrad and online deception in TikTok users. *Applied Psychology Review*, *1*(1), 20–33. https://journals.umt.edu.pk/index.php/apr

Fegan, R. B., & Bland, A. R. (2021). Social media use and vulnerable narcissism: The differential roles of oversensitivity and egocentricity. *International Journal of Environmental Research and Public Health*, *18*(17), 9172. https://doi.org/10.3390/ijerph18179172

Fennimore, A., & Sementelli, A. (2016). Public entrepreneurship and subclinical psychopaths: A conceptual frame and implications. *International Journal of Public Sector Management*, *29*(6), 612–634. https://doi.org/10.1108/IJPSM-01-2016-0011

Ferenczi, N., Marshall, T. C., & Bejanyan, K. (2017). Are sex differences in antisocial and prosocial Facebook use explained by narcissism and relational self-construal? *Computers in Human Behavior*, *77*, 25–31. https://doi.org/10.1016/j.chb.2017.08.033

Fichman, P., & Sanfilippo, M. R. (2016). *Online Trolling and Its Perpetrators: Under the Cyberbridge*. Lanham, MD: Rowman & Littlefield.

Fido, D., Rao, J., & Harper, C. A. (2022). Celebrity status, sex, and variation in psychopathy predicts judgements of and proclivity to generate and distribute deepfake pornography. *Computers in Human Behavior*, *129*, 107141. https://doi.org/10.1016/j.chb.2021.107141

Fisher, W. A., & Barak, A. (2001). Internet pornography: A social psychological perspective on internet sexuality. *Journal of Sex Research*, *38*(4), 312–323. https://doi.org/10.1080/00224490109552102

Fletcher, E. (2021). Romance scams take record dollars in 2020. *Federal Trade Commission*. Retrieved from www.ftc.gov/news-events/data-visualizations/data-spotlight/2021/02/romance-scams-take-record-dollars-2020#end2

Ford, D. P. (2013). Virtual harassment: Media characteristics' role in psychological health. *Journal of Managerial Psychology*, *28*(4), 408–428. https://doi.org/10.1108/JMP-12-2012-0398

Foster, J. D., Campbell, W. K., & Twenge, J. M. (2003). Individual differences in narcissism: Inflated self-views across the lifespan and around the world. *Journal of Research in Personality*, *37*, 469–486. http://dx.doi.org/10.1016/S0092-6566(03)00026-6

Fox, J., & Rooney, M. C. (2015). The Dark Triad and trait self-objectification as predictors of men's use and self-presentation behaviors on social networking sites. *Personality and Individual Differences*, *76*, 161–165. https://doi.org/10.1016/j.paid.2014.12.017

Freud, S. (1914/91). On narcissism: An introduction. In Sandler, J., Person, E., & Fonagy, P. (Eds.), *Freud's "On Narcissism: An Introduction"*. New Haven, CT: Yale University Press. https://doi.org/10.1080/00754170600563638

Freyth, L., & Batinic, B. (2021). How bright and dark personality traits predict dating app behavior. *Personality and Individual Differences, 168*, 110316. https://doi.org/10.1016/j.paid.2020.110316

Freyth, L., Batinic, B., & Jonason, P. K. (2023). Social media use and personality: Beyond self-reports and trait-level assessments. *Personality and Individual Differences, 202*. https://doi.org/10.1016/j.paid.2022.111960

Furian, L., & March, E. (2023). Trolling, the Dark Tetrad, and the four-facet spectrum of narcissism. *Personality and Individual Differences, 208*, 112169. https://doi.org/10.1016/j.paid.2023.112169

Furtner, M. R., Maran, T., & Rauthmann, J. F. (2017). Dark leadership: The role of leaders' Dark Triad personality traits. In Clark, M., & Gruber, C. (Eds.), *Leader Development Deconstructed: Annals of Theoretical Psychology*, vol 15 (pp. 75–99). Cham: Springer. https://doi.org/10.1007/978-3-319-64740-1_4

Gaia, J., Murray, D., Sanders, G., Sanders, S., Upadhyaya, S., Wang, X., & Yoo, C. (January 2022). The interaction of dark traits with the perceptions of apprehension. In *Proceedings of the 55th Hawaii International Conference on System Sciences*. Retrieved from https://hdl.handle.net/10125/79612978-0-9981331-5-7

Gaia, J., Ramamurthy, B., Sanders, G., Sanders, S., Upadhyaya, S., Wang, X., & Yoo, C. (2020). *Psychological profiling of hacking potential*. Paper presented at the Hawaii International Conference on System Sciences, Hawaii, USA.

Gaia, J., Sanders, G. L., Sanders, S. P., Upadhyaya, S., Wang, X., & Yoo, C. W. (2021). Dark Traits and hacking potential. *Journal of Organizational Psychology, 21*(3). https://doi.org/10.33423/jop.v21i3.4307

Gajda, A., Moroń, M., Królik, M., Małuch, M., & Mraczek, M. (2022). The Dark Tetrad, cybervictimization, and cyberbullying: The role of moral disengagement. *Current Psychology*. https://doi.org/10.1007/s12144-022-03456-6

Gamache, D., Savard, C., Faucher, J., & Cloutier, M. È. (2021). Development and validation of the stalking and obsessive relational intrusions questionnaire (SORI-Q). *Journal of Interpersonal Violence*, 08862605211042808. https://doi.org/10.1177/08862605211042808

Gammon, A. R., Converse, P. D., Lee, L. M., & Griffith, R. L. (2011). A personality process model of cyber harassment. *International Journal of Management and Decision Making, 11*(5–6), 358–378. https://doi.org/10.1504/IJMDM.2011.043409

Garcia, M. A., Lerma, M., Perez, M. G., Medina, K. S., Rodriguez-Crespo, A., & Cooper, T. V. (2023). Psychosocial and personality trait associates of phubbing and being phubbed in Hispanic emerging adult college students. *Current Psychology*, 1–14. https://doi-org.ezproxy.haifa.ac.il/10.1007/s12144-023-04767-y

Garcia, D., & Sikström, S. (2014). The dark side of Facebook: Semantic representations of status updates predict the Dark Triad of personality. *Personality and Individual Differences, 67*, 92–96. https://doi.org/10.1016/j.paid.2013.10.001

Garrido, E. C., Issa, T., Esteban, P. G., & Delgado, S. C. (2021). A descriptive litera-ture review of phubbing behaviors. *Heliyon* 7(5), e07037. https://doi.org/10.1016/j.heliyon.2021.e07037

Gavin, J., & Scott, A. J. (2019). Attributions of victim responsibility in revenge pornography. *Journal of Aggression, Conflict and Peace Research*, 11(4), 263–272. https://doi-org.ezproxy.haifa.ac.il/10.1108/JACPR-03-2019-0408

Geary, C., March, E., & Grieve, R. (2021). Insta-identity: Dark personality traits as predictors of authentic self-presentation on Instagram. *Telematics and Informatics*, 63, 101669. https://doi.org/10.1016/j.tele.2021.101669

Gibb, Z. G., & Devereux, P. G. (2014). Who does that anyway? Predictors and personality correlates of cyberbullying in college. *Computers in Human Behavior*, 38, 8–16. https://doi.org/10.1016/j.chb.2014.05.009

Giumetti, G. W., & Kowalski, R. M. (2022). Cyberbullying via social media and well-being. *Current Opinion in Psychology*, 45, 101314. https://doi.org/10.1016/j.copsyc.2022.101314

Giumetti, G. W., Kowalski, R. M., & Feinn, R. S. (2022). Predictors and out-comes of cyberbullying among college students: A two wave study. *Aggressive Behavior*, 48(1), 40–54. https://doi.org/10.1002/ab.21992

Giumetti, G. W., McKibben, E. S., Hatfield, A. L., Schroeder, A. N., & Kowalski, R. M. (2012). Cyber incivility @ work: The new age of interpersonal deviance. *Cyberpsychology, Behavior, and Social Networking*, 15, 148–154. https://doi.org/10.1089/cyber.2011.0336

Gnambs, T., & Appel, M. (2018). Narcissism and social networking behavior: A meta-analysis. *Journal of Personality*, 86(2), 200–212. https://doi-org.ezproxy.haifa.ac.il/10.1111/jopy.12305

Gonzalez, J. M., & Greitemeyer, T. (2018). The relationship between everyday sadism, violent video game play, and fascination with weapons. *Personality and Individual Differences*, 124, 51–53. https://doi.org/10.1016/j.paid.2017.11.045

Goodboy, A. K., & Martin, M. M. (2015). The personality profile of a cyberbully: Examining the Dark Triad. *Computers in Human Behavior*, 49, 1–4. https://doi.org/10.1016/j.chb.2015.02.052

GOV UK. (2015). Revenge porn. Retrieved from www.gov.uk/government/publications/revenge-porn

Greitemeyer, T. (2015). Everyday sadism predicts violent video game preferences. *Personality and Individual Differences*, 75, 19–23. https://doi-org.ezproxy.haifa.ac.il/10.1016/j.paid.2014.10

Greitemeyer, T., & Sagioglou, C. (2017). The longitudinal relationship between everyday sadism and the amount of violent video game play. *Personality and Individual Differences*, 104, 238–242. https://doi.org/10.1016/j.paid.2016.08.021

Grieve, R., Lang, C. P., & March, E. (2021). More than a preference for online social interaction: Vulnerable narcissism and phubbing. *Personality and Individual Differences*, 175, 110715. https://doi.org/10.1016/j.paid.2021.110715

Grieve, R., & March, E. (2021). "Just checking": Vulnerable and grandiose narcis-sism subtypes as predictors of phubbing. *Mobile Media & Communication*, 9(2), 195–209. https://doi.org/10.1177/2050157920942276

Grigg, D. W. (2010). Cyber-aggression: Definition and concept of cyberbullying. *Journal of Psychologists and Counsellors in Schools, 20*(2), 143–156. https://doi.org/10.1375/ajgc.20.2.143

Grijalva, E., & Harms, P. D. (2014). Narcissism: An integrative synthesis and dominance complementarity model. *The Academy of Management Perspectives, 28*(2), 108–127. http://dx.doi.org/10.5465/amp.2012.0048

Grubbs, J. B., Tahk, R., Fernandez, D. P., Fernandez, E. F., & Ley, D. (2023). Pornography and pride: Antagonism drives links between narcissism and perceived addiction to pornography. *Journal of Research in Personality* (2023), https://doi.org/10.1016/j.jrp.2023.104419

Gruda, D., McCleskey, J., & Khoury, I. (2023). Cause we are living in a Machiavellian world, and I am a Machiavellian major: Machiavellianism and academic major choice. *Personality and Individual Differences, 205*, 112096. https://doi.org/10.1016/j.paid.2023.112096

Gunasekara, P. B., & Senaratne, C. (March 2019). Psychopathy prediction and factorial classification on Twitter profiles. In *2019 IEEE 5th International Conference for Convergence in Technology (I2CT)* (pp. 1–3). IEEE.

Gylfason, H. F., Sveinsdottir, A. H., Vésteinsdóttir, V., & Sigurvinsdottir, R. (2021). Haters gonna hate, trolls gonna troll: The personality profile of a Facebook troll. *International Journal of Environmental Research and Public Health, 18*(11), 5722. https://doi.org/10.3390/ijerph18115722

Hacker. (January 28, 2023). In *Wikipedia*. Retrieved from https://en.wikipedia.org/wiki/Hacker

Hacktivism. (May 4, 2023). In *Wikipedia*. Retrieved from https://en.wikipedia.org/wiki/Hacktivism

Hamarta, E., Akat, M., & Akbulut, Ö. F. (2023). Dark Triad personality and online trolling: The mediating role of empathy. *European Journal of Psychology and Educational Research, 6*(1), 45–53. https://doi.org/10.12973/ejper.6.1.45

Hancock, J. T., Woodworth, M., & Boochever, R. (2018). Psychopaths online: The linguistic traces of psychopathy in email, text messaging and Facebook. *Media and Communication, 6*, 83–92. https://doi.org/10.17645/mac.v6i3.1499

Hand, C. J., Ingram, J., Glover, K., Brodie, Z. P., & Scott, G. G. (2022). Perceptions of female celebrity abuse on Twitter: Initial tweet valence, abuse volume, and observer Dark Tetrad characteristic effects. *Abuse Volume, and Observer Dark Tetrad Characteristic Effects*. https://ssrn-com.ezproxy.haifa.ac.il/abstract=4234899

Hand, C. J., & Scott, G. G. (2022). Beautiful victims: How the halo of attractiveness impacts judgments of celebrity and lay victims of online abuse. *Computers in Human Behavior*, 107157. https://doi.org/10.1016/j.chb.2021.107157

Hand, C. J., Scott, G. G., Brodie, Z. P., Ye, X., & Sereno, S. C. (2021). Tweet valence, volume of abuse, and observers' Dark Tetrad personality factors influence victim-blaming and the perceived severity of twitter cyberabuse. *Computers in Human Behavior Reports, 3*, 100056. https://doi.org/10.1016/j.chbr.2021.100056

Hanson, L., & Baker, D. L. (2017). "Corporate psychopaths" in public agencies? *Journal of Public Management & Social Policy, 24*(1), 21–41. https://digitalscholarship.tsu.edu/jpmsp/vol24/iss1/3

Hardaker, C. (2010). Trolling in asynchronous computer-mediated communication: From user discussions to academic definitions. *Journal of Politeness Research, 6*(2), 215–242. https://doi.org/10.1515/jplr.2010.011

Hare, R. D. (1999). *Without Conscience: The Disturbing World of the Psychopaths among Us.* New York, NY: Guilford Press.

Harewell, J. L., Pina, A., & Storey, J. E. (2021). Cyberstalking: Prevalence, characteristics, and impact. In Powell, A., Flynn, A., & Sugiura, L. (Eds.), *The Palgrave Handbook of Gendered Violence and Technology.* Cham: Palgrave Macmillan. https://doi.org/10.1007/978-3-030-83734-1_11

Harms, P. D., Marbut, A., Johnston, A. C., Lester, P., & Fezzey, T. (2022). Exposing the darkness within: A review of dark personality traits, models, and measures and their relationship to insider threats. *Journal of Information Security and Applications, 71*, 103378. https://doi.org/10.1016/j.jisa.2022.103378

Harper, C. A., Fido, D., & Petronzi, D. (2021). Delineating non-consensual sexual image offending: Towards an empirical approach. *Aggression and Violent Behavior, 58*, e101547. https://doi.org/10.1016/j.avb.2021.101547

Harper, C. A., Smith, L., Leach, J., Daruwala, N. A., & Fido, D. (2022). Development and validation of the beliefs about revenge pornography questionnaire. *Sexual Abuse.* https://doi.org/10.1177/10790632221082663

Harrison, A., Summers, J., & Mennecke, B. (2018). The effects of the Dark Triad on unethical behavior. *Journal of Business Ethics, 153*, 53–77. https://doi.org/10.1007/s10551-016-3368-3

Hassanein, M., Rady, S., Hussein, W., & Gharib, T. F. (2021). Predicting the Dark Triad for social network users using their personality characteristics. *International Journal for Computers & Their Applications, 28*(4), 204–211.

Hayes, N. L., Marsee, M. A., & Russell, D. W. (2020). Latent profile analysis of traditional and cyber-aggression and victimization: Associations with Dark Triad traits and psychopathology symptoms. *Journal of Psychopathology and Behavioral Assessment,* 1–14. https://doi.org/10.1007/s10862-020-09835-2

Hearn, J., & Hall, M. (2022). From physical violence to online violation: Forms, structures and effects: A comparison of the cases of "domestic violence" and "revenge pornography". *Aggression and Violent Behavior,* 101779. https://doi.org/10.1016/j.avb.2022.101779

Heatherington, W., & Coyne, I. (2014). Understanding individual experiences of cyberbullying encountered through work. *International Journal of Organizational Theory and Behavior, 17,* 163–192. https://doi.org/10.1108/IJOTB-17-02-2014-B002

Henle, C. A., & Blanchard, A. L. (2008). The interaction of work stressors and organizational sanctions on cyberloafing. *Journal of Managerial Issues, 20*(3), 383–400. www.jstor.org/stable/40604617

Herbst, T. (2014). *The Dark Side of Leadership: A Psycho-Spiritual Approach towards Understanding the Origins of Personality Dysfunctions: Derailment and the Restoration of Personality.* UK: Author House.

Hernández, M. P., Schoeps, K., Maganto, C., & Montoya-Castilla, I. (2021). The risk of sexual-erotic online behavior in adolescents – Which personality factors predict sexting and grooming victimization? *Computers in Human Behavior*, *114*, 106569. https://doi.org/10.1016/j.chb.2020.106569

Herron, M. M. (2021). Social media bullying in the workplace: Impacts on motivation, productivity, and workplace culture. In Ramos Salazar, L. (Ed.), *Handbook of Research on Cyberbullying and Online Harassment in the Workplace*, Chapter 4 (pp. 72–89). Hershey PA, USA: IGI Global.

Hertlein, K. M., & van Dyck, L. E. (2020). Predicting engagement in electronic surveillance in romantic relationships. *Cyberpsychology, Behavior, and Social Networking*, *23*(9), 604–610. https://doi.org/10.1089/cyber.2019.0424

Hillier, K., & Greig, C. (March 11, 2022). The art of the con: "Inventing Anna," "The Tinder Swindler" and gender. *The Conversation*. Retrieved from https://interaksyon.philstar.com/hobbies-interests/2022/03/11/212645/the-art-of-the-con-inventing-anna-the-tinder-swindler-and-gender/

Hogan, R., & Fico, J. M. (2011). Leadership. In Campbell, W. K., & Miller, J. D. (Eds.), *The Handbook of Narcissism and Narcissistic Personality Disorder: Theoretical Approaches, Empirical Findings, and Treatments* (pp. 393–402). New York: Wiley. https://doi.org/10.1002/9781118093108.ch35

Holt, T., Bossler, A., & Seigfried-Spellar, K. (2022). *Cybercrime and Digital Forensics: An Introduction* (3rd Edition). Abingdon: Routledge. http://ebookcentral.proquest.com/lib/ecu/detail.action?docID=6963530

Horowitz, M. (November 2021). Cybercrime predictions for 2022: Deepfakes, cryptocurrencies and misinformation. *Check Point® Software Technologies*. https://blog.checkpoint.com/2021/10/26/deepfakes-cryptocurrency-and-mobile-wallets-cybercriminals-find-new-opportunities-in-2022/

Hossain, M. A., Quaddus, M., Warren, M., Akter, S., & Pappas, I. (2022). Are you a cyberbully on social media? Exploring the personality traits using a fuzzy-set configurational approach. *International Journal of Information Management*, *66*. https://doi.org/10.1016/j.ijinfomgt.2022.102537

Hou, X., Ren, S., Rozgonjuk, D., Song, L., Xi, J., & Mõttus, R. (2023). The longitudinal association between narcissism and problematic social networking sites use: The roles of two social comparison orientations. *Addictive Behaviors*, 107786. https://doi.org/10.1016/j.addbeh.2023.107786

Hu, Y., Li, H., Yang, H., Sun, Y., Sun, L., & Wang, Z. (2019). Detecting stealthy attacks against industrial control systems based on residual skewness analysis. *EURASIP Journal on Wireless Communications and Networking*, *2019*(1), 1–14.

Huang, Y., Gan, X., Jin, X., Rao, S., Guo, B., He, Z., & Wei, Z. (2023). The relationship between the Dark Triad and bullying among Chinese adolescents: The role of social exclusion and sense of control. *Frontiers in Psychology*, *14*, 1173860. https://doi.org/10.3389/fpsyg.2023.1173860

Hughes, S., & Samuels, H. (2021). Dark desires: The Dark Tetrad and relationship control. *Personality and Individual Differences*, *171*, 110548. https://doi.org/10.1016/j.paid.2020.110548

Hussain, S. M., Sultan, S., Muniandy, V. D., & Haslindawati, N. (2022). An insight into the differences of psychological disparate motivations between hackers and crackers, *Journal of Correctional Issues*, *5*(1), 27–32. https://doi.org/10.52472/jci.v5i1.94

Hussain, Z., Griffiths, M. D., & Sheffield, D. (2017). An investigation into problematic smartphone use: The role of narcissism, anxiety, and personality factors. *Journal of Behavioral Addiction*, *6*(3), 378–386. https://doi.org/10.1556/2006.6.2017.052

Hussain, A., Khan, H., AJaml, I., & Akhtar, Y. (2023). Relationship of narcissism, Machiavellianism, and psychopathy personality traits with social media addiction among adults: Gender and marital status are in focus. *Journal of Social Sciences Review*, *3*(2), 1012–1021.

Hussain, Z., & Pontes, H. M. (2018). Personality, internet addiction, and other technological addictions: A psychological examination of personality traits and technological addictions. In Bozoglan, B. (Ed.), *Psychological, Social, and Cultural Aspects of Internet Addiction* (pp. 45–71). Hershey, PA: IGI Global:. https://doi.org/10.4018/978-1-5225-3477-8.ch003

Hussain, Z., & Pontes, H. M. (2019). Personality, internet addiction, and other technological addictions: An update of the research literature. In Bozoglan, B. (Ed.), *Multifaceted Approach to Digital Addiction and Its Treatment* (pp. 46–72). IGI Global. https://doi.org/10.4018/978-1-5225-8449-0.ch003

Hussain, Z., Wegmann, E., & Griffiths, M. D. (2021). The association between problematic social networking site use, Dark Triad traits, and emotion dysregulation. *BMC Psychology*, *9*, 160 (2021). https://doi.org/10.1186/s40359-021-00668-6

IC3. (2015). Internet crime complaint center: 2013 internet crime report. Accessed on August 9, 2016. Retrieved from www.ic3.gov/media/annualreport/2015_ic3report.pdf

Ibrahim, Y. (2010). Social Networking Sites (SNS) and the 'Narcissistic Turn': The politics of self-exposure. In *Social Computing: Concepts, Methodologies, Tools, and Applications* (pp. 1855–1868). IGI Global. https://doi.org/10.4018/978-1-60566-727-0.ch006

Iftikhar, M., & Tariq, S. (2014). Self-control, narcissistic tendencies and internet addiction among adolescents. *Journal of Arts & Social Sciences*, *1*(2), 37–52.

Ildirim, E. (2021). Personality factors predicting cyberbullying and online harassment. In Ramos Salazar, L. (Ed.), *Handbook of Research on Cyberbullying and Online Harassment in the Workplace*, Chapter 7 (pp. 130–152). Hershey PA, USA: IGI Global.

Insurance Fraud. (2022). Retrieved on February 1, 2022, from https://en.wikipedia.org/wiki/Insurance_fraud

Internet Live Stats. (2022). Internet users in the world. Retrieved from www.statista.com/statistics/273018/number-of-internet-users-worldwide/

Jabłońska, M. R., & Zajdel, R. (2020). The Dark Triad traits and problematic internet use: Their structure and relations. *Polish Sociological Review 212*(4), 477–495.

James, N. (2023, May 2). Cybersecurity Statistics 2023 [Updated]. *Astra*. Retrieved from www.getastra.com/blog/security-audit/cyber-security-statistics/

Jandaghi, G., Alvani, S. M., Matin, H. Z., & Kozekanan, S. F. (2015). Cyberloafing management in organizations. *Iranian Journal of Management Studies, 8*(3), 335–349. https://doi.org/10.22059/IJMS.2015.52634

Jauk, E., & Dieterich, R. (2019). Addiction and the dark triad of personality. *Frontiers in Psychiatry, 10,* 662. https://doi.org/10.3389/fpsyt.2019.00662

Jeffrey, C., Peltier, C., & Vannest, K. (2020). The effects of an online psychoeducational workshop to decrease anxiety and increase empowerment in victims of trolling and cyberbullying. *Journal of Online Learning Research, 6*(3), 265–296. Waynesville, NC USA: Association for the Advancement of Computing in Education (AACE). Retrieved on February 5, 2023, from www.learntechlib .org/primary/p/216915/

Jin, C. C., Wang, B. C., & Ji, A. T. (2019). The relationship between the Dark Triad and internet adaptation among adolescents in China: Internet use preference as a mediator. *Frontier Psychology, 10,* 2023. https://doi.org/10.3389/ fpsyg.2019.02023

Jin, C., Wang, B., Ji, A., & Zhao, B. (2022). Perceived parental monitoring and online deviant behavior among Chinese adolescents: A moderated mediation. *Journal of Child and Family Studies, 31*(10), 2825–2836. https://doi.org/10.1007/ s10826-022-02237-w

Johnson, L. K., Plouffe, R. A., & Saklofske, D. H. (2019). Subclinical sadism and the Dark Triad: Should there be a Dark Tetrad? *Journal of Individual Differences, 40*(3), 127–133. https://doi-org.ezproxy.haifa.ac.il/10.1027/1614-0001/a000284

Johnston J. E. (February 15, 2022). Think you couldn't be duped by a con artist? Think again. *Psychology Today.* Retrieved from www.psychologytoday.com/ intl/blog/the-human-equation/202202/think-you-couldnt-be-duped-con-artist-think-again

Jonason, P. K. (2014). Personality and politics. *Personality and Individual Differences, 71,* 181–184. https://doi.org/10.1016/j.paid.2014.08.002

Jonason, P., & Bulyk, R. (2019). Who uses Tinder? The Dark Triad traits, attachment, and mate value. *Studia Psychologica: Theoria et Praxis, 19*(1), 5–15. Retrieved from www.infona.pl/resource/bwmeta1.element.ojs-doi-10_21697_ sp_2019_19_1_01

Jonason, P. K., Kaźmierczak, I., Campos, A. C., & Davis, M. D. (2021). Leaving without a word: Ghosting and the Dark Triad traits. *Acta Psychologica, 220,* 103425. https://doi.org/10.1016/j.actpsy.2021.103425

Jonason, P. K., Li, N. P., Webster, G. D., & Schmitt, D. P. (2009). The Dark Triad: Facilitating a short-term mating strategy in men. *European Journal of Personality, 23*(1), 5–18. https://doi.org/10.1002/per.698

Jonason, P. K., Slomski, S., & Partyka, J. (2012). The Dark Triad at work: How toxic employees get their way. *Personality and Individual Differences, 52*(3), 449–453. https://doi.org/10.1016/j.paid.2011.11.008

Jones, D. N., & Figueredo, A. J. (2013). The core of darkness: Uncovering the heart of the Dark Triad. *European Journal of Personality, 27*(6), 521–531. https:// doi.org/10.1002/per.1893

Jones, D. N., Padilla, E., Curtis, S. R., & Kiekintveld, C. (2021). Network discovery and scanning strategies and the Dark Triad. *Computers in Human Behavior, 122*, 106799. https://doi.org/10.1016/j.chb.2021.106799

Jones, D. N., & Paulhus, D. L. (2010). Different provocations trigger aggression in narcissists and psychopaths. *Social Psychological and Personality Science, 1*, 12–18. http://dx.doi.org/10.1177/1948550609347591

Jones, D. N., & Paulus, D. L. (2009). Machiavellianism. In Leary, M. R., & Hoyle, R. H. (Eds.), *Individual Differences in Social Behavior* (pp. 93–108). New York, NY: Guilford Press.

Jones, D. N., & Paulhus, D. L. (2014). Introducing the short Dark Triad (SD3): A brief measure of dark personality traits. *Assessment, 21*(1), 28–41. https://doi.org/10.1177/1073191113514105

Jung, Y. E., Leventhal, B., Kim, Y. S., Park, T. W., Lee, S. H., Lee, M., ... & Park, J. I. (2014). Cyberbullying, problematic internet use, and psychopathologic symptoms among Korean youth. *Yonsei Medical Journal, 55*(3), 826–830. https://doi.org/10.3349/ymj.2014.55.3.826

Kalaitzaki, A., Laconi, S., Spritzer, D. T., Hauck, S., Gnisci, A., Sergi, I., ... & Sahlan, R. N. (2022). The prevalence and predictors of problematic mobile phone use: A 14-country empirical survey. *International Journal of Mental Health and Addiction*, 1–20. https://doi-org.ezproxy.haifa.ac.il/10.1007/s11469-022-00901-2

Kallis, R. B., & Meluch, A. L. (2021). Workplace cyberbullying and online harassment as an organizational threat: Exploring the negative organizational outcomes. In Ramos Salazar, L. (Ed.), *Handbook of Research on Cyberbullying and Online Harassment in the Workplace*, Chapter 9 (pp. 176–196). Hershey PA, USA: IGI Global.

Kanbur., E., & Kanbur. A. (2021). Phubbing at workplace. In Bingol, U. (Ed.), *Trending Topics on Social Media Researchers*, Section 2 (pp. 147–160). Berlin: Peter Lang Gmbh.

Kapidzic, S. (2013). Narcissism as a predictor of motivations behind Facebook profile picture selection. *Cyberpsychology, Behavior, and Social Networking, 16*(1), 14–19. https://doi.org/10.1089/cyber.2012.0143

Karasavva, V., Brunet, L., Smodis, A., Swanek, J., & Forth, A. (2023b). Putting the Y in cyberflashing: Exploring the prevalence and predictors of the reasons for sending unsolicited nude or sexual images. *Computers in Human Behavior, 140*, 107593. https://doi.org/10.1016/j.chb.2022.107593

Karasavva, V., & Forth, A. (2022). Personality, attitudinal, and demographic predictors of non-consensual dissemination of intimate images. *Journal of Interpersonal Violence, 37*(21–22), NP19265–NP19289. https://doi-org.ezproxy.haifa.ac.il/10.1177/08862605211043586

Karasavva, V., Swanek, J., Smodis, A., & Forth, A. (2023a). From myth to reality: Sexual image abuse myth acceptance, the Dark Tetrad, and non-consensual intimate image dissemination proclivity. *Journal of Sexual Aggression, 29*(1), 51–67. https://doi-org.ezproxy.haifa.ac.il/10.1080/13552600.2022.2032430

Karlsson, A. M. C., & Kajonius, P. J. (2020). Not only Trolls are Trolling the Internet: A study on dark personality traits, online environment, and commentary styles. *International Journal of Personality Psychology*, *6*, 12–23. https://doi.org/10.21827/ijpp.6.37214

Karthikeyan, C. (2020). Workplace cyberbullying and its impact on productivity, In Ramos Salazar, L. (Ed.), *Handbook of Research on Cyberbullying and Online Harassment in the Workplace*, Chapter 10 (pp. 197–214). Hershey PA, USA: IGI Global.

Karthikeyan, C. (2022). Workplace cyberbullying in organizations with criminal intent and subtle means: A very pleasant and safe organization culture brings in a better work culture in an organization. In *Handbook of Research on Digital Violence and Discrimination Studies* (pp. 568–588). IGI Global. https://doi.org/10.4018/978-1-7998-9187-1.ch025

Kasper, T. E., Short, M. B., & Milam, A. C. (2015). Narcissism and Internet pornography use. *Journal of Sex & Marital Therapy*, *41*(5), 481–486. https://doi.org/10.1080/0092623X.2014.931313

Katagelasticism. (2023, May 9). In *Wikipedia*. https://en.wikipedia.org/wiki/Katagelasticism

Kemp, S. (2023). Facebook statistics and trends. *DataReportal*. Retrieved from https://datareportal.com/essential-facebook-stats

Keskin, H., Akgün, A. E., Ayar, H., & Kayman, Ş. S. (2016). Cyberbullying victimization, counterproductive work behaviours and emotional intelligence at workplace. *Procedia-Social and Behavioral Sciences*, *235*, 281–287. https://doi.org/10.1016/j.sbspro.2016.11.031

Kim, J. H., & Kim, Y. (2019). Instagram user characteristics and the color of their photos: Colorfulness, color diversity, and color harmony. *Information Processing & Management*, *56*(4), 1494–1505. https://doi.org/10.1016/j.ipm.2018.10.018

King, Z., Henshel, D., Flora, L., Cains, M. G., Hoffman, B., & Sample, C. (2018). Characterizing and measuring maliciousness for cybersecurity risk assessment. *Frontiers in Psychology*, *9*(39). https://doi.org/10.3389/fpsyg.2018.00039

Kircaburun, K., Demetrovics, Z., & Tosuntaş, Ş. B. (2019). Analyzing the links between problematic social media use, Dark Triad traits, and self-esteem. *International Journal of Mental Health Addiction*, *17*, 1496–1507. https://doi.org/10.1007/s11469-018-9900-1

Kircaburun, K., & Griffiths, M. D. (2018). The dark side of internet: Preliminary evidence for the associations of dark personality traits with specific online activities and problematic internet use. *Journal of Behavioral Addictions*, *7*(4), 993–1003. https://doi.org/10.1556/2006.7.2018.109

Kircaburun, K., Jonason, P. K., & Griffiths, M. D. (2018a). The Dark Tetrad traits and problematic social media use: The mediating role of cyberbullying and cyberstalking. *Personality and Individual Differences*, *135*, 264–269.

Kircaburun, K., Jonason, P. K., & Griffiths, M. D. (2018b). The Dark Tetrad traits and problematic online gaming: The mediating role of online gaming motives and moderating role of game types. *Personality and Individual Differences*, *135*, 298–303. https://doi-org.ezproxy.haifa.ac.il/10.1016/j.paid.2018.07.038

Kircaburun, K., March, E., Balta, S., Emirtekin, E., Kışla, T., & Griffiths, M. D. (2022). The role of procrastination between personality traits and addictive mukbang watching among emerging adults. *SAGE Open*, *12*(1). https://doi.org/10.1177/21582440221085006

Kiziloglu, M., Dluhopolskyi, O., Koziuk, V., Vitvitskyi, S., & Kozlovskyi, S. (2021). Dark personality traits and job performance of employees: The mediating role of perfectionism, stress, and social media addiction. *Problems and Perspectives in Sinderman*, *19*(3), 533–544.

Koban, K., Stein, J. P., Eckhardt, V., & Ohler, P. (2018). Quid pro quo in Web 2.0. Connecting personality traits and Facebook usage intensity to uncivil commenting intentions in public online discussions. *Computers in Human Behavior*, *79*, 9–18. https://doi.org/10.1016/j.chb.2017.10.015

Kong, F., Wang, M., Zhang, X., Li, X., & Sun, X. (2021). Vulnerable narcissism in social networking sites: The role of upward and downward social comparisons. *Frontiers in Psychology*, 3921. https://doi.org/10.3389/fpsyg.2021.711909

Kowalski, C. M., Rogoza, R., Saklofske, D. H., & Schermer, J. A. (2021). Dark Triads, tetrads, tents, and cores: Why navigate (research) the jungle of dark personality models without a compass (criterion)? *Acta Psychologica*, *221*, 103455. https://doi.org/10.1016/j.actpsy.2021.103455

Kowalski., R. M., & Robbins, C. E. (2021). The meaning, prevalence, and outcomes of cyberbullying in the workplace. In Ramos Salazar, L. (Ed.), *Handbook of Research on Cyberbullying and Online Harassment in the Workplace*, Chapter 1 (pp. 1–22). Hershey PA, USA: IGI Global.

KPMG. (2013). *Global profiles of the fraudster: White-collar crime-present and future*. Retrieved from www.kpmg.com/Global/en/IssuesAndInsights/ArticlesPublications/global-profilesof-the-fraudster/Documents/global-profiles-of-the-fraudster-v3.pdf

Kramer, B. K. P., & Seda, M. A. (2017). What in the world were you thinking?! Inside the mindset of fraud perpetrators. *International Journal of Psychology Research*, *12*(3), 229–269.

Kristinsdottir, K. H., Gylfason, H. F., & Sigurvinsdottir, R. (2021). Narcissism and social media: The role of communal narcissism. *International Journal of Environmental Research and Public Health*, *18*(19), 10106. MDPI AG. Retrieved from http://dx.doi.org/10.3390/ijerph181910106

Kumpasoğlu, G. B., Eltan, S., Merdan-Yıldız, E. D., & Batıgün, A. D. (2021). Mediating role of life satisfaction and death anxiety in the relationship between Dark Triad and social media addiction. *Personality and Individual Differences*, *172*, 1–8, 110606.

Kurek, A., Jose, P. E., & Stuart, J. (2019). 'I did it for the LULZ': How the dark personality predicts online disinhibition and aggressive online behavior in adolescence. *Computers in Human Behavior*, *98*, 31–40. https://doi.org/10.1016/j.chb.2019.03.027

Laakasuo, M., Repo, M., Drosinou, M., Berg, A., Kunnari, A., Koverola, M., … & Sundvall, J. (2021). The dark path to eternal life: Machiavellianism predicts approval of mind upload technology. *Personality and Individual Differences*, *177*, 110731. https://doi.org/10.1016/j.paid.2021.110731

Lai, K., Jing, G., Zhao, J., & Xiong, X. (2023). How Dark Triad influences rumors spreading on social media? Mediating role of declining third-person effect. *Current Psychology*, 1–7.

Lamphere, R. D., & Lucas, K. T. (2019). Online romance in the 21st century: Deceptive online dating, catfishing, romance scams, and "mail order" marriages. In Chiluwa, I. E., & Samoilenko, S. A. (Eds.), *Deception, Fake News, and Misinformation Online* (pp. 475–488). Hershey: IGI Global.

Lancaster, M., Seibert, G. S., Cooper, A. N., May, R. W., & Fincham, F. (2019). Relationship quality in the context of cyber dating abuse: The role of attachment. *Journal of Family Issues*, *41*(6), 739–758. https://doi.org/10.1177/01925 13X19881674

Lauder, C., & March, E. (2023). Catching the catfish: Exploring gender and the Dark Tetrad as predictors of catfishing perpetration. *Computers in Human Behavior*, 107599. https://doi.org/10.1016/j.chb.2022.107599

Lazic, M. (2022). Shocking Insurance Fraud Statistics for 2022. *LegalJobs*. Retrieved from https://legaljobs.io/blog/insurance-fraud-statistics/

Lee, K., Ashton, M. C., Wiltshire, J., Bourdage, J. S., Visser, B. A., & Gallucci, A. (2013). Sex, power, and money: Prediction from the Dark Triad and honesty–humility. *European Journal of Personality*, *27*(2), 169–184. https://doi .org/10.1002/per.1860

Lee, B., & Paek, S. Y. (2020). Phishing and financial manipulation. In Holt, T., & Bossler, A. (Eds.), *The Palgrave Handbook of International Cybercrime and Cyberdeviance*. Cham: Palgrave Macmillan. https://doi .org/10.1007/978-3-319-78440-3_43

Lee, S. L. (2019). Predicting SNS addiction with the Big Five and the Dark Triad. *Cyberpsychology: Journal of Psychosocial Research on Cyberspace*, *13*(1). http:// dx.doi.org/10.5817/CP2019-1-3

Lee, S. L., & Lim, S. X. (2020). Predicting internet addiction with the Dark Triad: Beyond the five-factor model. *Psychology of Popular Media*. https://doi .org/10.1037/ppm0000336

Lee, S. L., Tan, Y. E., Tam, C. L., & Ahn, J. (2022). The facilitative effect of impulsiveness on the Dark Triad and social network sites addiction: The Dark Triad, impulsiveness, SNS addiction. *International Journal of Technology and Human Interaction (IJTHI)*, *18*(1), 1–15. https://doi .org/10.4018/IJTHI.297612

Lee, S. Y., Yao, M. Z., & Su, L. Y. F. (2021). Expressing unpopular opinion or trolling: Can dark personalities differentiate them? *Telematics and Informatics*, *63*, 101645. https://doi.org/10.1016/j.tele.2021.101645

Leite, Â., Cardoso, S., & Monteiro, A. P. (2023). Dark personality traits and online behaviors: Portuguese versions of cyberstalking, online harassment, flaming and trolling scales. *International Journal of Environmental Research and Public Health*, *20*(12), 6136. https://doi.org/10.3390/ijerph20126136

Li, W., Bizumic, B., Sivanathan, D., & Chen, J. (2022). Vulnerable and grandiose narcissism differentially predict phubbing via social anxiety and problematic social media use. *SSRN*. https://ssrn.com/abstract=4225316 or http://cx.doi.org/10.2139/ssrn.4225316

Lim, V. K. G. (2002). The IT way of loafing on the job – Cyberloafing, neutralizing and organizational justice. *Journal of Organizational Behavior*, *23*(5), 675–694. https://doi.org/10.1002/job.161

Lim, V. K., & Teo, T. S. (2022). Cyberloafing: A review and research agenda. *Applied Psychology*. https://doi-org.ezproxy.haifa.ac.il/10.1111/apps.12452

Linares, R., Aranda, M., García-Domingo, M., Amezcua, T., Fuentes, V., & Moreno-Padilla, M. (2021). Cyber-dating abuse in young adult couples: Relations with sexist attitudes and violence justification, smartphone usage and impulsivity. *PLoS One*, *16*(6), e0253180. https://doi.org/10.1371/journal.pone.0253180

Liu, A., Zhang, E., Leroux, E. J., & Benassi, P. (2022). Sexual sadism disorder and coercive paraphilic disorder: A scoping review. *The Journal of Sexual Medicine*, *19*(3), 496–506. https://doi-org.ezproxy.haifa.ac.il/10.1016/j.jsxm.2022.01.002

Liu, Y., & Zheng, L. (2020). Relationships between the Big Five, narcissistic personality traits, and online sexual activities. *Personality and Individual Differences*, *152*, 109593. https://doi.org/10.1016/j.paid.2019.109593

Liu, Y., Zhou, B., Ouyang, Y., Yang, B., & Xie, Q. (2023). Development and validation of Chinese form Short Dark Tetrad (C-SD4). *Heliyon*. https://doi.org/10.1016/j.heliyon.2023.e12929

Ljepava, N., Orr, R. R., Locke, S., & Ross, C. (2013). Personality and social characteristics of Facebook non-users and frequent users. *Computers in Human Behavior*, *29*(4), 1602–1607. https://doi.org/10.1016/j.chb.2013.01.026

Logic Bomb. (February 13, 2023). In *Wikipedia*. Retrieved from https://en.wikipedia.org/wiki/Logic_bomb

Lopes, B., & Yu, H. (2017). Who do you troll and Why: An investigation into the relationship between the Dark Triad Personalities and online trolling behaviours towards popular and less popular Facebook profiles. *Computers in Human Behavior*, *77*, 69–76. https://doi.org/10.1016/j.chb.2017.08.036

Lowe-Calverley, E., & Grieve, R. (2017). Web of deceit: Relationships between the Dark Triad, perceived ability to deceive and cyberloafing. *Cyberpsychology: Journal of Psychosocial Research on Cyberspace*, *11*(2). https://doi.org/10.5817/CP2017-2-5

Lykken, D. T. (1995). *The Antisocial Personalities*. Hillsdale, NJ: Erlbaum. https://doi.org/10.4324/9780203763551

Lyons, M., Gillies, N., & Brewer, G. (2019). Dark Triad traits, Facebook intensity, and intrasexual competition. *Personality and Individual Differences*, *141*, 157–159. https://doi.org/10.1016/j.paid.2019.01.012

Lyons, M., Messenger, A., Perry, R., & Brewer, G. (2020). The Dark Tetrad in Tinder®: Hook-up app for high psychopathy individuals, and a diverse utilitarian tool for Machiavellians? *Current Psychology*, *41*, 659–666. https://doi.org/10.1007/s12144-019-00589-z

Lyons, M., Messenger, A., Perry, R., & Brewer, M. (2022a). The Dark Tetrad in Tinder: hook-up app for high psychopathy individuals, and a diverse

utilitarian tool for Machiavellians? *Current Psychology, 41,* 659–666. https://doi
.org/10.1007/s12144-019-00589-z

Lyons, M., Rowe, A., Waddington, R., & Brewer, G. (2022b). Situational
and dispositional factors in rape cognitions: The roles of social media and
the Dark Triad traits. *Journal of Interpersonal Violence, 37*(11–12), https://doi
.org/10.1177/0886260520985499

Maasberg, M., Van Slyke, C., Ellis, S., & Beebe, N. (2020). The Dark Triad and
insider threats in cyber security. *Communications of the ACM, 63*(12), 64–80.
https://doi.org/10.1145/3408864

Maasberg, M., Warren, J., & Beebe, N. L. (January 2015). The dark side of the
insider: Detecting the insider threat through examination of Dark Triad personality traits. In *2015 48th Hawaii International Conference on System Sciences*
(pp. 3518–3526). IEEE.

Madan, A. O. (2014). Cyber aggression/cyber bullying and the Dark Triad: Effect
on workplace behavior/performance. *International Journal of Computer and
Systems Engineering, 8*(6), 1740–1745. https://waset.org/publications/9998533/
cyber-aggression-cyber-bullyingand-the-dark-triad-effect-on-workplace-
behavior-performance

Maftei, A., Holman, A. C., & Merlici, I. A. (2022). Using fake news as means
of cyber-bullying: The link with compulsive internet use and online moral
disengagement. *Computers in Human Behavior, 127,* 107032. https://doi
.org/10.1016/j.chb.2021.107032

Maimon, D., Babko-Malaya, O., Cathey, R., & Hinton, S. (November 2017).
Re-Thinking Online Offenders' SKRAM: Individual Traits and Situational
Motivations as Additional Risk Factors for Predicting Cyber Attacks. In *2017 IEEE
15th Intl Conf on Dependable, Autonomic and Secure Computing, 15th Intl Conf on
Pervasive Intelligence and Computing, 3rd Intl Conf on Big Data Intelligence and
Computing and Cyber Science and Technology Congress (DASC/PiCom/DataCom/
CyberSciTech)* (pp. 232–238). IEEE.

Mantilla, K. (2013). Gendertrolling: Misogyny adapts to new media. *Feminist
Studies, 39*(2), 563–570. https://doi.org/10.1353/fem.2013.0039

Manuoğlu, E., & Öner-Özkan, B. (2022). Sarcastic and deviant trolling in
Turkey: Associations with Dark Triad and aggression. *Social Media + Society,
8*(3). https://doi.org/10.1177/20563051221126053

Maple, C., Short, E., & Brown, A. (2011). *Cyberstalking in the United Kingdom:
An Analysis of the ECHO Pilot Survey.* National Centre for Cyberstalking
Research, University of Bedfordshire. Retrieved from https://paladinservice
.co.uk/wp-content/uploads/2013/12/ECHO_Pilot_Final-Cyberstalking-in-the-
UK-University-of-Bedfordshire.pdf

Marbut, A. R., & Harms, P. D. (2023). Fiends and fools: A narrative review and
neo-socioanalytic perspective on personality and insider threats. *Journal of
Business and Psychology,* 1–18. https://doi.org/10.1007/s10869-023-09885-9

March, E. (2019). Psychopathy, sadism, empathy, and the motivation to cause harm:
New evidence confirms malevolent nature of the Internet Troll. *Personality and
Individual Differences, 141,* 133–137. https://doi.org/10.1016/j.paid.2019.01.001

March, E. (2022). Psychopathy: Cybercrime and cyber abuse. In Marques, P. B., Paulino, P., & Alho, L. (Eds.), *Psychopathy and Criminal Behavior* (pp. 423–444). Academic Press. https://doi.org/10.1016/B978-0-12-811419-3.00015-7

March, E., Grieve, R., Clancy, E., Klettke, B., van Dick, R., & Hernandez Bark, A. S. (2021b). The role of individual differences in cyber dating abuse perpetration. *Cyberpsychology, Behavior, and Social Networking*, 24(7), 457–463. https://doi.org/10.1089/cyber.2020.0687

March, E., Grieve, R., Marrington, J., & Jonason, P. K. (2017). Trolling on Tinder (and other dating apps): Examining the role of the Dark Tetrad and impulsivity. *Personality and Individual Differences*, 110, 139–143. https://doi.org/10.1016/j.paid.2017.01.025

March, E., Grieve, R., Wagstaff, D., & Slocum, A. (2020a). Exploring anger as a moderator of narcissism and antisocial behaviour on tinder. *Personality and Individual Differences*, 161, 109961. https://doi.org/10.1016/j.paid.2020.109961

March, E., Litten, V., Sullivan, D. H., & Ward, L. (2020b). Somebody that I (used to) know: Gender and dimensions of dark personality traits as predictors of intimate partner cyberstalking. *Personality and Individual Differences*, 163, 110084. https://doi.org/10.1016/j.paid.2020.110084

March, E., Marrington, J. Z. (2021). Antisocial and Prosocial online behaviour: Exploring the roles of the Dark and Light Triads. *Current Psychology*. https://doi.org/10.1007/s12144-021-01552-7

March, E., & Marrington, J. Z. (2023). Antisocial and Prosocial online behaviour: Exploring the roles of the Dark and Light Triads. *Current Psychology*, 42(2), 1390–1393. https://doi.org/10.1007/s12144-021-01552-7

March, E., McDonald, L., & Forsyth, L. (2023). Personality and internet trolling: A validation study of a representative sample. *Current Psychology*, 1–4. https://doi.org/10.1007/s12144-023-04586-1

March, E., & Steele, G. (2020). High esteem and hurting others online: Trait sadism moderates the relationship between self-esteem and internet trolling. *Cyberpsychology, Behavior, and Social Networking*, 23(7), 441–446. https://doi.org/10.1089/cyber.2019.0652

March, E., Szymczak, P., Di Rago, M., & Jonason, P. K. (2022). Passive, invasive, and duplicitous: Three forms of intimate partner cyberstalking. *Personality and Individual Differences*, 189, 111502. https://doi.org/10.1016/j.paid.2022.111502

March, E., Szymczak, P., Smoker, M., & Jonason, P. K. (2021a). Who cyberstalked their sexual and romantic partners? Sex differences, dark personality traits, and fundamental social motives. *Current Psychology*, 1–4. https://doi.org/10.1007/s12144-021-02174-9

March, E., & Wagstaff, D. L. (2017). Sending nudes: Sex, self-rated mate value, and trait Machiavellianism predict sending unsolicited explicit images. *Frontiers in Psychology*, 8, 1–6. 2210. https://doi.org/10.3389/fpsyg.2017.02210

Marengo, D., & Settanni, M. (2023). Mining Facebook data for personality prediction: An overview. In Montag, C., & Baumeister, H. (Eds.), *Digital Phenotyping and Mobile Sensing: Studies in Neuroscience, Psychology and Behavioral Economics*. Cham: Springer. https://doi-org.ezproxy.haifa.ac.il/10.1007/978-3-030-98546-2_8

Marrington, J. Z., March, E., Murray, S., Jeffries, C., Machin, T., & March, S. (2023). An exploration of trolling behaviours in Australian adolescents: An online survey. *PLoS One, 18*(4), e0284378. https://doi.org/10.1371/journal .pone.0284378

Marshall, T. C., Lefringhausen, K., & Ferenczi, N. (2015). The Big Five, self-esteem, and narcissism as predictors of the topics people write about in Facebook status updates. *Personality and Individual Differences, 85,* 35–40. https://doi.org/10.1016/j.paid.2015.04.039

Martin, B. A., Chrysochou, P., Strong, C., Wang, D., & Yao, J. (2022). Dark personalities and Bitcoin®: The influence of the Dark Tetrad on cryptocurrency attitude and buying intention. *Personality and Individual Differences, 188,* 111453. https://doi.org/10.1016/j.paid.2021.111453

Masui, K. (2019). Loneliness moderates the relationship between Dark Tetrad personality traits and internet trolling. *Personality and Individual Differences, 150,* 109475. https://doi.org/10.1016/j.paid.2019.06.018

Matulessy, A., & Humaira, N. H. (2016). Hacker personality profiles reviewed in terms of the big five personality traits. *Psychology and Behavioral Sciences, 5*(6), 137–142. www.sciencepublishinggroup.com/j/pbs

Mayshak, R., Howard, D., Benstead, M., Klas, A., Skvarc, D., Harries, T., ... & Hyder, S. (2023). Dating in the dark: A qualitative examination of dating experiences in Dark Tetrad personalities. *Computers in Human Behavior, 143,* 107680. https://doi-org.ezproxy.haifa.ac.il/10.1016/j.chb.2023.107680

Mayshak, R., King, R. M., Chandler, B., & Hannah, M. (2020). To swipe or not to swipe: The Dark Tetrad and risks associated with mobile dating app use. *Personality and Individual Differences, 163,* 110099. https://doi.org/10.1016/j .paid.2020.110099

McCain, J. L., & Campbell, W. K. (2018). Narcissism and social media use: A meta-analytic review. *Psychology of Popular Media Culture, 7*(3), 308–327. http:// dx.doi.org/10.1037/ppm0000137

McKenna, F. (2020). Professional refunders are fraud hitmen for hire. [Blog post]. May 26. Retrieved from https://frankonfraud.com/fraud-trends/ professional-refunders-are-friendly-fraud-hitmen-for-hire/

Mckinlay, T., & Lavis, T. (2020). Why did she send it in the first place? Victim blame in the context of "revenge porn." *Psychiatry, Psychology and Law, 27*(3), 1–11. https://doi.org/10.1080/13218719.2020.1734977

McHoskey, J. W., Worzel, W., & Szyarto, C. (1998). Machiavellianism and psychopathy. *Journal of Personality and Social Psychology, 74*(1), 192–210. https:// doi.org/10.1037/0022-3514.74.1.192

McEwan, T. (2014, February). Personality differences: trolls and cyberstalkers aren't the same. *The Conversation.* Retrieved from https://theconversation.com/ personality-differences-trolls-and-cyberstalkers-arent-the-same-23309

Međedović, J., & Petrović, B. (2015). The Dark Tetrad: Structural properties and location in the personality space. *Journal of Individual Differences, 36*(4), 228–236. https://doi.org/10.1027/1614-0001/a000179

Mehdizadeh, S. (2010). Self-presentation 2.0: Narcissism and self-esteem on Facebook. *Cyberpsychology, Behavior, and Social Networking, 13*(4), 357–364. https://doi.org/10.1089=cyber.2009.0257

Meloy, J. R. (1998). *The Psychology of Stalking: Clinical and Forensic Perspectives*. San Diego, CA: Academic Press.

Ménard, K. S., & Pincus, A. L. (2012). Predicting overt and cyber stalking perpetration by male and female college students. *Journal of Interpersonal Violence, 27*(11), 2183–2207. https://doi.org/10.1177/0886260511432144

Menzel, J., Meier, M., & Maier, C. (January 2023). Online gaming and personality: Explaining gamers' cheating intention. In *Proceedings of the 56th Hawaii International Conference on System Sciences* (pp. 2346–2355). Retrieved from https://hdl.handle.net/10125/102921

Miech, K. (July 2022). Definition of cyberloafing – How much does it cost the employer? *Unrubble*. Retrieved from https://unrubble.com/Blog/definition-of-cyberloafing-how-much-does-it-cost-the-employer

Mihelič, K. K., Lim, V. K. G., & Culiberg, B. (2022). Cyberloafing among Gen Z students: The role of norms, moral disengagement, multitasking self-efficacy, and psychological outcomes. *European Journal of Psychology of Education*, 1–19. https://doi-org.ezproxy.haifa.ac.l/10 1007/s10212-022-00617-w

Millon, T. (2011). *Disorders of Personality: Introducing a DSM/ICD Spectrum from Normal to Abnormal*. 3rd ed. Hoboken, NJ: Wiley.

Millon, T., & Grossman, S. D. (2004). Personology: A theory based on evolutionary concepts. In Lenzenweger, M. F., & Clarkin, J. F. (Eds.), *Major Theories of Personality Disorder* (pp. 332–390). New York: Guilford Press.

Min, H., Pavisic, I., Howald, N., Highhouse, S., & Zickar, M. J. (2019). A systematic comparison of three sadism measures and their ability to explain workplace mistreatment over and above the Dark Triad. *Journal of Research in Personality, 82*, 103862. https://doi.org/10.1016/j.jrp.2019.103862

Miran, A., Yaseen, F., & Jabeen, S. (2023). Psychopathy and cyberbullying: The role of self-control as moderator among problematic smartphone users. *Gomal University Journal of Research, 39*(1), 69–79.

Modic, D., Palomäki, J., Drosinou, M., & Laakasuo, M. (2018). The Dark Triad and willingness to commit insurance fraud. *Cogent Psychology, 5*(:), 1469579. https://doi.org/10.1080/23311908.2018.1469579

Monacis, L., Griffiths, M. D., Limone, P., Sinatra, M., & Servidio, R. (2020). Selfitis behavior: Assessing the Italian version of the selfitis behavior scale and its mediating role in the relationship of dark traits with social media addiction. *International Journal of Environmental Research and Public Health, 17*(16), 5738, 1–17. https://doi.org/10.3390/ijerph17165738

Moody, G. D., Galletta, D. F., & Dunn, B. K. (2017). Which phish get caught? An exploratory study of individuals' susceptibility to phishing. *European Journal of Information Systems, 26*(6), 564–584. https://doi.org/10.1057/s41303-017-0058-x

Moor, L., & Anderson, J. R. (2019). A systematic literature review of the relationship between dark personality traits and antisocial online behaviours. *Personality and Individual Differences, 144*, 40–55. https://doi.org/10.1016/j.paid.2019.02.027

Morelli, M., Urbini, F., Bianchi, D., Baiocco, R., Cattelino, E., Laghi, F., … & Chirumbolo, A. (2021). The relationship between Dark Triad personality traits and sexting behaviors among adolescents and young adults across 11 countries. *International Journal of Environmental Research and Public Health, 18*(5), 2526. https://doi.org/10.3390/ijerph18052526

Mosley, M. A., Lancaster, M., Parker, M. L., & Campbell, K. (2020). Adult attachment and online dating deception: A theory modernized. *Sexual and Relationship Therapy, 35*(2), 227–243. https://doi.org/10.1080/14681994.2020.1714577

Muris, P., Merckelbach, H., Otgaar, H., & Meijer, E. (2017). The malevolent side of human nature: A meta-analysis and critical review of the literature on the Dark Triad (narcissism, Machiavellianism, and psychopathy). *Perspectives on Psychological Science, 12*(2), 183–204. https://doi.org/10.1177/1745691616666070

Muris, P., Otgaar, H., Meesters, C., Papasileka, E., & Pineda, D. (2020). The Dark Triad and honesty-humility: A preliminary study on the relations to pornography use. *Dignity: A Journal on Sexual Exploitation and Violence, 5*(1). https://doi.org/10.23860/dignity.2020.05.01.03

Musetti, A., Grazia, V., Alessandra, A., Franceschini, C., Corsano, P., & Marino, C. (2022). Vulnerable narcissism and problematic social networking sites use: Focusing the lens on specific motivations for social networking sites use. *Healthcare, 10*(9), 1719. MDPI AG. http://dx.doi.org/10.3390/healthcare10091719

Myers, S. (2006). Introduction to phishing. In Jakobsson, M., & Myers, S. (Eds.), *Phishing and Countermeasures: Understanding the Increasing Problem of Electronic Identity Theft*. Hoboken: Wiley.

Nadkarni, A., & Hofmann, S. G. (2012). Why do people use Facebook? *Personality and Individual Differences, 52*(3), 243–249. https://doi.org/10.1016/j.paid.2011.11.007

Naidu, S., Chand, A., Pandaram, A., & Patel, A. (2023). Problematic internet and social network site use in young adults: The role of emotional intelligence and fear of negative evaluation. *Personality and Individual Differences, 200*, 111915. https://doi.org/10.1016/j.paid.2022.111915

Navarro, R., Larrañaga, E., Yubero, S., & Villora, B. (2020). Ghosting and breadcrumbing: Prevalence and association with online dating behavior among young adults. *Escritos de Psicología-Psychological Writings, 13*(2), 46–59. https://doi.org/102431o/espsiescpsi.v13i2.9960

Navarro-Carrillo, G., Torres-Marín, J., & Carretero-Dios, H. (2021). Do trolls just want to have fun? Assessing the role of humor-related traits in online trolling behavior. *Computers in Human Behavior, 114*, 106551–48. https://doi.org/10.1016/j.chb.2020.106551

Necula, C. N. (2020). The relation between the Dark Triad and social media addiction, with the moderating role of social anxiety in young people. *Journal of Experiential Psychotherapy/Revista de PSIHOterapie Experientiala*, *23*(3), 47–59.

Nicol, S. (2012). Cyber-bullying and trolling. *Youth Studies Australia*, *31*, 3–4. Retrieved from http://journals.sfu.ca/ysa/index.php/YSA/article/viewFile/78r/98

Nikbin, D., Taghizadeh, S. K., & Rahman, S. A. (2022). Linking Dark Triad traits to Instagram addiction: The mediating role of motives. *Technology in Society*, *68*, 1–10. https://doi.org/10.1016/j.techsoc.2022.101892

Nitschinsk, L., Tobin, S. J., & Vanman, E. J. (2022). The Dark Triad and online self-presentation styles and beliefs. *Personality and Individual Differences*, *194*, 111641. https://doi.org/10.1016/j.paid.2022.111641

Nividita, J. (April 5, 2023). 90+ Cyber crime statistics 2023: Cost, industries & trends. *Astra*. Retrieved from www.getastra.com/blog/security-audit/cyber-crime-statistics/

Noakes, T., & Noakes, T. (2021). Distinguishing online academic bullying: Identifying new forms of harassment in a dissenting Emeritus Professor's case. *Heliyon*, *7*(2), e06326. https://doi.org/10.1016/j.heliyon.2021.e06326

Nocera, T. R., & Dahlen, E. R. (2017). Dark personality traits in cyber aggression among college students. In *63rd Annual Convention of the Southeastern Psychological Association*, Atlanta, GA.

Nocera, T. R., & Dahlen, E. R. (2020). Dark Triad personality traits in cyber aggression among college students. *Violence and Victims*, *35*(4), 524–538. https://doi.org/10.1891/VV-D-18-00058

Nocera, T. R., Dahlen, E. R., Mohn, R. S., Leuty, M. E., & Batastini, A. B. (2022). Dark personality traits and anger in cyber aggression perpetration: Is moral disengagement to blame? *Psychology of Popular Media*, *11*(1), 24–34. http://dx.doi.org/10.1037/ppm0000295

Nübold, A., Bader, J., Bozin, N., Depala, R., Eidast, H., Johan-nessen, E. A., & Prinz, G. (2017). Developing a taxonomy of Dark Triad triggers at work – A grounded theory study protocol. *Frontiers in Psychology*, *8*(293). https://doi.org/10.3389/fpsyg.2017.00293

Nurse, J. R., Legg, P. A., Buckley, O., Agrafiotis, I., Wright, G., Whitty, M., ... & Creese, S. (June 2014). A critical reflection on the threat from human insiders—its nature, industry perceptions, and detection approaches. In *International Conference on Human Aspects of Information Security, Privacy, and Trust* (pp. 270–281). Springer, Cham.

Nwufo, J. I., Nnadozie, E. E., & Beluonwu, M. I. (2023). Influence of Dark Triad and family functioning on Internet addiction among in-school adolescents in Nsukka Urban of Enugu State, Nigeria. *African Journal for the Psychological Studies of Social Issues*, *26*(2), 21–34.

O'Boyle, E. H., Jr., Forsyth, D. R., Banks, G. C., & McDaniel, M. A. (2012). A meta-analysis of the Dark Triad and work behavior: A social exchange perspective. *Journal of Applied Psychology*, *97*(3), 557–579. https://doi.org/10.1037/a0025679

Olckers, C., & Hattingh, M. (2022). The dark side of social media-cyberbullying, catfishing, and trolling: A systematic literature review. *EPiC Series in Computing – Proceedings of the Society – Integrating Digital World and Real World to Resolve Challenges in Business and Society, 84*, 86–99.

O'Meara, A., Davies, J., & Hammond, S. (2011). The psychometric properties and utility of the Short Sadistic Impulse Scale (SSIS). *Psychological Assessment, 23*(2), 523–531. https://doi.org/10.1037/a0022400

Ong, E. Y., Ang, R. P., Ho, J. C., Lim, J. C., Goh, D. H., Lee, C. S., & Chua, A. Y. (2011). Narcissism, extraversion and adolescents' self-presentation on Facebook. *Personality and Individual Differences, 50*(2), 180–185. https://doi.org/10.1016/j.paid.2010.09.022

Orhan, M. A., & Collisson, B. (2022). Who said there's no such thing as a free lunch? Customers' Dark Triad traits predict abuse of food refund policies. *Personality and Individual Differences, 190*, 111527.

Osborne, C. (June 18, 2022) How Tinder scammers steal your heart, then your money. *ZDNet/Finance*. Retrieved from www.zdnet.com/finance/todays-tinder-swindlers-how-scammers-steal-your-heart-then-your-money/

Osterholz, S., Mosel, E. I., & Egloff, B. (2023). # Insta personality: Personality expression in Instagram accounts, impression formation, and accuracy of personality judgments at zero acquaintance. *Journal of Personality, 91*(3), 566–582. https://doi-org.ezproxy.haifa.ac.il/10.1111/jopy.12756

Owen, T., Noble, W., & Speed, F. C. (2017). Trolling, the ugly face of the social network. In *New Perspectives on Cybercrime. Palgrave Studies in Cybercrime and Cybersecurity* (pp. 113–139). Cham: Palgrave Macmillan. https://doi-org.ezproxy.haifa.ac.il/10.1007/978-3-319-53856-3_7

Oxford Dictionaries. (2013). Selfie. Retrieved from www.oxforddictionaries.com/definition/English/selfie

Ozimek, P., Bierhoff, H., & Hanke, S. (2018). Do vulnerable narcissists profit more from Facebook use than grandiose narcissists? An examination of narcissistic Facebook use in the light of self-regulation and social comparison theory. *Personality and Individual Differences, 124*, 168–177. https://doi.org/10.1016/j.paid.2017.12.016

Paananen, A., & Reichl, A. J. (2019). Gendertrolls just want to have fun, too. *Personality and Individual Differences, 141*, 152–156. https://doi.org/10.1016/j.paid.2019.01.011

Pabian, S., De Backer, C. J., & Vandebosch, H. (2015). Dark Triad personality traits and adolescent cyber-aggression. *Personality and Individual Differences, 75*, 41–46. https://doi.org/10.1016/j.paid.2014.11.015

Pabian, S., & Vandebosch, H. (2023). The Dark Tetrad, online moral disengagement, and online aggression perpetration among adults. *Telematics and Informatics Reports*, 100089. https://doi.org/10.1016/j.teler.2023.100089

Padayachee, K. (2020). Understanding the relationship between the Dark Triad of personality traits and neutralization techniques toward cybersecurity behaviour, *10*(4), 1–19. https://doi.org/10.4018/IJCWT.2020100101

Padayachee, K. (2021). Joint effects of neutralization techniques and the Dark Triad of personality traits on gender: An insider threat perspective. In *Conference on Information Communications Technology and Society (ICTAS)*, 40–45. https://doi.org/10.1109/ICTAS50802.2021.9395053

Panatik, S. A., Abdul Raof, N. N., Yusof, J., Nordin, N. A., & Shahrin, R. (2022). Effect of Dark Triad personality on cyberbullying behavior among Malaysian university students. *The Eurasia Proceedings of Educational & Social Sciences (EPESS)*, *25*, 26–44.

Papapicco, C., & Quatera, I. (2019). "Do not make to eat to troll!": The dark side of web. *Online Journal of Communication and Media Technologies*, *9*(2), e201910. https://doi.org/10.29333/ojcmt/5764

Patchin, J. W., & Hinduja, S. (2015). Measuring cyberbullying: Implications for research. *Aggression and Violent Behavior*, *23*, 69–74. https://doi.org/10.1016/j.avb.2015.05.013

Paul, B. (2009). Predicting Internet pornography use and arousal: The role of individual difference variables. *Journal of Sex Research*, *46*(4), 344–357. https://doi.org/10.1080/00224490902754152

Paulhus, D. L., Curtis, S. R., & Jones, D. N. (2018). Aggression as a trait: The Dark Tetrad alternative. *Current Opinion in Psychology*, *19*, 88–92. https://doi.org/10.1016/j.copsyc.2017.04.007

Paulhus, D. L., & Williams, K. M. (2002). The Dark Triad of personality: Narcissism, Machiavellianism, and psychopathy. *Journal of Research in Personality*, *36*(6), 556–563. https://doi.org/10.1016/S0092-6566(02)00505-6

Pearson, C., & Hussain, Z. (2015). Smartphone use, addiction, narcissism, and personality: A mixed methods investigation. *International Journal of Cyber Behavior, Psychology and Learning (IJCBPL)*, *5*(1), 17–32. http://doi.org/10.4018/ijcbpl.2015010102

Pechorro, P., Karandikar, S., Carvalho, B., DeLisi, M., & Jones, D. N. (2023). Screening for dark personalities in Portugal: Intra-and interpersonal correlates, reliability and invariance of the Short Dark Tetrad Portuguese version. *Deviant Behavior*, *44*(4), 551–566. https://doi.org/10.1080/01639625.2022.2071655

Perenc, L. (2022). Psychopathic personality disorder and cybercriminality: An outline of the issue. *Current Issues in Personality Psychology*, *10*(4), 253–264.

Perez del Valle, J., & Hand, C. J. (2022). The role of scrupulosity, experiential avoidance, and the Dark Tetrad in problematic pornography use. *Sexual Health & Compulsivity*, *29*(1–2), 68–95, https://doi.org/10.1080/26929953.2022.2101168

Peterson, J., & Densley, J. (2017). Cyber violence: What do we know and where do we go from here? *Aggression and Violent Behavior*, *34*, 193–200. https://doi.org/10.1016/j.avb.2017.01.012

Petit, J., & Carcioppolo, N. (2020). Associations between the Dark Triad and online communication behavior: A brief report of preliminary findings. *Communication Research Reports*, *37*(5), 286–297. https://doi.org/10.1030/08824096.2020.186278

Pew Research Center. (June 12, 2019). *Internet/Broadband Fact Sheet*. Retrieved from www.pewinternet.org/fact-sheet/internet-broadband/

Pina, A., Bell, A., Griffin, K., & Vasquez, E. (2021). Image based sexual abuse proclivity and victim blaming: The role of dark personality traits and moral disengagement. *Oñati Socio-Legal Series*, *11*(5), 1179–1197. https://doi.org/10.35295/osls.iisl/0000-0000-0000-1213

Pina, A., Holland, J., & James, M. (2017). The malevolent side of revenge porn proclivity: Dark personality traits and sexist ideology. *International Journal of Technoethics (IJT)*, *8*(1), 30–43. https://doi.org/10.4018/IJT.2017010103

Pineda, D., Galan, M., Martinez-Martinez, A., Campagne, D. M., & Piqueras, J. A. (2022a). Same personality, new ways to abuse: How Dark Tetrad personalities are connected with cyber intimate partner violence. *Journal of Interpersonal Violence*, *37*(13–14), NP11223–NP11241. https://doi.org/10.1177/0886260521991307

Pineda, D., Martínez-Martínez, A., Galán, M., Rico-Bordera, P., & Piqueras, J. A. (2023). The Dark Tetrad and online sexual victimization: Enjoying in the distance. *Computers in Human Behavior*, 107659. https://doi.org/10.1016/j.chb.2023.107659

Pineda, D., Rico-Bordera, P., Martínez-Martínez, A., Galán, M., & Piqueras, J. A. (2022b). Dark Tetrad personality traits also play a role in bullying victimization. *Frontiers in Psychology*, *13*. https://doi.org/10.3389/fpsyg.2022.984744

Plouffe, R. A., Kowalski, C. M., Papageorgiou, K. A., Dinić, B. M., Artamonova, E., Dagnall, N., ... & Stalikas, A. (2023). The revised Assessment of Sadistic Personality (ASP-8): Evidence for validity across four countries. *Journal of Personality Assessment*, *105*(2), 149–162. https://doi.org/10.1080/00223891.2022.2055476

Plouffe, R. A., Smith, M, & Saklofske, D. H. (2019). A psychometric investigation of the assessment of sadistic personality. *Personality and Individual Differences*, *140*, 57–60. https://doi.org/10.1016/j.paid.2018.01.002

Po, L. C., Sher, C. Y., & Liu, Y. H. (2023). Progress and future directions for research on social media addiction: Visualization-based bibliometric analysis. *Telematics and Informatics*, 101968. https://doi-org.ezproxy.haifa.ac.il/10.1016/j.tele.2023.101968

Porter, S., Bhanwer, A., Woodworth, M., & Black, P. J. (2014). Soldiers of misfortune: An examination of the Dark Triad and the experience of schadenfreude. *Personality and Individual Differences*, *67*, 64–68. https://doi.org/10.1016/j.paid.2013.11.014

Porter, S., & Woodworth, M. (2006). Psychopathy and aggression. In Patrick, C. J. (Ed.), *Handbook of Psychopathy* (pp. 481–494). New York: Guilford Press.

Preotiuc-Pietro, D., Carpenter, J., Giorgi, S., & Ungar, L. (2016). Studying the Dark Triad of personality through Twitter behavior. In *Proceedings of the 25th ACM International Conference on Information and Knowledge Management* (pp. 761–770). http://dx.doi.org/10.1145/2983323.298382

Pyżalski, J. (2012). From cyberbullying to electronic aggression: Typology of the phenomenon. *Emotional and Behavioural Difficulties, 17*(3–4), 305–317. https://doi.org/10.1080/13632752.2012.704319

Rahman, M. S., & Muldoon, J. (2020). Dark side of technology: Investigating the role of dark personality traits and technological factors in managing cyberloafing behavior. *Journal of Strategic Innovation and Sustainability, 15*(3), 36–54.

Rajesh, T., & Rangaiah, B. (2022). Relationship between personality traits and Facebook addiction: A meta-analysis. *Heliyon, 8*(8), e10315. https://doi.org/10.1016/j.heliyon.2022.e10315

Ramamoorti, S., & Epstein, B. J. (2016). When reckless executives become dangerous fraudsters: Reward structures and auditing procedures need to be reformed to deter Dark Triad personalities. *The CPA Journal, 86*(11), 6–10.

Randazzo, M. R., Keeney, M., Kowalski, E., Cappelli, D., and Moore, A. (2004). *Insider Threat Study: Illicit Cyber Activity in the Banking and Finance Sector.* U.S. Secret Service and CERT Coordination Center/Carnegie Mellon University Software Engineering Institute. Retrieved from www.secretservice.gov/ntac/its_report_040820.pdf

Rauthmann, J. F. (2013). Investigating the MACH–IV with item response theory and proposing the trimmed MACH. *Journal of Personality Assessment, 95*(4), 388–397. https://doi.org/10.1080/00223891.2012.742905

Rauthmann, J. F., & Kolar, G. P. (2012). How "dark" are the Dark Triad traits? Examining the perceived darkness of narcissism, Machiavellianism, and psychopathy. *Personality and Individual Differences, 53*(7), 884–889. https://doi.org/10.1016/j.paid.2012.06.020

Reep-van den Bergh, C. M. M., & Junger, M. (2018). Victims of cybercrime in Europe: a review of victim surveys. *Crime Science, 7*(1), 1–15. https://doi.org/10.1186/s40163-018-0079-3

Reidy, D. E., Zeichner, A., & Seibert, L. A. (2011). Unprovoked aggression: Effects of psychopathic traits and sadism. *Journal of Personality, 79*(1), 75–100.

Resett, S., Caino, P. G., & Mesurado, B. (2022). Emotional problems, dark personality, sexting and grooming in adolescents: The role of gender and age. *CES Psicología, 15*(2), 23–43.

Resett, S., & González Caino, P. C. (2023). Psychometric properties of the revised trolling questionnaire in Argentinean adults. *Acta Colombiana de Psicología, 26*(2), 101–113. www.doi.org/10.14718/ACP.2023.26.2.9

Rivera, P. (2021). Tweepy: An easy-to-use Python library for accessing the Twitter API. *Tweepy.* Retrieved from www.tweepy.org

Robertson, S. A., Datu, J. A. D., Brawley, A. M., Pury, C. L., Mateo, N. J. (2016). The Dark Triad and social behavior: The influence of self-construal and power distance. *Personality and Individual Differences, 98*, 69–74. https://doi-org.ezproxy.haifa.ac.il/10.1016/j.paid.2016.03.090

Rochat, L., Orita, E., Jeannot, E., Achab, S., & Khazaal, Y. (2023). Willingness to pay for a dating app: Psychological correlates. *International Journal of Environmental Research and Public Health, 20*(3). https://doi.org/10.3390/ijerph20032101

Rohwer, E., Flöther, J.-C., Harth V., & Mache S. (2022). Overcoming the "Dark Side" of technology: A scoping review on preventing and coping with work-related technostress. *International Journal of Environmental Research and Public Health, 19*(6), 3625. https://doi.org/10.3390/ijerph19063625

Rood, M. L., & Schriner, J. (2021). The Internet never forgets: Image-based sexual abuse and the workplace. In Ramos Salazar, L. (Ed.), *Handbook of Research on Cyberbullying and Online Harassment in the Workplace*, Chapter 6 (pp. 107–128). Hershey PA, USA: IGI Global.

Rosen, L. D., Whaling, K., Rab, S., Carrier, L. M., & Cheever, N. A. (2013). Is Facebook creating "iDisorders"? The link between clinical symptoms of psychiatric disorders and technology use, attitudes and anxiety. *Computers in Human Behavior, 29*(3), 1243–1254. https://doi.org/10.1016/j.chb.2012.11.012

Rosenberg, J., & Egbert, N. (2011). Online impression management: Personality traits and concerns for secondary goals as predictors of self-presentation tactics on Facebook. *Journal of Computer-Mediated Communication, 17*, 1–18. https://doi.org/10.1111/j.1083-6101.2011.01560.x.

Rosenthal, S. A., & Pittinsky, T. L. (2006). Narcissistic leadership. *The Leadership Quarterly, 17*(6), 617–633. https://doi.org/10.1016/j.leaqua.2006.10.005

Ryan, T., & Xenos, S. (2011). Who uses Facebook? An investigation into the relationship between the Big Five, shyness, narcissism, loneliness, and Facebook usage. *Computers in Human Behavior, 27*(5), 1658–1664. https://doi.org/10.1016/j.chb.2011.02.004

Sabillon, R., Cano, J., Cavaller, V., & Serra, J. (2016). Cybercrime and cybercriminals: A comprehensive study. *International Journal of Computer Networks and Communications Security, 4*(6), 176–165.

Safaria, T., Nuqul, F. L., Purwandari, E., Ratnaningsih, I. Z., Khairania, M., Saputra, N., … & Mariati, L. I. (2020). The role of Dark Triad personality on cyberbullying: is it still a problem? *International Journal of Scientific & Technology Research, 9*(2), 4256–4260.

Salimi, S., Khojaste, L., Qazizadeh, F., & Abbasi, M. (2023). Designing a structural model for social media addiction based on the Dark Triad of personality: The mediating role of student social comparison. *Journal of Research in Psychopathology, 4*(12). https://doi.org/10.22098/jrp.2022.11336.1133

Sánchez-Medina, A. J., Galván-Sánchez, I., & Fernández-Monroy, M. (2020). Applying artificial intelligence to explore sexual cyberbullying behaviour. *Heliyon, 6*(1), e03218. https://doi.org/10.1016/j.heliyon.2020.e03218

Sanders, G. L., Upadhyaya, S., & Wang, X. (2019). Inside the insider. *IEEE Engineering Management Review, 47*(2), 84–91. https://doi.org/10.1109/EMR.2019.2917656

Sari, B. L., & Adriani, Y. (2022). Empathy as a mediator of the effect of Dark Triad personality, social support, and demographic factors on cyberbullying behavior in SMAN 10 Depok students. *TAZKIYA Journal of Psychology, 10*(2), 122–131. https://repository.uinjkt.ac.id/dspace/handle/123456789/66090

Satchell, L. P., Corr, P. J., & Latzman, R. D. (2022). Pirates with psychopathic personalities? The role of sub-clinical and normative traits in illegal streaming and downloading of media. *Journal of Research in Personality*, *96*, 104158. https://doi.org/10.1016/j.jrp.2021.104158

Savacı, G. Z., Bayraktar, B. K., & Özen, Ç. (2021). The impacts of behavioral factors on social media addiction. *Journal of Computer and Education Research*, *9*(18), 1059–1083. https://doi.org/10.18009/jcer.1013726

Savci, M. (2019). Social media craving and the amount of self-disclosure: The mediating role of the Dark Triad. *International Online Journal of Educational Sciences*, *11*(4), 1–10. https://doi.org/10.15345/iojes.2019.04.001

Savci, M., & Griffiths, M. D. (2019). The development of the Turkish Social Media Craving Scale (SMCS): A validation study. *International Journal of Mental Health and Addiction*. https://doi.org/10.1007/s11469-019-00062-9

Savci, M., Turan, M. E., Griffiths, M. D., & Ercengiz, M. (2021). Histrionic personality, narcissistic personality, and problematic social media use: Testing of a new hypothetical model. *International Journal of Mental Health and Addiction*, *19*, 986–1004. https://doi.org/10.1007/s11469-019-00139-5

Scarduzio, J., & Adams, M. (2022). 9 Exploring coworker online sexual harassment and risk: Factors of uncertainty and ambiguity for employees and organizations. In Engemann, K., Engemann, K., & Scott, C. (Eds.), *Volume III Organizational Risk Management: Managing for Uncertainty and Ambiguity* (pp. 171–188). Berlin, Boston: De Gruyter. https://doi.org/10.1515/9783110670202-009

Schade, E. C., Voracek, M., & Tran, U. S. (2021). The nexus of the Dark Triad personality traits with cyberbullying, empathy, and emotional intelligence: A structural-equation modeling approach. *Frontiers in Psychology*, *12*. https://doi.org/10.3389/fpsyg.2021.659282

Schoenherr, J. R., Lilja-Lolax, K., & Gioe, D. (2022). Multiple approach paths to insider threat (MAP-IT): Intentional, ambivalent and unintentional insider threats. *Counter-Insider Threat Research and Practice*, *1*(1), 1–23.

Schokkenbroek, J. M., Ponnet, K., Hauspie, T., & Hardyns, W. (2022). Malevolent monitoring: Dark Triad traits, cyber dating abuse and the instrumental role of self-control. In *71nd Annual ICA Conference*.

Scholz, D. D., Thielmann, I., & Hilbig, B. E. (2023). Down to the core: The role of the common core of dark traits for aversive relationship behaviors *Personality and Individual Differences*, *213*, 112263. https://doi.org/10.1016/j.paid.2023.112263

Schyns, B. (2015). Dark personality in the workplace: Introduction to the special issue. *Applied Psychology: An International Review*, *64*(1), 1–14. https://doi.org/10.1111/apps.12041

Scott, G. G., Boyle, E. A., Czerniawska, K., & Courtney, A. (2018). Posting photos on Facebook: The impact of narcissism, social anxiety, loneliness, and shyness. *Personality and Individual Differences*, *133*, 67–72. https://doi-org.ezproxy.haifa.ac.il/10.1016/j.paid.2016.12.039

Scott, G. G., Brodie, Z. P., Wilson, M. J., Ivory, L., Hand, C. J., & Sereno, S. C. (2020). Celebrity abuse on Twitter: The impact of tweet valence, volume of abuse, and Dark Triad personality factors on victim blaming and perceptions of severity. *Computers in Human Behavior, 103*, 109–119. https://doi.org/10.1016/j.chb.2019.09.020

Seigfried-Spellar, K. C., Villacís-Vukadinović, N., & Lynam, D. R. (2017). Computer criminal behavior is related to psychopathy and other antisocial behavior. *Journal of Criminal Justice, 51*, 67–73. https://doi.org/10.1016/j.jcrimjus.2017.06.003

Selzer, N., & Oelrich, S. (2021). Saint or Satan? Moral development and Dark Triad influences on cybercriminal intent. In Weulen Kranenbarg, M., & Leukfeldt, R. (Eds.), *Cybercrime in Context: The Human Factor in Victimization, Offending, and Policing* (pp. 175–194). Cham: Springer.

Servidio, R., Griffiths, M. D., & Demetrovics, Z. (2021). Dark Triad of personality and problematic smartphone use: A preliminary study on the mediating role of fear of missing out. *International Journal of Environmental Research and Public Health, 18*(16), 8463. https://doi.org/10.3390/ijerph18168463

Sest, N., & March, E. (2017). Constructing the cyber-troll: Psychopathy, sadism, and empathy. *Personality and Individual Differences, 119*, 69–72. https://doi.org/10.1016/j.paid.2017.06.038

Sevi, B. (2019). The dark side of Tinder: The Dark Triad of personality as correlates of Tinder use. *Journal of Individual Differences, 40*(4), 242–246. https://doi.org/10.1027/1614-0001/a000297

Shabahang, R., Aruguete, M. S., Shim, H., Hosseinkhanzadeh, A. A., & Azadimanesh, P. (2023). From skepticism toward celebrities to celebrity culture hate: Mediating role of perceived celebrity deception and perceived Dark Triad of celebrities. *Interpersona: An International Journal on Personal Relationships, 17*(1), 88–110. https://doi.org/10.5964/ijpr.9221

Shahnawaz, M. G., Nasir, S., & Rehman, U. (2020). Sadism and cyber aggression: Moral identity as a possible moderator. *Journal of Aggression, Maltreatment & Trauma, 29*(8), 969–983. https://doi-org.ezproxy.haifa.ac.il/10.1080/10926771.2019.1575302

Shiau, W. L., Dwivedi, Y. K., & Lai, H. H. (2018). Examining the core knowledge on Facebook. *International Journal of Information Management, 43*, 52–63. https://doi.org/10.1016/j.ijinfomgt.2018.06.006

Shim, J. W., Lee, S., & Paul, B. (2007). Who responds to unsolicited sexually explicit materials on the internet? The role of individual differences. *Cyber Psychology & Behavior, 10*(1), 71–79. https://doi.org/10.1089/cpb.2006.9990

Shrivastava, A. (2023). Social media addiction, Dark Triad traits, and the role of self-esteem among Indian GenZ. *International Journal of Indian Psychology, 11*(2), 2286–2300. https://doi.org/10.25215/1102.228

Siah, P. C., Hue, J. Y., Wong, B. Z. R., & Goh, S. J. (2021). Dark Triad and social media addiction among undergraduates: Coping strategy as a mediator. *Contemporary Educational Technology, 13*(4). https://doi.org/10.30935/cedtech/11104

Sindermann, C., Sariyska, R., Lachmann, B., Brand, M., & Montag, C. (2018). Associations between the Dark Triad of personality and unspecified/specific forms of Internet-use disorder. *Journal of Behavioral Addictions, 7*, 985–992. https://doi.org/10.1556/2006.7.2018.114

Slonje, R., & Smith, P. K. (2008). Cyberbullying: Another main type of bullying? *Scandinavian Journal of Psychology, 49*(2), 147–154. https://doi.org/10.1111/j.1467-9450.2007.00611.x

Smith A. D. (2021, June 21). The personality disorder we don't hear enough about. *Psychology Today*. Retrieved from www.psychologytoday.com/us/blog/and-running/202106/the-personality-disorder-we-dont-hear-enough-about

Smith, K., Emerson, D., Haight, T., & Wood, B. (2023). An examination of online cheating among business students through the lens of the Dark Triad and Fraud Diamond. *Ethics & Behavior, 33*(6), 433–460. https://doi.org/10.1080/10508422.2022.2104281

Smith, K. J., Emerson, D. J., & Mauldin, S. (2021). Online cheating at the intersection of the Dark Triad and fraud diamond. *Journal of Accounting Education, 57*, 100753. https://doi.org/10.1016/j.jaccedu.2021.100753

Smith, S. F., & Lilienfeld, S. O. (2013). Psychopathy in the workplace: The knowns and unknowns. *Aggression and Violent Behavior. 18*, 204–218. https://doi.org/10.1016/j.avb.2012.11.007

Smith, K., Mendez, F., & White, G. L. (2014). Narcissism as a predictor of Facebook users' privacy concern, vigilance, and exposure to risk. *International Journal of Technology and Human Interaction (IJTHI), 10*(2), 78–95. https://doi.org/10.4018/ijthi.2014040105

Smoker, M., & March, E. (2017). Predicting perpetration of intimate partner cyberstalking: Gender and the Dark Tetrad. *Computers in Human Behavior, 72*, 390–396. https://doi.org/10.1016/j.chb.2017.03.012

Soleimani Rad, H., & Abolghasemi, A. (2021). The role of psychological needs and Dark Triad traits of personality in selfie-taking behavior. *Journal of Modern Psychology, 1*(2), 12–25. https://doi.org/10.22034/JMP.2021.314664.1020

Sorokowski, P., Kowal, M., Zdybek, P., & Oleszkiewicz, A. (2020). Are online haters psychopaths? Psychological predictors of online hating behavior. *Frontiers in Psychology, 11*, 553. https://doi.org/10.3389/fpsyg.2020.00553

Spain, S. M., Harms, P., & LeBreton, J. M. (2014). The dark side of personality at work. *Journal of Organizational Behavior, 35*(S1), S41–S60. https://doi.org/10.1002/job.1894

Sparavec, A., March, E., & Grieve, R. (2022). The Dark Triad, empathy, and motives to use social media. *Personality and Individual Differences, 194*, 111647. https://doi.org/10.1016/j.paid.2022.111647

Sparks, B., Stephens, S., & Trendell, S. (2023). Image-based sexual abuse: Victim-perpetrator overlap and risk-related correlates of coerced sexting, non-consensual dissemination of intimate images, and cyberflashing. *Computers in Human Behavior*, 107879. https://doi.org/10.1016/j.chb.2023.107879

Srinivas, P. Y. K. L., Das, A., & Pulabaigari, V. (2022). Fake spreader is narcissist; real spreader is Machiavellian prediction of fake news diffusion using psycho-sociological facets. *Expert Systems with Applications, 207,* 117952. https://doi.org/10.1016/j.eswa.2022.117952

Statista. (2021). Global digital population as of January 2021. Retrieved from www.statista.com/statistics/617136/digitalpopulation-worldwide/. Accessed on 1 March 2022.

Statista. (2023a). Cyberbullying – Statistics & facts. Retrieved from www.statista .com/topics/1809/cyber-bullying

Statista. (2023b). Online dating worldwide – Statistics & facts. Retrieved from www.statista.com/topics/7443/online-dating/

Statista. (2023c). Facebook – Statistics & facts. Retrieved from www.statista.com/topics/751/facebook/#topicOverview

Stephenson, P., & Walter, R. (2012). Cyber crime assessment. In *2012 45th Hawaii International Conference on System Science (HICSS),* vol. 45, pp. 5404–5413, January 4–7. https://doi.org/10.1109/HICSS.2012.190

Stiff, C. (2019). The Dark Triad and Facebook surveillance: How Machiavellianism, psychopathy, but not narcissism predict using Facebook to spy on others. *Computers in Human Behavior, 94,* 62–69. https://doi.org/10.1016/j.chb.2018.12.044

Storey, J. E., Hart, S. D., Meloy, J. R., & Reavis, J. A. (2009). Psychopathy and stalking. *Law and Human Behavior, 33*(3), 237–246. https://doi.org/10.1007/s10979-008-9149.

Strickland, M. L., Love, H., & Kimmes, J. (2022). The interaction between adolescent cyber dating abuse and parenting on mental health outcomes. *Journal of Child and Family Studies,* 1–12. https://doi.org/10.1007/s10826-022-02433-8

Stuart, J., & Kurek, A. (2019). Looking hot in selfies: Narcissistic beginnings, aggressive outcomes? *International Journal of Behavioral Development, 43*(6), 500–506. https://doi.org/10.1177/0165025419865621

Sudzina, F., & Pavlicek, A. (2017). Propensity to click on suspicious links: Impact of gender, of age, and of personality traits. In *30th BLED E-Conference Digital Transformation, BLED 2017 Proceedings,* vol. 10, pp. 593–602. http://aisel .aisnet.org/bled2017/10

Sumner, C., Byers, A., Boochever, R., & Park, G. (December 2012). *Predicting Dark Triad personality traits from Twitter and a linguistic analysis of tweets.* Paper presented at the International Conference on Machine Learning and Applications, Boca Raton, FL.

Swenson-Lepper, T., & Kerby, A. (2019). Cyberbullies, trolls, and stalkers: Students' perceptions of ethical issues in social media. *Journal of Media Ethics, 34*(2), 1–12. https://doi.org/10.1080/23736992.2019.1599721

Sykes, G. M., & Matza, D. (1957). Techniques of neutralization: A theory of delinquency. *American Sociological Review, 22*(6), 664–670. https://doi.org/2089195

Symantec. (2023). 2023 cyber security report. Retrieved from https://pages .checkpoint.com/cyber-security-report-2023.html

Takezawa, M., Matsui, M., & Kawasaki, N. (2023). Narcissism and intimate partner violence using information and communication technology in Japan. *Journal of Family Violence, 38,* 931–940. https://doi.org/10.1007/s10896-022-00426-1

Tandon, A., Kaur, P., Ruparel, N., Islam, J. U., & Dhir, A. (2021). Cyberloafing and cyberslacking in the workplace: Systematic literature review of past achievements and future promises. *Internet Research.* https://doi.org/10.1108/INTR-06-2020-0332

Tang, W. Y., Reer, F., & Quandt, T. (2020). The interplay of gaming disorder, gaming motivations, and the Dark Triad. *Journal of Behavioral Addictions*, *9*(2), 491–496.

Tang, W. Y., Reer, F., & Quandt, T. (2022). The interplay of the Dark Triad and social media use motives to social media disorder. *Personality and Individual Differences*, *187*, 111402. https://doi.org/10.1016/j.paid.2021.111402

Tahoon, R. (2020). Mediating effects of dark personality triad and real and mediated social interaction on social media addiction and academic performance in university students. *Clinical and Experimental Psychology*, *6*(4), 1–10.

Themelidis, L., & Davies, J. (2021). Creating evil: Can sadism be induced? *Personality and Individual Differences*, *168*, 110358. https://doi.org/10.1016/j.paid.2020.110358

The Tinder Swindler. (December 5, 2022). In *Wikipedia*. Retrieved from https://en.wikipedia.org/wiki/The_Tinder_Swindler

Thomason-Darch, N. (2021). The Dark Tetrad of personality and the tendency to engage in revenge porn. *The Plymouth Student Scientist*, *14*(2), 651–668. http://hdl.handle.net/10026.1/18520

Timmermans, E., De Caluwe, E., & Alexopoulos, C. (2018). Why are you cheating on tinder? Exploring users' motives and (dark) personality traits. *Computers in Human Behavior*, *89*, 129–139. https://doi.org/10.1016/j.chb.2018.07.040

Treadway, D. C., Yang, J., Bentley, J. R., Williams, L. V., & Reeves, M. (2017). The impact of follower narcissism and LMX perceptions on feeling envied and job performance. *The International Journal of Human Resource Management*, 1–22. https://doi.org/10.1080/09585192.2017.1288151

Tripathi, N., & Lim, V. K. (2014). Moderating effect of Machiavellianism and perceived similarity on cyber incivility and its outcomes. In *Academy of Management Proceedings*, 2014(1), Academy of Management, Briarcliff Manor, New York, NY, p. 12000.

Tsoukas, A., & March, E. (2018). Predicting short- and long-term mating orientations: The role of sex and the Dark Tetrad. *The Journal of Sex Research*, *55*(9), 1206–1218. https://doi.org/10.1080/00224499.2017.1420750

Tucaković, L., Bojić, L., & Nikolić, N. (2022). The battle between light and dark Side of personality: How light and dark personality traits predict mating strategies in the online context. *Interpersona: An International Journal on Personal Relationships*, *16*(2), 295–312. https://doi.org/10.5964/ijpr.7869

Turan, M. E., Adam, F., Kaya, A., & Yıldırım, M. (2023). The mediating role of the dark personality triad in the relationship between ostracism and social media addiction in adolescents. *Education and Information Technologies*, 1–17. https://doi-org.ezproxy.haifa.ac.il/10.1007/s10639-023-12002-1

United States Department of Health and Human Services (January 2018). Laws, policies and regulations. Retrieved on June 14, 2019, from www.stopbullying .gov/laws/index.html

Vaknin, S. (December 28, 2008). The cyber narcissist. *Healthy Place*. Retrieved on March 1, 2022, from www.healthyplace.com/personality-disorders/ malignant-self-love/cyber-narcissist

Valentine, J. L., Miles, L. W., Mella Hamblin, K., & Worthen Gibbons, A. (2023). Dating app facilitated sexual assault: A retrospective review of sexual assault medical forensic examination charts. *Journal of Interpersonal Violence*, *38*(9–10), 6298–6322. https://doi.org/10.1177/08862605221130390

Valli, C. (2004). Non-business use of the WWW in three Western Australian organizations. *Internet Research*, *14*(5), 353–359. https://doi-org.ezproxy.haifa .ac.il/10.1108/10662240410566944

VandenBos, G. R. (Ed.). (2007). *APA Dictionary of Psychology*. American Psychological Association.

Vander Molen, R. J., Kaplan, S., Choi, E., & Montoya, D. (2018). Judgments of the Dark Triad based on Facebook profiles. *Journal of Research in Personality*, *73*, 150–163. https://doi.org/10.1016/j.jrp.2017.11.010

van der Vegt, I., Kleinberg, B., & Gill, P. (2022). Predicting author profiles from online abuse directed at public figures. *Journal of Threat Assessment and Management*. Advance online publication. http://dx.doi.org/10.1037/ tam0000172

van Geel, M., Goemans, A., Toprak, F., & Vedder, P. (2017). Which personality traits are related to traditional bullying and cyberbullying? A study with the Big Five, Dark Triad and sadism. *Personality and Individual Differences*, *106*, 231–235. https://doi.org/10.1016/j.paid.2016.10.063

Verbalyte, M., Keitel, C., & Howard, K. (2022). Online trolls: Unaffectionate psychopaths or just lonely outcasts and angry partisans?. *Politics and Governance*, *10*(4), 396–410. https://doi.org/10.17645/pag.v10i4.5790

Volkmer, S. A., Gaube, S., Raue, M., & Lermer, E. (2023). Troll story: The Dark Tetrad and online trolling revisited with a glance at humor. *PLoS One*, *18*(3), e0280271. https://doi.org/10.1371/journal.pone.0280271

Vranjes, I., Baillien, E., Vandebosch, H., Erreygers, S., & De Witte, H. (2017). The dark side of working online: Towards a definition and an Emotion Reaction model of workplace cyberbullying. *Computers in Human Behavior*, *69*, 324–334. https://doi.org/10.1016/j.chb.2016.12.055

Vyawahare, M., & Chatterjee, M. (2020). Taxonomy of cyberbullying detection and prediction techniques in online social networks. In Jain, L. C., Tsihrintzis, G. A., Balas, V. E., & Sharma, D. (Eds.), *Data Communication and Networks* (pp. 21–37). Springer. https://doi.org/10.1007/978-981-15-0132-6_3

Wang, P., Hu, H., Mo, P. K., Ouyang, M., Geng, J., Zeng, P., & Mao, N. (2022a). How is father phubbing associated with adolescents' social networking sites addiction? roles of narcissism, need to belong, and loneliness. *The Journal of Psychology*, 1–18. https://doi-org.ezproxy.haifa.ac.il/10.1080/00223980.2022.2034726

Wang, J., Nansel, T. R., & Iannotti, R. J. (2011). Cyber and traditional bullying: Differential association with depression. *Journal of Adolescent Health*, *48*(4), 415–417. https://doi.org/10.1016/j.jadohealth.2010.07.012

Wang, S., Zhu, X., Ding, W., & Yengejeh, A. A. (2022b). Cyberbullying and cyber-violence detection: A triangular user-activity-content view. *IEEE/CAA Journal of Automatica Sinica*, *9*(8), 1384–1405. https://doi.org/10.1109/JAS.2022.105740

Weatherbee, T. G. (2010). Counterproductive use of technology at work: Information & communications technologies and cyberdeviancy. *Human Resource Management Review*, *20*(1), 35–44. https://doi.org/10.1016/j.hrmr.2009.03.012

Widman, L., & McNulty, J. K. (2010). Sexual narcissism and the perpetration of sexual aggression. *Archives of Sexual Behavior*, *39*(4), 926–939. https://doi.org/10.1007/s10508-008-9461-7

Williams, K. M., Paulhus, D. L., & Hare, R. D. (2007). Capturing the four-factor structure of psychopathy in college students via self-report. *Journal of Personality Assessment*, *88*(2), 205–219. https://doi.org/10.1080/00223890701268074

Willis, M. L., Oliver, E., & March, E. (2023). Dating in the dark: Vulnerable narcissism predicts inauthentic self-presentation in online dating. *Telematics and Informatics*. https://doi-org.ezproxy.haifa.ac.il/10.1016/j.tele.2023.101985

Wilson, D. S., Near, D., & Miller, R. R. (1996). Machiavellianism: A synthesis of the evolutionary and psychological literatures. *Psychological Bulletin*, *119*(2), 285–299. https://doi.org/10.1037/0033-2909.119.2.285

Wilson, C., Sheridan, L., & Garratt-Reed, D. (2022). Examining cyberstalking perpetration and victimization: A scoping review. *Trauma, Violence, & Abuse*. https://doi.org/10.1177/15248380221082937

Wisse, B., Barelds, D. P., & Rietzschel, E. F. (2015). How innovative is your employee? The role of employee and supervisor Dark Triad personality traits in supervisor perceptions of employee innovative behavior. *Personality and Individual Differences*, *82*, 158–162. https://doi.org/10.1016/j.paid.2015.03.020

Wissink, I. B., Standaert, J. C., Stams, G. J. J., Asscher, J. J., & Assink, M. (2023). Risk factors for juvenile cybercrime: A meta-analytic review. *Aggression and Violent Behavior*, 101836. https://doi-org.ezproxy.haifa.ac.il/10.1016/j.avb.2023.101836

Withers, K. L., Parrish, J. L., Terrell, S., & Ellis, T. J. (2017). The relationship between the "Dark Triad" personality traits and deviant behavior on social networking sites. In *Proceedings of the Americas Conference on Information Systems (AMCIS)*, Boston, MA.

Wolfe, D. T., & Hermanson, D. R. (2004). The fraud diamond: Considering the four elements of fraud. *The CPA Journal*, *74*(12), 38–42. https://digitalcommons.kennesaw.edu/facpubs

World Health Organization. (2013). Global and regional estimates of violence against women: Prevalence and health effects of intimate partner violence and non-partner sexual violence. Retrieved from www.who.int/publications/i/item/9789241564625

World Health Organization. (2018). WHO releases new International Classification of Diseases (ICD 11). Retrieved on December 5, 2018, from www.who.int/news-room/detail/18-06-2018-who-releases-new-international-classification-of-diseases-(icd-11)

Wright, M. F., Huang, Z., Wachs, S., Aoyama, I., Kamble, S., Soudi, S., ... & Shu, C. (2020). Associations between cyberbullying perpetration and the Dark Triad of personality traits: the moderating effect of country of origin and gender. *Asia Pacific Journal of Social Work and Development, 30*(3), 242–256. https://doi.org/10.1080/02185385.2020.1788979

Wright, A. G. C., Pincus, A. L., Thomas, K. M., Hopwood, C. J., Markon, K. E., & Krueger, R. F. (2013). Conceptions of narcissism and the DSM-5 pathological personality traits. *Assessment, 20*, 339–352. https://doi.org/10.1177/1073191113486692

Wright, M. F., Wachs, S., Huang, Z., Kamble, S. V., Soudi, S., Bayraktar, F., Li, Z., Lei, L., & Shu, C. (2022). Longitudinal associations among Machiavellianism, popularity goals, and adolescents' cyberbullying involvement: The role of gender. *Journal of Genetic Psychology, 183*(5), 482–493. disinhibition

Wu, J., & Lebreton, J. M. (2011). Reconsidering the dispositional basis of counterproductive work behavior: The role of aberrant personality. *Personnel Psychology, 64*(3), 593–626. https://doi.org/10.1111/j.1744-6570.2011.01220.x

Wu, B., Zhou, L., Deng, Y., Zhao, J., & Liu, M. (2022). Online disinhibition and online trolling among Chinese college students: the mediation of the Dark Triad and the moderation of gender. *Cyberpsychology, Behavior, and Social Networking, 25*(11), 744–751. https://doi-org.ezproxy.haifa.ac.il/10.1089/cyber.2022.0046

Xu, X., Gao, L. F., Lian, S. L., Chen, Q., & Zhou, Z. K. (2022). How the Dark Triad associated with internet gaming disorder? The serial mediation of basic psychological needs satisfaction and negative coping styles. *Current Psychology*, 1–9. https://doi-org.ezproxy.haifa.ac.il/10.1007/s12144-022-03996-x

Yeo, V. C. S., Goh, S. K., & Rezaei, S. (2017). Consumer experiences, attitude and behavioral intention toward online food delivery (OFD) services. *Journal of Retailing and Consumer services, 35*, 150–162. https://doi.org/10.1016/j.jretconser.2016.12.013

Young, K. S., Griffin-Shelley, E., Cooper, A., O'mara, J., & Buchanan, J. (2000). Online infidelity: A new dimension in couple relationships with implications for evaluation and treatment. *Sexual Addiction & Compulsivity: The Journal of Treatment and Prevention, 7*(1–2), 59–74. https://doi.org/10.1080/10720160008400207

Yuan, G., Liu, Z., & An, Y. (2020a). Machiavellianism, mindfulness and cyberbullying among Chinese junior high school students: The mediating role of empathy. *Journal of Aggression, Maltreatment & Trauma, 29*(9), 1047–1058. https://doi.org/10.1080/10926771.2019.1667467

Yuan, C., Hong, Y., & Wu, J. (2020b). Does Facebook activity reveal your dark side? Using online language features to understand an individual's Dark Triad and needs. *Behaviour & Information Technology*, 1–15. https://doi.org/10.1080/0144929X.2020.1805513

Zerach, G. (2016). Pathological narcissism, cyberbullying victimization and offending among homosexual and heterosexual participants in online dating websites. *Computers in Human Behavior*, *57*, 292–299. https://doi.org/10.1016/j .chb.2015.12.038

Zhang, Z., Bian, S., Zhao, H., & Qi, C. (2022). Dark Triad and cyber aggression among Chinese adolescents during COVID-19: A moderated mediation model. *Frontiers in Psychology*, *13*, 1–9.

Zhang, S., & Leidner, D. (2014). Workplace cyberbullying: The antecedents and consequences. In: *Proceedings of the 20th Americas Conference on Information Systems*, AMCIS 2014. Savannah.

Zhang, S., Leidner, D., Cao, X., & Liu, N. (2022). Workplace cyberbullying: A criminological and routine activity perspective. *Journal of Information Technology*, *37*(1), 51–79. https://doi.org/10.1177/02683962211027888

Zhang, H., & Zhao, H. (2020). Dark personality traits and cyber aggression in adolescents: A moderated mediation analysis of belief in virtuous humanity and self-control. *Children and Youth Services Review*, *119*, 105565. https://doi .org/10.1016/j.childyouth.2020.105565

Zhou, Y. (2023). The benefits and dangers of online dating apps. *Canadian Journal of Family and Youth/Le Journal Canadien de Famille et de la Jeunesse*, *15*(2), 54–62. https://doi.org/10.29173/cjfy29872

Zweig, J. M., Lachman, P., Yahner, J., & Dank, M. (2014). Correlates of cyber dating abuse among teens. *Journal of Youth and Adolescence*, *43*(8), 1306–1321. https://doi.org/10.1007/s10964-013-0047-x

Index

#dark-triad (psychopath), 105
#psychopath, 104

Abell, L., 94
Abolghasemi, A., 97
abusive/toxic relationship, 253–254
academic cyberbullying, 307
Academic Escape, 29
Adams, M., 312
Adriani, Y., 123, 136
Afzal, W., 135
aggression. *See* cyberaggression
aggressiveness, xi, 120, 155, 200, 235, 262
Ahçi, Z. G., 321
Ahmad, H., 105
Ahmad, S., 105
Akat, M., 187
Akbulut, Ö. F., 187
Akdeniz, S., 321
Alavi, M., 128, 135
alcohol use, 19, 277
Alotaibi, F. M., 105
American Psychological Association (APA), 28
Amichai-Hamburger, Y., 252
Amon, M. J., 211
Anderson, J. R., 17, 25, 26, 330
Andreassen, C. S., 30, 32, 33, 60
anger, 33, 100, 102, 103, 106, 127, 157, 170, 219,
        220, 234, 245, 248, 254
anonymity, xv, xvi, xviii, xix, xxi, 21, 24, 65, 66, 114,
        122, 127, 134, 155, 158, 174, 177, 198, 199,
        232, 239, 240, 243, 260, 305, 308, 321
Ansari, S., 219
antisocial behaviors, 6
Antoniadou, N., 119, 125, 146
anxiety, xviii, 1, 4, 5, 8, 13, 14, 18, 19, 31, 33, 34,
        36, 37, 42, 45, 63, 64, 118, 155, 157,
        158, 170, 171, 173, 232, 234, 235, 248,
        254, 255, 260, 270, 271, 281, 308, 310,
        323, 327
appeal to higher loyalties, 204, 208, 304
Appel, M., 58, 59

Arabnia, H.R., 143
arrogance, 42, 122, 206, 240, 257
artificial general intelligence (AGI), 211
Asghar, J., 104
Asghar, M. Z., 105
ASKfm, 116
attention-deficit/hyperactivity disorder, 32
Australian Instagram user, 85
automobile insurance, 218
Aviram, I., 252
Azami, M. S., 135
Azzahra, K. A., 108

Babiak, P., 3, 6
Baheer, R., 313, 327
Balakrishnan J., 95
Balakrishnan, V., 143, 144
Balcerowska, J. M., 47, 64
Balta, S., 34, 38, 56, 68
Banchi, V., 43
Barberis, N., 53
Barelds, D. P., 14
Barry, C. T., 5
Baruch, Y., 308
Batinic, B., 53
Bayraktar, B. K., 61
Beluonwu, M. I., 58
Bergman, S. M., 60
Bertl, B., 15
Bhasin, D., 154
Bhogal, M.S., 259
Big Five personality traits, 44, 101,
        104, 131, 138, 177, 207, 208,
        238, 324
Bilal, A., 67
Bi-LSTM, 104
Björkqvist, K., 111
Błachnio, A., 66
Black hat hacking, 202, 209
Blais, J., 165, 323
Blanchard, A.L., 310
Bland, A. R., 63, 64

Blötner, C., 330
Board, B. J., 6
body image issues, 19, 235, 272
Bogolyubova, O., 100, 101
Bohns, V., x
Bonfá-Araujo, B., 17
Boochever, R., 102
Boyd, D. M., xii
Brailovskaia, J., 46, 65
Brand, M., 36
Branković, I., 165
Branson, M., 247, 256, 257
breadcrumbing, 248–251
    research findings, 251–253
Brewer, G., 94, 263
Brod, C., 33
Brown, W. M., 121, 132
Brubaker, P. J., 179
Buckels, E. E., 16, 173, 176–178
Budak, H., 321
Buffardi, L. E., 88, 89
Bui, N. H., 255
Bulyk, R., 237, 243
Bumble, 231, 236

Calvert, M., 61
Campbell, K., x
Campbell, W. K., 5, 62, 88, 89
Carpenter, C. J., 89
Carre, J. R., 210
Casale, S., 43, 46, 64
catfishing, 234, 236, 248–251
    research findings, 251–253
celebrity tweets, cyberbullying,
    139–143
Chabrol, H., 15
Charalampous, K., 144–146
Charlier, S. D., 19, 303, 312
Chatterjee, M., 116, 117
Chemistry.com, 231
Cheng, C., 28, 34, 118
Cheng, Z. W., 119
child pornography, xvi, 273
Chinese culture, 16, 137
Choi, W. H., 66
Choi, Y., 317
Christensen, L., x
Christie., R., 8, 9
Chung, K. L., 40, 55
Çıkan, F., 129
Clancy, E. M., 278
Cleckley, H., 6
clinical and psychiatric literature, 5
CNN-LSTM model, 105
Coalition Against Insurance Fraud, 218

coercion, 155, 241, 243, 271
Coffee Meet Bagel, 231
Cohen, A., 1, 308
Collisson, B., 221
compulsive Internet use, 29
Condemnation of condemners,
    204, 304
Cooke, D. J., 7
corporate crime, 304–305
corporate psychopaths, 7
corporate psychopathy, 12, 313
covert narcissist, 126
    grandiose in, 44–47
covert narcissists, 127
COVID-19 pandemic, 262
Craker, N., 167, 171, 173, 180, 330
credit cards, ix, 214
Cressey, D. R., 216, 217
criminal sadists, 11
cruel behaviors, 24, 176
Curtis, S. R., 210, 215, 216
cyber-abuse, xvi, xviii, xx, xxii, 17, 67, 140, 141,
    235, 258
cyber aggression, 17, 26, 110, 111, 118
    sample study
        non-Western cultures, 134–136
        Western cultures, 129–134
    in workplace cyber deviance,
        305–307
cyber crime, 17–20
cyber deviance, 17–20
    consequences of, 18–20
cyber-deviant behavior directed at individuals
    (CD-I), 303
cyber-deviant behavior directed at the
    organization, 303
cyber fraud, xvi
    practical implications, 324–326
cyber incivility, 308
cyber misconduct, xxii, 17, 19, 20
    Machiavellianism, 21–22
    narcissists, 21–22
    psychopathy, 23–24
    sadism, 24–25
cyber surveillance
    concept of, 157–158
    Machiavellianism, 162
    narcissism, 161
    psychopathy, 162
    sample study
        non-Western cultures, 165–166
        Western cultures, 163–165
cyber trolling, 38
cyber victimization, 119, 133, 135,
    144, 146

cyberaggression, 25
    comparative studies, 136–139
    as higher-level construct, 110–113
    Machiavellianism, 128
    narcissism, 125–128
    psychopathy, 124–125
    research findings, 148–153
    sadism, 128
    sample study
        psychopathy, 144–146
        narcissism, 146
        Machiavellianism, 146
        sadism, 147
cyberattacks, 135, 199, 204–205, 210, 320
cyberbullying, xxi, 17–19, 24, 25, 38, 82, 315
    academic, 307–308
    in adolescents, 19
    of celebrities, 139–143
    in children, 19
    cyber incivility, 308–309
    definition of, 309–310, 114
    IBSA, 308
    Machiavellianism, 128
    narcissism, 125–128
    psychopathy, 124–125
    sadism, 128
    sample study
        Machiavellianism, 146
        narcissism, 146
        non-Western cultures, 134–136
        psychopathy, 144–146
        sadism, 147
        Western cultures, 129
    types of, 116
    user's personality, 143–144
    victims, 117–119
    workplace cyber deviance, 305–307
cybercrime, xvi, xvii
    consequences of, 18–20
    definition, 198–200
    and fraud, 212
    future of, 320–321
    hacking, 201–207
    Machiavellianism, 200–201
    narcissism, 200–201
    practical implications, 324–326
    psychopathy, 200–201
    research findings, 223–230
    sadism, 200–201
cyberdating. *See* online dating
cyberflashing, 272–273
Cyberfraud. *See* fraud
cyberloafing, 303
    consequences of, 311–312
    research findings, 148–153

workplace cyber deviance, 310–311
cybersex, 23, 24, 67, 233, 269
cyberspace, xiii, xvi, xviii, xx, 22, 24, 65, 66,
        114, 120, 123, 127, 134, 198, 200, 209,
        221, 232
    antisocial behaviors in, 25, 136
    bullying behaviors in, 17
    features of, xviii–xix
    technological changes in, xxiii
cyberstalking, 38
    definition, 154–155
    duplicitous, 156
    invasive, 156
    Machiavellianism, 160
    narcissism, 159
    passive, 156
    psychopathy, 159–160
    research findings, 188–197
    sadism, 161
    sample study
        non-Western cultures, 165–166
        Western cultures, 163–165
    victim's, impact of, 156–157
cyberterrorism, 331
cynicism, 12, 108, 219

da Silva, P. G. N., 166
Dahlen, E. R., 130
Dark Tetrad traits
    cyber deviance and crime, 17–20
    cyber misconduct, 20–25
    Machiavellianism, 8–10
    narcissism, 2–6
    psychopathy, 6–8
    sadism, 10–12
DataProt, 213
Davies, J., 10
De Backer, C. J., 131
de Jesus Costa, B., 67, 258
deception/deceptive behaviors, ix, xi, 9, 128, 155,
        156, 170, 172, 186, 205, 206, 211, 216,
        240, 250, 277, 315
defense of necessity, 204, 208
Demircioğlu Z. I., 56, 129, 136, 245, 246
denial of injury, 204, 208, 304
denial of responsibility, 204, 208, 304
denial of the victim, 304
depression, xviii, 4, 5, 17–19, 31, 32, 34, 36, 42,
        117, 118, 157, 170, 234, 235, 246, 248,
        271, 274, 281, 310, 311, 321, 323
Devereux, P. G., 122, 130
Diagnostic and Statistical Manual
        (DSM-IV), 3, 5
Diagnostic and Statistical Manual of Mental
        Disorders (DSM), 4, 5, 28

Diagnostic and Statistical Manual of Mental Disorders (DSM-5), 61
digital media piracy
  costs, 213
  phishing, 213–215
  types of, 215
direct cyberbullying, 116
disempowerment, 170
distributed denial-of-service (DDoS) attacks, 199
domineering control, 154
doxing, 235, 331
Drouvelis, M., 249
drug abuse, 118
Duffy, A., 255
Duncan, Z., 243
Dunn, B. K., 215
The Dynamic Self-Regulatory Processing Model, 22

Egbert, N., 94
Egloff, B., 101
ego-defensiveness, 159, 163
egotism, 5, 126
eHarmony.com, 231, 237
Ehman, A. C., 117
Eksi, F., 66
emails, 19, 156, 158, 206, 214–216, 218, 231, 232, 302–304, 306, 308–310
Emerson, D. J., 221
emotion dysregulation, 19, 38
emotional coldness, 200, 207
emotional distress, 19, 249, 274, 282
emotional intimacy, 4, 233
Epstein, B. J., 325
erratic/impulsive behavior, 209
everyday sadists, 11
excessive Internet use, 18, 29

Facebook, xiv, xxi, 20, 22, 23, 27, 29, 30, 42, 43, 48, 49, 53, 57, 59, 64, 82, 116, 231
  Machiavellianism, 93–94
  narcissism, 86–88
    sample study
      non-Western cultures, 92–93
      Western cultures, 88–92
  practical implications, 322
  prevalence of, 81–82
  psychopathy, 93–94
  selfies, 95–100
  and Twitter, 100–109
  use of, 82–84
FaceTime, 231
face-to-face antisocial behaviors, 18
Fagade, T., 208
fake news, 117

Fan, C. Y., 126, 127, 146
fatigue, 31, 157
fear, 6, 8, 19, 23, 40, 45, 46, 48, 53, 68, 83, 84, 107, 118, 154, 155, 157, 166, 199, 219, 234, 240, 248, 249, 256, 277, 305
feelings of inadequacy, 44, 98, 159, 175, 240, 256
Fegan, R. B., 63, 64
Feinn, R. S., 129
Ferenczi, N., 88
Fico, J. M., 3
Fido, D., 282
Figueredo, A. J., 13
Fioravanti, G., 46, 64
Forsyth, L., 185
Forth, A., 265
Fox, J., 98, 99
fraud
  definition, 216–217
  Machiavellianism, 219
  psychopaths, 219
Freud, S., 2
Freyth, L., 53
friends-with-benefits, 266
Fritzon, K., 6
frustration, 170

Gaia, J., 209, 211
Gajda, A., 133
Galletta, D. F., 215
Gamache, D., 154
gambling, 27, 31, 35, 40, 310, 315
gaming disorder, 28, 61. *See also* online gaming
Gammon, A. R., 122, 123
Garcia, D., 84, 86
Geary, C., 82, 85
Geis, F.L., 8, 9
gender trolling, 168, 177
ghosting, 236, 260–261
  research findings, 263–266
Gibb, Z. G., 122, 130
Giumetti, G. W., 115, 129, 130, 308, 323, 329
global positioning systems (GPS), xxi, 155, 158, 236
Gnambs, T., 58, 59
Gonzalez, J. M., 40, 68
Goodboy, A. K., 130
Google, 95
Google+, 83
grandiose narcissism, 44–47, 83, 85
grandiosity, feelings of, xi
graphic and violent content, 84
Greig, C., x
Greitemeyer, T., 40, 68
Gray-hat hackers, 202, 209
Grieve, R., 45–47, 64, 82, 85, 314–316

Griffiths, M. D., 26, 29, 32, 60, 61, 95
Grigg, D. W., 110, 111
Grijalva, E., 4
grooming, 273
    research findings, 277–282
Gross, A. M., 117
Grossman, S. D., 3
Grubbs, J.B., 269, 276
Gunasekara, P. B., 108, 109
Gylfason, H. F., 180

hacking
    Black-hats, 202
    Gray-hats, 202
    insider threat, 203–205
    Machiavellianism, 205–207
    narcissism, 205–207
    psychopathy, 205–207
    and rationalization theory, 203–204
    sadism, 205–207
    White-hats, 202
Hamarta, E., 187
Hammond, S., 10
Hancock, J. T., 102, 103
Hand, C. J., 140–142
harassment, 17, 115, 132, 165, 214, 306
Hardaker, C., 172
Hare, R. D., 3, 6, 7
harmful online behavior, 20
Harms, P. D., 4, 203
Harrison, A., 17, 220
Hassanein, M., 104
hate speech, 84, 85, 184, 322–324
Hayes, N. L., 18, 26
health insurance, 218
helplessness, 33
Henle, C.A., 310
Hermanson, D. R., 217
Hernández, M. P., 270, 272, 281
heterosexual groups, 259
hidden webcams, xxi, 155
Hillier, K., x
Hogan, R., 3
home insurance, 218
homosexual groups, 259
Hong, Y., 103, 146
hook-up application, 237, 242
Hossain, M. A., 138
hostile attribution bias, 126
Hou, X., 61
Hughes, S., 11, 158
humiliation, 24, 115, 170, 177, 183, 234, 235,
    246, 261
Hussain, Z., 34, 36, 39, 40, 43, 52, 58, 61
hyper-intimacy, 154

I3 Theory of Aggression, 169
identity theft/fraud, 202, 218
Iftikhar, M., 61
image-based sexual abuse (IBSA), 271,
    279, 308
impulsivity, xi, 1, 6, 13, 36, 38, 39, 48, 54, 99,
    100, 103, 107, 136, 160, 163, 174, 178,
    200, 206, 212, 241, 245, 251,
    255–257, 312
indirect aggression, 113
indirect cyberbullying, 116
information and communication
    technologies, 308
insider threats, 203
insomnia, 33, 310
Instagram, 20, 23, 27, 42, 43, 48, 53, 54, 81–83,
    116, 231, 329
insurance fraud, 218
interaction of the Person-Affect-Cognition-
    Execution model (I-PACE), 36, 37
International Classification of Diseases (ICD
    11), 31
Internet, 22
Internet addiction, 22, 27, 29, 32. *See also* social
    network addiction
    prevalence rate of, 28
Internet dependency, 29
Internet haters, 171
Internet Interpersonal Orientation, 29
Internet problem behaviors, 29
Internet usage, 18, 27
Internet-communication disorder, 52
Internet-pornography-use disorder, 52
Internet-shopping disorder, 52
Internet-use disorder (IUD), 29, 51
interpersonal relationships, xiii, 4, 5, 28, 32, 43,
    123, 127, 165, 170, 186, 231, 240, 258
intimate relationships, cyberspace, 231–233
    consequences of, 233–236
    practical implications, 326–227
    research findings, 283–301
intimate-partner cyberstalking, 163
iPad, xvi
iPhone, 55
isolation, 117, 157, 329

Jabłońska, M. R., 18, 26
Ji, A., T., 55, 56
Jin, C. C., 28, 55, 56, 134
Johnson, L. K., 11, 15
Johnston J. E., x
Jonason, P., 237, 243
Jonason, P. K., 14, 26, 53, 249, 255, 263
Jones, D. N., 8, 13, 130, 205, 206, 209, 210
Jose, P. E., 132

Kajonius, P. J., 184
Kalaitzaki, A., 60
Kapidzic, S., 91
Karasavva, V., 262, 265, 266
Karlsson, A. M. C., 184
Karthikeyan, C., 302, 303, 307
Kasper, T. E., 276
katagelasticism, 181
Kaukiainen, A., 111
Kauten, R. L., 5, 6
Kawasaki, N., 260
Khan, S., 143
Kim, J. H., 93
Kim, Y., 93
Kircaburun, A., 56
Kircaburun, K., 25, 26, 29, 31, 66, 165, 166, 172
Kiziloglu, M., 58
Koban, K., 330
Kokkinos, C. M., 119, 125, 146
Kolar, G. P., 13
Kong, F., 46
Köse, A. G., 56, 136, 245, 246
Kowalski, R. M., 129, 329
Kramer, B. K. P., 217
Kumpasoğlu, G. B., 57
Kurek, A., 97, 132

Laakasuo, M., 211, 212
lack of confidence, 127
lack of conscience, 206
lack of empathy, x, 1, 4, 5, 9, 26, 36, 51, 67, 136, 137, 200, 206, 263, 271, 273, 279, 312
Lagerspetz, K. M., 111
Lang, C. P., 47
Latif, S., 135
Lauder, C., 251
Lebreton, J. M., 7, 8
Lee B., 215
Lee, S. L., 54, 55, 119
Lee, S. Y., 171, 172, 176, 181, 323
Lefringhausen, K., 88
Leidner, D., 306, 310
Leite, Â., 132, 165, 185
Li, A. Y. L., 28, 34, 118
life satisfaction, 4, 32, 34, 321
Lim, S. X., 55
Lim, V.K.G., 309, 316
Linguistic Analysis and Word Count (LIWC-22), 100, 103
Linguistic Inquiry and Word Count (LIWC), 107, 108
Linguistic Inquiry and Word Count (LIWC) 2007 software, 106
LinkedIn, 20, 27
Liu, Y., 16, 269

Liu, Y. H., 51
location-based-real-time dating (LBRTD) apps, 171, 173, 236, 237
long-term mating, 242, 243
Lopes, B., 26, 121, 124, 175, 183
low empathy, 1, 4, 6, 58, 120, 142, 277
low self-esteem, 18, 157, 170
Lowe-Calverley, E., 314–316
lower academic performance, 31
Lulz, 128, 169, 176
Lynam, D. R., 209
Lyons, M., 244, 280

Maasberg, M., 211, 325
Machiavellianism, xi, xxiii, 8–10
    cyber misconduct, 22–23
    cyber surveillance, 162
    cyberaggression, 128
    cyberbullying, 128
    cybercrime, 200–201
    cyberstalking, 160
    Facebook, 93–94
    fraud, 219
    hacking, 205–207
    social network addiction, 48–50, 66
    Tinder, 242
    trolling, 176
Maier, C., 39
maladaptive personality traits, 26, 39, 40, 54, 253–255, 271, 277
Mantilla, K., 168
Manuoğlu, E., 186
Marbut, A. R., 203
March, E., 45–47, 64, 82, 85, 99, 125, 131, 156, 158, 160, 163, 164, 167, 169, 171, 173, 175, 177–180, 182–185, 237, 239, 243, 245, 247, 251, 255–257, 271, 278, 330
Markos, A., 119, 125, 146
Marrington, J. Z., 131, 185
Marshall, T. C., 88, 89
Martin, M. M., 130
Masui, K., 185
Match.com, 231
Matsui, M., 260
Matza, D., 304
Mauldin, S., 221
Mayshak, R., 257, 258, 280, 326
McCain, J. L., 62
McDonald, L., 185
McHoskey, J. W., 14
McNulty, J. K., 269
Mehdizadeh, S., 90
Mehta, A., 154
Meier, M., 39
Meloy, J. R., 155

Ménard, K. S., 164, 324
Mendez, F., 91
Menzel, J., 39
Messenger, 20, 27
metaphor of the ledger, 204, 208, 304
Michie, C., 7
Microsoft Teams, 231
Miller, R. R., 8
Millon, T., 3
Mimicry Deception Theory, 205, 206
Min, H., 314, 316
Modic, D., 220
Mokros, A., 330
Monacis, L., 52, 95, 96
mood problems, 31
Moody, G. D., 215
Moor, L., 17, 25, 26, 330
Morelli, M., 271, 277, 278
Moseley, M. A., 101
Mukbang Watching, 31, 32
Muldoon, J., 317
Muris, P., 15, 267

narcissism, x, xi, xxiii, 2–6
    cyber misconduct, 21–22
    cyber surveillance, 161
    cyberaggression, 125–128
    cyberbullying, 125–128
    cybercrime, 200–201
    cyberstalking, 159
    dimensionality of
        non-Western culture, 65–66
        Western cultures, 63–65
    Facebook
        non-Western cultures, samples from, 92–93
        Western cultures, samples from, 88–92
    hacking, 205–207
    social network addiction, 41–44
    Tinder, 239–241
    trolling, 174–175
    vulnerability, 46, 47, 64, 259
narcissistic personality disorder (NPD), 5
Nasir, S., 128
National Centre for Cyberstalking Research, 155
Navarro-Carrillo, G., 173, 181
Near, D., 8
Necula, C. N., 57
neuroticism, 45, 127, 276
neutralization techniques, 204, 207, 208
neutralization theory, 304
Nikbin, D., 36, 42, 54, 84
Nitschinsk, L., 85
Nnadozi, E. E., 58
Noakes, T., 307
Nocera, T. R., 130, 147

non-Western cultures
    cyber aggression, 134–136
    cyber surveillance, 165–166
    cyberbullying, 134–136
    cyberstalking, 165–166
    Facebook, 92–93
    social network addiction, 54–58, 62
        dimensionality of, 65–66
    trolling, 185–187
nudity, 84, 85
Nurse, J. R., 203
Nwufo, J. I., 58

Oelrich, S., 201
OKCupid.com, 231
Oliver, E., 251
O'Meara, A., 10
Öner-Özkan, B., 186
Ong, E. Y., 92
online academic bullying (OAB), 307
online cheating, 221
online consumer fraud, 218
online dating, 231, 236. *See also* Tinder
    abuse, 246–248
online gaming, 23, 25, 26, 39
online harassment. *See* harassment
online trolling. *See* trolling
Orhan, M. A., 221
Osterholz, S., 101
OurTime.com, 231
Özen, Ç., 61
Ozimek, P., 92

Pabian, S., 131, 133
Padayachee, K., 204
Paek, S.Y., 215
Pallesen, S., 30, 32, 33, 60
panic attacks, 157, 310
Papapicco, C., xv, 182
paranoia, 170, 219, 234, 248
Pasalich, D. S., 255
pathological narcissism, 3–5, 97
Paul, B., 266, 275
Paulhus, D. L., 8, 13, 130
Pavlicek, A., 216
Pearson, C., 34, 61
Pechorro, P., 330
Perenc, L., xviii, xx
phishing, 18, 200, 206, 207, 212
    fraud, 216–217
    insurance fraud, 218
phubbing, 30, 31, 33, 34, 45, 47, 64
physical aggression, 113
Pietschnig, J., 15
Pina, A., 261, 264, 265, 279

Pincus, A. L., 164, 324
Pineda, D., 279, 280
Plouffe, R. A., 11, 15, 16
Po, L. C., 51
political sadists, 11
Pontes, H. M., 43
PopCornBox Games, 55
pornography, 266–270
    research findings, 274–276
Porter, S., 10
post-traumatic stress disorder (PTSD), 170, 310
Preotiuc-Pietro, D., 106, 108
primary psychopathy, 85
privacy, 91
privacy rights, 211
problematic Internet use, 29
psychological health, 28, 29, 117
psychopathic personality traits, xi, xvii, 7, 12, 24,
        200, 211, 212, 219, 267, 324
psychopathy, x, xxiii, 6–8, 38
    cyber misconduct, 23–24
    cyber surveillance, 162
    cyberaggression, 124–125, 144–146
    cyberbullying, 124–125, 144–146
    cybercrime, 200–201
    cyberstalking, 159–160
    Facebook, 93–94
    fraud, 219
    hacking, 205–207
    social network addiction, 66–67
    Tinder, 241
    trolling, 175
Python-based library, 104, 105

Quatera, I., xv, 182

Rahman, M. S., 317
Rajesh, T., 59
Ramamoorti, S., 325
Randazzo, M. R., 19
Rangaiah, B., 59
rationalization theory, 203–204
Rauthmann, J. F., 13
real-life relationships, 232
recklessness, 38, 54
Reddit, 179
Rehman, U., 128
Reidy, D. E., 11
relational aggression, 113
Resett, S., 281
restlessness, 33
Revenge Porn Helpline, 262
revenge porn proclivity, 19, 234, 235, 261
revenge pornography, 261–262
    research findings, 263–266

Rietzschel, E. F., 14
risky sexting, 235, 270, 277, 278
Robertson, S. A., 12
romance scams, x, 234, 235
romantic game-playing, 160
Rooney, M. C., 98, 99
Rosen, L. D., 90
Rosenberg, J., 94
Ryan, T., 90

sadism, xi, 10–12
    cyber misconduct, 24–25
    cyberaggression, 128
    cyberbullying, 128
    cybercrime, 200–201
    cyberstalking, 161
    hacking, 205–207
    social network addiction, 50–51
    Tinder, 242
    trolling, 176–177
    social network addiction, 67–68
sadistic personality disorder, xi, 10
Safaria, T., 135, 323
Sagioglou, C., 40, 68
Saklofske, D. H., 11, 15, 16
Salimi, S., 58
Samuels, H., 11, 158
Sánchez-Medina, A. J., 132, 328
Sari, B. L., 123, 136
Satchell, L. P., 213
Savacı, G. Z., 61
Savci, M., 31, 41, 56, 61
Sawicki, A, 47
Scarduzio, J., 312
Schade, E. C., 138
schadenfreude, 169, 179
Schyns, B., 3
Scott, G. G., 99, 116, 139–142
secondary psychopathy, 85
secure sockets layer, 214
Security as a Service, 214
Seda, M. A., 217
Seibert, L. A., 11
Seigfried-Spellar, K. C., 209, 324
self-centered impulsivity, 7
self-centeredness, xi, 39, 42, 63
self-confidence, 36, 42, 125, 126
self-esteem, xvi, xviii, 4, 5, 32, 34, 35, 42, 43,
        57, 64, 89, 90, 93, 95, 97, 98, 100,
        101, 116, 118, 121, 125, 126, 183, 184,
        240, 250, 256, 270, 282, 313,
        321, 330
self-harm, 118, 157, 170
selfies, 21, 24, 95–100
self-interest, 8, 121, 128, 137, 241

Selfitis Behavior Scale (SBS), 95
self-monitoring, 22, 36, 37, 49, 55, 94, 250
self-promotion, 21, 36–38, 44, 48, 49, 53, 56,
 57, 84, 87, 88, 90, 94, 200, 240, 249,
 250, 268
self-reported psychopathy, 144, 145
Selzer, N., 201
Senaratne, C., 108, 109
sense of entitlement, xi, 4, 206, 258, 315
Servidio, R., 53
Sest, N., 178, 179
Sevi, B., 238, 242
sexting, 270–272
 research findings, 277–282
sexual deception, 242
sexual sadism, 11, 269
sexual violence, 25
Shabahang, R., 139
Shahnawaz, M. G., 128, 129, 136
shame, 157, 170
Sheffield, D., 61
Sher, C. Y., 51
shopping, 27
short-term mating, 238, 240–242, 244, 249, 268,
 272, 274, 275
Shrivastava, A., 58
Siddique, A., 135
Sihwi, S. W., 108
Sikström, S., 84, 86
sleep and eating patterns, 29
sleep problems, 31, 274
Slonje, R., 19
smartphones, xii, xvi, 30, 33–35, 38, 45, 46, 53,
 56, 61, 215
Smith, A. D., 10, 217
Smith, K., 91
Smith, K. J., 221, 222
Smith, M., 16
Smith, P. K., 19
Smoker, M., 164
Snapchat, 42, 43, 48, 83, 231
social aggression, 113
social dominance, 15, 45, 119, 173
social insurance, 218
social media bullying, 115
social network addiction, 57, 58, 317
 attraction to, 34–36
 definition of, 27–30
 forms of, 30–32
 Machiavellians, 48–50
 narcissism, 41–44
  non-Western cultures, 62
  sample study
   non-Western culture, 65–66
   Western cultures, 60–61

non-Western cultures, 54–58
outcomes of, 32–34
personalities and, 36–40
practical implications, 321
psychopathy, 47–48
research findings, 69–80
sadism, 50–51
sample study
 Machiavellianism, 66
 narcissism
  Western cultures, 63–65
  non-Western culture, 65–66
 psychopathy, 66–67
 sadism, 67–68
 vulnerable/covert narcissist, 44–47
 Western cultures, 51–54
social network craving, 31
social network disorder, 29
social network site addiction, 29, 64
social networking, 27
Social Online-Self-Regulation Theory, 92
social phobia, 32, 232
social-personality literature, 4
sociosexuality, 238
software-as-a-service (SaaS), 214
Soleimani Rad, H., 97
Sorokowski, P., 170, 184, 323
Sparks, B., 282
spear phishing, 215
SpyWare, xxi, 155
Srinivas, P. Y. K. L., 117
Steele, G., 175, 177, 183
Stephenson, P., 201
Stieger, S., 15
Stiff, C., 157, 166, 322
stress, 34, 57, 157, 271, 327
structured equation modeling
 (SEM), 135
Stuart, J., 97, 132
substance abuse, 170, 310
substance use, 19, 35
successful psychopaths, 7
Sudzina, F., 216
suicidal behaviors, 19
suicidal ideation, 118, 170, 235, 246,
 270, 310
suicide attempts, 117, 118
suicide ideation, 118
Sumner, C., 105, 106, 322
Sykes, G. M., 304
Symantec, 199
Szyarto, C., 14

Taghizadeh, S. K., 35, 36
Tahoon, R., 29, 37, 54

Takezawa, M., 260, 327
Tandon, A., 329
Tang, W. Y., 36, 38, 39, 52
Taremian, F., 135
Tariq, S., 61
text messages, xii, 19, 20, 31, 158, 215, 270, 273, 303, 304
text-based cyberbullying, 130
Thomason-Darch, N., 262, 265
thrill-seeking behavior, 122, 125, 147, 164, 178, 184
Timmermans, E., 240, 244
Tinder, ix, 231, 235–239
    Machiavellianism, 242
    narcissism, 239–241
    psychopathy, 241
    research findings, 242–246
    sadism, 242
The Tinder Swindler (film), ix
Tobin, S. J., 85
Tran, U. S., 15, 138
Tripathi, N., 316
trolling, 17, 24, 25
    definition, 166–169
    Machiavellians, 176
    narcissism, 174–175
    psychopathy, 175
    research findings, 188–197
    sadism, 176–177
    sample study
        non-Westernized cultures, 185–187
        Western cultures, 177–185
    victims of, 170–171
Turan, M. E., 58
Tweepy, 104, 105
Twitter, xiii, xiv, 20, 27, 57, 59, 82, 83, 100–109, 116, 139, 144, 231, 322, 329
Twitter Search API, 106

U.S. Cybersecurity and Infrastructure Security Agency, 203
U.S. Department of Health and Human Services, 115
United States, 89, 91, 117, 132, 147, 218, 221, 237, 242, 248, 251, 263, 275, 282
Uses and Gratifications Theory, 47, 64, 82, 83

Vaknin, S., 22
Valli, C., 310
valuable possessions, insurance for, 218
van der Vegt, I., 103
Van Geel, M., 131
Vandebosch, H., 131, 133
Vander Molen, R. J., 96, 102
Vanman, E. J., 85
verbal aggression, 113

vigilance, 91
Villacís-Vukadinović, N., 209
violent graphic content, 85
violent intimate-partner behaviors, 159, 163
vishing. *See* voice phishing
visual-based cyberbullying, 130
vocal minorities, 172
voice phishing, 215
Volkmer, S. A., 173, 185
Voracek, M., 15, 138
Vranjes, I., 306
vulnerability, xvii, 18, 43, 119, 121, 127, 234
vulnerable narcissism, 44–47, 83, 85, 163
Vyawahare, M., 116, 117

Wagstaff, D. L., 271, 278
Wallace, D., 259
Walter, R., 201
Wang, B. C., 55, 56
Warranting Theory, 116
Weatherbee, T. G., 303
website defacement, xvii
well-being, 28, 29, 32, 33, 63, 156, 157, 215, 271, 306, 311, 312, 327, 329, 330
Western cultures
    cyber aggression, 129–134
    cyber surveillance, 163–165
    cyberbullying, 129–134
    cyberstalking, 163–165
    Facebook, 88–92
    social network addiction, 51–54, 60–62
        dimensionality of, 63–65
    trolling, 177–185
WhatsApp, ix, xiii, 20, 27, 83, 310
White, G. L., 91
White-hat hackers, 202, 209, 211
Widman, L., 269
Willis, M. L., 251, 252, 263
Wilson, C., 161
Wilson, D. S., 8
Wisse, B., 14
Withers, K. L., 84, 85
Wolfe, D. T., 217
Woodworth, M., 10, 102
workplace cyber deviance
    consequences of, 310–311
    corporate crime, 304–305
    cyber aggression, 305–307
    cyberbullying, 305–307
        Machiavellianism, 312–314
        narcissism, 312–314
        psychopathy, 312–314
        research findings, 316
        sadism, 312–314

workplace cyber deviance (cont.)
  cyberloafing
    Machiavellianism, 314–316
    narcissism, 314–316
    practical implications, 328–329
    psychopathy, 314–316
    research findings, 316–317
    sadism, 314–316
  definition, 302–304
  future of, 320–321
  neutralization theory, 304
  research findings, 318, 319
World Health Organization (WHO), 31
Worzel, W., 14
Wright, M. F., 137, 138
Wu, B., 186
Wu, J., 7, 8, 103, 146

Xenos, S., 90
Xu, X., 57

YouTube, 32, 82, 83, 116
Yu, H., 26, 121,
    124, 175, 183
Yuan, C., 103, 146

Zajdel, R., 18, 26
Zeichner, A., 11
Zerach, G., 259, 260
Zhang, H., 134
Zhang, S., 135, 306, 310
Zhao, H., 134
Zheng, L., 269
Zoom, 231
Zoosk, 231

9 781009 416863